THE STORY OF AUSTRALIA

Robert Lewis
in association with

national museum australia

RANDOM HOUSE AUSTRALIA

A Random House book
Published by Penguin Random House Australia Pty Ltd
Level 3, 100 Pacific Highway, North Sydney NSW 2060
www.penguin.com.au

First published by Random House Australia in 2017

Addresses for the Penguin Random House group of companies can be found at global.penguinrandomhouse.com/offices

National Library of Australia
Cataloguing-in-Publication Entry

Authors: Lewis, Robert; National Museum of Australia
Title: The story of Australia
ISBN: 978 0 85798 314 5 (pbk)
Target Audience: For secondary school age
Subjects: Aboriginal Australians – History; Australia – Discovery and exploration; Australia – History
Other Creators/Contributors: National Museum of Australia
Dewey Number: 994

Cover design by Ingo Voss, Voss Design
Internal design and typesetting by Midland Typesetters, based on original design by Ingo Voss, Voss Design
Cover images: **NMA images** – Mothers and Widows badge, photo by Jason McCarthy; toy kangaroo with fundraising badges from World War One, photo by Jason McCarthy; Heidelberg dress, photo by George Serras; Warburton Mission: Leaving Time by Judith Yinyika Chambers, photo of artwork by Jason McCarthy; Klondike flag; Maris Pacifici map, photo by George Serras; hand-coloured lantern slide – Ned Kelly in armour; Hills hoist model; photograph – Hughie McClelland with his stockmen bring in a mob of ewes for shearing 1950; portrait of Australian soldiers in uniform with rifles in hand; Life. Be in it., photo by Sam Birch; cannon from HMB *Endeavour*, photo by George Serras; portrait of a soldier, woman and child; Certificate of Registration for A. Jedrzejowski, photo by Rasha Ajaj; wood carving – female human figure, photo by Dean Golja; Australian mining: prospecting for gold; Prototype No 1 Holden sedan, photo by Lannon Harley; Harvest of Endurance: A History of the Chinese in Australia 1788–1988 'Before the Gold Rush', photo by Matt Kelso; Debrie Parvo model 'L' camera, photo by George Serras; wooden model canoe, photo by Dean Golja medallion portrait of navigator and explorer Captain James Cook, photo by George Serras; New South Wales Postal Service mail box, photo by Jason McCarthy; Circular Quay in 1848; Race to the Gold Diggings board game; photograph – group of adults and children – Empire Day 1907. **Dreamstime images** – bushfire/wildfire close-up at night © Roger Rosentreter; changing colours of Uluru © Matthew Weinel; the national flag of Australia © Rafael Ben-ari; the Great Barrier Reef in Queensland State © Filipe Frazao.
Internal map design by Tango Media Pty Ltd
Internal images © National Museum of Australia, unless otherwise stated.
Printed in Hong Kong

CONTENTS

FOREWORD

The Story of Australia is the story of who we are and where we have come from. It is the journey of us, a rich and diverse journey, with many twists and turns along the way.

In the chapters of this book, you will read about people, places, events, ideas, emotions and interactions. You will find success, harmony, love and greatness, but there is also failure, fear, violence, pettiness and hate. There are things to be proud of and things to regret.

Like *The Story of Australia*, the National Museum of Australia tells the stories of this great nation. It brings these tales to life in many ways, in particular through the careful selection of objects that speak to us of the past, and present. What especially excites me about *The Story of Australia* is the opportunity to select objects from our collections to illustrate many of the key people, events and themes in Australian history explored in the book.

When you see, for example, the wide range of materials and artefacts used by Aboriginal people over millennia, you begin to gain a very real sense of the human ingenuity and technological innovation that has been a feature of the entire span of human history. Or when you look at the image of a gold cradle at the beginning of the chapter that explores the transformative impact of gold discoveries in Australia from the 1850s, you can imagine what the experience would have been like.

The Story of Australia has been written with a close eye on the Australian Curriculum and pays particular attention to those parts of our history that children will learn in school. This makes it an excellent reference for school history. But it is also a great resource for helping all of us, young or old – children, parents or grandparents – to understand more fully the big themes in Australia's past, while also providing fascinating insights into important, defining moments. In doing so, it leaves space for you to share your own personal stories with each other and contemplate and discuss what may lie ahead for the future story of Australia.

I invite you to take a journey through *The Story of Australia* to understand what has happened in our history, when these things happened, how they happened, why they happened and by whom and to whom they happened. I encourage you to consider where this story may lead in the future and how young people today will influence our unfolding narrative. And I also urge you to visit the National Museum of Australia in Canberra to see for yourself how we tell the stories of Australia and Australians.

Dr Mathew Trinca
Director
National Museum of Australia

Earliest Australia and the First Australians

The Australian landform has changed continuously and slowly over millions of years. The first Australians had to adapt to enormous changes in the environment, and developed an affinity with the land, which shaped their way of life.

Pangaea

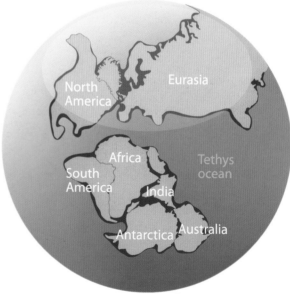

Laurasia and Gondwana

THE FORMATION OF THE AUSTRALIAN CONTINENT

The Australian continent has been shaped by hundreds of millions of years of natural processes, and by at least 50,000 years of human influence. The continent gained its present shape about 6000 years ago, when rising sea levels created the shoreline that is recognisable today. Evidence of these changes can still be seen in areas of modern Australia.

Pangaea, Gondwana and Sahul

Since as early as the 16th century, scientists have noted that the shapes of some continents seem to fit together. Others have pondered why identical or similar animals, plants and rocks can be found on adjacent continents. Today, the commonly accepted scientific theory, based on geological and biological evidence, is that the Earth's landmasses sit on tectonic plates. These plates float on a mass of liquid rock and move very slowly across the earth. Scientists believe Australia and all the other continents were once a single landmass known as Pangaea, which formed about 300 million years ago.

About 200 million years ago, the plates that formed Pangaea slowly started to drift apart, creating two separate supercontinents: Laurasia, which became North America and Eurasia; and Gondwana, which separated into South America, Africa, India, Antarctica and Australia. This was during the Mesozoic Era, which includes the age of the dinosaurs. Australia separated from Gondwana about 100 million years ago as part of the continental mass called Sahul. Sahul included Australia, New Guinea and areas that are now covered by the Timor Sea and the Arafura Sea. Sahul was separated from the nearest Asian landmass, called Sunda, by a deep channel called the Timor Trough. This deep ocean trough created a physical barrier that stopped animals from spreading between Sahul and Sunda, with the exception only of rats and bats. Over time, animals that were specific to the region and not found anywhere else began to evolve.

Modern World

Ancient fauna

Dinosaur fossils have been discovered in many parts of Australia. At Lark Quarry, near Winton, Queensland, about 3000 dinosaur footprints were discovered in the rock. One theory is that the tracks were caused by a stampede of dinosaurs escaping a predator 95 million years ago. At Broome in Western Australia, there are dinosaur footprints embedded in rock from 130 million years ago. Riversleigh World Heritage Site in the Boodjamulla National Park of north-east Queensland contains fossils of mammals from the Pliocene and Pleistocene epochs, spanning about 20 million years. These include many megafauna, which are

A cast of a diprodoton foot.

the larger ancestors of animals such as kangaroos, wombats, lizards, koalas, snakes and emus. For example, the diprotodon is related to the modern wombat but was the size of a hippopotamus.

Ancient landmarks

The Australian landmass formed from west to east over time. The Pilbara region of Western Australia features rock dating from 4.4 billion years ago. That is only 150 million years younger than the formation of Earth. There are examples of the oldest life form on earth, stromatolites, in Shark Bay, in the Gascoyne region of Western Australia. These are rocks formed when tiny microorganisms bind together tiny grains of sand to create 'living' rocks. The fossilised ones in the Gascoyne region date from 3.5 billion years ago.

We can see the impact of powerful natural forces in many familiar features of our current landscape.

Earthquakes, volcanoes, shifting rock plates and the tilting of the landmass all helped change the land. One great change was the draining of the inland sea. About 80 million years ago, the inland sea started to evaporate and slowly moving rock plates pushed against each other. The weakest parts crumpled and lifted to form the mountains we know as the Flinders Ranges in South Australia.

The rocks of Cradle Mountain in Tasmania were laid down about 600 million years ago, but the spectacular valley that exists today was carved out by glacial ice action much more recently, between 20,000 and 10,000 years ago.

Uluru in the Northern Territory used to be under the sea. It is an inselberg, or 'island mountain', made up of layers of sandstone. Most of its bulk is under the surface, possibly as far as five or six kilometres down. The sea drained, and about 400 million years ago massive natural forces tilted the inselberg 90 degrees onto its end. The surrounding rock eroded over the following 300 million years, leaving the formation we know as Uluru protruding above the surface.

Meanwhile, the famous beehive-shaped rock formations of the Bungle Bungle Range in the Purnululu National Park of Western Australia were created when sediment was deposited by seawater in the Ord Basin 375–350 million years ago. When the sea retreated, rainfall and wind blowing from the Tanami Desert in the Northern Territory helped smooth and shape the rocks.

About 800 million years ago, the entire east coast of Australia was lifted, creating a deep inland hollow that allowed the sea to pour in. Then about 600 million years ago Australia began to separate from Antarctica.

Snider-Pelligrini Wegener fossil map

This map shows how the modern land areas of South America, Africa, India, Antarctica and Australia share both plant and animal fossil remains in common. This must mean that they were once connected in one landmass – Gondwana – and that they broke away and drifted apart over time.

The continents are still drifting. Australia is moving north at 6.7 centimetres a year, about the same growth rate as our fingernails, and is expected to crash into northern Borneo and southern China – in a few hundred million years. It could then form a new supercontinent.

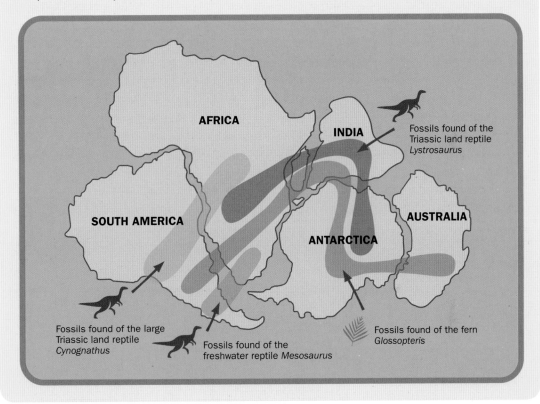

AFRICA

INDIA

Fossils found of the Triassic land reptile *Lystrosaurus*

SOUTH AMERICA

AUSTRALIA

ANTARCTICA

Fossils found of the large Triassic land reptile *Cynognathus*

Fossils found of the freshwater reptile *Mesosaurus*

Fossils found of the fern *Glossopteris*

Ancient rainforests

Great rainforests dominated the environment during the Gondwanan period. Queensland's Daintree Rainforest is the largest remnant of Australia's rainforest flora of 100–50 million years ago. It represents the closest living remnant of the vegetation type in which all of Australia's marsupials evolved.

The rainforest contains flora that account for eight evolutionary stages in Earth's history: the Age of Pteridophytes (vascular plants such as ferns), the Age of Conifers and Cyades (trees), the Age of Angiosperms (flowering plants), the break-up of Pangaea and then Gondwana, flora and fauna developments during 35 million years of isolation, the spread of songbirds, the transfer of Asian plants to the Australian continent, and the Pleistocene ice ages of 2.5 million to 10,000 years ago.

Ten million years ago to today

In relatively recent geological history, Australia has continued to be shaped by geological forces and changes to the climate. The Nullarbor Plain and the Murray River have both been inundated by the sea, which then drained away, leaving marine fossils and salt behind. Tasmania has been exposed and then submerged eight times, as has Papua New Guinea.

In the past two million years, there have been 19 climatic cycles known as 'glacials' and 'interglacials'. During glacials the climate cooled and more water was locked up in ice, resulting in lower sea levels. During interglacials, the climate warmed, ice melted and subsequently sea levels rose, inundating the low-lying edges or rims of Sahul. The last glacial began about 120,000 years ago and sea levels lowered by more than 100 metres. During this period there was less sea and more land, making it easier for humans to cross from one land area to another.

Lake Mungo, in New South Wales, was originally formed about 150,000 years ago, but then dried up during a dry climatic period. Then followed a cold period from 60,000–75,000 years ago, when water was locked up as ice. About 60,000 years ago the climate warmed again, and the water was released. Water flowing from the Great Dividing Range to the east filled the lakes again. People were able to live around Lake Mungo, and they have left a rich archaeological record. The arrival of another ice age between 22,000 and 18,000 years ago meant the lake dried up again, making it uninhabitable.

Lake Mungo

The history of Lake Mungo is one of Australia's greatest examples of how natural change has influenced human occupation.

Sixty thousand years ago the Willandra Lakes area, which includes Lake Mungo, had a cooler climate with less evaporation, so rivers flowed into and filled the lake system.

Humans arrived there at least 45,000 years ago, possibly even longer. They found a very rich environment, with freshwater fish and shellfish, animals, reptiles and birds.

It was about 40,000 years ago that a young woman died, was burned, and then her bones were crushed, burned again and then buried. This is the oldest known cremation in the world.

Around the same time, a man estimated to be about 40 years old died in the same region. He was buried respectfully and carefully, and had a large amount of ochre spread over his chest. The ochre was brought from about 150 kilometres away and must have been very valuable.

We do not know why these two people were buried so differently, but both burials show that it was important to people of that time for the dead to be treated in particular ways.

During the period that Mungo Lady and Mungo Man died, changes to the climate brought great dust storms. By 19,000 years ago the lakes had dried up, and humans had abandoned the area, leaving only the clues that modern archaeologists are using to understand the history of the continent, and the people who had lived in it.

The natural processes that have created Australia are still happening. Tasmania was last joined to the Australian mainland about 12,000 years ago, before a warming climate melted ice and the sea rose to flood all but the highest peaks. Bondi Beach in New South Wales formed over the past 6000 years, when sea levels reached their approximate levels of today. The limestone cliffs of the south-eastern coast of Victoria called the 'Twelve Apostles' were formed about 20 million years ago, but have been eroding ever since. Water and wind gradually create cliffs, which erode into isolated pillars of rock called 'stacks'. The endless force of wind and waves erode the base of these stacks, eating them away until they fall apart. One of these stacks collapsed as recently as 2009.

THE FIRST AUSTRALIANS ARRIVE

Australia formed over a period of 4.4 billion years; the earliest forms of humans (hominids) developed during the past six or seven million years. Evolution of the human brain led to the earliest humans learning to use tools about two million years ago. *Homo erectus* (or 'upright man') developed into today's *homo sapiens* ('wise' or 'knowing man') between 200,000 and 150,000 years ago.

Some Aboriginal Dreaming stories say that people have always inhabited Australia, and had originated here. Others tell foundation stories of Ancestral Beings who came from across the sea and shaped the new land. Current archaeological and scientific evidence (such as

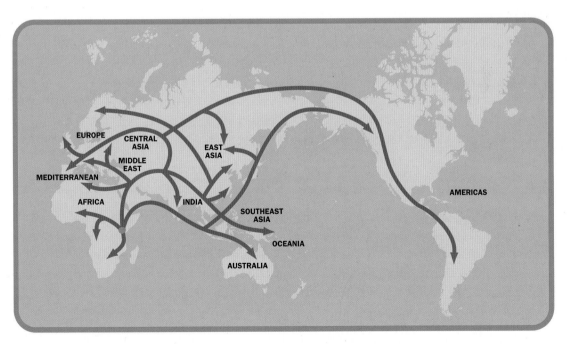

The orange dot on the map shows where it's believed hominids dispersed from southern Africa to the rest of the world.

DNA, which reveals the biological origins of groups of people) suggests that the first people arrived at least 50,000 years ago.

There are two popular theories of how humans spread across the globe. One is the multi-regional theory, in which homo sapiens developed simultaneously out of earlier human forms in different regions of the world. The other, known as the 'out of Africa' theory, argues that homo sapiens developed first in east Africa and began to move out to the rest of the world along varying paths, beginning around 70,000 years ago.

DNA studies also suggest that Australian Aboriginal people, Papua New Guinean highlanders and the Mamanwa people in the Philippines may originally have been part of the same group – one of the first groups to leave Africa and migrate by a coastal route. This route would have taken them across the mouth of the Red Sea, around the southern coast of the Arabian Peninsula, India, the Bay of Bengal, and into south-east Asia and then New Guinea and Australia. Scientists estimate that it could have taken as little as a few thousand years for people to migrate this far.

How did humans reach Australia?

Historians and scientists do not know exactly where Australia's first human inhabitants came from, or where they would have first landed. People could never have walked onto the Australian continent, as no complete land bridge between Asia and Australia has existed during the span of human history. It is more likely that the first inhabitants arrived in small canoes. The approximate distance of the sea that had to be crossed in human times was between 90 and 150 kilometres. There are two alternative routes of this crossing.

One is a southern route sailing over the deep sea trough between Timor and Australia. Small islands could have broken the journey into shorter parts, and summer north-west winds blow strongly from Timor towards Australia. The other is a northern route across West Papua, but this would have required more skill in sailing if it were a deliberate journey.

Whichever route the first Australians took, the sea would have been at least 50 metres lower than it is today, the land would have extended further, and as a result they would have arrived at a place that is now under water and at least 200 kilometres from the present coast.

Historians can only speculate on why people came to Australia and whether it was accidental or deliberate. A group of people out fishing could have been caught in an unexpected storm or current, and swept away, finally hitting the Australian coast. Or people might have seen smoke in the distance from bushfires started by lightning, or they might have watched birds migrating and realised that they were coming from or going to land nearby. Perhaps there were population pressures or starvation in their lands of origin at that time, which forced them to seek better prospects elsewhere. There could also have been several separate voyages over thousands of years and not necessarily one mass journey.

These migrations of people might have been from a single population source (one group of people only), or they might have been from several journeys over time from different places.

The extinction of megafauna

There are three current theories for explaining why Australia's megafauna became extinct.

Australia was inhabited at various times by at least 88 species of megafauna, animals similar to today's native animals but far bigger. There were heavy short-faced kangaroos, rhinoceros-sized wombats, huge flightless emu-like birds with slashing claws, seven-metre long carnivorous lizards, and 50-kilogram snakes.

Most species of Australian megafauna had disappeared by 130,000 years ago, during a period of drier climate and well before humans arrived. But between eight and 14 species may have co-existed with humans for a short time, perhaps for a few thousand years. These included the diprotodon (wombat), geryornis (emu) and sthenurus (kangaroo). This is indicated by ancient cave paintings of megafauna-like animals in parts of northern Australia.

The first theory claims that the last megafauna were wiped out by hunting. The megafauna were generally slow and therefore easy to hunt, but there has been no historical evidence of humans killing megafauna, or of them having the tools to do so. Human tools and megafauna fossils were found together at Cuddie Springs in Queensland during archaeological excavations between 1996 and 2009, but this could be explained by natural disturbances in the soil mixing the fossils and tools together.

A second theory says that natural climate change made the environment colder and drier and changed the megafauna's habitat, depriving them of vegetation and water. However, some megafauna species survived the worst of that period of change and lived into warmer times when humans were around.

A third theory is that fire, both natural and then manmade, changed the animals' environment. The human use of fire changed the vegetation that the megafauna had evolved with, and encouraged the spread of a different type of vegetation – the fire-tolerant plants that replaced the megafauna's main food plants.

The *megalania prisca*, which measured approximately 7 metres long, is believed to be the biggest lizard ever to have inhabited Australia. The megalania was featured in Australia Post's Australian Megafauna stamp series in 2008.

One scientific study has even suggested that the latest of these migrations might have been as recent as 4200 years ago, with DNA evidence showing the genetic influence of people from India in some Indigenous populations.

A changing continent

When the first people landed in the north of Australia, they would have found an environment very like the one they had just left. It would have been teeming with birds, fish, animals, reptiles and edible plants – many of which would have been familiar to them. Other parts of Australia varied in their climate, environment and fauna and flora, but the descendants of the first settlers would not have reached these areas for thousands of years.

The early inhabitants would have experienced changes in the climate and their environment and adapted their habits accordingly. In the approximately 50,000 years between the first settlement and the European invasion, sea levels rose. The change would have been hardly noticeable in some places, about 25 millimetres per year, and obvious and rapid in others, with high tides increasing by up to a metre per week.

Some early Australians along the east and south-east coast would have seen and been affected by fire or lava flows from volcanic eruptions. These eruptions would have destroyed trees and grasses, covered soil in rock, and possibly changed the flow and nature of local creeks. The most recent volcanic eruption in Australia was in the Mount Gambier area in South Australia about 4500 years ago.

Any change in the natural environment also affected its ecosystems, which either thrived or adapted to the new conditions introduced to the area.

HUMAN IMPACTS ON THE ENVIRONMENT

Fire

Naturally occurring fire shaped the Australian environment for hundreds of thousands of years, but the coming of humans meant that fire was used to control and shape the environment in new ways.

Originally, Australia was predominantly a rainforest. As the continent slowly broke from Gondwana and moved north, the climate became drier. By the Pleistocene era (between two million and 10,000 years ago), plants that could adapt to dry conditions – the scleromorphs – flourished in most areas west of the Great Dividing Range along the east coast of Australia. These plants, such as the casuarina, had small, tough, leathery leaves, which minimised water loss and allowed the plant to conserve nutrients. The moisture-loving rainforest vegetation of old Gondwana became restricted to the eastern coastal fringe. The rainforest at Daintree National Park in Queensland is one of the few remaining examples of Gondwanan rainforest in Australia.

Between 38,000 and 26,000 years ago, the rainforests had almost disappeared, and between 20,000 and 7500 years ago, fire-dependent plants such as eucalypts and kangaroo grass displaced the older plants. This was mainly due to a technique called 'firestick farming',

The use of fire

Joseph Lycett (c.1817), *Aborigines using fire to hunt kangaroos*, National Library of Australia.

This colonial painting illustrates how Aboriginal people deliberately used fire to create an environment that suited them – to create grassy spaces that encouraged kangaroos to graze, as well as leaving thick bush to provide shelter for them.

The kangaroos, gathered in a small area in the trees, were flushed out by a controlled fire and would break into the open areas, where hunters awaited them. The fire would not destroy the whole forest patch, as the wind would push it towards the grass, where it would die out. This whole process was planned, precise, predictable and logical. The consequence of having fire as an ally was that the people were mobile, and able to move to different patches at different times to take advantage of the diversity that burning provided, and they had an obligation to constantly look after the process.

which was developed by Aboriginal people to shape and manage the environment in a way that made life easier for them. Most tropical ecologists agree that the north Australian savannah – the landscape of grass and scattered trees that covers about a third of the Australian landmass – was fostered and spread by human use of fire.

Many of the earliest European visitors and settlers to eastern Australia commented on the number of bushfires they saw burning. Historians now generally agree that Aboriginal people used fire to create different types of habitat, including thickly wooded areas where animals could shelter, and open grassy areas that provided rich grazing grounds for animals such as

kangaroos. Fire was also used to create patches where the tree canopy was cleared to allow light in for the growth of useful plants.

The dingo

A second way in which human habitation changed the Gondwanan environment was through the introduction of a new animal – the dingo. The earliest archaeological evidence for the dingo dates its arrival from south-east Asia to Australia about 4000 years ago. Recent DNA analysis suggests the dingo may have arrived earlier than this – even up to 18,000 years ago – and that it originated in China, but there is no archaeological evidence yet to support this theory.

Pelt of a thylacine (Tasmanian Tiger).

The dingo was welcomed into Aboriginal life for its ability to live with humans. It helped clean up bones and scraps from camp sites, provided warmth on cold nights, and may have helped hunters by forcing kangaroos to cluster more closely, making them easier to hunt. It also provided a source of food if necessary. The dingo was soon incorporated into Aboriginal beliefs and Dreaming stories.

The dingo had a major impact on some of its native carnivore competitors, especially the marsupial lion (*thylacoleo carnifex*) and the Tasmanian tiger (*thylacinus cynocephalus*; otherwise known as the thylacine), which in turn affected the natural ecosystem. The dingo was a superior predator and caused the extinction of the marsupial lion throughout Australia and the Tasmanian tiger on the Australian mainland. Tasmania had been cut off from the rest of Australia before the dingo arrived, so the dingo did not make it to Tasmania before the last land bridge disappeared. The Tasmanian tiger was able to survive there until the arrival of Europeans.

ABORIGINAL AND TORRES STRAIT ISLAND LIFE BEFORE EUROPEAN COLONISATION

At the end of the last glacial period around 10–12,000 years ago, the climate warmed. The melting ice caused the sea level to rise, drowning large areas, including the land bridge that once connected Australia to Papua New Guinea, and leaving only high mountain peaks exposed as islands.

By about 3000 years ago sea levels stabilised, and 18 of the 100 islands existing at that time were suitable for permanent settlement. Melanesian people occupied these islands, which are known today as the Torres Strait Islands.

What we know about Aboriginal and Torres Strait Islander life before European colonisation comes from a variety of sources. These include the oral histories of Aboriginal and Torres Strait Islander people, scientific and archaeological evidence, the records of early European settlers, and the work of anthropologists who studied contemporary Aboriginal and Torres Strait Islander societies firsthand and then applied that information backwards to earlier generations, arguing that life would have been the same then. And while such findings describe traditional Aboriginal life and customs pre-European settlement, these practices are still relevant and exercised in many Indigenous communities today.

Over time Aboriginal people occupied the whole of mainland Australia. The population size of an area depended on that area's ability to provide what people needed in order to live.

Most people lived on the coastal and riverine areas, which could sustain semi-permanent occupation. The increasingly arid areas of central Australia and the west gradually became less densely populated. The inhabitants there were the most mobile, likely to travel from place to place in search of seasonal food sources.

The different environments meant that people developed various tools, weapons and decorations specific to that area. For example, a desert person's shelter would be very different from that belonging to a coastal or river person. However, there were still fundamental similarities in the way people organised their society.

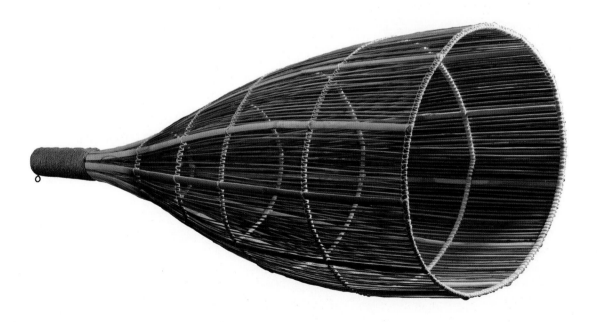

A fish scoop featuring a cylindrical wooden handle with a truncated end decorated with plaited string. The fish scoop is made up of thin sticks tied to five circular wooden braces with white string.

Social organisation

Aboriginal people lived in small independent societies. The basic social unit was the band, which was made up of 15 to 35 core members who were closely related by birth or marriage. Members would be gained or lost by marriage.

There might be several extended families in a band. Each band had its own exclusive region or Country, but could move more widely around the area with the permission of other bands. Several bands might constitute a tribe, a large group in a specific area or Country, and with a common identity, often based on a claim of descent from a common Ancestral Being.

There was no common language among all Aboriginal people. Historians believe that there were about 250 separate Aboriginal languages spoken around the time of the settlement of Europeans in 1788, with perhaps 700 dialects between them.

Several tribes might meet and travel together for part of a year. Periodically there would be gatherings, in which people would arrange marriages, make agreements with other groups, trade valuable goods such as ochre or special types of rock, settle disputes and carry out significant ceremonies.

There were respected Elders in each group, and decisions were usually taken by consensus of the Elders.

Gender roles

Some aspects of men's lives were kept secret from women and vice versa. Boys and girls would be initiated in secret and sacred gender-specific ceremonies. They would learn the special laws, objects and events that only they could know, see, use or take part in. These initiation rituals often involved circumcision or having a front tooth knocked out (for boys), being scarred (both boys and girls), or having a finger joint removed (girls). All groups had some sort of initiation ceremony for girls and for boys, which differed across the country.

Male family members would negotiate the marriage of girl children into another band. Senior men might have several wives. Some were often much younger than their husband and chosen to look after him in his old age. Some relationships were forbidden to ensure that genetically close relatives did not marry. However, if a man died his brother may have been obliged to marry a wife or wives and take responsibility for any children.

Photograph of an unknown Aboriginal man, showing tribal scarring. Early 20th century.

Childhood

Responsibility for children's education and upbringing was shared among the members of the band. The focus of early childhood life until initiation was to learn the skills needed for survival, and the proper behaviour and obligations within the society.

Toys were used to help children develop hunting and gathering skills – boys would have small spears to throw at targets, whereas girls would have a small digging stick and a bag or piece of bark for gathering food.

There were hunting and chasing games, including ones using balls made from grass or fur tied with string. It's said that Tom Wills, one of the main founders of Australian Rules football in 1859, got the idea and the basic rules of the sport from a game called marngrook, which he saw Aboriginal children play where he lived in western Victoria. It involved chasing, kicking and catching a ball made out of skins.

Beliefs, knowledge and spirituality

Aboriginal people were great biologists and naturalists. Their lives depended on observing all aspects of the natural world, such as animal behaviour, plant growth, soil and water conditions, weather patterns, and the movement of the stars in the sky. They understood the connectedness of all these things.

Behind all nature were Ancestral Beings, creators who were tied to special places. Oral stories, art and ceremonies were used to pass on knowledge of what today is called 'the Dreaming'. These are sacred stories explaining aspects of the creation, and were often part of 'songlines'.

Songlines are a long sequence of short verses that form a song map of an Ancestral Being's journey in creating natural features of the environment. Elders would take children to points in

A head ornament with animal teeth, from Northern Territory. Collected c.1932.

the songline and tell stories and sing the verses, thus helping children create a mental map of their Country. Stories could also be secular, providing explanations for natural phenomena such as how a bird got its colours or how the echidna got its quills. These stories usually had a moral lesson to teach children how to behave.

The Law was laid down in the Dreaming and all behaviour was governed by the Law. The Law existed to define the right behaviour in every aspect of life and to make clear each person's responsibilities and duties.

The kinship system structured people's relationships, obligations and behaviour towards each other, and this in turn defined such matters as who would look after children if a parent died, who could marry whom and who would care for the sick.

How we know about the ancient past

Knowledge of the ancient Aboriginal past depends on archaeology and the study of objects found at key sites. Up to the 1950s, scholars believed that people had occupied Australia for less than 10,000 years. New discoveries and changes in the methods of dating remains pushed that estimate out to more than 10,000 years by 1962, to 20,000 years by 1965, to 30,000 years by 1969, and then to 40,000 years by 1973. Today most people set 50,000–60,000 years ago as the time of first settlement. Some have said it could be over 100,000 years, but the evidence for this claim is debatable.

Archaeologists study human and animal bones, stone tools, caves and rock shelters, middens, plants, earth mounds, burial sites, stone arrangements, carved trees, fish traps, language and DNA. Meanwhile, anthropologists focus on observing modern Indigenous social groups, and studying written records and oral stories.

The main ways of studying this biological and geological matter are through stratigraphy (seeing a sequence of layers over time), radiocarbon dating (accurate only to about 40,000 years ago), and new techniques of finding electrons trapped in remains, in which heat and light are used to identify and date them.

Some key sites in the study of ancient Aboriginal people include:

- Jinmium in the Northern Territory, where some have suggested a date of human occupation of 128,000 years ago (though other scientific evidence has suggested a date of only 10,000–20,000 years);
- Koonalda Cave on the Nullarbor Plain, which has 20,000-year-old artwork;
- Malakunanja II (also called Madjedbebe) rock shelter in Arnhem Land, currently the oldest confirmed site of human occupation, dating from at least 50,000 years ago;
- Kow Swamp in Victoria, where human remains dating from about 20,000 years ago were excavated; and
- Preminghana in Tasmania, which features complex rock engravings.

The principle of reciprocity or mutual exchange was central to most aspects of community life. Gifts were given at events such as initiation or marriage, and people shared food or other valued goods with those from whom they had received benefits in the past.

Reciprocity (mutual exchange) and obligation extended to caring for the land. The land gave life and in return people were obliged to care for it. This included burning an area at the right time and in the appropriate way to reduce fuel that could otherwise lead to an uncontrollable and destructive fire.

As in all societies, there were undoubtedly outstandingly talented individuals – great explorers, artists, storytellers, engineers, healers, actors, dancers, hunters, diplomats, comedians and spiritualists – among Indigenous peoples. There was also a belief in magic and spirits. There were spells for love, for harming enemies or rivals, as well as for good and bad luck. As there was no system of writing to record individual deeds, such people remain largely unknown to us today. But it was a society in which every person knew their role and their responsibilities, and in which individualism had to give way to the interests of the group.

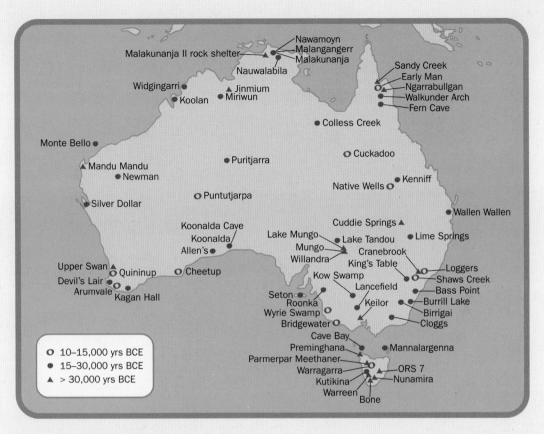

This map indicates areas in Australia where fossils have been located from 10,000 up to more than 30,000 years before the Common Era.

Shelter

Aboriginal people usually lived without clothing, although in cold areas possum-skin rugs and cloaks were used for warmth. Many groups lived in simple temporary shelters, as they were semi-nomadic and moved seasonally to follow their food sources. In some places where there was a reliable and regular source of food, people might build semi-permanent huts for shelter.

Early European explorers such as George Grey noted huts on mounds around the Murray River. At Lake Condah in Victoria, the Gunditjmara people gathered and arranged rocks to create channels that guided eels into holding pools, providing fresh food for several months. The Gunditjmara also used the local volcanic rocks to build a permanent base on which they could add tree branches and bark for shelter. They also used the local volcanic rocks to build permanent bases on which they added fresh bark and branches to create huts for their seasonal visits during the eel season.

Central Australian desert grass shelter. 1926.

Coastal camp site on the shores of the Coorong, South Australia. 1847.

Finding food

Generally, the most reliable food supply came from gathering rather than hunting. Bands learned to manage resources effectively, in a way that did not require a European form of agriculture.

People ate any and all food available in their local environment – animals, birds, reptiles, shellfish, insects, fruit, vegetables. However, individuals had 'totems', which were special animals, birds, fish, reptiles or plants that were associated with that person from birth. It was the individual's responsibility to care for and respect his or her totem, and its wellbeing. This helped to ensure that no resource was ever exhausted.

In some areas taboos were placed on certain foods, making them forbidden to the whole group. One example is found in Rocky Cape in north-west Tasmania. Based on the remains of ancient camps discovered there, archaeologists realised that the Tasmanian Aboriginal people had suddenly stopped eating fish. No fish bones were found above a particular level in the soil, indicating that no fish had been consumed after that time. There were also no tools for cleaning scales from fish beyond that same level. It therefore seems that eating fish had become taboo for the group. A possible explanation might be that the people had become ill after eating fish, and had removed it from their diet to avoid further illness. This taboo may have then become part of the Law, which was observed for several thousand years.

Food-finding was broadly gender-based, usually the responsibility of women and children. Roots and tubers were dug out of the ground, shellfish and plants were pulled out of shallow water, and fruits and greens were picked from trees, grass and bushes, or cut out of plants, such as tree ferns. Seeds would be ground to make a paste, which could then be eaten raw or cooked on hot coals.

A hafted stone hatchet.

People had learned over millennia how to treat toxic plants to remove poison and make them edible; in fact, the same techniques are still used today in certain places. A wide variety of medicinal plants were grown and developed to treat illnesses and infections. People knew not to exhaust a supply of food but to leave some to provide the next year's 'crop', even replanting seeds in preparation. People sometimes dried and stored surplus amounts for special gatherings and celebrations.

Some Aboriginal people in the north knew about vegetation gardens from Torres Strait Islander people, who used them extensively. At least ten plants found and cultivated in south-east Asia also grow in Australia, including taro, arrowroot, yams, wild rice, native millet and macadamia nuts. However, Aboriginal people did not feel the need to cultivate their own gardens.

There were also animals that could be domesticated – kangaroos, wallabies, wombats, pelicans, bush turkeys, cassowaries, emus, ducks and geese. Some groups would pen different kinds of birds until they were ready to use them, but animal husbandry – deliberate breeding – was not practised.

Tools

People carried few possessions when they travelled from place to place. Larger items such as grinding stones could be left behind because they would still be there when the group returned to that spot.

A woman's tool kit usually included a digging stick, a bark bowl, a string bag and needles made of bone. She might also have string made from fibres or hair wrapped around her waist, as well as ornaments of shells or animal teeth.

Men usually hunted with spears, clubs and boomerangs. There were different spears for different purposes, such as for fishing, hunting or fighting. Spear throwers, short sticks with a notch or hook at one end into which the spear end fitted, acted as an extension of the thrower's arm, and allowed the spears to be hurled with far greater force, and over longer distances. Men might also have shields and a hafted axe (an axe head tied or glued to a wooden handle) slung in a hair or fibre belt.

The oldest boomerang to have been found in Australia is about 10,000 years old. Other societies, including in India and in the United States, also developed boomerangs seemingly independently at about the same time. The oldest known boomerang is from Poland. It was made about 23,000 years ago from mammoth tusk.

Yirrkala basket made from fibre and vegetable dyes.

Animals could also be caught by using clubs, pits, traps and nets. Fish could be caught from land or from boats by spears, nets, traps, line and hook (often the special role of women), stunned by poison, or even simply caught by hand. At night, fire was sometimes used to attract fish. There are ancient stone remains at Brewarrina in New South Wales, where fish were trapped in artificial ponds when the water level of the Darling River dropped below the stone arrangement.

Aboriginal people had a variety of other tools available, including rocks that were shaped to allow cutting and scraping. About 6000 years ago, new and specialised tools such as points, backed blades and thumbnail scrapers became common. This technology has also been found in Asia and may have been brought from there, or may have been developed independently.

Studies suggest that, on average, Aboriginal people had to spend around five hours a day hunting and gathering, or 35 hours a week, to source enough food to sustain themselves. By comparison, in 1750 the average British worker had to labour for 80 hours a week to survive.

Health and population stability

Aboriginal diets were potentially very healthy, but depended on a variety of food being available at all times. A study of pre-1788 Aboriginal bones from the Murray River region of Victoria and South Australia

Kimberley stone spear point shaped by striking the edges with another rock.

showed that most of the children had several periods of interrupted growth, suggesting that sufficient food was not always available. Flood, fire or drought could easily destroy a major food source for at least a year.

Archaeological evidence indicates that Aboriginal people suffered diseases similar to those that were common worldwide, including trachoma, intestinal parasites, skin diseases, hepatitis B, arthritis, and infections. However, many diseases that normally afflict large populations living in close contact, such as influenza, measles, rubella, smallpox and cholera, had not reached Australia. Some ancient skeletal remains show excessive wear on teeth from eating seeds that were coarsely ground into a flour or paste, resulting in the erosion of molars and probobaly painful exposure of nerves.

For Aboriginal people, the most common causes of death were by injury (including violence), disease and sorcery – where a person has seemingly used spirits or supernatural powers to harm another person.

Funeral customs differed according to the area. Bodies might be buried in the ground (common in eastern and southern Australia), cremated, placed in hollow trees or in log coffins, wrapped in bark, or placed on platforms before being put in bark coffins, caves or rock shelters (all very common in the north). Many remains have been found with some belongings or artefacts (such as a decorative headband made of animal teeth) buried with them.

Contact, conflict and exchange

Each band had its own Country and was self-sufficient and sustainable, but there was often contact between bands, especially for the exchange of desirable goods that could only be found in a particular area. A specific type of stone might be greatly valued for its high quality in making blades, or a special shell for certain decorations, or a type of ochre for various ceremonies. These would be traded or exchanged over hundreds of kilometres. For example, pearl shell from the Kimberley area was traded across multiple territories and over 1700 kilometres to the central Australian, western desert and Adelaide areas. Ochre, highly prized for rock art and for painting bodies in ceremonies, might have to be brought in if no ochre quarries existed in a band's Country.

A mid-20th century model or toy of a traditional Torres Strait Islands canoe with sail. 1948.

Trading, and sometimes hunting, could prompt one band to enter another band's Country. There were ways of seeking permission to do so that avoided any conflict. However, contacts between groups were not always peaceful, and conflict and violence could occur. Some Aboriginal groups were known to be aggressive. One occasional practice was to raid another band to kidnap women. This sometimes occurred because men were often not allowed to marry until they were fully initiated, which could be later in their adult life.

Laws of reciprocity obliged people to share. These laws also imposed obligations to seek violent retribution for actions that broke the Law. In some cases, the punishment might be symbolic rather than real. For example, the accuser would be allowed to fend off spears thrown at him by the accused. But punishment could also be violent, and involve spearing and bashing with clubs. Many ancient skeletons show men with broken arm bones caused by warding off blows, and women with head injuries caused by being hit either with clubs or digging sticks. A revenge killing could in turn lead to pitched battles in which several people would die.

Art and ceremonies

Aboriginal people in every part of Australia expressed themselves through art. The art could be found on the ground, the body, trees, rocks, and everyday implements such as shields, baskets and skin cloaks. Art expressed knowledge about identity and demonstrated the people's relationship to land, sea and sky. It depicted the interdependence of all things and how everything was integrated through the ancestral heroes of the Dreaming.

Rock art is one of the earliest art forms in all ancient societies. Rock art in Makassar, Indonesia, that features hand stencils and pig-like creatures has been dated at about 40,000 years old. In El Castillo, Spain, hand stencils and signs on rock walls are a similar age.

There are many rock art sites throughout Australia. Rock engravings found at Koonalda on the Nullarbor Plain in South Australia have been dated at more than 20,000 years old. The oldest rock art found in Australia is in the Northern Territory, and features charcoal drawings that have been dated at 28,000 years old.

A wooden sculpture of a female human figure with facial features outlined and geometric designs on the body.

Painted rock galleries are also found in several places. People in different regions had unique styles of depicting Dreaming stories and the Dreaming ancestors, or for painting people, animals or their own hands. One style found in west Arnhem Land is the Mimi (or Mimih), which feature small stick-like figures in action poses. Another distinctive style is the Wandjina figures found in the Kimberley. This shows people with large round heads and usually no mouth. An earlier example from the same region is the Bradshaw style, now called Gwion Gwion, showing dynamic figures decorated with tassels, bags or headdresses.

Around 3000 years ago, people in western Arnhem Land began to paint figures with visible internal organs in their rock art. This is known as 'X-ray art'. These figures later appeared on bark paintings from the area. Bark paintings from eastern Arnhem Land use complex geometric designs and carry many layers of meaning. Each tribe owns a wide range of patterns and designs.

In the deserts of central Australia, people used dots and lines to decorate their bodies and in sand art, and this has become the dot style of modern central Australian art. One of the earliest forms of human adornment found anywhere in the world, painted beads, was found in a rock shelter in the Pilbara around 30,000 years ago.

A ceremonial dance. This would be a public rather than private ceremony, as the artist seems to have painted himself observing, and there may also be women watching. 1850.

Ancient rock painting that features a human figure, fish and emus painted in red and white ochres on a red rock wall in northern Queensland. Date unknown.

Pastel drawing representing the markings on the underside of a possum skin cloak from south-eastern Australia, 1999. Possum skin cloaks are a significant aspect of Aboriginal cultural heritage from Victoria and other parts of south-eastern Australia. The designs marked on the underside of the coat represent clan identity, animals, plants and natural features.

In south-eastern Australia, men's tools were elaborately decorated with delicate carvings and possum fur cloaks were marked with symbolic designs scarred into the inside of the skin.

Across the continent, Aboriginal art is a complex system of representation, which continues to play an important role in the transmission of both secular and sacred knowledge today, illustrating the Law and values laid down in the Dreaming.

Most music involved the use of clap sticks, and often boomerangs were used. The didgeridoo, seen now as symbolising Aboriginal music, was used only in northern Australia, and was usually made of straight stringybark, ironbark trunks or branches that had been hollowed out by ants. Ceremonies could be public and mixed, or sometimes secret and for males or females only. They involved music, songs and dances, with participants painted with ochre in special symbolic designs.

TASMANIA AND THE TORRES STRAIT ISLANDS

Two areas of Indigenous Australia differed most from the rest. They were Tasmania and the Torres Strait Islands.

Tasmania

About 12,000 years ago, the end of the last ice age, the Glacial Maximum, led to the seas between Tasmania and the mainland beginning to rise. By around 8000 years ago, Tasmania was completely isolated. Prolonged isolation led to Tasmanian people using tools that were different from those developed on the mainland. For example, hafted axes (those with a wooden handle), boomerangs and spear throwers were not used in Tasmania.

Eight main groups lived in Tasmania in about 60 bands. Most spent a large part of the year near the coast, but moved to inland areas to exploit seasonal food sources.

Tasmanian people used shells to carry water, and large pieces of kelp were made into bags. They also wore cloaks made from kangaroo and possum skins to keep warm. They developed canoes, which were often more sophisticated than those of the mainland, to hunt seals and mutton birds. In the west, people built strong dome-shaped huts to protect them from the bitter winters.

The Torres Strait Islands

About 22,000 years ago, at the end of the Glacial Maximum, the sea level around Australia was about 120 metres lower than it is today. As the climate started to warm and the ice melted, the sea level increased, and rose rapidly between 8000–14,000 years ago. About 6000 years ago the sea reached its present level around Australia and created the Torres Strait, separating the Australian mainland from New Guinea.

People who had inhabited the area for perhaps 60,000 years were now cut off, living on the higher areas of lands that became islands. They were able to travel to and from the Australian mainland in their canoes and sailing craft, as these Torres Strait Islands were like stepping stones for trading contacts between New Guinea, the islands themselves, and the Cape York Peninsula in Northern Queensland. This led to a continuous mixing of people and cultures from the three influences.

The people of the Torres Strait Islands are Melanesians. Their appearance, language, social structure, land use and ownership, and customs differ from those of Aboriginal people from the mainland.

Before European settlement, there were also clear differences between the Torres Strait Islanders. People who lived on the eastern islands were more practised in agriculture and were likely to be gardeners or farmers, while people in the central islands were mainly fishermen. In the west, people were predominantly hunters – of turtles, dugongs, geese and ducks. These divisions were not absolute and people across all islands practised some form of agriculture, fishing and hunting.

Torres Strait Islander identity is expressed as a unique sea culture. Central to the belief system is the sea hero Tagai, who is represented by a vast constellation of stars. Other ancestral heroes are important on the various islands. To the Meriam speakers of the eastern islands, Malo-Bomai is a central figure. Through these heroes, the world was ordered so that everything and everyone had a place and a path to follow.

During the 50,000–60,000 years in which people first occupied and then spread throughout Australia and then the Torres Strait Islands, there was very little contact with any people other than the Makassar fishermen, from what is now Indonesia.

The development of new technologies in 15th-century Europe, which enabled explorers to sail across oceans and navigate their way around the world, meant that this isolation was about to end. The Indigenous people of Australia were about to encounter Europeans. The Aboriginal group who would first experience that world-shattering meeting was the Eora people of the Sydney area. They would have to deal with a totally alien culture that would change their world.

A modern painting of the traditional Malo-Bomai story of the Torres Strait Islands. 1999. The Malo-Bomai is the native tale of a man called Malo who'd been separated from his three brothers as they'd sailed from New Guinea. Malo continued to sail the seas alone until his canoe was hit by a massive wave. But because of Malo's incredible power, he was able to transform into a whale, and then into many other sea creatures, in order to cross the Torres Strait to reach Mer. The Meriam people believed him to be a powerful supernatural being and Malo was named the god of the eight clans of Meriam, establishing laws and ceremonies. 'Bomai' is Malo's sacred name.

Discovery and Colonisation

The discovery of a sailing route to Asia exposed Australia to the rest of the world. Britain established a settler colony, claiming the land was 'owned by nobody'. But what was 'settlement' to the newcomers was 'invasion' to the Indigenous people of the Sydney region, whose way of life was challenged by colonial forces.

A 1595 map of the Pacific area with no sign of Australia, only speculation that there must be land in that area.

PUTTING AUSTRALIA ON THE MAP

Mystery

Australia and other southern lands did not appear on the earliest world maps, as no map-maker knew of the lands' existence. The ancient Greeks had known that the earth was a sphere as early as 800 to 480 BC. They believed that there had to be a southern land to balance the masses of land they knew existed in the northern hemisphere. They drew an area on their maps to show where they thought this great southern land would be. Early maps even showed imaginary people and fantastic scenes of sea monsters, strange animals and mermen and mermaids drawn on this land.

Growth of the spice trade

At the end of the 15th century, there was no known way for Europeans to sail to Asia. Valuable spices such as pepper, cinnamon, cardamom and ginger had long been brought from the Middle East or Spice Islands to both China and Europe along the 'Silk Road'. This was a series of overland trading routes through China, India, Persia (modern Iran) and Arabia

An image of an early 17th-century exploration ship, on a postcard publicising a competition for schoolchildren about the 300th anniversary of the discovery of the Torres Strait in 1606.

(modern Saudi Arabia and surrounding areas of the Middle East), on to the trading port of Venice, in Italy, and then to the rest of Europe. Much greater quantities could be transported more quickly in ships – if ships could reach Asia. A northern route across the Arctic Circle was not possible because of ice, which proved to be a deadly obstacle. A southern route seemed impossible because no ships had sailed around the southern tip of Africa or South America, and returned. The ships were too fragile, the seas too dangerous, and the sailors' ways of navigating were not reliable enough.

European discovery

This changed in 1488 when Portuguese explorer Bartholomew Diaz sailed around the southern tip of Africa, entered the Indian Ocean, and returned safely, proving that a southern route was possible. Ten years later, a fleet led by Vasco da Gama reached India using this same route. Eventually, this sea route brought European ships and settlements to the area north of Australia. The explorer Luis de Torres had sailed into the Pacific Ocean from Peru in 1605, and in 1606 sailed between New Guinea and Australia, through what is now known as the Torres Strait. De Torres did not map any part of Australia, but with European ships and trading settlements in the area, and now able to approach from the north, east and west, it was inevitable that the Australian coast would soon be discovered.

The north of the continent of Australia was mapped in 1606 by Captain Willem Janszoon. He was exploring part of the west coast of Cape York looking for commercial possibilities. Janszoon was captain of the *Duyfken*, a ship based in Java, Indonesia. At the time Indonesia was a Dutch colony that allowed easy access to the spices of the East Indies (South and Southeast Asia).

The first European contact with the west coast of Australia was in 1616, when Dutchman Dirk Hartog landed at Shark Bay near Carnarvon. This was due to the discovery by navigators of the 'Roaring Forties', the wind between the latitudes of 40 and 50 degrees. Sailors caught these strong winds and their ships raced eastward from the bottom of Africa before turning north and heading for the East Indies. This was a far quicker way to the Indies, but it also meant that ships were more likely to sail close to the coast of Western Australia if they went too far east before they headed north.

Sometimes they went *too* close and were wrecked on the reefs and islands off the coast. The most infamous example of this was the *Batavia* in 1629. Most of the 322 people aboard survived on a handful of small islands. However, some of them mutinied and murdered at least a hundred of their fellow survivors before being arrested when a rescue ship finally arrived. Most of the mutineers were executed but two were marooned on the mainland. Their fate is unknown.

Van Diemen's Land and New Holland

In 1642, Anthony van Diemen, the governor of Batavia (now Jakarta, Indonesia) sent Abel Tasman to explore the Australian coast further. Tasman discovered and mapped the southern part of Tasmania, named it Van Diemen's Land after the governor, and claimed it for the Netherlands. He then sailed on to New Zealand. In 1644 he undertook another expedition that mapped much of north-east Australia, and named the land New Holland.

By 1681 most of the north, west and south coast of Australia (New Holland) had been mapped, although nobody knew where the landmass ended or what its eastern coastline looked like.

Makassan contacts

Trade and interaction between mainland Australia and the islands to the north was frequent in the 18th and 19th centuries and probably earlier. Each year between November and December, when the start of the monsoon season was heralded by lightning, a fleet of boats from Makassar in Sulawesi sailed to the waters of northern Australia.

Each year 20 to 60 of these boats or *praus* visited Australia, each with a crew of 30 to 40 people. They came to gather the trepang (a sea slug) and tortoise shells from the shallow coastal waters of the north of Australia, near Broome, and around in an arc to the Gulf of Carpentaria. The trepang was picked off the sea floor at low tide, boiled down in great metal pots, then dried and taken back to Makassar for export to China.

The sea slug was used as a flavour-enhancing additive to food and also as a stimulant and an aphrodisiac. The Makassans would be in Australia for several months until the winds turned and they could sail back.

The Makassans had an impact on the local people, such as the Yolngu people of Arnhem Land. They introduced tobacco and cloth, and influenced local language, food, stories and ceremonies. Their influence also led to modified canoe styles and the use of glass and metal axes.

Some Aboriginal men or boys travelled on the praus back to Makassar, but this was not a regular or long-term migration experience. There is no evidence that Aboriginal language or customs had any influence on the Makassans on their return home.

The earliest archaeological record of any Makassan contact with Aboriginal people is rock art dating from at least 1644. However, some archaeologists believe that the regular trepang trade started some time later, possibly by about 1700, and certainly by 1760. It ended in 1906, when the South Australian Government, which then controlled the Northern Territory, restricted licences to local trepangers.

An example of the influence of cultural contact – a pipe brought by Makassan traders.

James Cook

The best known historical account of European discovery of Australia came when Lieutenant James Cook sighted and mapped most of the east coast of the continent in 1770. This led to the settlement of Australia by the British 18 years later.

Scientific mission

Cook was a British naval officer and expert navigator and map-maker. In 1769 he was sent as leader of a joint British Royal Society and Royal Navy scientific expedition to Tahiti to observe the transit or crossing of the planet Venus across the face of the Sun. Scientists were confident that by observing and timing the transit from several different locations on the globe, they would be able to work out the distance between the Earth and the Sun, and from there the size of the solar system. This knowledge would also help sailors to navigate more accurately and safely.

Once Cook had made his scientific observations, he opened a set of secret naval orders, which he had been given before leaving Britain. The instructions were secret because the Pacific was just starting to be explored and mapped by Europeans. If other nations found out that Cook's voyage was not only for science but also to expand Britain's empire and trade, they might have

A bark painting that depicts two Makassan praus (ships) by Birrikidji Gumana, Yirrkala, 1966.

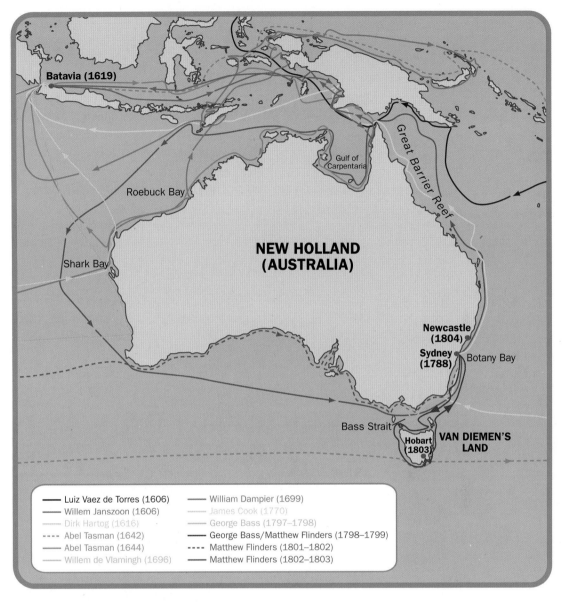

This map shows important exploration routes between the 17th and 19th centuries that established Australia's location on the global map.

Map labels:
Batavia (1619)
Gulf of Carpentaria
Great Barrier Reef
Roebuck Bay
NEW HOLLAND (AUSTRALIA)
Shark Bay
Newcastle (1804)
Sydney (1788)
Botany Bay
Bass Strait
Hobart (1803)
VAN DIEMEN'S LAND

Legend:
- Luiz Vaez de Torres (1606)
- Willem Janszoon (1606)
- Dirk Hartog (1616)
- Abel Tasman (1642)
- Abel Tasman (1644)
- Willem de Vlamingh (1696)
- William Dampier (1699)
- James Cook (1770)
- George Bass (1797–1798)
- George Bass/Matthew Flinders (1798–1799)
- Matthew Flinders (1801–1802)
- Matthew Flinders (1802–1803)

sent rivals to the area and stopped potentially important discoveries that might lead to wealth and new territory.

Cook's secret orders instructed him to continue sailing in the Pacific Ocean after his Transit of Venus observations to see if he could find the supposed Great South Land that was believed to balance the landmasses of the northern hemisphere. He was to search for it east of New Zealand. If he didn't find it, this would confirm that the land did not exist, and he was then to sail west towards New Holland.

Hartog's plate

When Dutch explorer Dirk Hartog landed at Shark Bay, Western Australia, in the 17th century, he nailed a pewter plate to a post he had placed on Dirk Hartog Island. The Dutch inscription read in translation:

On the 25th October, arrived here the ship Eendracht *of Amsterdam; the first merchant, Gilles Mibais, of Luyck; Captain Dirk Hartog, of Amsterdam; the 27th ditto set sail for Bantam; undermerchant Jan Stoyn, upper steersman, Pieter Dockes, from Bil, Ao, 1616*

This is the oldest known artefact of European contact with Australia.

In 1696 another Dutch explorer, Willem de Vlamingh, landed on the same island and found the plate half-buried in sand. He replaced it with a new plate that copied Hartog's words and added some of his own. De Vlamingh took the original plate back to Holland, where it is now on display in the Rijksmuseum in Amsterdam. Vlamingh's own plate was later removed, and is now on display in the Western Australian Maritime Museum in Perth.

Cook's discoveries

Cook explored the area east of New Zealand and proved that the great landmass the ancient Greeks had supposed was there did not exist. He then circumnavigated New Zealand and headed west.

After his first sighting of Point Hicks on the east coast of Australia, Cook sailed north along the coast, mapping and naming places, anxious to land and communicate with the local people. The first place he did land, on 29 April 1770, he named Stingray's Harbour (soon changed to Botany Bay). The botanist Joseph Banks thought this would be a perfect place for a settlement, despite his tense first encounter with the local people.

Cook sailed past the entrance to what he named Port Jackson, which is more commonly known today as Sydney Harbour, but he did not sail into it.

When Cook landed at various places along the east coast, he had little success communicating with the Aboriginal people. This changed when his ship was nearly sunk on the Great Barrier Reef and he managed to sail it into the mouth of the Endeavour River, the site of today's

Porcelain figure of Captain Cook made in the late 1840s.

Cooktown. The crew beached the ship and repaired it. During this time he and the scientists aboard, including Joseph Banks, met with the local people, the Guugu Yimithirr. Banks and Cook recorded several words of their language, including the first record of the name 'kangaru', or 'kangaroo'. After a seven-week stay while the ship was repaired, Cook recorded his judgement that:

'the Natives of New Holland . . . may appear to some to be the most wretched People upon Earth; but in reality they are far more happier than we Europeans, being wholly unacquainted not only with the Superfluous, but with the necessary Conveniences so much sought after in Europe; they are happy in not knowing the use of them . . . The earth and Sea of their own accord furnishes them with all things necessary for Life.'

Entry after 23 August 1770, James Cook, *Journal of H. M. S.* Endeavour, *1768–1771,* National Library of Australia

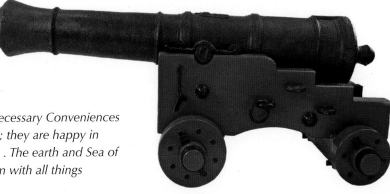

A cannon from Captain Cook's *Endeavour,* thrown overboard in 1770 in the Great Barrier Reef off Cooktown, when Cook's ship was in danger of sinking.

A needlework map showing the route of Captain Cook's voyages of discovery, including the east coast of Australia.

From the Endeavour River, Cook sailed on and reached the northernmost part of the coastline on 22 August 1770 at Possession Island. He named all of eastern Australia New South Wales and claimed it for the British Crown.

Cook returned to Britain and deposited the records of his voyage with the officials in charge of the Navy. The knowledge he gained, together with the knowledge of the great naturalist Joseph Banks, would later be key influences in the colonisation of Australia.

Cook's discovery of the eastern part of Australia meant that the land could be mapped as a continent by 1771. But, of course, Australia was not known by that name back then. 'New Holland' was used to refer to the western half of the continent, and 'New South Wales' to the east.

In 1772 two French ships on a scientific expedition of discovery, and commanded by Marc-Joseph Marion-Dufresne, landed in Van Diemen's Land (known today as Tasmania). After that there were no recorded European voyages to Australia until 1788.

Previous discoveries of Australia?

There have been theories that Cook was not the first to map the east coast of Australia. One claim is that Chinese explorers under the Admiral Zheng He had landed on the eastern coast of Australia in 1422 (and, on a separate part of Zheng He's expedition, on the western coast of Australia), but this theory has no satisfactory evidence to support it. There have also been claims that the Portuguese sailor Cristóvão de Mendonça mapped much of the east coast in 1522, but again no convincing evidence exists.

DECISION TO SETTLE

During the 1770s and the 1780s Britain faced new global challenges. Britain had American colonies, to which it sent convicts, but the American colonies revolted and British transportation of convicts ceased. (This was the American Revolutionary War, 1775–1783.) As a result, Britain was forced to keep their convicts in gaols, or in old ships called 'hulks', which were converted to become prisons and kept in rivers such as the Thames at London. An alternative place of transportation had to be found to relieve the problem of the overcrowded and disease-ridden prisons and hulks.

Britain had also engaged in a naval war with the French, Dutch and Spanish. The Dutch, Portuguese and Spanish had established many ports in Asia to load their cargoes of spices for Europe, and these were places where Britain's enemies could re-supply and repair their warships. Britain did not have such an advantage. It feared that its possessions in India might be attacked from the sea, and it could not provide and keep a fleet in good repair to protect India. Britain therefore needed its own naval base in that part of the world.

In 1785 the British decided that a base at Das Voltas Bay in present-day Namibia on the south-west coast of Africa was the best solution. They would send convicts there to create a naval base that would be close enough to protect India. However, when they sent people to assess and report on the location and its conditions, the area was found to be barren and disease-ridden.

James Cook

James Cook (born 1728; died 1779) was one of the world's great explorers.

At 18 he started working on coal and coastal trading ships, and transferred to the Royal Navy at 26.

He served during the Seven Years' War (1756–1763) against the French in Canada, and became an expert navigator and chartmaker.

He sailed in three epic voyages of discovery into the Pacific, mapped huge areas of the region and the coast of New Zealand, proved that there was no Great South Land, discovered the east coast of Australia and sailed closer to Antarctica than anyone had ever done before.

He married Elizabeth Batts and had six children, none of whom lived to adulthood.

Cook was killed by local people in Hawaii.

Joseph Banks

Sir Joseph Banks (born 1743; died 1820) was a wealthy young man who paid a huge sum to be part of Cook's first world voyage. His staff of eight (two other naturalists, two artists, two workers from his farm who were brought to help look after the plants and animals he collected, and two servants) strained the accommodation on the ship, especially after Banks began gathering specimens wherever the ship went. Many of the plants and specimens they gathered were destroyed when the *Endeavour* was holed on the Great Barrier Reef, but others survived and were re-planted at Kew Gardens on his return.

Banks sponsored or supported many other expeditions, but his main impact on Australian history was his evidence during an inquiry that led to the decision to send a convict settlement to Botany Bay.

Convicts kept in hulks working at building embankments.

An alternative had to be found, and Botany Bay in New South Wales was declared a suitable naval base. It had several advantages: a good harbour and a healthy climate, the reports of Cook and Banks suggested that there were not many existing inhabitants, and the location already 'belonged' to Britain after Cook had claimed it in 1770.

New South Wales was also reasonably close to trade opportunities with India, the East Indies, and the South American coast, as well as to the Pacific Islands, which seemed to promise a good supply of timber for masts and flax for sails – materials essential for running a fleet. Timber in particular was important – building just one British warship required 3000 mature trees. For the masts, ships needed tall, straight trees, which could be obtained from the Norfolk Island pines that grew in New Zealand and on Norfolk Island.

So on 19 August 1786, the British Government decided to send a fleet of convicts with military guards and officials to New South Wales. It was an expensive operation and Botany Bay was more remote from Asia and India than had been preferred, but it was the best solution available.

More than 1000 people would be sent 19,000 kilometres across the world on an eight- to nine-month voyage through almost uncharted waters to a place where nobody had settled before. It was a challenging mission!

The convicts

The first group of convicts to be sent to Botany Bay were selected from prisoners who had been sentenced to transportation – usually for seven or 14 years, or life. Some of these convicts had already been in prison for several years – more than 40 per cent had been sentenced in 1784 or earlier. They were drawn from hulks, from the main prison, Newgate, in London, and from various county prisons, including Bristol, Suffolk, Norfolk, Cardiff, Derby, Worcester and York.

Official records differ but there were approximately 568 males and 191 females on the First Fleet. Their ages ranged from 13 up to 62 years for the oldest man, and possibly 82 years for the oldest woman. Most were aged between 20 and 39 and were English, but there were also some Irish, Welsh and Scottish people. Some prisoners were Jewish, and might have been European Jews who had come to England and then been arrested and tried for local crimes. There were also 11 people identified as 'African', who were probably either freed slaves or from the West Indies, which was then a colony of Britain.

Some of the convicts bound for Botany Bay were at least halfway through their sentences. The women seem to have been randomly selected. At least some of the men originally chosen seem to have been rejected because of their health, and others may have been included because of their occupations. At least 163 male and 67 female convicts had useful skills – as carpenters, brick-makers, weavers, farmers or gardeners – but most seem to have been unskilled labourers.

Most of the convicts do not seem to have been the worst criminals, but nor were they all poor victims of a harsh system that brutally punished petty property crimes, as some might suggest. Britain was at the start of the Industrial Revolution. Many rural labourers were crowding into cities to work in the manufacturing industries that flourished due to mechanisation. There were no social services for the orphaned, the poor, the homeless, the unemployed or the disabled, so people had to find other ways to survive. Most of the criminals first sent to Botany Bay had been convicted of theft of goods, and a minority for violent crimes such as highway robbery.

There were also 25 convicts' wives and a few children who were permitted to go, plus a few children who were born on the way. This group was considered to be the first free settlers to arrive in Australia on the First Fleet.

The First Fleet

The fleet or convoy of 11 ships – six transport ships, three supply ships and two naval escorts – was under the command of Captain Arthur Phillip, who had been appointed governor of the new colony in 1786, well before the fleet left England. The ships were all under six years old, and seaworthy. The convict transport ships were *Alexander, Charlotte, Friendship, Lady Penrhyn, Prince of Wales* and *Scarborough*; the food and supply ships were *Golden Grove, Fishburn* and *Borrowdale* and the naval escorts were HMS *Sirius* and HMS *Supply*.

Preparation for voyage

As captain of the First Fleet, Phillip was responsible for the health of the convicts, the ships' crews, and the officers and marines who would guard the new colony, as well as for the equipment and supplies required for a successful voyage. Most importantly, he needed to ensure that the settlement could be self-sufficient within two or three years. Phillip tried to provide everything they could possibly need on board, including clothes, tools,

Convicts due for transportation would make – or pay to have made – love tokens for their families and loved ones to remember them by. The tokens were usually coins with their surfaces smoothed and then inscribed. This example is inscribed on one side 'David Freeman, born the year 1798, banished 17th June 1818'. The other side is inscribed 'Dear Sarah, when this you see, remember me when in some foreign country'. The tokens were also known as 'leaden hearts'.

wheelbarrows, ploughs, firearms and seeds of all kinds. The objects and culture of one world was about to be transplanted in another.

Apart from the necessities for voyage and settlement, trees and plants were also taken on board – orange, lime, lemon, quince, apple, pear, fig, sugarcane, vines, strawberries, oak and myrtle. Bibles and religious tracts were donated by a Christian society after an appeal by the Archbishop of Canterbury for spiritual books for the settlement. Kittens, puppies and Governor Phillip's greyhounds and rabbits also went on the voyage.

The voyage

The fleet left Portsmouth, southern England, on 13 May 1787 and stopped at Teneriffe (in the Canary Islands off the west coast of Africa), Rio de Janeiro in Brazil, and Cape Town in South Africa for supplies. The journey from Cape Town to Botany Bay had only been sailed three times before, by Abel Tasman in 1642, then Tobias Furneaux as part of Cook's second expedition in 1773, and James Cook himself during his third voyage in 1777. The First Fleet was an extraordinary undertaking for a fleet of transport ships. None of the sailors, crew, officials or marines had ever been to Botany Bay. Although the crew and officials expected to be able to return, the convicts knew that they probably never would. They were sailing into exile.

The boats left Cape Town packed with pigs, goats, poultry, horses, oxen, bulls, sheep, additional plants, fresh water and food for the animals. The ships ran into fogs, fierce gales and stormy seas as they sailed close to the Antarctic Circle. Disease and the freezing cold temperatures killed many of the animals and plants. Several people fell overboard in the high seas and fierce winds. In these conditions there was little hope of saving anyone, though incredibly some were rescued.

Apart from the threat of extreme weather, conditions aboard also held elements of danger. The convict ships had to be specially fitted out to provide the crew with security against any attempts at mutiny. Barriers were built to keep the convicts separate from the crew on the decks.

The most unhygienic part of the ship was below deck, where the convicts slept in hammocks crammed together. There were no portholes, and no candles at night (for fear of fire), so the convicts would spend half their day in darkness, in heat or cold depending on the weather, in filthy conditions and with no privacy. Rats, cockroaches and lice thrived in this unsanitary environment.

The fleet sailed south of Van Diemen's Land and then north for the final approach to Botany Bay. The journey had lasted eight months and one week. The number of deaths reported varies in different records – from 23 to 48. This was significantly fewer than had perished during the much shorter and easier Atlantic crossings of convict ships between Britain and the American colonies.

The arrival

The ships of the fleet arrived separately over two days, at the proposed settlement site at Botany Bay. Phillip was disappointed that the Botany Bay of a fierce summer January of 1788 was not the pleasant and fertile land that Cook and Banks had described in May 1770.

Phillip investigated the area and found an entry to a harbour that Cook had named Port Jackson but not entered. He sailed in and chose a place that was better suited for a new settlement – initially he was going to call it Albion, the poetic name for England, but soon changed it to Sydney Cove, named after British Home Secretary Thomas Townshend, Lord Sydney, who was in charge of the venture.

In the meantime, the British were astonished to see two French ships also arrive in Botany Bay, just a couple of days before Phillip was about to transfer his fleet to Sydney Cove.

Arthur Phillip

Governor Arthur Phillip (born 1738; died 1814) worked on a whaling ship from age 15, and then joined the Royal Navy in 1755 (coincidentally the same year as James Cook). He began as a captain's servant but eventually became a captain himself in 1786.

He was fluent in German, Portuguese and French, and worked as a spy against the French for the British Government. He served in the Royal Navy during the Seven Years' War, then joined the Portuguese Navy as a mercenary and fought in a war against Spain from 1774 to 1778.

Phillip was appointed to lead the convict fleet to Botany Bay and was involved in every aspect of its planning. Phillip's naval career had made him acutely aware of the problem of scurvy on long trips and he made sure the First Fleet took on supplies of fresh fruit.

Phillip was a man of the Enlightenment, the period of the 18th century that saw the blossoming of a spirit of scientific inquiry, respect for learning, and a belief in knowledge and reason rather than superstition. He was determined that there would be no slavery in the new colony, and believed that the convicts should be treated fairly and allowed to work or farm.

Captain and Governor Arthur Phillip shown on a 150th anniversary medallion. 1938.

These ships, *L'Astrolabe* (named after a scientific instrument used for navigation by the stars) and *La Boussole* (the French word for 'compass'), were on a scientific expedition of the Pacific commanded by Jean-François de Galaup, comte de La Pérouse. While the French expeditioners were at Botany Bay, they were responsible for several 'firsts' on Australian soil – the first Christian services, the first burial, the first garden, the first fortress. Their landing site is now the suburb of La Perouse, and their arrival is commemorated each year. The French ships stayed six weeks and then left for France, never to be seen again. It wasn't until 1964 that the remains of the wreck of *La Boussole* were found on a reef off one of the Santa Cruz Islands in the Pacific.

ESTABLISHING THE NEW COLONY

On 26 January 1788, Captain Arthur Phillip and an official party from the First Fleet sailed into Port Jackson on HMS *Supply* and stepped ashore at Sydney Cove. A few convicts and marines had already prepared a flagpole with the pre-1801 version of the Union Jack flag (without the red cross of St Patrick that represents Ireland) flying from it. A marine guard fired a volley from his weapon and Phillip and the other officials toasted the British king, George III, and the royal family.

Members of the Eora, the Aboriginal people of the Sydney region, looked on, hidden. Some of them would have seen Cook's ship in Botany Bay in 1770. The Eora people's reactions were now mixed. Some signalled to the strangers to go away, and shook weapons in a threatening manner, but others demonstrated hospitality by showing the British where to get fresh water.

Over the next 20 years the British settlement would struggle, then grow from a small, isolated prison to a brash and expanding society.

The legal claim to New South Wales

There were several ways in which a nation could take possession of another country according to accepted European law in the late 18th century.

A postage stamp mural commemorating the landing of the First Fleet at Sydney Cove, 1788.

One was by discovery and possession or settlement. If the new land belonged to no-one or the occupants had no system of law, it could be claimed by the new occupiers. This concept of an unclaimed land became known as 'terra nullius'. A second way was by invasion and conquest, leading to a treaty or agreement with the defeated local people. A third was by negotiation and agreement, where the land was purchased by the newcomers with the agreement of the original owners.

James Cook claimed sovereignty by discovery in 1770, and Governor Arthur Phillip claimed it by possession and settlement on 26 January 1788. In 1992 the High Court of Australia decided in the famous Mabo case (see chapter 11) that these claims to Australia had wrongly assumed that New South Wales was 'terra nullius', because the Indigenous people did in fact have their own systems of law and ownership of the land.

Britain's claim to sovereignty did not mean that the Aboriginal people could be treated violently – they were supposed to be protected by British law. Before the First Fleet sailed, King George III had told Governor Phillip to try to have friendly relations with the Aboriginal people and to protect them from harm by the new settlers:

> And if any of [the King's] subjects shall wantonly destroy [the Aboriginal people] or give them any unnecessary Interruption in the exercise of their several occupations' then it is [the King's] Will and Pleasure that you do cause such offenders to be brought to punishment according to the degree of the Offence.

The early days of settlement

Governor Phillip chose Sydney Cove because it offered a sloping ground that would not be flooded, a source of fresh water in the form of the Tank Stream, and a deep water anchorage, so that ships could come in close to shore to be easily unloaded.

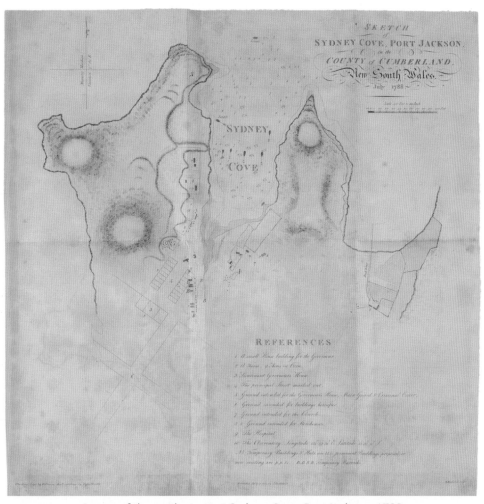

A map of the settlement at Sydney Cove, Port Jackson, 1789.

A First Fleeter – Esther Abrahams

Esther Abrahams was 16 in 1786, when she was tried in London for stealing 24 metres of black lace valued at 50 shillings – a substantial amount of money at that time. She was found guilty and sentenced to seven years' transportation to New South Wales. While in gaol she became pregnant, and gave birth to a daughter, Roseanne, who was sent with her to Sydney.

Abrahams was aboard the *Lady Penrhyn* of the First Fleet, and became the de facto wife of the ship's first lieutenant, George Johnston.

In New South Wales in 1808, Johnston overthrew Governor Bligh, making Abrahams briefly and unofficially the first lady of the colony.

Abrahams and Johnston eventually married in 1814 and had seven children. Esther died in 1846, a wealthy woman. One of her great-great-great-grandchildren, Sir David Martin, became governor of New South Wales in 1988, the bicentennial of the landing of the First Fleet and Abrahams' arrival in Sydney.

There were about 1000 people in the new society, including the governor, a chaplain, a surveyor, a judge, several naval surgeons, 16 officers, 192 marines, 548 male convicts, 188 female convicts, 42 wives and 37 children of marines or convicts.

In the two weeks after the first landing, the convict transports and the supply ships were unloaded, transforming the area into a noisy, busy worksite. The convicts chopped down trees, cleared ground, split logs, dragged stores and supplies ashore, built rough fences, and set up canvas tents or made rough bark shelters.

Convict parties were set to work constructing the first permanent buildings – two solid wooden rooms to protect the stores, then a barracks for the marines, followed by a brick house for the governor, which was completed in June 1789. Officials, officers and convicts had to find ways to build their own houses from the bricks made in kilns from local clay.

A First Fleeter – James Ruse

James Ruse (born 1760; died 1837) was a First Fleet convict who arrived with only 18 months of his seven-year penalty still to serve. He is famous in Australia because of his claim, carved by himself on his own headstone, which reads: 'And when I arrived in this colony I sowed the first grains'. He is believed to be the first person to plant wheat in the new colony.

In fact, he did not plant the first grains but he was the first ex-convict to do so, in 1789. He was given a land grant at Parramatta and by early 1791 he was growing enough food to feed himself and his wife, and to be taken off the government supplies. His success showed that the vision of a colony of self-sufficient ex-convict farmers on small farms might become a reality.

While Phillip had set aside land around Sydney Cove for different groups and purposes, most of those areas grew as a rough and largely unplanned jumble during the first few years.

The food problem

The First Fleet brought two years' supply of dried food such as grain, flour and salt meat. This was rationed out at a fixed rate to the new colonists, both convicts and officials, who had to find their own way of cooking their meals. Women received two-thirds of a man's rations.

Phillip realised, when allocating sections of land, that one of the most important tasks was to clear an area to grow food to keep the settlement going. The governor's instructions from Britain were clear: convicts were to be put to work on large public farms to cultivate food for the common good, which would replace the rations that would run out after two years. The orders also authorised him to grant farming land to convicts when their term of transportation had ended, including additional land for their wife and children, together with tools, seeds, grain and rations for two years. Phillip wanted to create a self-sufficient agricultural society like the one he knew in Britain.

But there were major problems with this plan: most of the convicts did not want to work clearing the land; the local soil was suitable for growing vegetables and fruit on a small scale, but not for the large supplies of grain needed by the government farms; summer, the season in which they'd arrived, was not the best time for planting; and, though they did not know it, the First Fleet had landed during a severe drought year.

As time went on, it was apparent that the British officials had not anticipated the harsh conditions the new environment presented. The wood in the native trees was harder than the

Members of the First Fleet recorded the birds, animals and plants that were totally new to them.

soft wood of European trees, so the cutting tools the colonists had brought with them were less effective. The earth was hard and dry, so ploughs became snagged and could not turn the soil.

In 1789, a transport ship bringing fresh supplies didn't arrive, as it had struck an iceberg on the journey out from Britain. Phillip had to ration food carefully, and he earned gratitude from some and hostility from others when, on 1 November 1789, he ruled that every person, whether convict or free, and regardless of their station in life, would receive the same reduced ration. He did not reduce the women's ration, as many were looking after children or feeding babies.

But the convicts kept coming. In June 1790, the Second Fleet arrived, and the Sydney settlers were shocked at the terrible state of the convicts on board. The Second Fleet had been contracted to private businesses, which were less concerned about ensuring for the health of the convicts. They had starved and locked the convicts below decks for much of the voyage, with illness raging through them. Of the 1026 convicts who had embarked, 256 men and 11 women died during the journey. Half of those who survived had to be hospitalised on arrival.

From the beginning of settlement, Governor Phillip had sent out parties to explore the surrounding land. They followed the Hawkesbury-Nepean River and soon found new areas suitable for the settlement to expand into. By June 1791 large public farms had been established by the Parramatta River at Parramatta and Toongabbie. Private land grants were given to some convicts to start small farms.

The new farmers began to adapt to the new conditions. They learned to hoe rather than plough, and discovered which local plants would help cure scurvy – a disease caused by vitamin-C deficiency, which afflicted the settlers when they landed. The settlers became more observant of their surroundings, developing their understanding of the environment over time. Within a few years the food crisis had passed and the settlement was able to feed itself.

Managing the convicts

Although the new settlement was being farmed by convicts, there were no gaolers watching over them. The marines refused to keep watch over the convicts, as they claimed that their job was to protect the settlement from attack or rebellion, not to force people to work. So Phillip used convict overseers to supervise the government work parties clearing the land.

If they chose, convicts could undertake private work in their time off from government work. Many hired themselves out to build houses for the officers and officials. In the first weeks of the settlement, several convicts even turned up at Botany Bay and tried to get the French scientific ships under La Pérouse to take them aboard.

The female convicts were not made to work. On the voyage to Australia, some women formed relationships with sailors or marines, and as a result gained protection and favourable treatment. After the fleet landed at Sydney Cove, some of these relationships were recognised through marriage, and many women were employed by the officials and officers as cooks and domestic servants.

A needlework sampler of Botany Bay created by ten-year-old Margret Begbie between the late 18th and early 19th century. Samplers were developed as a way of recording history, and learning embroidery played an important role in educating young girls in 'feminine skills'.

Interacting with the Aboriginal people

There are no Aboriginal records of how the Eora people reacted to what to them was the invasion of 1788. Before British settlement, the Eora only had experience of themselves and their neighbouring groups to create their understanding of the world. The sudden intrusion of a totally different people must have been puzzling and almost certainly threatening.

The interaction between the newcomers and local people was complex and varied. From the evidence of First Fleeters who wrote about their experiences, it appears that the Eora people initially ignored and avoided the new settlement as much as possible. Governor Philip had been instructed to 'conciliate' the local people, but he wanted to go further and engage with them. He did this in the violent but common way of the time: he kidnapped individuals in order to try to communicate with and understand them.

Contact with the settler culture

In November 1789 Governor Phillip ordered a party to capture an Eora man, so that he could learn about Aboriginal language and customs. They first captured an Aboriginal man called Arabanoo, and shortly after two men named Bennelong and Corby, who were kept as prisoners but otherwise treated well.

In May 1790 Bennelong escaped and was seen back with his tribe at Manly. Shortly after this, Governor Phillip went to Manly and tried to persuade him to return. In an event that has baffled historians as to its meaning, Bennelong drew Phillip in towards him. Then another man, named by a witness as Willermering, picked up a spear and threw it into Phillip's shoulder, severely injuring the governor. This may have been a matter of Law – payback – for the capture of Bennelong or for intruding on their Country.

To this day, historians are not sure whether Willermering was trying to kill Phillip or just wound him. The fact that the design of the spear point was not the usual killing style suggests that Willermering may not have intended to kill Phillip, but to punish him according to Indigenous ritual. Philip recovered and the spearing seems to have marked a change in the attitude of the local Aboriginal people towards the newcomers: many Eora started to 'come in', living openly and peacefully with the Europeans in Sydney Town.

When Phillip left New South Wales for Britain in 1792, Bennelong and a teenaged Aboriginal man from the same tribe voluntarily went with him. The younger man's name was Yemmerrawanie, and he had occasionally been a servant at Phillip's table. In May 1794, Yemmerrawanie died from a chest complaint in Britain, becoming the first Aboriginal person to die on English soil. His headstone is still there, in a churchyard in Eltham, near London.

Bennelong, ill, homesick and depressed, returned to Sydney in 1795 and lived in his own brick hut at what is now called Bennelong Point, the site today of the Sydney Opera House. On his return he was able to live in the two societies – his Aboriginal one and the British colonial one. He died in 1813.

Bennelong's experiences show the complexities of contact between the Aboriginal people and the colonists. There were instances of friendship, with some individuals such as the First Fleet officer Watkin Tench befriending several Aboriginal people, and engaging with them enthusiastically, learning their language and culture. There were also many cases of Aboriginal people and Europeans, especially women, helping and sharing with each other, such as with mutual support during childbirth. Many Eora became very fond of the tea, sugar, flour and alcohol the British had introduced, and traded weapons and tools for them, or took jobs as bottle washers and serving girls to earn them.

Aboriginal people were also quick to adapt some of the new technology that became available to them, especially glass and metal, which were superior to stone, bone or wooden points and blades. Many Aboriginal men became sailors, and one of them, Bungaree, may have been responsible for introducing the spear thrower to northern Australian people.

But there were other aspects of the European culture that they rejected. The Eora could see no sense in the hot, uncomfortable clothes of the British or the hard work that many convicts were made to do. When Phillip had the first captured Eora man, Arabanoo, watch the flogging of a convict to show how justice worked according to the British system of that time, Arabanoo showed only 'disgust and terror'. Europeans, many of whom were violent themselves, were nevertheless shocked by the occasional open violence of Aboriginal men towards Aboriginal women, and of the violence between women themselves.

A portrait of Bennelong, titled: *Portrait of Bennilong* [sic]*; a native of New Holland, who after experiencing for two years the luxuries of England, returned to his own Country and resumed all his Savage Habits.*

There was also occasional physical conflict between the settlers and Aboriginal people in the early years of the settlement. Soldiers sometimes fired on the Eora people if they felt threatened, and the Eora soon learned to leave armed soldiers alone. However, the bush became a dangerous place for unarmed convicts to wander alone or in pairs. They were likely to be targeted by the Eora, perhaps because they were invaders, or because they had disturbed a sacred place, or as payback for some injury inflicted on the local people.

Disease

The greatest killer of the Eora people was disease. Aboriginal people were devastated in 1789 by smallpox, a disease to which they had no immunity. There is still much debate among

An example of friendly but wary contact – trading fish. 1825.

historians about whether smallpox was released in Sydney by accident, through transmission by clothing or blankets, or whether it was released deliberately by the British settlers. There is even a theory that the disease was transmitted by contact with Indonesian fishermen in northern Australia, and gradually moved down the waterways that were used for travel by Aboriginal people, although this is the least likely explanation.

Whatever the cause, the result was horrific. An estimated half of the local population was killed. The victims suffered a high fever, severe headaches, backaches, vomiting and rashes throughout the body, including in the mouth and throat. People could not speak or breathe properly, or swallow water, even though they had an agonising thirst.

Arabanoo, the first Eora man kidnapped, also witnessed the death of his people from smallpox. Lieutenant David Collins reported Arabanoo's grief at the results of his family's demise: 'All dead! All dead!' he cried. He returned from the British settlement to nurse some of his family and caught the disease himself, dying shortly after. Arabanoo was buried in Governor Phillip's garden.

Expansion to Norfolk Island

One of the instructions Phillip had been given by the British Government was to send a party north-east to Norfolk Island as soon as possible. The British believed that there were good supplies of the flax plant (from which sails and ropes could be made for ships) and tall, straight, strong Norfolk Island pine trees (from which ships' masts could be constructed).

A small party was sent there in February 1788, but they soon discovered that the flax was unsuitable for sail-making, and the pine trees had hollow interiors, which meant they could not be used as masts.

A new society and culture

By 1791 Governor Phillip's health was poor, probably from kidney stones, which caused occasional but severe pain in his side. He returned to Britain in 1792. The new settlement he had helped create in New South Wales was a society with several social groups: the government officials, the marine officers, the marines and their families, the convicts, the free wives and children of the convicts, and the local Eora people, though there was much mixing between several of the groups. It had survived the early threat of starvation, and had grown in size and number as more convict fleets arrived, and people spread to the rich soils of the Hawkesbury-Nepean River. But it was not a thriving society. The international situation that had helped create the settlement soon changed.

Other Aboriginal responses to European contact

Pemulwuy (born c. 1750; died 1802) resisted the invasion of his land in New South Wales. In 1790 he killed John McIntyre, Governor Phillip's gamekeeper, and from 1792 he led raids on settlers in the outlying areas. One of the colony's officials, David Collins, believed that the attacks were the result of the settlers' own misconduct, including the kidnapping of Aboriginal children.

A military party was sent out to catch Pemulwuy with orders to kill as many Aboriginal people as could be found. None were.

In 1797 Pemulwuy led a raid on the government farm at Toongabbie in New South Wales. He was tracked down, wounded and imprisoned but managed to escape. In 1801 he was declared an outlaw and later shot dead. Governor King wrote about him as 'a terrible pest to the colony, [but] a brave and independent character'. Pemulwuy's head was cut off, preserved in spirits and sent to Sir Joseph Banks for study. During Prince William's visit to Australia in 2010, Aboriginal elders requested that Pemulwuy's head be returned from Britain, but the location of the head is not known.

Bungaree (birth unknown; died 1830) came in with the remnants of the Aboriginal people of Broken Bay, near Sydney, to settle in the town. He sailed with Matthew Flinders in the *Investigator* between 1801 and 1802, and was the first Aboriginal person to circumnavigate Australia. In 1804 he escorted some Aboriginal people who had come from Newcastle to Sydney and acted as a diplomat and helper for them.

In 1815 he was part of the Eora group that was given a farm and he was presented with a plaque that read: 'Bungaree: Chief of the Broken Bay Tribe'. The group did not stay on the farm and were given a fishing boat and net as an alternative.

In 1817 Bungaree travelled with explorer Phillip Parker King to north-western Australia and again helped as an interpreter and diplomat between the European and local people.

Britain had been at war with France since 1793, and this pushed the New South Wales settlement well down the list of British Government priorities. The East India Company – the body that controlled trade between India and Britain – had its trade monopoly renewed, so there was no longer any chance for trade between India and New South Wales to grow. The vital naval supplies that were supposedly on Norfolk Island had been found not to exist.

And so two of the possible reasons for establishing the settlement of New South Wales had disappeared. Its only remaining value seemed to be as a prison. New South Wales would have to look after itself and not draw money from the British Government, and earn its keep as an effective gaol. The next three governors would try to achieve this.

NEW GOVERNORS AND NEW PROBLEMS

As the colony developed, new problems appeared. With settlers from Britain arriving and convicts being freed at the end of their sentences, there were demands for the place to be run more as a free settlement than as a gaol. There were also clashes of interest between the officers, who wanted to make profits, and the governors, who were supposed to run the colony for the benefit of all.

Although Arthur Phillip returned to Britain in 1792, his replacement, Governor John Hunter, did not arrive until 1795. Between these years the colony was ruled by the senior military officers Major Francis Grose, acting governor from 1792 to 1794, and then Major William Paterson, until 1795. These men had arrived in 1790 with the New South Wales Corps, which was the British regiment that replaced the First Fleet's marines.

The Rum Corps and the colonial economy

The officers of the new regiment hoped to become rich during their posting to New South Wales. They were looking for land grants, and to make money through buying and selling goods. Acting governors Grose and Paterson granted land and assigned convicts more freely to the new officers than Governor Phillip had to the First Fleet marines. Grose also closed down the colony's government farms, in an attempt to encourage private enterprise, while continuing to let the government bear the cost of feeding and clothing assigned convict workers. This allowed the new officers to increase their wealth at the government's expense: they received free or cheap labour from the convicts, then the officers sold the products of that labour to the government store.

The convicts had to work for the landowner for a certain duration each day, but after that could hire themselves out in return for payment.

The British Government had not provided the new colony with currency for general circulation. Only the officials and military had access to money. Because the officers were the only ones with money they were able to buy goods straight off incoming ships, and sell them to ex-convict merchants or middle men. These merchants carried out the selling of goods to individual convicts, who used anything they could for the exchange, including other products, notes promising to pay, even foreign coins cut into pieces.

There was also great profit to be made in rum. 'Rum' was the name used for any alcoholic spirits produced by a process of distilling – wheat or corn or some other food that contained sugar was added to yeast and boiled off. The boiling converted the sugar into ethanol, or alcohol. This was then used as currency.

The officers could buy goods from the ex-convict merchants and pay them in rum that had been brought in on the trading ships. They were also able to use rum to pay the convicts for extra labour on the officers' farms. As a result of this, the New South Wales Corps earned the nickname 'Rum Corps' later in history.

As more people were given land, there was greater demand for equipment and supplies to maintain and cultivate it. This meant more ships bringing goods to New South Wales, more buying and selling, and more need for services in the town. The settlement's economy was starting to develop.

Hunting whales and seals in southern waters also helped the fledgling economy. Whale oil burned in lamps was Europe's main source of lighting other than candles, and seal-skin top hats were the height of fashion in London. Whalers and sealers stopped off at Sydney to get supplies – barrels to store the oil, ropes, nails, food, medicines, salt and such – and offloaded their catch for transportation back to Europe.

Many people were starting to thrive in the colony, but it was both far rougher and more equal than the Britain that most people had left. There were some who looked on the development of the new society with distaste. The two Protestant religious leaders Reverend Richard Johnson and Reverend Samuel Marsden believed that the colony was becoming an ungodly place, where the sanctity of the Sabbath (Sunday) was violated by work or by drinking and gambling. They also worried about the strength of Catholicism – about one third of all convicts were Irish, and most of these were Catholic. They looked to the new governor to restore Protestant order.

The new governors

John Hunter 1795–1800

Governor John Hunter arrived in 1795 with instructions to tackle the rum economy, make the settlement more self-sufficient and therefore cheaper for the British Government, keep local prices down and control the trading of the military officers. He was an older man, aged 60 when most officials and officers were in their 30s and, as a naval officer, was used to unquestioning obedience. Hunter found that his attempts to reduce the buying power of the officers, and to get rid of rum, made him many enemies among the officers. His opposers were able to undermine him back in Britain, and he was recalled from New South Wales in 1800 by the British Government.

Philip Gidley King 1800–1806

In Hunter's place came Governor Philip Gidley King, who cut back the number of convicts assigned to work for the officers, and put them to work for the government on useful projects such as constructing roads and public buildings. King also approved more land grants so that ex-convicts would be able to create small farms and feed themselves.

He re-introduced the policy of having the government buy goods from merchant ships, and re-sell them at a cheaper price than would be the case if the officers had bought them for re-sale. King's policies challenged the trading monopoly that the Rum Corps had gained, and provided competition, bringing down prices. Slowly, more currency came into the economy, and this broke the use of rum as a means of payment for work completed.

King created many public works (including a church, a granary, a schoolhouse, mills, a bridge, factories and offices) and cut the proportion of people drawing rations from the government stores from 72 per cent in 1800 to 32 per cent in 1806. But he created powerful enemies, and as his health declined, he was openly opposed by many officers. Once again the British Government listened to the words of the critics rather than the governor, and he was recalled in 1806.

William Bligh 1806–1808

King was replaced by another naval captain, Governor William Bligh. Bligh was ordered to restore the colony's image as a deterrent against crime – the British Government was worried that transportation to New South Wales was being seen as an opportunity to accumulate wealth rather than as punishment. Bligh was a strict disciplinarian and was known to be blunt and direct, even abusive. He swore violently at people and frequently flew into bad tempers, alienating those who were the subject of his verbal attacks. His behaviour had led to a mutiny on the naval ship *Bounty* in 1789. There would soon be another mutiny against him.

Governor Bligh started imposing better order on Sydney streets. From 1788, houses had been built without any real pattern or planning, and the town was a sprawling mess. Bligh began evicting people from the houses they had built without permission, which caused great resentment among the home dwellers.

When Bligh abolished rum as a form of payment, three wealthy ex-convict merchants, Simeon Lord, Henry Kable and James Underwood, wrote a letter of protest to him. Bligh abused and gaoled them, and made it clear that if people did not accept his decisions they would suffer. Bligh also clashed with some of the settlement's biggest landowners, such as John Macarthur, whom he threw in gaol. He also upset the New South Wales Corps officers and harshly criticised the troops.

On 26 January 1808, exactly 20 years after the foundation of the colony, Major George Johnston of the New South Wales Corps led a detachment of soldiers to Government House, where they arrested Bligh. This would later be referred to as the 'Rum Rebellion', in reference to the New South Wales Corps' nickname. Despite its name, the rebellion did not really involve rum but was an attempt by powerful people to remove the man they saw as threatening and undermining their commercial interests and their power in the colony.

Bligh was kept under house arrest for a year, and refused to return to Britain to face an inquiry. He managed to sail to Van Diemen's Land, where he tried to get Lieutenant Governor David Collins to support him in taking back control in Sydney. Collins refused, and Bligh went back to Sydney.

Bligh finally agreed to return to Britain, and Johnston was charged with treason. The British Government convicted Johnston and therefore seemed to be supporting Bligh, but their verdict made it clear that they believed Bligh was at least partly to blame for the troubles. The New South Wales Corps was recalled, and a new governor, Lachlan Macquarie, was sent to take over from Bligh. Governor Macquarie would dramatically re-shape the way New South Wales was developing.

A 19th-century folk art diorama portraying Governor William Bligh's arrest by the local militia during the Rum Rebellion in Sydney in 1808.

3 Expanding Settlement: The Colonies to 1850

After years of struggle, the colony started to develop and expand. Explorers opened up new areas for settlement around Australia. Though the colonies remained British, the growing number of locally born people meant that a new element of identity, an awareness of an 'Australianness', was also beginning to develop.

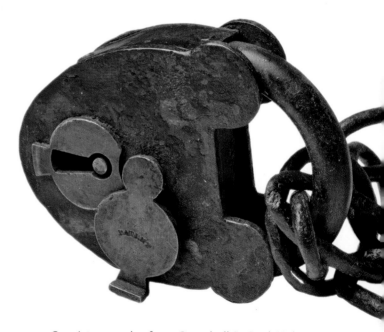

Convict manacles from Campbell St Gaol, Hobart, used between 1837 and 1960.

MACQUARIE'S NEW SOUTH WALES

In its early years, the British colony of New South Wales comprised the entire eastern half of Australia, including Van Diemen's Land (Tasmania) from 1803, although only very small parts were populated by the European settlers. Between 1788 and 1810, settlements in New South Wales and Van Diemen's Land remained small and isolated, and struggled to survive. The arrival of Governor Lachlan Macquarie in New South Wales set the settlements on a new path.

Lachlan Macquarie arrived in New South Wales in 1810 with his wife, Elizabeth, to replace Governor Bligh. His instructions from the British Government were clear: improve the colonists' morals, encourage marriage, provide for the education of the young people in the colony, stamp out the use of rum, and increase the agricultural and pastoral development of the colony.

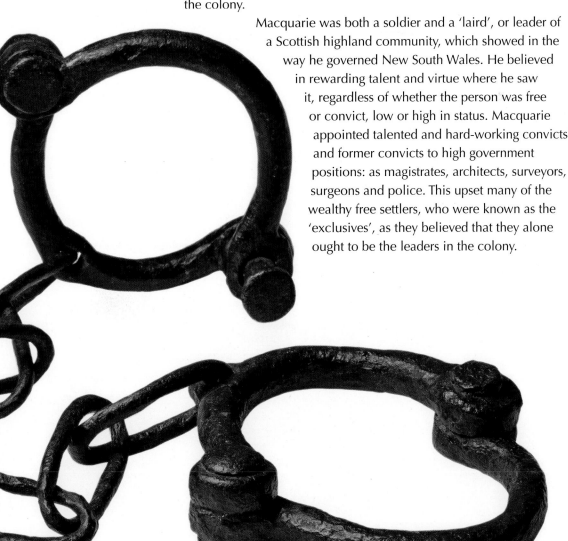

Macquarie was both a soldier and a 'laird', or leader of a Scottish highland community, which showed in the way he governed New South Wales. He believed in rewarding talent and virtue where he saw it, regardless of whether the person was free or convict, low or high in status. Macquarie appointed talented and hard-working convicts and former convicts to high government positions: as magistrates, architects, surveyors, surgeons and police. This upset many of the wealthy free settlers, who were known as the 'exclusives', as they believed that they alone ought to be the leaders in the colony.

Relations with Aboriginal people

Macquarie arrived at a time when many settlers were moving west from the harbour. Some Aboriginal people in these areas resisted this invasion of their Country, and conflict between the settlers and Aboriginal people became more common. When several settlers were killed, Macquarie responded by sending out troops to stop the violence.

In one expedition south of Sydney in 1816, 14 Dharawal people – men, women and children – were killed when the troops attacked their camp. This stopped much of the resistance to settlement in that area. Macquarie initiated a series of annual meetings in Parramatta of all the Aboriginal people of the area, where he would distribute blankets and food, and assert his authority as governor. He also created a school for Aboriginal children in Parramatta. Many people attended, although not regularly, as they were more concerned with their own economic and cultural life.

Building program and expansion

Macquarie began an ambitious building program in Sydney and the 'Macquarie towns' he had helped establish – Windsor, Wilberforce, Pitt Town, Richmond and Castlereagh, all located on or around the Hawkesbury River. Macquarie used convict labour and local materials to build roads, churches, hospitals, lighthouses and barracks. He set out a new

Developing colonial life. Hyde Park, 1842.

town plan for Sydney, and compensated people whose houses had to be torn down to create an ordered street grid.

In 1813 Macquarie authorised the explorers Gregory Blaxland, William Lawson and William Wentworth to search for a way across the ridges of the Blue Mountains. These mountains were blocking expansion to the west. Several exploration parties in the past had already tried to find a way through but were unsuccessful. Convict John Wilson might have discovered a route over the mountains in 1798, but his claims were kept quiet – John Hunter, the governor of that time, was scared that, if Wilson's claims were true, convicts might use this route to escape from Sydney.

Although Macquarie needed to find new agricultural land, he was reluctant to allow settlement to expand as it would be difficult to control people once they spread beyond Sydney. It would also be expensive, as the government would have to spend money providing magistrates and soldiers in the new areas. After the 1813 party reported their success, Macquarie had a road built across the mountains, and appointed military guards to limit the number and type of people who could travel to the rich Bathurst plains. Within two years, settlers were ignoring the restrictions and moving into the grazing area with flocks of sheep. The plains were already inhabited by the original Aboriginal owners, and this soon led to bloody resistance.

Convict policy

Macquarie introduced a policy that relied on convicts' specialised skills to develop the settlement. When convicts arrived, officials recorded each person's details, including their place of origin, religion, their ability to read and write, their previous occupation and skills, and any distinguishing physical features. Those with skills became valuable to the government and to settlers.

Before Macquarie's time, convicts and freed convicts had lived wherever they could. Most lived in shared houses in The Rocks area of Sydney, with some of them even owning homes. Macquarie built a barracks to accommodate the convicts on government work gangs during the week. This meant improved supervision, which forced the convicts to work harder.

A government shirt issued to convicts. 1830.

Convicts whose sentence of transportation had expired were allowed to return to Britain if they could afford the fare. Most could not, so there were growing numbers of 'emancipists' (those who had been pardoned before the end of their sentence) and ex-convicts in the new society. Macquarie did not discriminate against former convicts, and even employed and promoted some if they were talented and reformed. Macquarie also continued to give land grants and government supplies to those who had set up small farms that would help grow crops and feed the colony.

The most common convict experience was of 'assignment' – being loaned out to a settler as a worker. The settler had to feed, clothe and provide basic medical care for the assigned convicts in his or her care, but did not pay them. In many cases the convicts were also able to work for pay outside their duties – either for their assigned master, or for someone else. This arrangement suited all parties: the settler had cheap labour; the government didn't have to pay to look after the convicts; the convicts could make extra money outside their work hours. It also meant that people could develop their farms and add to the colony's productivity more quickly.

A government-issued convict jacket, circa 1850s.

Convicts on assignment had the right to make official complaints if the master was not providing the set quantity of food and clothing, but the magistrates were more likely to side with their free neighbours than the convicts.

If a convict was considered to be well behaved, they might earn 'a ticket of leave' before their sentence expired. This was a licence that allowed them to live with greater freedom within the colony. As a result, they could work for themselves and be productive members of the community. If they then misbehaved, their ticket of leave could be cancelled, and they returned to being subject to all the restrictions on convicts.

At the end of his or her sentence, a convict was given a certificate of freedom to show that they were now free. As late as the 1820s, some freed convicts received land grants, although this was less common after 1808, when the British Government ordered the colonial governors to restrict the system.

Punishment and reformation

The word 'transportation' can create the image of the government chain gang: prisoners with their legs in chains or hobbles, swinging a pick to break rocks for buildings or roads. Chain gangs existed, but it was more common for convicts to be assigned to free settlers as labourers.

Another image many have of the convict system is one of brutal punishment: chains, whipping, bread and water rations, small prison cells and iron bars. This was certainly true for some, but only if they were found to have committed further offences after arriving in the colony. The sentence of transportation to New South Wales from Britain was meant to punish and reform convicts without the need for further physical punishment once the convicts arrived.

Within a few years, harsher places were established for convicts who committed crimes after their arrival. These were at Newcastle, Norfolk Island, Port Macquarie, Moreton Bay, Macquarie Island and Port Arthur. Most convicts did not serve time at these places, but those who did soon learned that they were to be avoided if possible.

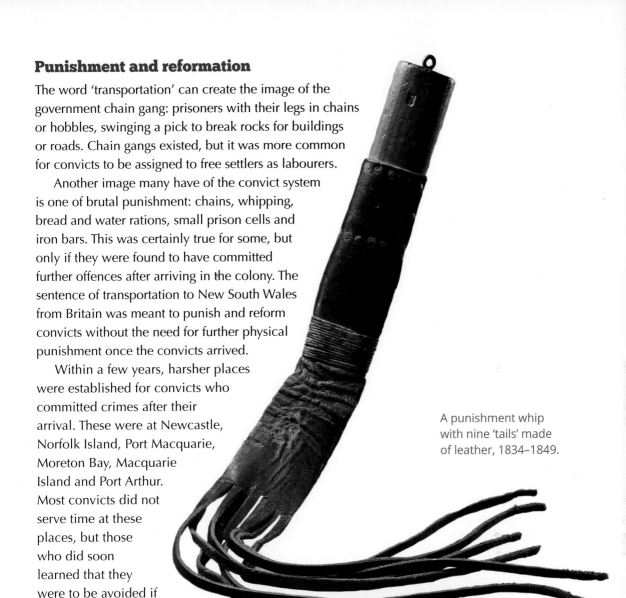

A punishment whip with nine 'tails' made of leather, 1834–1849.

Female convicts

Women made up about one-fifth of the convicts sent to Australia. The women were of all ages, but most were in their twenties and thirties. About half were Irish. As with the men, most had been sentenced to transportation because they were found guilty of theft. Juries often valued the property stolen at a low cost because they knew that conviction for theft of expensive items meant hanging, not transportation. It is a myth that people were transported because they stole something as petty as a handkerchief or a loaf of bread.

In the first few decades of the colony, female convicts were left to themselves to find accommodation and work. Women were also sent to female factories as places of secondary punishment if they committed crimes once they had arrived in the colony.

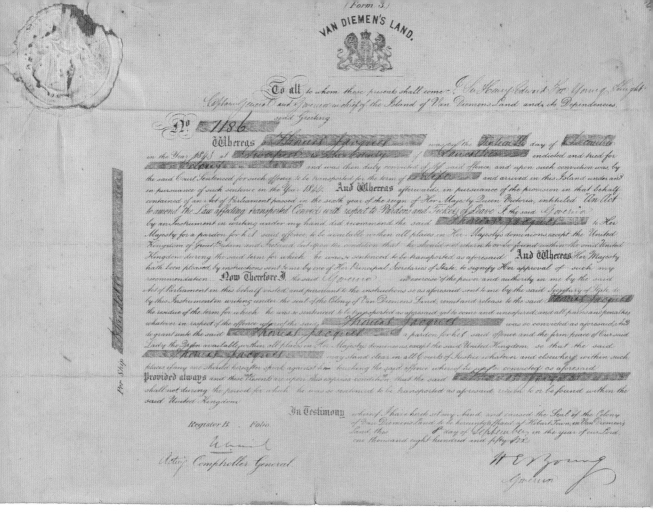

Convict pardon for Thomas Jacques of Van Diemen's Land by the governor, dated 8 September 1856.

A female factory was a walled prison, where newly arrived transported female convicts waited until they were assigned to a settler. They had to work at such tasks as washing clothes and sheets, unravelling rope for re-use, or weaving and spinning.

Many women arrived pregnant or with their children, some of whom might have been born during the voyage. Once an assigned woman had given birth, her baby was sent to an orphanage until the woman had served out her time and could claim the child back.

Between 1801 and 1856, 13 female factories were established in New South Wales and Van Diemen's Land. The Parramatta Female Factory, established by Macquarie in 1821, was the largest.

Opposition to Macquarie and changing attitudes to transportation

Under Governor Macquarie's progressive policies, wealthy ex-convicts had greater opportunities to become leaders in settlement society. This was opposed by free and wealthy settlers who believed in leadership through a traditional class structure. Those settlers did not want to mix with people they considered their social inferiors and complained to politicians in Britain.

The situation in Britain was also changing, and this worked against Macquarie's policies. By 1816 the British Government worried about how effective transportation was in deterring crime in Britain. Transportation was supposed to be a punishment, not just an exile. It was the second harshest punishment available after hanging. But as convict success stories from New South Wales became known in Britain, criminals were even starting to request or be given transportation as a way to improve their lives.

At around the same time, there was an increase in crime in Britain. In 1815, after 20 years of war with France, Britain demobilised (sacked) 400,000 soldiers who were no longer needed. Many of these soldiers could not find jobs and turned to crime, so the government needed transportation to be a deterrent, not a reward, to help control criminal behaviour.

Macquarie's policies were expensive. Convicts were being kept by the government, which had to feed and clothe them (rather than the convicts being assigned to settlers who bore those costs). As more convicts were sent to New South Wales and Van Diemen's Land, Britain needed the governor to spend less on each criminal, not more.

The British Government was also being increasingly influenced by committed Christian 'evangelicals' who argued that transportation corrupted convicts' morals, and created a degraded and godless society.

In 1816 the government appointed an investigator, John Thomas Bigge, to report on the state of the colony. The government made it clear to Bigge what it wanted, and he was chosen because he would find evidence to support that view. While Macquarie saw the convict system as a way of contributing to the development of the colony, the British Government and Bigge saw it primarily as a system of punishment. Bigge investigated and relied heavily on the evidence and ideas of Macquarie's enemies, the free-settler exclusives, and his report was critical of Macquarie's methods and priorities. As a result, Macquarie was recalled to Britain in 1821.

A stricter convict system in New South Wales

Lachlan Macquarie was replaced in New South Wales by Major-General Sir Thomas Brisbane from 1821 to 1825, and then Lieutenant-General Sir Ralph Darling from 1825 to 1831. Van Diemen's Land had a number of governors between 1803 and 1824, when Colonel George Arthur was appointed governor.

Both Governor Darling and Governor Arthur were military men who had recently fought against France. They were ready to be tough in implementing what the British Government wanted in the 1820s, including making the convict system harsher. Under the stricter system more convicts had to be part of government work gangs, they would be assigned only to free settlers, and tickets of leave and conditional pardons were not given as readily as they had been under Macquarie's governorship.

VAN DIEMEN'S LAND

Van Diemen's Land had originally been claimed by the Dutch explorer Abel Tasman in 1642, and between 1772 and 1802 the island had been visited by 11 separate exploration parties.

In 1803, New South Wales Governor Philip Gidley King sent a small party to Hobart, as he was worried about the possibility of French expeditions settling the area. The first permanent settlement was established that same year when a group of 49 British officials, military, convicts and free settlers sailed from Sydney to Van Diemen's Land. They landed at Risdon Cove, near present-day Hobart, and established it as British by their presence.

The British Government was also concerned about the possibility of land claims by the French. Not knowing that Governor King had acted independently, the British Government sent out a party from England under Colonel David Collins. That party first settled unsuccessfully in Port Phillip Bay at Sorrento (Victoria), and then moved to establish Hobart.

Founding a settlement

The first weeks of a new coastal settlement, such as Hobart, typically involved anchoring the ship close to the shore and then transferring supplies on land. Convicts would be sent to chop down trees for firewood and logs for fences and houses. The settlers would set up canvas tents or make temporary bark shelters. Ground would be set aside for a vegetable garden, and animals – horses, cattle, sheep, goats, pigs, chickens – would be placed in rough yards and tethered, or allowed to roam free.

Areas would be defined for the officials, the soldiers, any free settlers and the convicts. Parties would set out to explore the immediate area and to shoot any game for food. If there was suitable clay, a brick kiln would be set up. Settlers would obtain water in buckets from the source of fresh water. At night there would be many cooking fires with people clustered around them.

Over time the settlement would spread with streets marked out, usually on a grid pattern, and roads appearing, as people used tracks regularly. Settlers would claim land and start building shacks or more substantial houses. The settlement would gradually expand as people set out to find new areas to claim and to pasture their animals.

The small group that settled Hobart brought very few supplies. In 1805 the official in charge of Van Diemen's Land, Lieutenant-Governor Collins, sent convicts out with guns to kill kangaroos for food. But many did not return. Some were attacked by the local Aboriginal people, but others were accepted and ended up living with them, becoming the first 'bushrangers'.

The Mairremmener, the Black War and the Flinders Island reservation

In 1804, only a year after Van Diemen's Land was settled, there was a violent clash between a large group of Aboriginal people, the Mairremmener, and the settlers at Risdon Cove. The records are not definite, but the Mairremmener were probably on a kangaroo hunt. There was a confrontation between the hunters and the soldiers at the settlement, and soldiers fired shots, killing some of the Mairremmener and wounding others. The causes of the conflict and the extent of the casualties are debated by historians. The clash permanently soured relations between the local people and the settlers.

For the first 20 years of the colony there were few other clashes. But as new settlements spread south from Launceston and north from Hobart through the midlands, they intersected with the traditional seasonal east–west movement of Aboriginal people across the area. Before 1824, on average fewer than two clashes per year were recorded, though there may have been more that were unrecorded. By 1830, the number of reported clashes was 222.

Aboriginal people resisted the invasion in Tasmania because their whole way of life was being destroyed – their food sources, their water supplies, their hunting and gathering patterns, their sacred sites, their culture and their very lives. In response to these intrusions they attacked shepherds and travellers, burned farms and crops, and slaughtered or crippled animals. An estimated 170 settlers were killed. It is likely that the majority of Aboriginal deaths was from diseases introduced by the new settlers and for which Aboriginal people had no natural immunity, but undoubtedly many Aboriginal people were shot by the settlers. The period of increased conflict was known as the Black War. Of the estimated 1500 Aboriginal people in Tasmania in 1824, only 350 are thought to have survived by 1831.

In response to violence towards the invaders, the Governor of Van Diemen's Land, George Arthur, declared martial law. He organised an event called the Black Line to trap the Aboriginal people and force them into a reservation. Over 2000 armed settlers and soldiers moved in a line across the island for six weeks in October and November of 1828. Only two Aboriginal people, one a child, were trapped. The rest probably slipped past the camps of men during the night.

By 1831 resistance by the remaining Aboriginal people had become futile. George Augustus Robinson was employed by Lieutenant-Governor Arthur to bring as many Indigenous people as possible to a settlement on Flinders Island, off the north-east coast of Tasmania.

A British military musket. Aboriginal warriors quickly learned that the time to reload between single shots from such weapons gave them the chance to attack with their spears. This musket was used against miners at the Eureka Stockade (1854), and the Lambing Flat anti-Chinese race riot (1861).

Robinson set out for the west coast with a group of Aboriginal people, including a woman named Truganini. She seemed to have acted as diplomat, negotiator and interpreter for him, with the message that the Aboriginal people were all being killed, that it was no use fighting any more, that Robinson was their friend, and he would take them to a safe and good place. They were able to collect a number of Indigenous people to take back to Flinders Island.

In early 1833, there were 220 Aboriginal residents at Wybalenna on Flinders Island. It was a bleak and exposed place, and the Aboriginal people huddled together in a small settlement without immunity to many introduced diseases. Soon the people began to die. By October 1847, when Wybalenna was abandoned and the people moved to Oyster Cove, only 46 had survived. Truganini herself died in Hobart in 1876; however, many Tasmanians still trace their heritage to the pre-European people.

Other changes in Van Diemen's Land

When Lieutenant-Governor Arthur first arrived in the colony of Van Diemen's Land in 1824, he had orders from Britain to restore the effectiveness of transportation as a punishment and a deterrent to crime. Arthur established the harsh settlement at Port Arthur, increased the number of chain gangs used to build roads, and imposed stricter rules on both the assigned convicts and the settlers who were in charge of them. Convicts were only entitled to a ticket of leave for good conduct or some special service (such as helping in the capture of bushrangers).

In 1823 Van Diemen's Land was separated legally from New South Wales. Within a few years it would become the staging point for the creation of yet another settlement, the Port Phillip District, which would eventually become Victoria. At the same time three other colonies were starting to develop: South Australia, Queensland and Western Australia.

CREATING NEW SETTLEMENTS

As the populations of New South Wales and Van Diemen's Land grew, explorers ventured into unknown areas in the north, south and west. They were often aided, willingly or unwillingly, by Aboriginal people and their knowledge of the country. Settlers began to move beyond the original settlement areas, officially and unofficially.

Flinders and Bass

Matthew Flinders (born 1774; died 1814) was a great navigator and chart-maker and one of the most renowned explorers in Australia's colonial history. He was a British naval officer who had served with William Bligh (Governor of New South Wales 1806–1808) and had seen action in war.

Flinders first arrived in New South Wales in 1795, during which he became friends with the ship's surgeon, George Bass (born 1771; disappeared 1803). Soon after arriving in the colony, Flinders and Bass made two trips of exploration along the New South Wales coast. In 1796, they sailed in a tiny boat called *Tom Thumb*, which was less than three metres long. Bass and

Opposite: Relics of convict discipline including shackles, guns, whips and a ball and chain.

Flinders explored rivers near Port Jackson (Sydney), which led to new settlements in the region. In 1798, they sailed in a larger ship, the *Norfolk*, around Van Diemen's Land, proving that it was an island. Flinders named the waterway separating Tasmania from the Australian mainland Bass Strait, and an island in the strait is called Flinders Island.

Matthew Flinders – the man who gave Australia its name

Matthew Flinders, explorer, was born in Donington, Britain, in 1774. His main achievement was proving that New Holland and New South Wales were the one land, and that the mainland was separate from Van Diemen's Land.

On a trip back to Britain in 1803, Flinders was forced to call in to the French colony of Mauritius for repairs to his ship. Shortly before this, the war had broken out between France and England, and Flinders was arrested as a suspected spy. He showed a letter of support from the French Baudin expedition that he had met in 1802. The letter affirmed his role as an explorer rather than a spy, but he was detained under open arrest for the next seven years. Flinders had many opportunities to escape but refused to break his word that he would not try.

During his imprisonment he wrote an account of his voyages for publication. In 1804, he wrote to Joseph Banks and included his map of Australia as a separate island, recommending that the island then called New Holland in its western half and New South Wales on its eastern side be called Australia, after the traditional legendary name of 'Terra Australis', or south land. Banks did not even open the map.

Flinders was eventually freed in 1810 and returned to England. He worked on his

Men of Stamina — **Matthew Flinders**

book, *A Voyage to Terra Australis*, but died the day after it was published in 1814. He did not see a copy of it in published form.

Governor Macquarie was aware of Flinders' attempts to have the continent called Australia and recommended this name to the British authorities. They finally accepted the suggestion and in 1824 the land became officially known as Australia.

A wrought-iron fisherman's style stream anchor from Matthew Flinders' ship, *Investigator*.

Flinders returned to England in 1800 and married the following year. The British Government asked him to explore the New South Wales and New Holland coast again. So between 1802 and 1803, Flinders sailed the ship *Investigator* and he and his crew became the first to circumnavigate Australia. He mapped coastal areas for the first time and proved that New South Wales and New Holland were both part of the same single land mass.

George Bass was not on the *Investigator*. He sailed from New South Wales for South America in 1803 and was never heard from again.

Official exploration parties continued to discover and report back on the existence of attractive land in south-eastern Australia and the south-western corner of New Holland. Explorers were keen to find useful land and to

A model of Flinders' cat Trim, who circumnavigated Australia with him.

gather scientific information about the unique animals and plants of the country. Those who followed the larger rivers were impressed by their fertile plains.

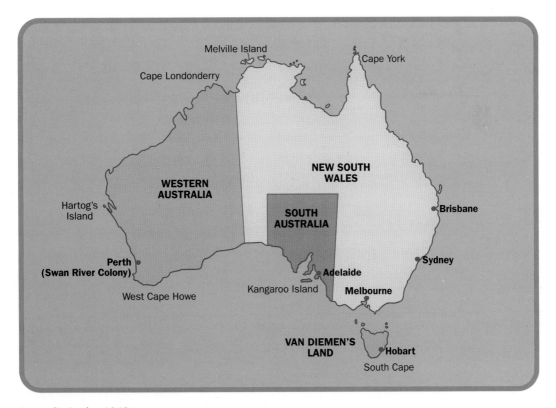

Australia in the 1840s.

Some exploration parties were very large, such as that of Major Mitchell in 1836, which opened up the huge grasslands in south-west Victoria to settlement. Mitchell's party rode horses, had supply carts drawn by oxen, and even had a flock of sheep for food. Other large parties included servants and some had Aboriginal guides who acted as interpreters and diplomats when they entered the Country of other Indigenous people.

Four new settlements

Four new settlements that would eventually become state capitals were created between 1824 and 1835 as a result of the exploration parties' reports to governors. The settlements had several features in common: they were on or close to good harbours, they had reliable fresh water supplies, they were on land usually not subject to flooding, and they were well-timbered, which would provide materials required to build the new settlements.

Brisbane 1824

The earliest settlement in what became Queensland was the convict outpost at Moreton Bay (Brisbane) in 1824, created after the explorer John Oxley reported on its potential in 1823. The settlement became a notoriously brutal place of secondary punishment – that is, a place where convicts who committed a crime in Australia, on top of the crime they'd been convicted for in Britain, were sent for punishment. The outpost's superintendent, Captain Patrick Logan, was murdered by escaped convicts, or Aboriginal people, or both, in 1830. The convict settlement was closed in 1842 and the area inland from Brisbane, known as the Darling Downs, was occupied by pastoralists coming north with their sheep. Brisbane became the main port for the region.

PROCLAMATION

By His Excellency JOHN HINDMARSH Knight of the Royal Hanoverian Guelphic Order, Governor and Commander-in-Chief of

HIS MAJESTY'S PROVINCE

OF

SOUTH AUSTRALIA

In announcing to the COLONISTS of HIS MAJESTY'S PROVINCE OF SOUTH AUSTRALIA the establishment of the Government, I hereby call upon them to conduct themselves on all occasions with order and quietness, duly to respect the laws, and by a course of industry and sobriety, by the practice of sound morality and a strict observance of the Ordinances of Religion, to prove themselves worthy to be FOUNDERS of a great and free Colony.

It is also, at this time especially, my duty to apprise the Colonists of my resolution to take every lawful means for extending the same protection to the NATIVE POPULATION as to the rest of His Majesty's Subjects, and of my firm determination to punish with exemplary severity all acts of violence or injustice which may in any manner be practised or attempted against the NATIVES, who are to be considered as much under the Safeguard of the law as the Colonists themselves, and equally entitled to the privileges of British Subjects. I trust, therefore, with confidence to the exercise of moderation and forbearance by all Classes in their intercourse with the NATIVE INHABITANTS, and that they will omit no opportunity of assisting me to fulfil His Majesty's most gracious and benevolent intentions towards them by promoting their advancement in civilization, and ultimately, under the blessing of Divine Providence, their conversion to the Christian Faith.

By His Excellency's Command,

ROBERT GOUGER, Colonial Secretary.

Glenelg, 28th December, 1836.

GOD SAVE THE KING   26

GLENELG : Printed by authority by ROBERT THOMAS AND CO., Government Printers

A government proclamation recognising South Australia as a new colony and stating that no 'violence or injustice' be enacted against the local Aboriginal people. 1836.

Perth 1829

The Swan River Colony (Perth) was established as a settlement of 450 free people in 1829, in the area British explorer Captain James Stirling had identified during a sea voyage in 1827. Stirling had reported that the area had good soil, although he did not travel far from the river. He reported that the area could be a port for promoting trade in the Indian Ocean. A settlement there would also stop possible French and American interest in the area.

The Swan River Colony was to be a new type of British colony: funded by private investment, and with little cost to the British Government and no convicts. The idea was that settlers would buy land, but they would not gain full ownership of it until it was partially cultivated. Settlers would also be given more land for every free labourer they brought with them.

The settlers arrived, and the colony was symbolically founded when a tree was cut down by Helen Dance, the wife of the captain of one of the ships. The new settlers soon discovered that the soil was in poor condition, and some had to move to Guildford to grow food. The settlers also preferred to use Fremantle as the port. Local merchants charged exorbitant prices for goods, and many of the free labourers were soon unemployed as much of the land was not arable.

The colony developed very slowly and by 1850 fewer than 6000 people lived in Western Australia, mostly in Perth and Fremantle.

Adelaide 1836

The settlement of Adelaide in 1836 was an exercise in planned free colonisation as another alternative to convict transportation. The idea was for the British Government to sell the land to wealthy settlers. The government would use the money to send out poor but worthy people (that is, free settlers) from Britain to work on the new farms. These workers would eventually earn enough money to buy land for themselves, thus perpetuating the process. The colony would expand in a controlled way and it would finance itself. As the settlers were free, the new colony would not have to rely on convicts for its development.

This theory had been worked out by Edward Gibbon Wakefield, a man who never visited South Australia. Ironically, he thought out his ideas while in a gaol cell, serving time for eloping with a 15-year-old heiress. Wakefield was a persuasive writer, and his published ideas about systematic colonisation influenced key decision-makers.

The early settlers to the Adelaide area were mainly British, but later included German farmers who had left the region of Germany called Prussia because their government was imposing a prayer book that did not reflect their own religious beliefs. They settled in the Adelaide Hills and were responsible for planting the first vineyards in the Barossa Valley.

Melbourne 1835

The first settlements in the Port Phillip District, near modern-day Melbourne, were established in 1803 and then in 1826. Both failed. The 1803 settlement was created at Sorrento on Port Phillip Bay by a party of officials, convicts and a few free settlers. The purpose of this settlement was to warn off any attempt by suspected nearby French voyagers to claim it. The site did not have fresh water and the soil was poor. The settlement packed up after a few months and in 1804 headed to Van Diemen's Land, minus one of the most famous characters of early colonial Australian history, the convict William Buckley.

Buckley had escaped from the settlement, walked around the bay, and lived for 32 years with an Aboriginal family before suddenly appearing at the new settlement set up in Melbourne by John Batman and others in 1835.

In 1826, a settlement from Sydney was founded in response to reports of possible claims by France. The settlement, in Corinella, 114 km south-east of Melbourne, was abandoned two years later due to poor soil, lack of fresh water and no sign of French incursion. The successful establishment of the new colony at Melbourne in 1835 came as a result of pressure for land in Van Diemen's Land. Although the number of sheep continued to increase, and with them their valuable export product of raw wool, there was not enough land available for the pastoralists to expand their flocks. The pastoralists in Van Diemen's Land looked to the seemingly endless grasslands across Bass Strait.

The Batman treaty

In 1835 a group calling themselves the Port Phillip Association developed a plan to send sheep from Van Diemen's Land to the area of New South Wales known as the Port Phillip District. They sailed to the mouth of the Yarra River in Port Phillip Bay, an area that had been surveyed and identified in 1803 as a potential site for settlement. The party, led by John Batman, proceeded to do something unique in Australian history – they made a treaty with the local Aboriginal people.

Before leaving Launceston, the party had drawn up a document, which they referred to again when they gathered a group of Wurundjeri people, including eight elders, together

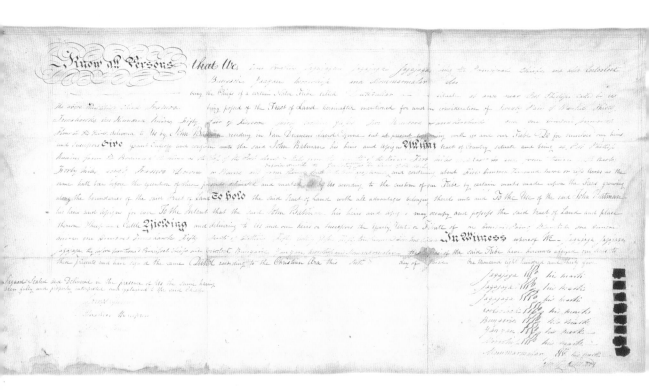

Batman's 'treaty' or agreement with Aboriginal leaders of the Kulin Nation to give his party the right to graze sheep in return for annual gifts. 1835.

William Buckley

William Buckley (born 1776; died 1856) was a British soldier who was transported to New South Wales for theft. He was part of the small settlement at Sorrento in Victoria, which was set up to show the French that the area was not available to claim.

While at Sorrento, Buckley and some other convicts escaped. The others soon surrendered and were taken to Hobart when the Sorrento settlement failed, but Buckley stayed hidden. He eventually walked around to the opposite side of Port Phillip Bay and was adopted by an Aboriginal family, who apparently believed he was a recently deceased relative returned to them. Buckley had taken this man's spear from his grave and the family recognised it. He lived with the group for the next 32 years and became knowledgeable in their language and culture.

In 1835 when the John Batman party arrived at the site that would become Melbourne, Buckley heard the news and went to meet them. He had virtually forgotten how to speak English but soon re-learned it. He now had to make a great decision – to return to his old civilisation or to continue with the new one. Buckley stayed with the Europeans, though he admitted he often regretted that choice.

Buckley was pardoned and remained in the new settlement doing odd jobs.

John Batman

John Batman was born in New South Wales in 1801, the son of a transported convict and his wife, who had paid to come with him. He moved to Van Diemen's Land in 1821, leaving behind a pregnant girl.

Batman bought some poor pastoral land and became a skilled bushman. He helped

John Batman

capture the bushranger Matthew Brady and became a bounty hunter, rounding up Aboriginal people to be sent to Flinders Island. Batman was part of a raid that killed at least ten people, including two wounded women whom Batman shot because he could not carry them with him. He effectively adopted two Aboriginal boys whose parents were killed in this raid.

Despite his father's convict background, Batman was able to mix and negotiate with wealthy people and was sent by the private company, the Port Phillip Association, to make an agreement with Aboriginal people for the purchase of a huge area of land around what is now Melbourne.

The document recording that purchase had no legal validity and could not bind either party. It was quickly annulled by the British Government. Though the 'treaty' was never officially recognised, it represents an approach that was not commonly taken in relations with Aboriginal people.

Batman brought his wife and eight children to the new settlement of Melbourne and built a house there in 1836. He died of syphilis in 1839.

in Port Phillip Bay. Batman added their names to the document, as well as various squiggly lines beside each name as a form of signature of consent from the Aboriginal people, possibly taking them from clan marks he saw on trees. He paid the Aboriginal leaders in beads, axes and cloth, and promised an annual payment of food.

Batman also picked up dirt and leaves and gave them to the leaders, signifying the making of an agreement. His party included several Aboriginal people from New South Wales, and it may be that by design or accident the procedure with the dirt and leaves was recognised by the local leaders as a *tanderrum*, a 'welcome to country' custom similar to a smoking ceremony and a recognised way of coming to an agreement in Aboriginal culture. The process may have been familiar to the local Wurundjeri people, but it could not have been understood in the same way by both sides. To the Europeans, it was understood as a transfer of property; to the local people, it was at best seen as a promise by the strangers that they would behave properly and obey Aboriginal Law while they were in the area.

Batman's party returned to Launceston to collect sheep and other goods they would need to establish their colony, and then headed back to the settlement, which was variously called Barebrass, Bareport, Bareheep, Barehurp and Bareberp. It was officially named Melbourne in 1837.

Batman's Land Deed or Treaty was declared void by the New South Wales governor, Richard Bourke. As the whole Port Phillip District was officially Crown Land (owned by the British Government), the land contained within could not be traded away by anybody else. But pastoralists had started to pour into the new area and there was nothing the governor could do to stop them. He made the best of a bad situation by appointing a police magistrate to the Port Phillip District, who would have the power to try to enforce the appropriate laws.

Even before the New South Wales governor had rejected the treaty, other parties, including one led by John Pascoe Fawkner, had also arrived and taken up land. They did not accept the legal authority of the Deed, and simply claimed the land for themselves.

Aboriginal responses to colonisation

The colonies were already inhabited by people who had owned this land for many thousands of years. Aboriginal people did not 'own' the land in the British legal sense, but their right of possession of their territory was as strong and as real as European property titles. As settlers pushed into new areas, they came in contact with the Aboriginal people whose land was being invaded and occupied, and whose food and water resources and sacred sites were being disrupted.

The settlers did not see it in this way – they believed, or chose to believe, that they were legally occupying territory that was mostly unused by the Indigenous inhabitants, and who therefore did not really own it.

As European settlements spread and grew, the original inhabitants were confronted with something totally outside their experience of the way people and the world behaved. Sometimes settlers arrived while the Aboriginal owners were exploiting a seasonal food source in another part of their traditional Country. When they returned they would find strangers settled without permission in their territory.

The Aboriginal people had to decide how to respond to this invasion: whether to resist, or flee, or try to share with the newcomers. All three were tried in different places at different times.

Explorers 1817–1849

John Oxley explored the Lachlan River west of Bathurst in 1817, and the Macquarie River northwest of Bathurst and across to Port Macquarie in 1818.

Allan Cunningham explored the north of Bathurst in 1823. He also moved through the New England area northwest of Sydney in 1827 and the area south of Brisbane in 1828.

Hamilton Hume and William Hovell explored the area from Lake George (near present-day Canberra) to the western side of Port Phillip Bay (present-day Geelong) in 1824.

Charles Sturt explored along the Macquarie River west to present-day Bourke between 1828 and 1829, the Murrumbidgee River and then the Murray River to the sea at Victor Harbour between 1829 and 1830.

Major Thomas Mitchell, between 1831 and 1836, followed the Darling River, then the Lachlan River, the Murray River, and overland to Portland, discovering the 'Australia Felix' – the western district of Victoria – before going back to Goulburn. Settlers followed in the wheel tracks of his cart to occupy the rich lands he discovered.

Angus McMillan and Pawel Strzelecki explored the Gippsland area of Victoria at separate times – McMillan in 1839 and Strzelecki in 1840.

The midlands and west coast of Van Diemen's Land were explored and opened up by different people in the early 1800s – Thomas Laycock in 1807, William Wedge in 1825 and 1828, Jorgen Jorgensen in 1826, Henry Hellyer and Joseph Fossey in 1827 and George Robinson between 1830 and 1833.

The south-west of Western Australia was also explored by different people –Thomas Bannister between 1830 and 1831, Alexander Collie in 1831, George Grey in 1839, Francis Gregory between 1846 and 1848, and John Septimus Roe between 1848 and 1849.

A postcard featuring explorer Charles Sturt, who followed the Murray River to the sea.

Harmony/disharmony

Some of the early encounters between settlers and the Indigenous people were cautiously friendly. Governors tried to maintain peace and harmony between the settlers and the Indigenous people. Officially the law was to be applied equally and evenly to both groups – any violence by settlers towards Aboriginal people was considered unlawful as was violence by Aboriginal people towards settlers. In effect, that was not always the case.

In 1838, 11 stockmen, both convict and ex-convicts, murdered up to 30 Wirrayaraay people on Myall Creek Station in northern New South Wales. In a rare example of applying the law equally to all, the government prosecuted the killers. Initially the stockmen were found not guilty, but after a public uproar they were re-tried, and seven of the 11 were convicted and hanged. The other four were released when the key Aboriginal witness mysteriously disappeared and could not give evidence against them.

Not all settlers were hostile towards the local people. Some tried to live amicably with Indigenous people while still maintaining their own claim on the area; these settlers allowed the local people to stay on the land rather than forcing them off it. Some settlers provided or shared food supplies, learned the locals' language and ways, and showed respect and consideration.

Some Aboriginal people developed loyalties to the Europeans. In October 1835 Derrimut, described by the settlers as a 'native chief', warned the new settlers at Melbourne that an 'up country tribe' was planning to massacre them. The grateful colonists erected a headstone over Derrimut's grave in 1864 to commemorate his 'noble act'.

In other places, settlers and Aboriginal groups were not able to collaborate effectively and the settlers pushed the Aboriginal people off the land. The danger here was that those being forced into a new area might be trespassing on a hostile group's Country, which could lead to conflict between the two Aboriginal groups. Convict William Buckley described several incidents of territorial rivalry between groups among the Wathaurong people of the Geelong area, in which many men, women and children were killed because of land disputes.

Resistance

In some places Aboriginal resistance to invasion and colonisation was effective and sustained. In the Darling Downs area of Queensland, several Aboriginal groups would meet to resist invasion by attacking settlers and demanding that they leave. They quickly learned not to challenge large armed groups of European settlers, instead targeting isolated shepherds, hutkeepers or families, and destroying their huts, animals and supplies. About 50 Europeans were killed in the Darling Downs area in the 1840s, and this resulted in an estimated 300 Aboriginal deaths in retaliation.

In the Swan River Colony (what is now Western Australia), resistance was led by a Nyungar warrior named Yagan. He led a series of raids against settlers in 1831 and 1832 and was subsequently declared an outlaw and imprisoned. He escaped and took revenge for the death of his brother by killing two settlers. As a result, he was again declared an outlaw, tracked down and shot. Yagan's head was removed and eventually sent to Britain. It was stored in Liverpool Museum, where it was studied for many years, until it was buried

Settlers often made brass breastplates for an Elder in an Aboriginal group in an attempt both to make that person feel important, and to create someone whom settlers could deal with as a leader.

Windradyne

Windradyne (born about 1800; died 1829) was a leader of the Wiradjuri people who resisted the European invasion of the Bathurst area.

The movement of settlers into the area disrupted traditional Wiradjuri hunting, camp sites, water supplies and sacred sites. During the early 1820s, the Wiradjuri attacked and killed settlers. In 1823 Windradyne was arrested for his involvement in the death of two shepherds, but was released a month later.

Europeans began retaliating violently against Aboriginal groups and the Wiradjuri responded with more violence of their own. The settlers had firearms and horses, but the Wiradjuri were able to use the environment more effectively to carry out hit-and-run attacks.

In 1824 Governor Thomas Brisbane declared martial law, which meant that soldiers and settlers could legally attack Aboriginal people. Windradyne was declared an outlaw and a reward was offered for his capture.

Windradyne gathered his people and they walked nearly 200 kilometres to Parramatta, to the annual feast and meeting organised by the government for the Aboriginal people. He knew that such a public occasion would protect his people from any attack. They were formally pardoned there by Governor Brisbane.

Windradyne then lived on the property of a friendly settler until 1829, when he was involved in a tribal fight and died after wounds he received became infected.

in 1964 with other human remains. Western Australian Aboriginal man Ken Colbung eventually tracked down the skull. He formally buried it in Yagan's native soil in 2010, 177 years after the Nyungar warrior's death.

Acceptance

There were also instances during the colonial period in which Aboriginal people 'came in' – they accepted the reality of the new settlement by engaging with the British settlers, even taking occasional jobs on farms or pastoral properties.

In 1842, 20 young Aboriginal men joined the Victorian Native Police, a body created by the government to track offenders. It was supported by some local Elders as it gave them influence with the colonial government. The Native Police was an attractive option for young Aboriginal warriors. They were equipped with a uniform, a horse, firearms and pay, and they could exercise power over other people. The Native Police were removed from the restrictions of having to follow the rules of their Elders, but in turn had to follow the orders of a white officer. A Native Police force was also established in New South Wales and South Australia, but the largest and longest-serving one was in Queensland, between 1848 and 1905. The Queensland Native Police force was especially brutal in attacking Aboriginal people on the frontier of settlement between Indigenous and new settlers.

THE PEOPLING OF THE COLONIES

Transported convicts were the main source of migration to the colonies until the 1830s, when the bigger source was free migrants.

New South Wales (including Queensland) received about 80,000 convicts between 1788 and 1830, and only 3000 more in the 1840s.

Van Diemen's Land received around 30,000 between 1803 and 1840, but then another 30,000 in the 1840s after transportation to New South Wales virtually stopped in 1840.

The Swan River settlement in Western Australia received about 10,000 convicts between 1850 and 1868.

Victoria and South Australia claimed to be 'free', but over 1700 'Pentonvillians' sent to Australia arrived in Victoria in the 1840s. These were convicts from England's Pentonville prison who had not been sentenced to transportation but who

Porcelain figure of William O'Brien, an Irish nationalist political rebel transported to Tasmania in the 1840s. Made 1848.

had agreed to be sent to Australia for the remainder of their sentence. Most Pentonvillians were taken by squatters – pastoralists who settled on land without having any legal claim to it – and used as cheap labour.

By the late 1830s powerful movements against transportation were developing in Britain, and then later in Australia. The 1830s were a time of great agitation in Britain against slavery, led by the religious people known as 'evangelicals'. They argued that transportation was a 'lottery', with no certainty that an assigned convict would get a good master. It was also, they claimed, a form of slavery, which corrupted and brutalised the convicts, and had a bad influence on the whole society.

In 1838 the Molesworth Committee of the British Parliament recommended that transportation to New South Wales under the assignment system cease. All convicts were now to be sent to Van Diemen's Land, where it was believed they could be better controlled.

In the late 1840s some wealthy squatters proposed to reintroduce

The *Success* was launched in 1790 and used as a convict ship. It was turned into a floating museum in the 1890s and was exhibited in the United States in the 1920s.

transportation as a source of cheap labour (such as shepherds). Strong resistance to this developed in the colonies. Opponents of transportation formed the Australasian Anti-Transportation League in Van Diemen's Land, and it had many supporters in New South Wales, Victoria and South Australia. Their main arguments were that convict labour would keep free settlers out of jobs, and that the 'convict stain' needed to be removed from the developing society.

Transportation to Van Diemen's land was officially ended in 1853.

The name Van Diemen's Land was changed to Tasmania in 1856, to try to separate it from its convict origins.

Meanwhile, transportation continued in Western Australia between 1850 and 1868, as the colony was struggling to establish itself and required cheap convict labour. Most convicts in Western Australia worked on government projects to build roads and public buildings that would help the colony develop.

Assisted migrant schemes

The population balance between convicts/ex-convicts and free settlers began to change during the 1830s, when greater numbers of free settlers started arriving. There was also a great gender imbalance: in the 1830s men outnumbered women in the colonies by about four to one in the cities, and eight to one in country areas.

By 1840 many people wanted to migrate to Australia to improve their lives. The Industrial Revolution in Britain had created a struggling working class, many of whom lived in unhygienic homes. The failure of the Irish potato crop during the 1840s created mass starvation in Ireland, and stimulated an exodus of people to other countries. Most British and Irish emigrants chose the United States as their destination, because it was closer than Australia, making the voyage safer and cheaper. But a system of free emigration helped encourage settlers to come to Australia.

Silver snuff box presented by emigrants in thanks for a safe voyage. The underside is inscribed: *A Trifling Token OF ESTEEM from the Emigrants of THE LADY ANN TO Capt. Wm. Maxton Octr. 1854.*

The assisted passage scheme subsidised working families who wanted to emigrate to the colonies. The colonial governments would pay the cost of the emigrants' passage to the colonies, plus a further few weeks' living expenses after that. This was funded by the sale of land in the colonies to settlers. Immigration agents in Britain chose the fittest, healthiest, most 'useful' settlers who could afford to bring themselves to the colonies. At a time when the colonies' economies were booming, strong workers would be snapped up by farmers and other employers.

There was no similar scheme for assisting immigrants from countries other than the United Kingdom (mainly England and Ireland). As a result, the Australian colonies developed a very different ethnic profile from other immigrant nations of the time. The United States, for example, received large numbers of immigrants from Germany, Italy, Russia and other countries.

The voyage

The free immigrants' voyage from Britain and Ireland to the colonies was long, uncomfortable and challenging – yet it offered new opportunities most people in Britain would not be exposed to if they remained at home.

All immigrants came on sailing ships. The voyage would take three to four months and passengers lived in large dormitories. Blankets drawn around their beds provided the only

The peril of the sea voyage. This postcard shows the sailing ship *Ditton* in 1908, but the danger of storms was present in all sea voyages during the 19th century.

privacy. Separate dormitories were set up below deck for families, single men and single women. On one ship, for example, which brought Cornish settlers to South Australia in 1848, there were 66 married males, 64 married females, 49 single males and 51 single females. There were also 121 children aged under 14, and 21 infants. Six children were born during the trip and 12 people died, including nine children.

All aspects of life – eating, sleeping, talking, praying, arguing, drinking, playing, reading, being ill, dying, giving birth, going to the toilet – took place in the one enclosed area. People could go on deck if the weather was fine but often it was not. People could wash but with no privacy; bodies soon stank and lice and rats were always present.

Ships often sailed through raging seas and storms. Possessions would be hurled around the dormitory if they were not secured. Food and drink would spill from mugs and plates, the ship would never be still and people felt seasick. The greatest threats were fire, as there always had to be fires going to cook food; illness, which spread rapidly among the tightly packed passengers; and shipwreck.

Most ships arrived safely, but there were tragedies. One of the worst was the *Cataraqui* in 1845. It left England with 369 passengers and 41 crew members. During the voyage six children died and five were born. As the ship neared Australia a terrible storm struck, and the ship was wrecked on rocks off King Island, north of Tasmania. Only eight crew members and one passenger survived.

DEVELOPING AN ECONOMY IN THE COLONIES

From the beginning of settlement in 1788, people in the colony of New South Wales tried to achieve two economic outcomes: to be able to feed themselves, and to create wealth. These aims led to people actively participating in buying, selling, growing, making and trading.

As early as the 1790s whalers and sealers in southern waters used Sydney as a port. They bought supplies there and traded their own catches. Their catches included sealskins for hats, coats, waistcoats and boots; sandalwood for incense; trepang or sea cucumber for medical purposes in Asia; and seal and whale oil for fuel in lamps. The colonial merchants exported these goods to Asia and England, but the merchants were acting as middlemen, buying from the non-local producers to sell on again to others. This trade was for private profit, but it helped to stimulate broader economic activity in the colony.

Sea cucumber, or trepang, which regularly brought Makassan fishermen to the northern Australian coastline.

Real economic development could only occur when goods were produced in the colonies and traded overseas. This started with livestock – cattle and sheep. Initially most livestock in Australia was for eating, but once new areas started to open up for settlement, people in New South Wales, Van Diemen's Land and later Victoria also raised sheep to produce wool, as well as for meat and sheepskin to sell.

Wool

In 1830 the export value of goods such as animal skins, trepang and sandalwood was double that of wool. By 1840, however, wool exports were three times the value of all other exports. Internationally, Australia's share of the wool trade rose from 8.1 per cent in 1830 to 47 per cent in 1850, displacing the previous wool giant, Germany. The wool industry began to transform the early Australian economy. Australia, as the saying went, was starting to ride on the sheep's back.

There were several reasons for the success of wool: sheep were suited to the climate of the south-eastern edge of Australia; there were vast grazing areas, adequate fresh water, and the absence of a natural predator other than the dingo, which was quickly brought under control by the settlers.

The Spanish merino

The best wool at the time of settlement was the Spanish merino. Deliberate breeding programs by a few wool growers in colonial Australia quickly saw the quality of wool improved.

This process began when New South Wales Governor John Hunter sent Captains Henry Waterhouse and William Kent to the Cape of Good Hope, South Africa, in 1796 to buy cattle. When they arrived Captain Philip Gidley King, who was also aboard the ship on

Eliza Forlonge

Eliza Forlonge (born 1784; died 1859) is also a significant figure in the Australian wool industry. John and Eliza Forlonge were Scottish merchants. They decided to send their sons to Australia to seek their fortune in the wool industry. Eliza and her two sons prepared for this by going to the wool capital of the world, Germany, to learn about fleeces.

Eliza walked for over 200 kilometres through sheep country, selecting the best quality Saxon merino sheep for her new flock, and paying for them with gold coins sewn into her corset. She padlocked a brass collar on each sheep she bought so that she could recognise it, and gathered her flock together at the end of her buying trip.

She then walked the 97 sheep she had purchased over 300 kilometres to the port of Hamburg, to ship them to England, and then to Australia. The surviving 75 sheep were landed in Hobart in 1829.

Eliza went on another buying trip to Saxony and bought a second flock, which went to Launceston and later to Goulburn.

She sailed to Van Diemen's Land with her two sons before moving to the Port Phillip district in 1838, and finally settled near Euroa, north of Melbourne.

Some of the Saxon merinos the Forlonge family introduced to Tasmania, Victoria and New South Wales were crossbred with other sheep to reinvigorate the merino breed and to make it the most successful wool in the world from the 1840s, and Australia's main export.

his way home to England, persuaded them to buy 26 Spanish merinos. A number of the sheep died on the voyage back to Australia but John Macarthur, a prominent businessman, immediately offered to buy the surviving sheep. Though the offer was refused, a few sheep were later distributed to Macarthur and to other exclusives such as the Reverend Samuel Marsden.

In 1804 Macarthur bought more Spanish fine wool merino sheep. Skilful breeding and selection between Spanish and Saxon merinos resulted in the development of a hardy animal that produced high quality wool suited to the industrial spinning machines used for manufacturing textiles in England. By 1890 the weight of a merino ram in Australia was several times the weight of the original rams owned by Macarthur.

For a long time, Australian history books celebrated John Macarthur as the founder of the Australian wool industry. More recently it was realised that his wife, Elizabeth Macarthur, was the key person behind the successful development of the merino fleece in Australia through her work breeding varieties of the merino sheep to produce superior wool. She did much of this during her husband's absence, while he was defending himself in Britain against the overthrow of Governor Bligh.

The wool industry
The wool industry was also helped by the availability of convict shepherds who were cheaper to employ than free settler shepherds. Later, after the loss of the convicts, the new

A 'holey dollar' introduced as currency in New South Wales. The middle of existing foreign coins were punched out and new engraving added, creating two coins to help overcome the lack of local currency.

technology of cheap wire-fencing meant that large numbers of sheep could be controlled without workers.

The British invested a lot of money in the development of the Australian wool industry. This money went towards increasing the sheep population, the spreading out of settlers to more areas with their flocks, and the construction of basic roads and small towns to provide services to the growers and their workers. The spread of sheep and cattle grazing (known as pastoralism) also led to increased contact with Aboriginal people as the introduced animals damaged sacred sites and displaced the main native grazer, the kangaroo. Violence and cultural destruction followed, and so did more involvement of Aboriginal people in the industry. The Wiradjuri warrior Windradyne, for example, initially resisted the expansion of settlement, but surrendered and then worked on a pastoral property, where he died in 1829.

The rise and fall of Australian exports

Wool was not the only source of wealth in the economy but it was the major export. The discovery of copper in South Australia in 1842 led to the development of mining in that area and the immigration of Cornish miners with their expert skills. Wheat was also an important crop in all colonies, and production increased after the development of the Ridley stripper in South Australia in 1843, which made wheat harvesting much quicker and easier there.

It was not all profit and expansion, however. Late in the 1830s there was a slump in the British textile industry. People were buying less material in Britain, which meant that there was less production, which in turn meant less demand for wool used to manufacture the cloth, and a consequent fall in wool prices. Many growers in Australia fell into debt or had to kill their sheep and walk off the land. In 1843, growers developed a process for boiling down the bodies of sheep to produce tallow or fat for candles. This meant that they at least had a small source of income until the price of wool rose again. Between 1843 and 1851 an estimated 45 million sheep and 250,000 cattle were used in this way.

The economic recovery started with the discovery of gold in the 1850s. This triggered a huge wave of immigration, which in turn required a significant increase in food production of all kinds.

Changing the environment

The development of pastoralism and agriculture as a result of European settlement meant that a far greater population could inhabit Australia than had been possible under a hunter-gatherer economy. But this also caused great changes to the environment, especially the south-eastern crescent of land from Brisbane to Adelaide, plus Tasmania and the south-west corner of Western Australia.

The creation of European farms meant that trees were chopped down in large numbers, and sheep and cattle were introduced into areas where they competed with kangaroos for grass and quickly ate out some species of native grasslands.

Sheep and cattle also eroded creek beds and trampled down riverine plants that grew along the banks or floodplains of rivers. The pattern of European occupation interrupted the traditional Aboriginal fire regime and this changed the environment significantly, with undergrowth encroaching in wooded areas and forest areas spreading. This created hotter and more destructive bushfires. The Victorian bushfire of February 1851 is estimated to have burned about one quarter of the whole colony, an unprecedented impact.

Introduced species of fruit trees and bushes were spread by birds, and these choked out some native plants and interfered with natural water flows. Willow trees and blackberry bushes were – and still are – two of the biggest offenders.

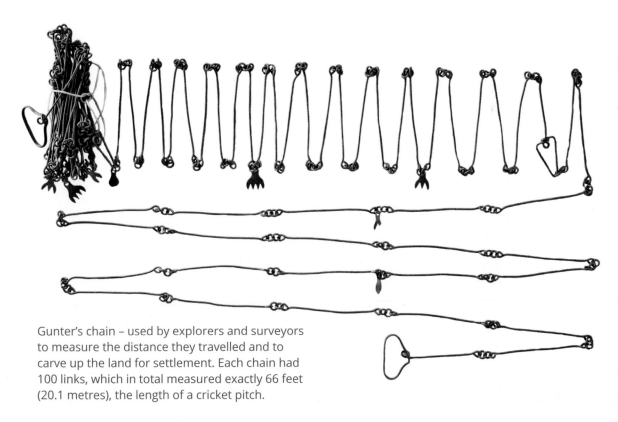

Gunter's chain – used by explorers and surveyors to measure the distance they travelled and to carve up the land for settlement. Each chain had 100 links, which in total measured exactly 66 feet (20.1 metres), the length of a cricket pitch.

LIVING AND WORKING IN THE COLONIES

Life in the cities

As the colonies grew, so did the demand for services – food, clothes, entertainment, transport, medical treatment, education, tools, repairs, legal advice and banks. By 1850, all the foundation settlements had developed extensively and rapidly, there were many shops selling the latest fashions and luxuries, and there was even gas lighting in some streets. There were schools, libraries and churches. However, the streets also had deep gutters blocked by rubbish, with horse manure everywhere, and most roads were still dirt rather than paved and were either muddy in winter or dusty in summer.

There were rough and rundown areas where people crowded together in terrible, unsanitary conditions.

Sydney

The city of Sydney grew greatly under Governor Lachlan Macquarie. He used convict labour and skills to design and build a range of public buildings, and he created specialised areas for markets and manufacturers. The area around Sydney Harbour became crowded, but further out, houses were set on larger areas of land and could have their own gardens. The western side became the working city and the lower classes crowded into The Rocks area.

Several substantial villages were established around or near Sydney – Windsor, Parramatta, Liverpool, Campbelltown, Wilberforce, Pitt Town, Richmond, Castlereagh and, further north, the town of Newcastle. Most of these became staging points connecting Sydney to the hinterland.

Circular Quay, Sydney, N. S. W. in 1848

Hobart

Hobart was the largest city in Tasmania, with Launceston its main rival town. Shops, government offices, churches and schools were all located in the centre, while manufacturing areas were in the outskirts. Wealthier people started to congregate in a new suburb in the north of the city. The towering Mount Wellington pushed settlement along the rivers rather than around the centre of the original settlement.

Perth

The Swan River Colony was proclaimed in 1829 and renamed Western Australia in 1832. Perth started as three separate settlements in the new colony: Fremantle as the port area, Guildford at the head of the Swan River as the agricultural area, and Perth between them as a service centre. Specialist areas developed around each of the three settlements. Sandbars and the shallowness of the Swan River made development on both sides of the river difficult until the first bridge was opened in 1843. By 1850 there was also a canal and established tracks, but Perth was still a very small colony.

Adelaide

South Australia became a separate colony from New South Wales in 1836. Adelaide started as the city with the largest founding population, planned carefully from the beginning. It quickly developed a retail, commercial and professional area (for legal and government buildings). A ring of parks separated the city from the surrounding suburbs. Low land prices encouraged high rates of home ownership. Adelaide developed a working area to the north and west, near the port.

Melbourne

Melbourne also developed around a central grid. Land was expensive in the centre – where the areas of commerce, the law and government and food and animal markets were situated – so suburbs grew around it. Housing clustered near the shoreline of the bay, up the Yarra River and to the inner north, where the land was lower and swampy and therefore cheaper, and where factories were established. Victoria became a separate colony in 1851.

Brisbane

Brisbane was slow to develop until 1842, when it was opened as a free settlement. There were problems with the city area, as it was difficult for cargo vessels to unload due to shoals and obstructions near the mouth of the river. The site also had poor fresh water and poor soil. As a result, villages began to grow outside Brisbane. Ipswich grew as the main supply base for the inland Darling Downs once settlers started expanding there with their flocks of sheep. South Brisbane developed as the commercial area, Kangaroo Point developed as an industrial and residential area, and Fortitude Valley housed new immigrants. As Brisbane was so far south in Queensland, there was no certainty that it would become the capital city until the 1850s. Queensland became a separate colony in 1859.

Way of living

In the various settlements, wealthier people had large houses, could employ maids and gardeners, provided tutors for their children, and built their homes on high ground away from the heat, dust and smells of the main city areas. Skilled tradespeople had smaller but still substantial homes. The working class often lived in cramped and poorly ventilated housing, and because they weren't always guaranteed work, they couldn't afford fresh food all the time. The inner areas rapidly developed into manufacturing or industrial suburbs.

In the mid-19th century, women had an average of six children during their lifetime. Statistics for New South Wales for 1856 to 1866 showed that one in ten children died before age one, and two in ten died by age ten. Some mothers also died during childbirth due to poor medical practices. Scientists did not understand until the 1880s that bacteria could cause infections, so infection was common. Death rates from infections that are readily controlled today by antibiotics (penicillin was not developed until the 1940s) were very high.

Working class children were expected to work in the home and outside it. They would look after younger siblings, gather and chop firewood, feed chickens, and help with the heavy washing. Most children would be expected to work outside the house from the age of 12, either as an apprentice in a trade, or a labourer in a domestic service.

Most children had a basic education. There were a few public schools, usually set up by the churches and partly subsidised by the government. These schools accepted all pupils and taught basic literacy. Few families could afford to send their children to small private schools. There had been some institutions set up to educate Aboriginal children, such as Governor Macquarie's Native Institution in New South Wales, and the Merri Creek Aboriginal School in Melbourne, but education of Aboriginal children was mostly left to the missionaries.

Life in the country

In the country, 'squatters' were pastoralists who had brought in the first flocks and simply stayed on the land without buying it – although colonial governments made these squatters pay rent from 1836 onwards. Many of the squatters built substantial houses with wide verandahs, glass windows (glass was imported and very expensive), quality furnishings, and well maintained vegetable and flower gardens.

Many other free settlers lived as basically as the convicts assigned to them – in miserable bark huts with rough furniture and shutters for windows, surviving on tea and damper and mutton for most meals, and isolated from their neighbours.

Among the country settlers, life was hardest for women and children. While the men worked on the land, women and children were cut off from others, unable to call on help in times of danger or crisis from wanderers, convicts or snakes, and they too worked very long and hard days.

Many Aboriginal people formed a large part of the workforce as shepherds, wool washers, drovers, cattlemen, domestic servants and gardeners. They had useful skills, but were not paid equal wages to other workers, and usually lived in separate camps on properties, or on the fringes of settlements.

SOCIETY AND CULTURE

As the ratio of convicts to free settlers dropped, society began to change. The 'currency lads and lasses' – the nickname given to freeborn children of the convicts who were 'local currency', rather than the superior British currency called 'sterling' – became a more influential segment of the population. These children tended to be healthier and taller than their parents as the quality of food improved. They had no doubt that they belonged in the colony, and were not the forced inhabitants that their parents were.

Increased numbers of assisted migrants also changed the balance of the population, bringing in many poor but respectable people who were hardworking and ambitious. Although the settlers were still trying to recreate British culture, in the form of food, fashions, plants and animals, they were also responding and adapting to what was Australian. One of the most common decorative motifs of the time was the kangaroo.

Britain continued to be the primary source of immigration, which only began to vary more when the gold rushes began in the 1850s.

Governing the people

From 1788 the governor was in effect a dictator in New South Wales, though he was expected to follow the laws of Britain, and to account for all his actions to the British Government. In 1810 the governor could decide when religious services could be held, the rights of people to assemble together, whether people could marry, whether a person was sane or not, how much people could drink, how much those being provided with rations by the government would get to eat, and what should be taught in schools. He could pardon people, grant tickets of leave to convicts and make land grants to any person.

In New South Wales, the power and influence of the governor was slowly reduced by the creation of a Legislative Council. In 1823 the British Parliament passed an Act to allow the governor to appoint a council for advice. Initially, the council was not democratic: its members were not elected by public vote, nor could the general public stand to be elected. The councillors were men of property and influence appointed by the governor. But it was a step forward as the council could represent the interests of the colony rather than Britain's interests and the council also had a say in passing laws, which had been the sole power of the governor. The council was democratised in 1843, when it was expanded to 36 members, 24 of whom were public elected (though only by voters who owned a certain value of property) and only 12 of whom were appointed by the governor.

The free press

The development of a free press allowed the interests of the colony to be expressed. In 1824, William Charles Wentworth and Robert Wardell first published *The Australian* newspaper. (This has no connection to the current newspaper of the same name.) Wentworth, a former explorer and NSW-born son of a convict, used the paper as a platform to fearlessly criticise government policies that he disagreed with. He supported the rights and power of the emancipist class – those from a convict background over those of the exclusives, who prided themselves on their social superiority as free and wealthy settlers. Free postage of newspapers to inland areas meant that people remote from the cities could be kept informed about important local and international events.

Civil rights

For the colonies to be truly democratic, the political system had to acknowledge the civil rights of convicts and ex-convicts. Convicts could take employees or masters to magistrates or courts to protect their interests as subjects of the Crown. Ex-convicts were allowed to sit on civil juries from 1823 and on criminal juries from 1833. This demonstrates that ex-convicts were gradually being regarded as legitimate citizens, and gaining rights that the governor could not overrule.

By 1850 all six Australian colonies and their capital cities had been established. They were growing, and free settlers were slowly outnumbering convicts, changing the nature of the colonies. Gold would soon be discovered in New South Wales, Victoria, Queensland and Western Australia, and this would supercharge the rate at which each of these colonies developed.

Photograph of Port Arthur paupers, circa 1870s. Between 1830 and 1877, convicts who had re-offended after their arrival in Van Diemen's Land and New South Wales were imprisoned in the remote location of Port Arthur, Tasmania. The paupers were known as the aged mentally and physically ill convicts who had remained in Port Arthur after it ceased to be a place of punishment.

4 Gold Changes Australia: 1850 to 1900

The discovery of gold was one of the most significant events in Australian history. The gold rush brought huge numbers of immigrants into the colonies, which changed the country economically, socially, politically and culturally. Technology developed from this newfound wealth and improved Australia's communication with the world.

A gold cradle. These humble machines were used by thousands of prospectors during the gold rushes.

GOLD

Before 1851, Australia had a predominantly pastoral and agricultural economy. The discovery and mining of the precious metal gold created a new export resource. Between the 1850s and the 1870s, gold displaced wool as Australia's most valuable export.

Gold had been found in Australia before 1851. The difference at this critical moment in Australia's history was that many men had returned from the 1849 California gold rush, and they brought with them knowledge of where to look to find gold, and the skills to extract it.

Gold was valuable because many countries' governments, including the British Government, used it to provide value for their currency. Every note or coin represented a fixed quantity of gold and, theoretically, a person could swap the note or coins for an equivalent amount of gold. If a government increased its holdings of gold it could print more currency, and use that currency to buy goods from overseas.

In effect, gold increased the country's wealth and buying power. Gold stimulated commerce and

Panning for gold in a stream.

benefited both the nation that found it and sold it, and also the nation that bought it and increased its gold stocks.

Gold was found in all six colonies of Australia between 1850 and 1900. The first gold rushes occurred in New South Wales, and were the result of Edward Hargraves' claim that he had discovered a potentially large quantity of gold.

Edward Hargraves

Hargraves was born in Britain in 1816, went to sea at 14, and arrived in New South Wales in 1832. In 1849, he sailed off to the California gold rush in the United States of America.

Though he was unsuccessful there, he brought back to New South Wales an understanding of the type of area where gold might be located, and a knowledge of the best method to extract this metal from creeks.

The New South Wales Government, realising the potential value of a gold rush in terms of immigration and increased wealth, offered a reward to the person who could find large quantities in that colony. Hargraves enlisted the help of John Lister, who claimed to have found traces of gold near Bathurst, and the three Tom brothers, William, James and Henry. With them, Hargraves found specks of gold near Bathurst in 1851. He went to Sydney to publicise the find and claim the reward, leaving Lister and the brothers behind to continue looking for a larger gold find that would support his claim. Hargraves was made Crown Commissioner of the Goldfields and given an even greater reward, but did not share either reward with Lister or the Tom brothers.

Hargraves' discovery of gold created a rush to the Bathurst area by people already living in New South Wales. Men quit their jobs and headed by foot or by cart to the diggings. Sometimes their families came with them, but often they would remain behind. Once the news of the gold discovery spread, people from the other colonies joined in the rush. Within months, they were joined by prospectors from Europe, Britain, the United States and China.

Gold rush immigration

The discovery of gold caused a rush of immigration to Australia. In 1841, the non-Indigenous population of Australia was 220,961; by 1851 it had grown to 437,665 and in 1861 rose to 1,168,149. During the 1850s Victoria and New South Wales were the two colonies most affected by gold.

Of the half a million people who left the United Kingdom for Australia in the 1850s, about a third had their migration costs paid by colonial governments in the hope that they would become pastoral workers.

Prospectors would use a round shallow tin pan to sieve through the residue and dirt in the water to find nuggets of gold.

Other founders

The spectacular success of a few lucky miners was matched by equally spectacular failures.

Joseph Wills discovered tin near the Queensland–New South Wales border in 1870 and showed it in a pub. The lump of metal was taken to Sydney by one of the drinkers, where someone recognised its value and started a rush there. Wills had not pegged out a claim and missed out. His headstone reads:

> Here lieth poor Wills who found out tin
> But very little did he win
> He paved the way for others' gain
> And died neglected for his pain.

In 1893, Paddy Hannan set off for a rush in Western Australia with a small party, which got separated from the main group of prospectors. His party wandered off the track east of Coolgardie and stumbled over the richest goldfield in history. Hannan was then nearly shot by another miner who mistook him for an emu. Though Hannan had made some profit out of the discovery, he preferred a life of solitary prospecting and died living off the reward money paid to him by the Western Australian Government. A statue of Hannan was erected in Kalgoorlie.

Leslie Menzies was prospecting in Western Australia in 1894. He later claimed in a very colourful story that when he jumped off his camel he landed onto ground strewn with gold nuggets. He loaded six tonnes into wheelbarrows and wheeled them 160 kilometres south to Coolgardie, shouted the town £4000 worth of champagne (at a time when the annual wage of a working man was about £150), and cashed in £750,000 worth of gold – over $250 million in today's values.

One digger, whose name remains unknown, had a share in a Bendigo gold mine in the early 1860s. He sold it to another man, John Boyd Watson, for one shilling – the equivalent of about $25 today. The digger then shouted Watson a drink out of the shilling he had just been paid. Watson later became the richest man in Australia from the mine.

The other two-thirds paid their own way and most of these came to seek gold. Sixty thousand others came from Europe, mostly from Germany and Italy, 10,000 from the United States, and 5000 from New Zealand and the South Pacific. Half of these newcomers were aged between 21 and 35 and two-thirds were male. Sixty per cent of the gold migrants went to Victoria and 25 per cent to New South Wales.

Forty-two thousand prospectors arrived from China, and this contributed to the experiences and attitudes that developed after Federation into the White Australia policy. This was colonial governments' policy at various times, and supported by most Australians in the era, to limit the numbers of Chinese and other non-European migrants to Australia.

The gold rush immigrants began to arrive in large numbers in 1852. They brought their own languages and dialects, religious beliefs, political views, values and customs into the developing Australian society. Some immigrants mixed with the broader community, while others preferred to stay in national groups. This added to racial and religious tensions, especially between Irish Catholics and English Protestants. Many English people looked down on the supposedly 'peasant' Irish, and many from Europe and the United States believed themselves racially superior to the Chinese.

The European immigrants of the gold period were generally more skilled and literate than most previous immigrants, and had the means to pay their own fare to Australia on the chance they would become rich. Some prospectors did become fabulously wealthy or did very well, but most just made a basic living. Many found nothing and lost their investment. The migrants who did best were often those with the entrepreneurial sense to go into businesses that supported the diggers. They realised that while only some diggers found gold, *all* diggers needed to buy food and drink, tents, mining equipment, carts, wheelbarrows and entertainment.

The increased population created by the gold rushes stimulated local production of food and materials, housing, road-building, overseas investment and government expenditure. A large number of the immigrant miners stayed in Australia. This created demand for housing and services, which in turn created employment and wealth. The impact of the gold boom can still be seen in Melbourne, Ballarat and Bendigo today, as many of these cities' large buildings are made of expensive bluestone, material that only the wealthy and successful could afford to use.

Children's gold-diggings themed game from the 1850s.

When the surface gold ran out, only mining companies could afford the equipment and machinery required to dig out and crush gold from quartz.

Three types of gold mining

Alluvial fields

The earliest goldfields were alluvial fields: gold nuggets were on or near the surface of the ground, or in sand or soil that when washed and sifted left the gleaming specks of gold behind. Anybody could collect this – the only tools needed were a pick, shovel and a sieve. This alluvial gold was exhausted within a few weeks by the first wave of diggers, and after this it became much harder to find any gold, let alone to strike it rich.

Deep sinking

Gold could also be found trapped underground in the beds of ancient rivers (known as gold seams). Miners had to dig down, creating a mine shaft by hauling the dirt out in buckets and dumping it somewhere nearby. The narrow shafts were dangerous and could collapse, and the miners had to rig sails to funnel air down to the digger.

This whole process was called deep sinking, and meant that the miners had to camp in the one spot for weeks, maybe months, while they dug deeper and deeper and hoped to intersect with the old gold layer.

Hitting the gold seam became the dream and the last hope of many diggers. Most shafts missed the gold seam, so even though the miners may have spent weeks digging, with constant expenses to be paid, they gained nothing.

99

THE "GOLDEN EAGLE" NUGGET.
Weight *1135 ozs, 15 dwts.* Discoverers J. J. Larcombe and Son at Larkinville, West: Aust: Jan: *1931.* *Illustrations to — Photograph —*

The Golden Eagle was one of the biggest gold nuggets discovered in Australia. It was found by 17-year-old Jim Larcombe in 1931 and weighs over 30 kilos.

Quartz mining

Gold was also found embedded in quartz rock, which had to be crushed to remove the metal. This required large heavy crushing machines called stampers, which were operated by expensive steam engines. This type of mining could only be carried out by large-scale companies, not individual miners, so quartz mining took over when the gold from alluvial and deep-sinking mining ran out.

The licence system

When diggers arrived on the goldfield they had to buy a licence to mine. This was because the gold was legally owned by the British Crown. A licence was an agreement between the miner and the Crown, through the colonial government, that allowed the miner to extract the Crown's gold.

The licence gave the miner the right to claim a small area, about two metres square, and to dig there for gold. Usually several miners would join together and share their area, meaning that they had a much larger space to work in. The licence raised money that was used to pay for government services on the goldfield, especially the provision of police to keep law and order.

The miners had to pay for a licence each month, regardless of whether they found gold or not. Many tried to save on this expense by not getting one, but the goldfields' authorities carried out inspections. Men who had no licence tried to run away or hide and were hunted down by police, many of whom behaved brutally towards the diggers.

Most police had left the force at the start of the gold rushes and had gone to dig for gold themselves. They were replaced by new police, some of whom were ex-convicts, lazy or corrupt, or all three. The police were poorly paid, and there was great temptation for them to take bribes. There was also corruption in the form of bribes paid to other officials, favours done, and officials who looked the other way to help friends.

The miners lived in tents, in primitive and unhygienic conditions. The slow process of deep sinking meant that on a field such as Ballarat, in Victoria, the large miner population had plenty of time to discuss their grievances against the authorities.

Aboriginal people actively engaged in a variety of roles on the goldfields, including finding and trading gold.

The background to the Eureka Stockade

The most famous rebellion in Australian history occurred in Ballarat, at the deep sinking area known as the Eureka Lead – named in hope after the ancient Greek word 'Eureka!'. This phrase means 'I've found it!', and was supposedly cried out by Archimedes (287–212 BCE) when he found the solution to a particularly difficult question he was puzzling over.

In Victoria in October 1854, a drunken miner named James Scobie was killed in a dispute with a pub owner called James Bentley. Bentley was accused of the murder but was later released by the police magistrate, John Dewes, who had accepted a bribe to grant the hotel a licence. About 4000 diggers met outside Bentley's hotel to protest against the injustice. They pelted the hotel with stones, and then somebody set it alight. Three diggers, Andrew McIntyre, Thomas Fletcher and Michael Westerby, were arrested for this crime.

On 11 November, a large crowd gathered again, and set up the Ballarat Reform League. The league demanded various reforms that had been made popular by political protestors in

Women at Eureka

The typical image of the Eureka Stockade is one of men in battle – soldiers, police and troopers fighting miners. A photograph taken at the 50th anniversary of the event in December 1904 shows about 50 men survivors – but there are also at least seven women there to remind us that Eureka was an experience shared by all.

Women were involved in many different ways at Eureka: the flag was probably stitched by women, and there were women inside the stockade, supporting their partners, when the government troops attacked on 4 December 1854. One woman loaded rifles for her husband, while another distracted soldiers to allow her husband to slip away so as not to be captured. One unknown woman was killed by a mounted trooper as she pleaded for the life of her husband. Her name is not recorded on any lists or memorials, but her coffin was buried with the others the next day.

The design of the Eureka flag, used here as a modern republican symbol.

Britain known as the Chartists. These demands included manhood suffrage (a vote for every adult male, regardless of whether they owned property or not), payment of members of parliament (so that ordinary men could afford to become members of parliament) and representation of the diggers in parliament.

On 16 November, Victorian Governor Charles Hotham set up an inquiry into corruption on the goldfields. On 20 November, Bentley was tried and convicted of the death of Scobie, and on the same day McIntyre, Fletcher and Westerby were found guilty of burning down Bentley's hotel. Members of the Ballarat Reform League were infuriated by this and on 27 November sent a delegation to Hotham, demanding the release of the three men.

Hotham was a former naval officer and used to total and unquestioning obedience. He refused to listen to the delegation's 'demands', saying instead he would only listen to 'requests'. The diggers met again on 29 November, and in a show of defiance to the authorities, many burned their licences and swore allegiance to each other under a new flag, the Southern Cross, which had been stitched together overnight, probably by a group of miners' wives. They were now led by one of the Irish diggers, Peter Lalor. The licence burning and, especially, the swearing of an oath of loyalty to each other could be seen as an act of treason or rebellion; the government had to react. It called up more police and soldiers to Ballarat, and ordered a licence hunt on the day after many miners had burned their copies.

The Eureka Stockade

On 30 November 1854, the diggers threw together a stockade or rough fort made of wooden logs or slabs in which the unlicenced miners could gather and be protected against more licence hunts. The diggers collected guns and swords, some making pikes or spears, and prepared themselves for battle. The leaders sent out messages for more diggers to join them from other goldfields.

By this stage it was Saturday afternoon, 2 December. There had never been a licence hunt on a Saturday afternoon or a Sunday, so many diggers felt safe and left the stockade to enjoy the evening in their own tents.

Just before dawn on Sunday 3 December, the forces of British authority in Victoria, in the form of 276 soldiers, mounted troops, foot police and civilian officials of the goldfields, crept up on the stockade. Nobody knows who fired first, but gunfire soon erupted.

The attackers rushed at the diggers' flimsy defence and quickly stormed in. In about 15 to 20 minutes the fight was over. An estimated 30 diggers were dead, some of them killed in bloodlust after having been wounded or having surrendered. Five soldiers had also died, most of them young men aged between 19 and 22.

The attackers started burning tents to flush out any remaining diggers, and destroyed and looted the compound. The leader of the resistance, Peter Lalor, lay hidden until he could be smuggled out to safety, his left arm shattered by a bullet. His arm was later amputated.

A few months after the attack, 13 captured leaders of the rebellion were put on trial. All were acquitted by the jury of citizens in Melbourne, who in effect were telling the government that these men were not rebels and traitors, but free men

Postcard advertising Western Australia's gold yield.

who had been pushed too far by a poor goldfield administration. Soon after the trial, most of the Ballarat Reform League's original demands for political reforms were included in the new Victorian constitution. It seems they would have been included anyway, regardless of the Eureka Stockade.

The events of the Eureka Stockade continue to divide people in Australia. Was it a rebellion and an attempt to win justice against tyranny? Or was it merely a protest by tax evaders? The symbol of the event, the Eureka flag, has been used by many different groups since that time, particularly left-wing parties such as the Eureka Youth League (an Australian Communist Party group), and various trade unions and republican organisations. Eureka is often linked to Chartism in England and the move across Europe in the mid-19th century for greater political rights.

The era of the individual miner in Victoria ended soon after the Eureka rebellion. The remaining gold was trapped in quartz, which meant only companies with expensive machinery had access to the precious metal. The remaining diggers mostly became mine employees.

Gold in other colonies

Gold rushes occurred in the other colonies, though the rushes were most intense in Victoria. There were rushes in New South Wales in the 1860s (Kiandra, Lambing Flat, Young, Forbes and Gulgong), in Queensland between the 1860s and 1880s (Gympie, Charters Towers, Palmer River and Mount Morgan), and in Western Australia in the 1890s (Coolgardie and Kalgoorlie).

All these rushes followed a similar pattern to that of Victoria: the initial rush, where a few would strike it rich but most would not; Chinese miners would then arrive in large numbers; the local economy would boom temporarily; the suppliers and service providers would make the most money before the rush moved on, leaving behind many largely abandoned settlements. However, the Western Australian goldfields of Kalgoorlie and Coolgardie were the exceptions because the vast amount of gold there made permanent mining possible.

An artistic representation of Chinese gold miners in 19th-century Australia.

CHINESE IMMIGRATION

Other than the British, the largest immigrant group to come as a result of the gold rushes was the Chinese.

The middle of the 19th century was a period of large-scale movement by the Chinese to several countries, including the United States, Peru, the Philippines, Brazil, Cuba and Malaya as well as to Australia. Initially the Chinese immigrants were indentured labourers, which meant workers hired themselves to an employer for an agreed amount of time, known as the period of indenture.

There were both 'push' and 'pull' factors behind this large-scale emigration. The southern part of China suffered a series of wars and rebellions from 1851, as well as a series of floods from 1849. European nations had taken control by force of several Chinese ports, opening China to the west. As the use of slaves in western countries was abolished between 1824 and

1863, business people saw the chance to use cheap Chinese labour as an alternative. Many workers were indentured, and many became part of a 'bound labour' system operated by lenders in China.

The gold rushes to Australia were part of this 'bound labour' system. The Chinese gold seekers borrowed money from lenders in their home region to pay for their voyage to Australia and stay on the goldfields. Later they had to repay the borrowed money with interest. The workers were free to leave at any time but would not do so while they owed the debt.

Working habits

Chinese gold seekers travelled in large groups, working under a supervisor or headman. They also lived as a community, separate from the other miners. Unlike the other diggers who used mine shafts to collect gold, the Chinese sifted through the discarded dirt and clay known as 'mullock', seeking small specks that had been missed. This process used a lot of water from shared sources, which often created tensions between the Chinese and other miners.

Although there were differences among the European miners, they noted the much larger distinctions between themselves and the Chinese – in the way that they dressed, worked, spoke, ate and worshipped. Nearly all Chinese gold seekers were men, as almost no Chinese

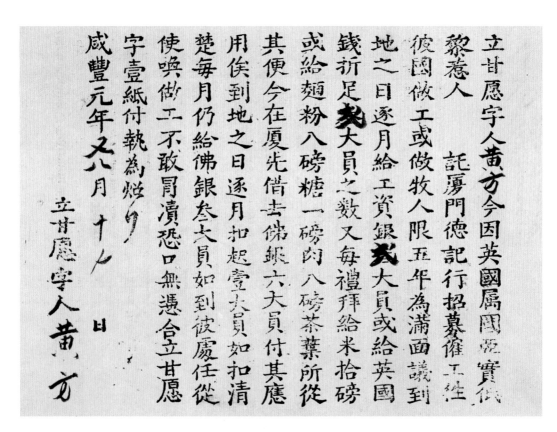

Chinese labour indenture certificate between Ng Hong and John Simpson issued in Sydney in 1851.

women had emigrated to work or be near their husbands. In 1856, there were more than 4000 Chinese men in the colonies, and six Chinese women.

All of these factors made the Chinese distinct among the varied European, British and Australian diggers, and a target for possible resentments. Added to this was the belief held by many British people at the time that there were superior and inferior races, and that the British were above the Chinese.

Limitations to immigration

Chinese people started to arrive in large numbers from 1855. The Victorian Government, reflecting the racial attitudes and fears of the day, passed a law to limit Chinese immigration once it seemed that this immigrant group would be different from the others. The government made Chinese people pay a tax to enter the colony, and also limited the number of Chinese passengers that any ship could carry. The Chinese found a way around that problem by landing in Robe in South Australia and trekking overland to the central Victorian goldfields, thereby avoiding the tax collectors in the usual entry ports of Melbourne and Geelong.

As new rushes started, including those in New South Wales and especially Queensland in the 1870s, this process of Chinese migration to the goldfields was repeated. By the close of 1876, in Queensland's Palmer River goldfield, Chinese merchants and miners numbered 18,000 – 90 per cent of the total population of diggers in that area.

Although there was often resentment and hostility shown towards the Chinese, there was little physical violence. Two notable exceptions were on the Buckland River in Victoria in 1857, and at Lambing Flat near Young, New South Wales, in 1860–61. In both cases, Chinese immigrants were assaulted and some were killed, but police and troops intervened and prosecuted the ringleaders.

In the 1870s and 1880s the issue of Chinese immigration was again taken up by unions and colonial governments, who feared that cheap Chinese labour in trades such as furniture-making were threatening wage levels. This led to colonial governments renewing their limitations on the number of Chinese who could be carried on each ship.

There was also outrage over a widespread scam whereby Chinese immigrants would be naturalised as citizens, then return to China and sell or pass on their naturalisation certificates to Chinese labour organisers, who would use the certificates to allow workers to enter Victoria as 'citizens' rather than as bonded labourers. In this way, it looked as though the person named on the naturalisation paper had just gone to China for a short break.

The late 1800s

Nearly all colonies passed laws restricting Chinese immigration in the late 1880s and 1890s. In 1896, New South Wales and Victoria made the restrictions broader by applying them to all non-Europeans.

These restrictions on Chinese immigration to Australia were successful and the number of Chinese residents in Australia declined. The Chinese people already living in Australia at the time of Federation were accepted, but few newcomers were allowed to join them under the increasingly restrictive laws that were passed in the lead-up to and after Federation.

In the major cities, Chinese people were sometimes harassed by local larrikins – groups of young troublemakers in the inner suburbs – and many people still resented them as cheaper competitors in the labour market. But those who lived in suburbs or country towns as families or individuals, rather than part of a large and separate group, had an active and valued place in their communities as market gardeners, hawkers and restaurant owners.

Many successfully blended their Chinese cultural heritage with their new European cultural ways, and were part of thriving and peaceful local communities. Some became respected leaders in business, such as the Sydney tea merchant Mei Quong Tart, and influential community leaders Lowe Kong Meng and Louis Ah Mouy in Melbourne. At the Federation celebration of 1901 in Melbourne, the Chinese dragon became a colourful and admired part of the celebratory procession, symbolising the Chinese community's role in Australian society.

Chinese immigrants particularly helped develop the economy and community in the northern areas of Australia, where they often became traders and merchants. There was a belief that European people could not do manual work in the tropical northern areas. Chinese immigrants filled a need for cheap and effective labour in these parts, which meant that by 1878 Chinese people outnumbered Europeans in the main northern settlements of Broome and Darwin.

UNLOCKING THE LAND

Squatters and selectors

Mass immigration following the discovery of gold led to the demand to 'unlock the land'. From settlement in 1788, the British Government had claimed ownership of all the land and had given it away in grants to settlers. The government had not been able to stop other settlers from occupying land at no cost as pastoralists – called 'squatting'.

As a result, squatters occupied huge areas of grasslands by the 1850s and amassed wealth. This wealth enabled them to be elected to the upper houses of colonial parliaments, which meant the parliaments would not pass laws to make the squatters buy the land – though they did have to pay rent to the government for it. Unsurprisingly, newcomers to Australia wanted part of that land in order to create their own farms.

The mass migration of free people after the gold rushes increased the pressure to unlock the land. During the 1860s and 1870s, governments in New South Wales, Victoria, Queensland and South Australia managed to pass laws to give small farmers, or 'selectors', the opportunity to buy land. The key to selection was always fresh water – usually a river or creek. If a property had access to water, it could survive. If it had no water source within its boundaries it would probably fail, as rainfall was too unreliable in most parts of Australia to allow successful farming.

The squatters developed ways to counteract the challenge to them. One practice was to pay another person to claim land along the river or creek, and then the squatter would take the land over. A tactic like this was called 'dummying', as the buyer was a 'dummy', not a real claimant. Or the squatter might select the only area with water on it, making the rest of

This postcard dated 1906 shows a typical bush post office from the mid–late 19th century. The explanation on the back notes: 'There is rarely a postman to deliver mail in these districts, and the settlers therefore call for their letters on the days when the mail comes in – a time of great excitement.'

the area useless to selectors. This was called 'peacocking'.

The squatters' attempts to stop the selectors from gaining their land was costly. They had to borrow money to purchase the land, and as a result some went broke during the next poor season.

The hardship of selection became a major theme of the writer Arthur Hoey Davis, known as Steele Rudd. His 'Dad and Dave' stories, later made popular as a radio series, showed the challenges and endurance needed to run a selection by salt-of-the-earth families.

Despite its difficulties, the selection process succeeded in creating rural communities. Towns expanded, especially when railways were extended. The communities also created social mixing that reduced the class tension between the lordly

Postcard showing timber workers at the Huon, Tasmania, circa 1913.

squatters and the humble selectors. The squatter may have been rich, able to live in a big house and employ local people, but he and his family still needed to interact socially in all sorts of ways – at local shops, church services, as employee and employer, fighting floods or bushfires, playing or watching sport, and at the local school.

Bushrangers

The gold and selection eras were also the time when bushrangers flourished in Australia.

Bushrangers, outlaws who operated in country areas, occasionally attacked coaches carrying gold. But these vehicles were often well protected and the bushrangers preferred the easier pickings of individuals coming from the goldfields or isolated homesteads. Bushrangers were also more likely to steal cattle, horses and sheep from small farmers, as the property of the wealthier squatters was better secured.

Ben Hall

Most bushrangers were hard men who lived violent lives and died violent deaths. A few had a reputation as gentlemen. One bushranger who was genuinely admired by many was the New South Wales farmer Ben Hall. Hall had lost his property during a drought in 1862 and his wife ran off with another man. Hall drifted into crime. He claimed never to have killed anyone, but he did participate in robberies that his gang committed. Hall was eventually betrayed and shot in 1865 while trying to escape a police ambush.

Ned Kelly

Ned Kelly remains the most controversial bushranger in Australian culture. Kelly was born in 1855. His father, John 'Red' Kelly, was a transported convict from Ireland and his mother, Ellen Quinn, was the daughter of a free Irish immigrant.

Both the Kelly and Quinn families were involved in crime after they moved to a small selection in Greta in north-western Victoria. Ned Kelly was in trouble even as a 14-year-old – for assaults, helping the bushranger Harry Power, and stealing cattle and horses.

In 1878, Constable Alexander Fitzpatrick arrived at the Kelly house to arrest him and his younger brother

A medal awarded to the Faithfull boys in 1876 for resisting Ben Hall's gang. Their father had three copies made so that each would have one.

Dan for stealing horses. Fitzpatrick claimed he was attacked by Dan and mother Ellen, and shot in the wrist by Kelly. Ellen was tried and sent to prison, which Kelly claimed was an injustice, and which inflamed his hatred of the police.

While on the run, Kelly ambushed the camp of four police at Stringybark Creek near Mansfield, Victoria. He killed Constables Lonigan and Scanlan, and Sergeant Kennedy; Constable McIntyre survived. Kelly claimed that he was acting in self-defence and that the police would have shot him on sight.

On the run, Kelly and his gang robbed banks and homesteads. During this time Kelly, helped by gang member Joe Byrne, dictated the famous 'Jerilderie Letter', an impassioned 8000-word justification of his actions, and condemnation of what he claimed was police persecution.

The final showdown came when Kelly prepared to take on police at Glenrowan, near the Kelly house at Greta. The gang took over a hotel and held around 60 local people hostage, while the four outlaws donned their homemade armour and prepared to shoot police. Part of their plan was to rip up the railway lines on a nearby bend and wreck a special train that was carrying police reinforcements, Aboriginal trackers from Queensland, civilians and journalists.

The plan failed when one of the hostages, local school teacher Thomas Curnow, talked his way into being released, and waved down the train before it reached the broken lines. Kelly was captured in a prolonged shoot-out. The other three

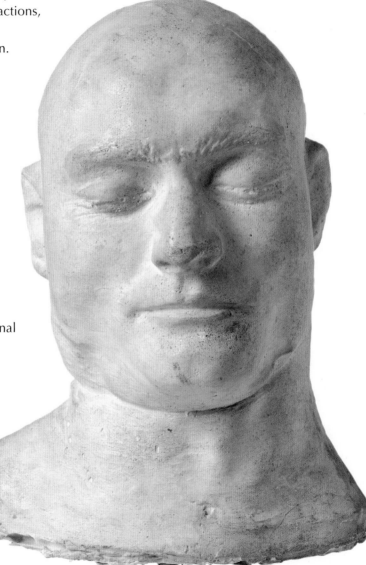

Death mask made of Ned Kelly after he was hanged in 1880.

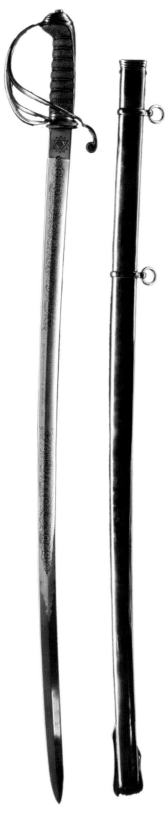

gang members were killed, along with three of the hostages, including a 13-year-old boy.

Kelly was tried for the murder of Constable Lonigan at Stringybark Creek. That was the killing that the surviving policeman, Constable McIntyre, could give the strongest evidence for in court. Kelly was found guilty and hanged on 11 November 1880, despite a petition signed by over 30,000 of Melbourne's 1880 population of 280,000.

Kelly's defenders claim that he was a leader, a protector and a champion of oppressed settlers. His detractors claim he was a brutal petty thief and bank robber who murdered police and endangered many innocent lives.

Explorers

The amount of land available to squatters and selectors increased significantly as a result of inland exploration. Before 1860, most inland exploration had been in the eastern half of the Australian continent, as there was a greater concentration of people there. In the second half of the 19th century, with the eastern half of the continent now well known, explorers focused on a south-to-north crossing, and west-to-east exploration to fill in the gaps on the map.

Exploration parties varied from small groups to huge assemblies of people equipped with transport and food animals, bullock-drawn wagons, tents, desks, tonnes of firewood, and even boats. These parties were not entering empty spaces, but following areas that were already known and mapped by the Indigenous people, through songlines. Songlines are sequences of songs that describe the creation and significance of key features in the landscape. The most successful explorers used Aboriginal guides as 'diplomats' to help them travel through the land. The explorers usually ignored existing Indigenous place names and substituted new ones for the features they 'discovered'.

The European inland explorers moved from the west, the south and the east, hoping to encounter rich grazing lands, great rivers and exciting new scientific discoveries.

Sword with scabbard presented to Sergeant Arthur Steele by grateful pastoralists following the capture of Ned Kelly.

While they found good pastoral country, particularly in Queensland and in parts of Western Australia, they also found plenty of arid desert.

In 1855 to 1856 and in 1858, Augustus Gregory mapped much of the north-east. He trekked from Port Curtis north of Brisbane, along the Burdekin River, through the Barkly Tableland, across part of Arnhem Land and into the Kimberley area in Western Australia.

During 1860 and 1861, the largely incompetent Burke and Wills party travelled north from Melbourne to the swampy land of Cape York in Queensland, and died tragically trying to return.

Meanwhile, explorer John McDouall Stuart tried several times in 1861 and 1862 to make a south–north crossing from Adelaide and succeeded. In doing so, Stuart set the track that would become the Overland Telegraph Line.

The Burke and Wills expedition

The 1860–61 Burke and Wills expedition was an attempt to travel more than 3000 kilometres across Australia from south to north, both to explore an unknown part of Australia, and also to map out a potential route for the proposed telegraph connection from northern Australia to the south.

The expedition was a disaster for many reasons. The exploring party was too large and consisted of 19 men, 23 horses, six carts carrying 20 tonnes of equipment, and 26 camels. It took eight weeks to cover the first 750 kilometres, using the same route that the regular mail cart took just over a week to cover. Burke was a poor leader and an inexperienced bushman. Many of the party quarrelled, and were sacked. The party had to be split several times for it to keep progressing.

Eventually four men, Robert O'Hara Burke, William Wills, John King and Charles Grey, made it to the swamps just five kilometres from the Gulf of Carpentaria.

On the way back the three survivors (Grey had died by then) reached Cooper Creek, but twice just missed relief parties there that believed they were dead. The three explorers had food and water with them, and received help from the local Yandruwandha people, until Burke fired his revolver at one of them and alienated them. Both Burke and Wills died, possibly of scurvy (vitamin C deficiency), or of a vitamin B1 deficiency – perhaps because they had not followed the Yandruwandhas' way of treating the seeds of a local grass that neutralised a dangerous enzyme.

King found his way back to the local people, and was helped by a rescue party.

Robert O'Hara Burke's water bottle, from the Burke and Wills 1860–61 expedition to reach the top of Australia from the south.

A carved and mounted emu egg commemorating the fatal Burke and Wills expedition. It was created by Peter Harris, whose home lies on the route the explorers took.

In the west, John Forrest, Andrew Forrest, Ernest Giles and Peter Warburton crossed the Great Victoria Desert, the Sandy Desert, and the Gibson Desert between 1869 and 1879 to finally discover the aridity of Australia's heart, while Alexander Forrest explored the Kimberley area, which led to its opening as a pastoral area for cattle.

Tommy Windich, Indigenous guide

The best of the explorers relied upon the experience, knowledge and diplomatic skills of Aboriginal guides, such as Tommy Windich. A Kokar Aboriginal man, he was born near Mount Stirling in Western Australia. Windich helped early land seekers and government surveyors, and accompanied an expedition into the country east of York in 1866. As a police tracker and native constable, he assisted in the arrest of the Aboriginal men who had killed a local pastoralist, Edward Clarkson.

Windich went with John Forrest on three expeditions between 1869 and 1874, and with Alexander Forrest in 1871. As both Forrest brothers were surveyors who could navigate land by astronomical observation, they were never in danger of being lost in wide open deserts, but they did rely heavily on their Aboriginal trackers in the daily search for drinking water and for feed for the horses. Windich usually scouted ahead and was expert at finding wells or waterholes in the rocky outcrops.

As tokens of appreciation, the government gave Windich gifts for his services, and the Forrest brothers thanked him for his support. In February 1876, a tombstone was erected over his grave at Esperance Bay with the words: 'He was an aboriginal native of Western Australia, of great intelligence and fidelity, who accompanied them on exploring expeditions into the interior of Australia, two of which were from Perth to Adelaide. Be Ye Also Ready'.

Explorers' memorial

In Fremantle, Western Australia, is a monument created in 1913 to the explorers Panter, Harding and Goldwyer. The three men were killed by Aboriginal people while exploring in search of pastoral land near Broome in 1864. A search party sent out by explorer Maitland Brown found their bodies. Brown's party killed several Aboriginal people, claiming that they, too, had been attacked and were acting in self-defence.

*THIS MONUMENT WAS ERECTED BY
C. J. BROCKMAN
AS A FELLOW BUSH WANDERER'S
TRIBUTE TO THE MEMORY OF
PANTER, HARDING AND GOLDWYER
EARLIEST EXPLORERS AFTER GREY AND
GREGORY OF THIS
'TERRA INCOGNITA', ATTACKED AT
NIGHT BY TREACHEROUS NATIVES
WERE MURDERED AT BOOLA BOOLA
NEAR LE GRANGE BAY
ON THE 13 NOVEMBER 1864.
ALSO AS AN APPRECIATIVE TOKEN OF
REMEMBRANCE OF
MAITLAND BROWN
ONE OF THE PIONEER PASTORALISTS
AND PREMIER POLITICIANS OF THIS
STATE, INTREPID LEADER OF THE
GOVERNMENT SEARCH AND PUNITIVE
PARTY. HIS REMAINS TOGETHER WITH
THE SAD RELICS OF THE ILL
FATED THREE RECOVERED AT GREAT
RISK AND DANGER FROM LONE
WILDS REPOSE UNDER A PUBLIC
MONUMENT IN THE EAST PERTH
CEMETERY
'LEST WE FORGET'*

In 1994 a second panel was added underneath the original one. It gave a different version of events:

*THIS PLAQUE WAS ERECTED BY PEOPLE
WHO FOUND THE MONUMENT
BEFORE YOU OFFENSIVE.
THE MONUMENT DESCRIBED THE
EVENTS AT LA GRANGE FROM ONE
PERSPECTIVE ONLY:
THE VIEWPOINT OF THE WHITE
'SETTLERS'
NO MENTION IS MADE OF THE RIGHT
OF ABORIGINAL PEOPLE TO DEFEND
THEIR LAND OR OF THE
HISTORY OF PROVOCATION WHICH
LED TO THE EXPLORERS' DEATH.
THE 'PUNITIVE PARTY' MENTIONED
HERE ENDED IN THE DEATHS OF
SOMEWHERE AROUND TWENTY
ABORIGINAL PEOPLE
THE WHITES WERE WELL ARMED AND
EQUIPPED AND NONE OF THEIR PARTY
WAS KILLED OR WOUNDED.
THIS PLAQUE IS IN MEMORY OF THE
ABORIGINAL PEOPLE KILLED AT LA
GRANGE. IT ALSO COMMEMORATES ALL
OTHER ABORIGINAL PEOPLE WHO
DIED DURING THE INVASION OF THEIR
COUNTRY
LEST WE FORGET
MAPA JARRIYA-NYALAKU*

Technology

Developments in technology helped transform Australia during the second half of the 19th century. The first 'Industrial Revolution' began in Britain in the 1750s, when steam engines were used to replace human labour. By 1830, one man and a boy assistant operating a machine could produce more cloth than 20 hand-weavers in the same amount of time. This advance in technology helped develop inventions and innovations that have changed living and working conditions for people around Australia.

Machinery and electricity

Steam engines were commonly used in Australia from the 1850s. They were used for a variety of operations, such as to crush quartz to release gold, power trains and river boats, hammer metal in iron foundries, pump water into irrigation ditches, roll pastry in industrial biscuit factories, and print newspapers.

Later in the century, electricity became the source of power for these machines, which further increased their efficiency. Electricity also replaced gas for street lamps and then home lighting. The very first football game to have been played under electric lighting at night was in Melbourne in 1879.

By the end of the 1890s many country towns, such as Tamworth, Young and Broken Hill in New South Wales, and Nhill in Victoria, all had their own generators to produce electric street lighting. Brisbane was the first capital city to have its city centre electrified, as early as 1882, followed by Melbourne and Perth in 1894, Adelaide in 1899, Sydney in 1904 and Hobart in 1905.

The invention of the typewriter in the late 19th century provided a new area of employment.

In the 1880s, hydraulic lifts were developed in the United States of America. This meant that buildings could now be taller than five stories, the height that people could comfortably walk up stairs regularly. The physical shape and appearance of capital cities started to change as buildings became much taller.

Advances in manufacturing techniques and equipment meant that thin strands of wire could be mass-produced and used as cheap paddock fencing. This allowed farmers to control their animals more easily, reduced the number of shepherds required, and led to a more effective use of the land.

The sewing machine

The sewing machine particularly affected women's work and lives. Women could make their own clothing at home more quickly and efficiently if they had the money to buy the new machine. Mass production of clothing and shoes made these goods more affordable for ordinary people. Much of the production was done in factories, and changes in factory laws from the 1880s in all colonies gradually improved the hours, pay and conditions of work for women, men and children.

However, the development of the sewing machine also introduced 'sweatshops'. Here the manufacturers forced women to work long hours for a small rate of pay per piece produced in their own homes. Conditions for these piece workers could not be regulated in the same way as work in a factory.

Communications

The first electric telegraph line was built in 1854 to connect Melbourne and the port of Williamstown, just a few kilometres away. This made information about ships' arrivals much faster and more reliable.

The benefits of this form of near-instant communication quickly became obvious, and the capital cities of the colonies were connected to each other by the telegraph between 1858 and 1877. South Australia and Victoria were connected in 1858; New South Wales and Victoria in 1858; Queensland and New South Wales in 1861; Tasmania and Victoria in 1859 (but not reliably until 1869); Western Australia and South Australia in 1877.

The development of telephones in the late 19th century transformed personal and business communications.

By 1861 there were 110 telegraph stations spread across the eastern colonies, and by 1867 Victoria alone was sending 122,000 messages a year, compared to about 7.92 million in the United States and 5.78 million in Britain.

The next step was to connect the colonies to the rest of the world. This was done when the first message was sent from Darwin, which was linked in 1872 to the rest of the world by a submarine cable, and internally to Adelaide via the overland telegraph, also completed in 1872. This brought news and commercial information much more quickly and put Australia in touch with events as they happened anywhere in the world.

Telephones also started to become more accessible to the wealthy and to businesses. The first telephone system in Australia connected the offices of the Robinson brothers in Melbourne and South Melbourne in 1879. The first telephone exchange, or central point linking different telephone subscribers, was opened in Melbourne the following year. By 1884, around 20 calls per day were operated via the exchange, and by 1901 there were approximately 33,000 phones across Australia.

Overland Telegraph

One of Australia's great engineering feats in the second half of the 19th century was the construction of an overland telegraph from Port Augusta to Darwin. This line linked the Australian colonies to the world and reduced the 'tyranny of distance', which had kept the colonies isolated from timely knowledge of world events.

The mission
By the 1860s most of the colonies were connected to one another by telegraph, but messages to and from Britain took 60–80 days by mail ship. A telegraph cable extending from Europe to India and then Java was established in 1864. Two further cables were required to connect the large Australian cities to Europe: an undersea cable between Java and Darwin, then an overland cable between Darwin and one of the Australian capital cities.

South Australia, Queensland and Victoria all wanted the transcontinental Australian telegraph line to lead into their own colony. (This is why the Burke and Wills expedition was sent out – to find a route to the north of Australia that started from Victoria.) South Australia won the right after John McDouall Stuart successfully travelled from Adelaide to Darwin in 1862. The telegraph line followed his route, which was a distance of over 3000 kilometres through some of the harshest land in the middle of Australia.

How it worked
The overland telegraph system worked by having a telegraph operator tap out morse code on a key. The key sent electrical impulses along a wire. The signal had to be recorded and repeated 11 times to cross the continent. Repeater stations had to be built for this, and were manned 24 hours a day.

The operation
The overland telegraph was built by three teams operating simultaneously: one in the northern section, the others in the central and southern parts. Each team had carpenters, blacksmiths, cooks, managers, storemen,

linesmen and surveyors. All equipment – 3000 metal poles, 3000 kilometres of wire, insulators, batteries, food and medical stores – had to be carried by horses, bullocks and camels. The hole for each pole had to be dug by hand.

Mission accomplished!

The Overland Telegraph Line was completed in 1872, and the connection made with the undersea cable at Darwin. Church bells rang in Adelaide. Messages could now travel to London in seven days, rather than 70.

Conflict

The telegraph was not always beneficial to everybody, especially to local Indigenous people. In 1874, the repeater station at Barrow Creek was attacked by local Kaytetye people, possibly as retaliation for settlers abusing Kaytetye women or because the telegraph construction team fenced off a major waterhole and refused the Kaytetye people access to it.

One operator, John Franks, was speared in the chest and died soon after. Three others, James Stapleton, Ebenezer Flint and Aboriginal worker Jemmy, were wounded. The injured men sent a message through to Adelaide, 2000 kilometres away. A doctor was brought in to try to send medical advice to the dying Stapleton. His wife was also there, sending her final message of love as he died. Stapleton tapped out his last message in reply: 'God bless you and the children'. A police party was sent to arrest the attackers. As reprisal, an unknown number of Aboriginal people, possibly as many as 90, were killed, with no prisoners brought back to face trial.

A morse code printing machine from the late 19th century.

C. Y. O'Connor

Charles Yelverton O'Connor (born 1843; died 1902) was an Irish migrant to New Zealand who moved to Western Australia in 1891 and completed two of the most significant engineering feats in the colony's history.

His first great achievement was building a deep water harbour at Fremantle to attract ocean-going mail ships. The first steamer docked there in 1897.

O'Connor then turned his attention to the water supply for the Kalgoorlie and Coolgardie goldfields. These were important for the Western Australian economy, but they were in an arid area where poor water supplies would quickly cause disease among the miners. The only way to supply water was to build a dam near Perth, then pump the water 500 kilometres to Kalgoorlie. The pumping also had to send the water uphill, as Kalgoorlie is 300 metres higher above sea level than Perth.

O'Connor's plan, and O'Connor himself, were brutally criticised by a local newspaper. The plan was called wasteful, and he was accused of incompetence and corruption. He suffered depression and illness.

On 8 March 1902, O'Connor successfully led a pumping test over the most difficult part of the water pipe route. Two days later, he committed suicide. He left a note saying that he knew the pipeline would work and that it would be better for another man who was not burdened by the controversy to finish the project.

On 24 January 1903, Sir John Forrest – the first premier of Western Australia and a great supporter of O'Connor – turned on the water to Kalgoorlie. He praised O'Connor's vision and determination.

There is now an eerliy moving statue of O'Connor in the waters off the beach named after him in Fremantle.

The typewriter also led to economic and social change. Women were believed to be quicker and more accurate typists, and were cheaper to employ. This led to the replacement of male workers, who had dominated the clerical job sector, with females, and the opening of a new area of employment to unmarried, literate middle-class women.

Steam power

Steam power was initially used on ships to supplement sails, then replaced them completely, cutting down the time of international sea travel. The use of this type of energy meant that ships could be made bigger and stronger, but this additional weight did not make them slower as the powerful engines could move them quickly and reliably.

In 1788, the 35-metre-long supply ship *Borrowdale* of the First Fleet took approximately 250 days to bring 216 passengers from England to Sydney. In 1888, the 110-metre-long steam-and-sail-driven *Australasian* took 50 days to deliver 640 passengers to Sydney via Melbourne. In 1909, the 168-metre-long steam-driven *Osterley* delivered 1100 passengers to Sydney, Melbourne and Brisbane in 45 days.

Opposite: A great symbol of a revolution in communications. Millions of telegraph poles appeared in cities, towns and the outback from the 1850s.

The opening of the Suez Canal in 1869 further reduced the travel time between England and Australia, benefiting individuals and trade. Steam power also made the ships more comfortable, allowing for a more pleasant and hygienic voyage, by the provision of electric lighting, ventilation and refrigeration of food.

Within the colonies, steamships navigated the Murray and Darling rivers, delivering supplies to the homesteads along the banks and towing barges of wool. The first steamships carried loads along the rivers in 1853. These paddle-driven steamers had a very shallow draft, meaning that there was very little of the boat beneath the water. This enabled the ship to come close to shore to load and unload. The wool was shipped to inland ports linked to that other great innovation, the railway, which then took the wool to the seaports, where the fleece would be transported to British and European factories.

Railway system

Australia's first steam railway was built in Melbourne in 1854 to carry goods and passengers between the port and the city.

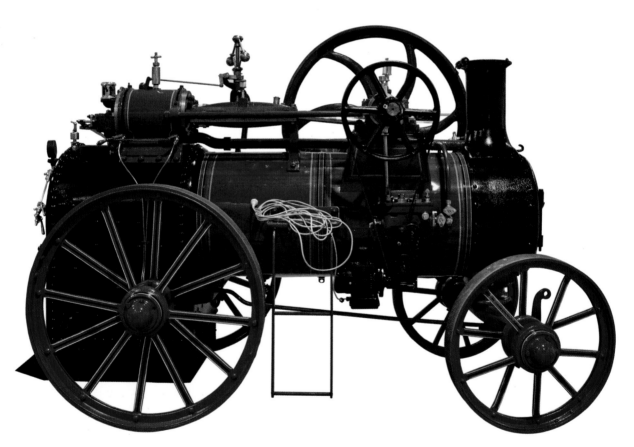

The Industrial Revolution in Britain created powerful steam machinery that was imported to Australia.

JUBILEE.

The steam train linked the bush to the cities and opened new areas to development.

Each colony developed its own railway system, and this led to the use of three different gauges, or widths between the rails: 5 feet 3 inches (1600 mm) in Victoria, Tasmania and the part of South Australia that connected with Victoria; 3 feet 6 inches (1066 mm) in Queensland, Western Australia and other parts of South Australia; and 4 feet 8 ½ inches (1435 mm) in New South Wales. (The different gauges existed because different colonial governments awarded contracts to different British firms.) This meant that people and goods had to be unloaded onto other trains at the borders when travelling between colonies that had different gauges.

Up to the 1870s, most railway systems were built around the capital cities of the colonies, but during the 1870s the principal mountain ranges had been crossed and the work of construction was able to proceed more rapidly and cost-effectively.

The greatest growth between 1871 and 1901 was in New South Wales, Victoria, Queensland and Western Australia. As land was opened up for farming, the rail system provided a way of transporting the agricultural and pastoral produce to the main colonial ports, and this helped settlers move in quickly, knowing that they could effectively market their products.

The rail system also led to the development of country towns along the rail lines. Railway maps of Australia in 1901 show a series of spidery lines leading inland from each of the capital cities, as well as crossings in places to provide connections. Each capital city also developed its own system of suburban railways, and these allowed suburbs to spread out from the capital city as people were able to take cheap rail trips between home and work.

The development of wool presses reduced the cost of transporting wool.

Agricultural technology

Technological developments also improved farming productivity. The stump-jump plough revolutionised wheat farming by opening up huge areas of land where the main vegetation was the mallee tree. Mallee trees have extensive and thickly matted underground roots just below the surface soil. The soil could not be turned by normal ploughing, as the plough would get tangled in the roots and not move forward.

The only way to turn mallee areas into farms was by cutting down the trees, which wasn't so hard to do, but then also grubbing out each tree's thick and tangled roots – a virtually impossible task. That is, until the perfection of the stump-jump plough by South Australian farmer Richard Bowyer Smith in 1876. This plough would not try to rip through the mallee tree roots but would jump over it, plough the next lot of land until the next tree root, then jump again. In this way, the roots did not have to be grubbed out, but the land could grow a crop between them.

Agricultural and pastoral productivity were also improved by many other technological developments. In 1877, Frederick Wolseley patented the world's first mechanical sheep-shearing equipment. Hand shearers could still match and beat the new machine for speed, but the electric machines required less skill from the user and could cut closer to the skin, increasing the wool yield.

A combined wheat stripper and thresher, the prototype of which was developed in 1884 by 19-year-old inventor Hugh McKay, allowed ears of wheat to be stripped from the stalk, threshed to remove the grain, cleaned and bagged all in one continuous operation. McKay would later establish the famous Sunshine Harvester machine factory to manufacture the machines, become a major employer, and be involved in a famous court case that would establish the principle of a fair minimum wage for all workers.

The process of refrigeration, which was perfected in 1879, enabled meat and other food to be frozen and sent overseas, thereby creating a new export industry. In 1881, 499 tonnes of frozen meat were exported. By 1900 it was over 51,000 tonnes.

In the 1890s, Christian Koerstz developed a cheap and efficient wool press that decreased the labour costs of packing fleeces by hand, protected fleeces better during transportation, and saved money by reducing the space a wool bale took on ships.

In 1901, William Farrer successfully crossbred different types of wheat, resulting in a tougher, more resilient variety suited to the Australian method of machine harvesting. He named this wheat strain 'Federation', in honour of the six colonies coming together for the Federation of Australia. It was the leading variety planted in Australia between 1910 and 1925.

In 1885, the South Australian Government started Roseworthy Agricultural College to educate young farmers in the latest scientific principles of agriculture. This was followed by Victoria's Dookie Agricultural College in 1886 and New South Wales' Hawkesbury Agricultural College in 1891.

ABORIGINAL AUSTRALIANS

The dynamics of development in the second half of the 19th century placed Aboriginal people increasingly in the margins of, if not invisible to, European Australia. The role of Aboriginal people in helping explorers is one example of the complexity of Indigenous colonial experience. There was continuing conflict in some areas of Australia and cooperation in others: Aboriginal people became a significant part of local workforces, but many suffered isolation on the edges of white settlements, with people not living fully in either the Aboriginal or the European world.

There were hundreds of incidents of bloody conflict as colonists intruded into new frontier areas of Queensland, the Northern Territory and Western Australia. One of the worst examples occurred in 1861 when 19 settlers – men, women and children – were massacred at Cullin-la-ringo station in central Queensland by the local Kairi Kairi people. The killings may have been payback for the brutality of local graziers 80 kilometres away, who were possibly poisoning waterholes and shooting local people. The European settlers retaliated, and more than 200 Indigenous men, women and children were massacred.

In some instances Aboriginal people resisted strongly for many years but could only delay the invasion of pastoralism and its destruction of their culture. Eventually resistance became impracticable. Many Aboriginal individuals and communities had to make the hard choice between trying to survive within the new economy or remaining outside it, despite the invasiveness of European occupation.

Employment

Some Aboriginal men joined the Native Police. This body trained young men to work under a European officer to forcibly control and disperse local Aboriginal people. Native policemen

A large group of Aboriginal and non-Aboriginal people formally posed at the Point McLeay Mission Station, now known as Raukkan (its original Ngarrindgeri name) in South Australia, 1885.

were usually posted to areas away from their own country and people. They sometimes became willing participants in violence towards other Aboriginal people, killing on orders. This was particularly true in areas where past feuds existed.

Many Aboriginal people worked for the pastoralists as cooks, domestics and skilled stockmen. Others, in the longer-settled areas, tended to be isolated economically and socially on the fringes of town settlements, often living in terrible circumstances in makeshift shelters.

Living conditions

Christian missionaries provided shelter, protection, food, education and medical care – but often at the price of conversion to Christianity and the suppression of their culture. Some missionaries tried to prohibit local languages while others recorded them and translated the Bible into those languages, thereby helping to keep them alive.

The colonial governments also set up a protectorate system. This was based on the idea that Aboriginal people would willingly create self-sufficient agricultural communities if they

Opposite: Illuminated letter to Graham Berry dated March 22nd 1888. William Barak led a group of men from Coranderrk to Melbourne to farewell former Premier Graham Berry (1822–1904) before his return to England. They presented him with spears, boomerangs and other artefacts, along with the illuminated 'address'. The gifts were offered as thanks for Berry's assistance in maintaining the station against the advice of the Aboriginal Protection Board. Born in 1824, William Barak was an Aboriginal leader of great diplomatic skill. He is reputed to have witnessed the arrival of John Batman and his party at Port Phillip as a child.

To the Hon.ble Graham Berry.

Melbourne, March 22nd/86.

We have come to see you because you have done a great deal of work for the Aborigines. —

I feel very sorrowful and first time I hear you was going home I was crying. you do all that thing for the Station when we were in trouble. when the Board would not give us much food and clothes and wanted to drive us off the land we come to you and told you our trouble and you gave us the land for our own as long as we live and gave us more food and clothes and blankets and better houses and the people all very thankful.

And now you leave this country. Victoria to go to England where we may never see you no more. we give you small present with our love, when you go away keep remembering the Natives for the Natives will remember you for your doing good to Coranderrk. —

We had a trouble here in this country. but we can all meet up along "Our Father" we hope that God will lead you right through the water and take you safe to England and keep you in the straight way and give you eternal life through Jesus Christ Our Saviour. —

Signed   Barak   ×
Chief of the Yarra Yarra tribe of Aborigines,
Victoria Australia.

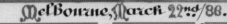

Bertdrak ×	Mooney +	Patterson ×
Kata warmin +	Manton ×	Cogle ×
Wort ee ilum +	Hamilton +	Stewart ×
Ngiaqueon +	Rowan ×	Logan ×
Derrinil ×	Were ×	Gable ×

could be protected from local Europeans. The price for this security was the Europeanisation of their culture, the loss of their freedom, and having their lands and lives controlled in ways that treated them as virtual prisoners. In these agricultural communities, Indigenous people had to get permission to leave the area, to marry and to work.

In 1860 Simon Wonga, a Wurundjeri man, approached William Thomas for land for the Wurundjeri people. The land granted was not suitable and Wonga led a deputation to Melbourne. This led to the establishment of Coranderrk Station under the supervision of John Green who became recognised as a friend and respected leader. The farm won agricultural show awards during the 1870s and early 1880s. However, the Aboriginal people were not able to own the land, the profit from the produce was not used to improve the place, and there was still central control of people's lives. When Green was sacked and Coranderrk threatened with closure, William Barak, who succeeded Wonga as leader, organised a political campaign of letters, petitions and marches, which led to an inquiry in 1881 and kept Coranderrk open. However, in 1886, legislation was passed to separate 'half-caste' or mixed-heritage Aboriginal people from protectorates. This forced 60 people to be evicted from Coranderrk, making the workforce too small to keep the farm viable. It slowly drifted into disuse and the land was taken over by local white farmers.

LIVING AND WORKING IN CITIES AND THE BUSH

Infrastructure

Most of the immigrants who poured into the colonies after the gold rush made their way to the larger colonial cities and added to the process of urbanisation. Most immigrants were themselves urban people, whose skills were appropriate for city rather than country life.

The capital cities were located on rivers and ports, which made them effective both as economic hubs and communication hubs. This in turn stimulated population growth.

The major cities were the seats of government and public service, the centres of manufacturing, trade, commerce and services. They were the first places to have paved roads rather than dirt ones.

The city centres had parks, entertainment venues, department stores and modern fashion shops. Tall buildings started to change the skyline, and gas, then electric street lighting made streets safer. Wealthier people began to move out of cities, creating new suburbs and making the cities more commercial and less residential.

These suburbs spread further and further out, especially as public transport snaked out from the city centre. Public transport developed from horse-drawn to electric trams, and steam and then electric trains from the 1880s.

Towns also developed as governments built railways into rural areas. A town would have shops, a post office, a blacksmith, a bank, a school, several churches, a police station, a library, a School of Art, hotels, a mechanics institute (a place for working people to meet and study), a racing club, sports oval and a church hall.

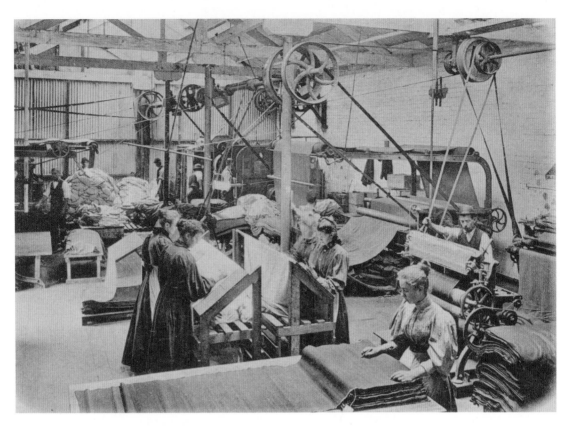

Mechanisation and industrialisation helped the development of factories, and both skilled and unskilled employment in cities.

Sanitary conditions

There were ugly sides to urbanisation. Conditions in some parts of the cities were terrible. Houses were old, rat-infested and unsanitary.

Few homes had an indoor toilet – only a pit in the small backyard, which would attract flies in summer and become a stinking sludge in winter. The waste that was collected from yards where there was a pan toilet might be dumped by the weekly 'night soil' collectors onto waste ground to create a foul-smelling oozing slime. If not, it might be sold to market gardeners as fertiliser. As water was often drawn from the same river that waste was dumped in, diseases caused by contaminated water were common and deadly.

Two of the greatest improvements in the latter part of the 19th century were the development of sewerage systems to remove human waste through underground pipes, and the provision of fresh water into houses through pipes from reservoirs. These were both expensive processes, and became the main responsibility of special government bodies.

The results were dramatic. In Sydney, after a fresh water supply system from reservoirs was introduced in the 1890s, the infant mortality rate dropped from 103.7 deaths per 1000 live births in 1901 to 80.6 in 1905, and 74.7 in 1910.

A successful manufacturer

Macpherson Robertson's success is an example of how colonial manufacturing could start from nothing.

Robertson was the son of a Scottish carpenter who came to Australia with his family during the gold rush. The family did not strike it rich, and Robertson had to leave school to become an apprentice at a confectionary firm.

In 1880 he began making novelty sweets in the shape of dogs, mice, horses and other animals in the bathroom of his family's home in Fitzroy, Victoria. He later claimed his process for this involved using an old nail-can as a furnace, heating sugar in a second-hand tin boiler, and pouring the mixture into moulds he'd created.

Robertson carried the sweets on a tray on his head – about half his own body weight – and would walk many kilometres, selling to shopkeepers. He later bought a tricycle to carry his product around.

By the late 1880s he had moved into a factory, MacRobertson Steam Confectionery Works, with over 30 employees. He travelled overseas and came back with innovations in packaging, marketing and products. He introduced chewing gum and fairy floss to Australia. Employees and customers were offered rewards for devising advertising jingles, and messages for 'conversation lollies'.

Government policies that supported local manufacturers gave Robertson an opportunity to spread nationally and he soon had large factories in every colony, employing thousands of workers.

Robertson was a model employer and was a noted and generous philanthropist. In 1967, the Australian institution of MacRobertson sweets was bought out by Cadbury Schweppes.

Working conditions

Most work was still physical. Men worked six or five and a half days a week. They would arrive home dirty and exhausted after their eight to ten-hour day. Factory legislation from the 1880s onwards helped improve and regulate working hours and conditions, but work could still be dangerous and unhygienic. Eleven years after factory legislation had been introduced, and compulsory education had supposedly stopped children from working in factories, a Melbourne investigation found that children were still employed in these places – working with unguarded machines, up to 60 hours a week for one-sixth of a man's wage.

Women worked in factories, from home, or as maids and housekeepers. House work, whether as an employee or at home, was physically demanding. Women had to gather and chop wood, wash clothes and sheets and wring them out by hand, scrub floors and steps, sweep and dust and polish, and cook over open fires or big cast iron stoves, often in poorly ventilated kitchens and in scorching summer heat.

Children were also expected to help out. In the bush and rural areas, children worked by chopping kindling for fires, feeding the animals, milking the cows, and helping at shearing and harvest time.

Harvest time on a family farm.

Sport and leisure

As Australians became wealthier, lived in established communities and experienced improved working conditions, they had more leisure time. Football, cycling, cricket, rowing, athletics and woodchopping were all popular leisure pursuits. Large numbers of spectators also watched them, as well as horse races and boxing. Both men and women were enthusiastic spectators at football matches, especially the Australian Rules form in Victoria, South Australia, Tasmania and Western Australia.

Some of the great heroes during the late 19th century were the world champion rowers. As a boy in Grafton, New South Wales, Henry Serle used to row his brothers and sisters five kilometres each day to school and back. In 1889, aged 22, he went to London and won the world championship for scullers, and a prize of £1000 – equal to about ten years of wages for a

The Pattison Shield awarded to Victor Trumper as the highest run scorer in inter-colonial cricket for the season 1898–1899.

working man. He died on the way back to Australia, and 170,000 people lined the streets of Sydney for his funeral. In 1868, the first cricket team from Australia to tour England was an all Aboriginal team.

Religion

Religion was important in most people's lives. Most Australians were christened, married and buried within a Christian faith. In 1871 between 60 and 70 per cent attended church regularly. The 1881 census showed that 96 per cent of Australians were Christians, 2 per cent of another religion, and 2 per cent of no religion. Even small country towns might have two or more churches of different religious denominations.

The churches played a significant role in education, charity, social and personal values, social mixing and civic leadership. They led campaigns against drunkenness, child labour abuses and prostitution. They provided help to the unemployed, the homeless, the destitute and the orphans at a time when politicians did not consider this part of the state's responsibility. Churches were also active in missionary activities among Aboriginal people. From time to time, strong antagonism and rivalry was evident between the majority group, Protestants, and the quarter of the population who were Roman Catholics.

CHANGING AND ADAPTING TO THE ENVIRONMENT

The opening of new lands to pastoralism and mining involved land clearing, fencing and changing natural watercourses. All these greatly affected the environment, bringing onto the land ever-growing numbers of people and increasing the productivity of the land for both local foods and exports.

Introduced species

During the 1860s and 1870s, 'acclimatisation societies' became popular. These were groups of people who believed that Australia would benefit from the introduction of European species of animals and plants, whether for food, sport or just as reminders of the landscape and environment of their homeland (usually Britain). This practice caused environmental disaster. The list of introduced species that had a detrimental impact on the Australian environment is long – prickly pear made paddocks unusable; salmon and trout displaced local fish; cats devastated small native animals and birds; feral dogs formed packs and tore sheep and lambs to pieces. Camels, which had been imported for transportation and for exploration of arid areas, had an impact on soils, vegetation and waterholes. Mice and foxes were also devastating.

Human impacts included the periodic slaughter of native animals, such as koalas and platypuses for their fur, kangaroos because they were competitors for food and water and sometimes broke fences, and dingos because they were responsible for the slaughter of sheep and lambs.

Rabbits

Of the introduced animals, rabbits had possibly the worst effect. Rabbits had been brought on the First Fleet in 1788, but the first evidence they were a problem was in Tasmania in 1827, when they were reported to be running about in their thousands on large estates.

Their impact on the mainland started to be felt in 1859, when pastoralist Thomas Austin imported 24 rabbits to his property near Geelong in Victoria for hunting. These rabbits were a hardy crossbred type different from normal domestic rabbits, and they thrived in Australia. They bred and spread into new territory rapidly, eating native grasses and stripping paddocks bare. This reduced the number of sheep that could be grazed, as well as the food supply and habitats of native animals. Rabbits' burrowing caused soil erosion as the disturbed soil was more easily washed away by rain.

The rabbits spread north into New South Wales and Queensland, and ate and bred their way into South Australia and across the Nullarbor Plain into Western Australia. The Western Australian Government built an 1800-kilometre-long rabbit-proof fence to stop their progress, but if one gate was left open it meant the whole strategy was useless. Soon rabbits swarmed in.

A mounted platypus specimen. Attitudes to native animals have changed over time, from exploitation to conservation.

Sheep

Sheep also caused enormous changes to the land. They grazed best in the temperate eucalypt woodlands of the east coast and the south-west of Western Australia. Their hard hooves and grazing of native vegetation compacted the soil, suppressing native grasses and allowing other species to dominate and change the environment.

Natural disasters

Numerous natural disasters struck the colonies in the second half of the 19th century. A heatwave in south-eastern Australia in 1895 to 1896 killed 437 people, including 47 in Bourke, in New South Wales.

Cyclone Mahina hit Queensland near Cooktown in 1899. It sank the Thursday Island-based pearling fleet, drowning at least 307 crewmen and more than 100 Indigenous people.

The cyclone created a storm surge that destroyed vegetation and property for five kilometres inland in some places.

The Black Thursday bushfires in Victoria in 1851 killed 12 people, a million sheep, thousands of cattle, and countless wildlife as it burned around one quarter of the total area of the colony. Scientists believe that the devastation was so great because Aboriginal fire practices had been disrupted by European settlement, leading to a build-up of fuel in the bush.

In 1852, a flood at Gundagai in New South Wales killed at least 78 of the town's 350 residents. One local Aboriginal man, Yarri, rescued 49 people. The local Indigenous people knew how badly and quickly the Murrumbidgee River flooded, but the newcomers had ignored their advice and built on the floodplain with dire consequences.

Human adaptation and conservation

It was not all destruction, however. People quickly learned to create dams on their property, especially after wire fencing was introduced from the 1850s and 1860s and animals could be contained in fixed areas. These dams created small ecosystems – places where a whole community of plants, animals and insects lived in a system of mutual support.

In 1878, a pastoralist on Kallara Station near Bourke in New South Wales drilled down and struck fresh water. This water came from what is called the Great Artesian Basin, a vast underground lake that lies under 22 per cent of Australia. This water can be drawn up to provide drinking water for animals, and thus opened up new areas of scrubby land to pastoralism – though at a very low number of animals per hectare.

Governments also encouraged the development of irrigated agriculture along the flat plains bordering the Murray River. This involved creating canals from the river, and then pumping the water onto crops. As a result, new settlements developed at Renmark in 1887 and Mildura in 1888 as food production regions.

The first government-enacted natural conservation measures were passed in the 1860s, including the creation of reserved areas. In 1862, the Tasmanian Government passed a law to protect native birds and their eggs from hunters during the nesting season. Victoria and New South Wales later adopted a similar law.

In the 1870s, the Tasmanian Government protected kangaroos when other states were slaughtering them. In 1879, the first national park in Australia – and only the second one in the world – was created near Sydney. This represented a change in thinking about nature and the environment – that it was not a place to exploit but one to conserve in its natural state.

In the 1880s, many field naturalist clubs were formed. Members would go on bushwalks to study and appreciate native flora and fauna. In 1887, Victoria established a part of Ferntree Gully, on the outskirts of Melbourne, as a conservation area. In 1891, South Australia did the same with Belair, in the hills near Adelaide. In 1888, the New South Wales Government set aside the huge area of Centennial Park, in Sydney, and in 1894 the Western Australian Government created Kings Park, near the centre of Perth.

OCEANA SERIES C.　　　ARTESIAN BORE, Australia

A postcard showing an artesian bore. Tapping underground water made it possible for settlers to graze cattle in new areas. Posted 1905.

A DEVELOPING ECONOMY

The economies of most of the colonies boomed in the second half of the 19th century. The greatest developments were in mining, followed by wool production, and the cattle and sugar-cane industries. The boom was a result of a combination of natural resources, manual labour, technological developments, overseas investment, a long series of good rainfall years, and the suppression of Aboriginal resistance to the occupation of new areas.

Though gold was the most important and lucrative mineral, the mining of other metals also created wealth in the colonies. During the 1880s and 1890s the focus of mineral wealth changed to silver, lead and zinc at Broken Hill, New South Wales, and copper at Mount Lyell, Tasmania. By 1900, minerals represented one-third of the value of Australia's exports.

Migration and natural population growth stimulated expansion in the cities. As the population increased, so did the need for services, goods, food, clothing, entertainment and tools. Some local manufacturers, sheltered by protection policies in some colonies (see page 146), developed large businesses, employing thousands of people.

A booming agricultural industry

By 1901 cattle, sheep, horses, wheat, oats, maize (corn), barley and hay had spread almost to their geographical limits, and had been a major influence on Australian economic, social and environmental developments in the 19th century.

1814. Australian Sheep Shearing Shed.

Wool was one of the two bases of Australia's wealth in the 19th century, together with gold.

Successful agricultural and pastoral production required capital investment, secure and productive land, reliable water supplies (whether groundwater, rivers or rain), a labour supply, markets, ways of getting to markets and technological innovation.

Initially cattle were the preferred animal of farmers, as they could tolerate harsh conditions, defend themselves against dingos, and handle most climates. Stock routes were developed to take cattle to internal markets or to railways linked to the ports. The stock routes needed watering points and this meant intrusion on, and often destruction of, Aboriginal resources and sacred sites. Pastoral and agricultural expansion led to the collapse or movement of Aboriginal populations through displacement, disease and sometimes killings.

Sheep were more profitable, but required shepherds (until the development of cheap wire fencing in the 1850s), and more moderate climates. In the 1880s, the number of sheep in Australia increased from 50 million to 100 million before the drought of the late 1890s reduced numbers. Experimental breeding improved the quality of wool, while the expansion of the railways meant that wool could be taken more quickly and cheaply to ports around the country. Refrigeration, developed by Thomas Mort, meant that frozen meat would arrive fresh in the export country.

Pastoralists learned to manage water on their property through the use of storage dams, windmills and water tanks, all of which increased the carrying capacity of the land. The breeding of specialised sheepdogs reduced the number of shepherds required, making growing wool more profitable.

Queensland cane fields

During the 1860s, there was a shortage of Australian labour in the cotton and sugar industries in Queensland. Cotton remained a minor crop, but once workers were brought to Australia from Indonesia, Sri Lanka, and especially the Pacific Islands, sugar cane became widespread and profitable. About 60,000 Pacific Island labourers were brought to Australia between the 1860s and 1900 to work in the sugar cane fields of Queensland. Historically, the Pacific Island workers were often called 'Kanakas', from the Hawaiian word for 'man', but the word took on a derogatory meaning and is no longer used.

Many of the early Pacific Island labourers were 'blackbirded' – kidnapped. They were enticed or forced onto ships, then taken to Queensland and made to work under appalling conditions. The death rate of Pacific Island labourers in the early years of cane farming was 15 times that of other men of the same age.

Even after this 'blackbirding' stopped and workers arrived on freely made agreements, called indentures, the death rate remained three times higher than that of workers in other labouring jobs. A typical agreement signed by a Pacific Island labourer lasted for three years and involved long hours of hard work in unhygienic conditions but provided them with the possibility for greater wealth than they could have hoped for in their home islands.

Many labourers renewed their agreement several times and saved money, setting themselves up with their families on their own farms. As the colonies negotiated over what a federated nation of Australia would look like, the prevalence of Pacific Islander labour in northern Queensland threatened to keep Queensland out of the new

A pink dress made from wool from the Springfield merino. William Pitt Faithfull established the Springfield Merino Stud in 1838 with ten rams selected from the Macarthur Camden Park stud.

Broken Hill Silver Mines, N. S. W.

Economic development led to the expansion of mining.

nation. The other colonies wanted the new nation to be a 'white' Australia, and this would be threatened if any colony still imported and used 'black' labour.

DEMOCRACY, POLITICS AND IDENTITY IN THE COLONIES

The end of convict transportation to the eastern colonies in 1853 and the spread of Chartist ideas on the goldfields and at the Eureka Stockade helped the process of democratisation in Australia.

Developing responsible democracy

Colonial laws were implemented by the Legislative Council, which consisted of members appointed by King George III. But in 1850 the British Government agreed to allow each colony, except Queensland (which was part of New South Wales until 1859) and Western Australia (which was still a tiny settlement), to develop a new set of fundamental principles or laws by which they would be governed. These constitutions would include self-government, which involved the right of each colony to elect its own parliaments and to make most laws for itself.

New South Wales, Victoria and Tasmania gained the right to have popularly elected Legislative Assemblies in 1855. This was followed by South Australia in 1856, Queensland in

1859 and Western Australia in 1890. This new, more democratic system allowed the public to elect members who would represent the needs and interests of the community.

The lower house and the upper house

The colonies all had a 'bicameral', or two-house, system of parliament: a Legislative Assembly (the lower house) and a Legislative Council (the upper house).

Government was formed in the Legislative Assemblies, and these assemblies had the greatest power to make laws. The Legislative Assemblies were elected by manhood suffrage, which meant every adult man (aged 21 and over) would be able to vote. This was a very advanced democratic idea for the time. In Britain, for example, only about one in five adult males could vote, as men had to own a certain value of property in order to be able to vote.

Although women would not get the vote until 1894 in South Australia and 1899 in Western Australia, and not until after Federation in the other colonies, Australia was one of the world's earliest adopters of the female franchise. It was 1928 before women in Britain could vote.

Legislative Councils in the colonies still retained some undemocratic aspects, such as a property qualification for membership, and in some cases multiple voting rights for property owners.

Payment for parliamentarians and the secret ballot

The introduction of payment of Members of Parliament, starting with Victoria in 1870, meant that ordinary working people, and not just the wealthy, could afford to stand for Parliament.

Another significant democratic development was the introduction of the secret ballot. In 1856, Victoria and then Tasmania were the first places in the world to introduce this system. It was designed to stop bribery and intimidation: if votes were cast in public and another person could see how a voter marked his ballot paper, then potentially the voter could be bribed or intimidated. The secret ballot helped to make sure that a person could vote freely.

Free education

Another important democratic development was the introduction of free and compulsory education, which allowed children to attend school up to the age of 13 without having to pay any fees. This would improve literacy

The slate was once an essential classroom tool. Students would write on the slate with a special pencil, and then wipe the slate clean by rubbing it with a rag – or with spit and a sleeve.

YOUNGSTER:- "Father, teacher says I've gotter bring a penny wi' me to school termorrer ter buy a slate pencil wi' !"

PARENT:- "Go it! Go it! that makes ninepence-'alfpenny I've spent on yer education already."

PHIL MAY

A joke about the small cost of free and compulsory education – and some parents' attitudes towards it. Date unknown.

rates within the generation so that people could read, be better informed, and therefore become more responsible voters. Free, compulsory and secular (non-religious) education until age 14 was first introduced in Victoria in 1872, and adopted soon after by the other colonies, well before its implementation in Britain in the late 1890s.

Nationalism and the growth of a national identity

The mid- to late-19th century was also a time of developing nationalism – the identification of a group of people by language and culture as being part of a single and separate nation. The British and the French already had a strong sense of national identity. The Americans had gained theirs during their revolution against Britain in 1776 and the civil war of the 1860s. The people of many small German-speaking states had come together in 1871 to form the new nation of Germany. Several Italian-speaking states had done the same to create the nation of Italy, also in 1871. An Australian sense of national identity was developing as the separate colonies increased their contact and became more conscious of the common features of a united Australia.

Australian artists and writers

This growing nationalism was evident in a variety of creative fields. The Heidelberg School of the 1880s, which included painters Frederick McCubbin, Tom Roberts, Arthur Streeton, Clara Southern and Charles Conder, attempted to capture and celebrate the beauty of the country's light, heat and dryness, and Australian bush themes. Ellis Rowan was an internationally acclaimed botanical artist, who specialised in painting landscapes, flora and fauna.

Writers such as Henry Lawson, Banjo Paterson, Adam Lindsay Gordon and Steele Rudd all wrote about the bush. Sometimes the life they presented was harsh, often romantic, but all were treating it as distinctly Australian. Miles Franklin's *My Brilliant Career*, published in 1901, revolves around a teenage girl facing the challenges of growing up in rural Australia. Popular literature used scenes and motifs unique to Australia, particularly the bush and kangaroos.

Architecture
Architects also started to express ideas about Australia in their designs. The Queenslander house solved the problem of heat and humidity by having the house set on tall posts, allowing air to flow underneath the building to cool it. In Sydney and Melbourne the Federation style of housing developed, with more space between buildings, and often with Australian flora and fauna as decorative elements in windows, doors and even roof ornaments.

Political writing
Two books, both by one-time principals of private schools in Melbourne, had a great impact. William Fitchett's *Deeds that Won the Empire* provided stories of British military heroes as inspirational reading for schoolchildren, and revolved around themes of war, the Empire and civic duty. It was written in 1897, the year of Queen Victoria's Diamond Jubilee, and had been reprinted 29 times by 1914.

The style of home pictured was popular from around 1890 to 1915, and came to be known as the Federation style. Advertising postcard, circa 1910.

Charles Pearson's *National Life and Character* predicted the rise of Asian and African nations, and the decline of the British Empire. Pearson's views were very influential in the 1901 debates on White Australia and were used as a justification for the policy of excluding non-Europeans for fear that they would provide unfair competition for white Australians.

The Ashes

Sport helped develop both colonial loyalties and national pride. In 1877 a combined New South Wales and Victoria cricket team defeated the English team in their first test match in Australia. In 1882 a mock obituary for English cricket was published after an Australian team again defeated the English visitors, saying that the 'body will be cremated and the ashes taken to Australia'. The following year, a group of Melbourne women jokingly

Camels and Afghan cameleers

The first camel to arrive in Australia was 'Henry', brought here from Teneriffe in the Canary Islands, in 1840. In 1846, Henry was part of John Ainsworth Horrocks' exploration party around Spencer Gulf in South Australia. Henry was managed by an Aboriginal goatherder, Jimmy Moorhouse.

During the trip, Horrocks was about to shoot a bird when Henry bumped him and the man shot himself in the hand and jaw. Horrocks died from infection of the wounds, and Henry was destroyed – but not before biting a stockman on the head during the process.

In 1860, 24 camels and three cameleers were used for the Burke and Wills expedition. An estimated 2000 cameleers and 15,000 camels were brought mainly from north-western India in the period between 1870 and 1900. The use of camels was vital in various exploring parties, then in supporting part of the construction of the Overland Telegraph Line and in the transport of supplies for the Port Augusta to Alice Springs rail link, known as the Afghan Express, and today as 'The Ghan'. The symbol of today's train is an Afghan man and a camel.

The cameleers were called 'Afghans', but they came from areas we know today as Afghanistan, Balochistan, Kashmir, Sindh, Pakistan, Egypt, Iran, Turkey and the Punjab. The cameleers spoke many different languages but they were all united in their religion, Islam. The men were brought out on three-year contracts and usually lived on the outskirts of inland towns. There was some conflict as they competed against European bullock teams for transportation contracts.

The most successful cameleer was Abdul Wade (possibly originally Wahid or Wadi). He arrived in Australia in 1879. In 1893, he managed the Bourke Camel Carrying Company before setting up his own business importing camels and cameleers. In 1895 he married Emily Ozadelle, with whom he had seven children.

Wade could be seen arriving at the copper fields of New South Wales on a white camel, and dressed as a European gentleman. He once challenged a rival to a long-distance race between his camel and his rival's horse. The horse died halfway.

presented a small urn containing the ashes of a bail to the touring English captain, and the 'Ashes' trophy was born.

Other political ideas and ideologies

Alongside the rise of a more democratic government in Australia, the second half of the 19th century saw the growth of many new social theories and political ideas.

Late-19th century attitudes to race could be considered complex and even contradictory. They ranged from a belief in full equality to a belief in the superiority of some races over others. This variety of attitudes would be evident in debates in 1901 about what sort of nation Australia should be.

Wade was respected by his employees and was naturalised in 1902. However, he was not fully accepted by his European rivals, who mocked his 'Afghan-ness'. In 1923 he left his family, gave up his passport, and returned to Afghanistan, and then to Britain, where he died in 1928.

A key element in communication and economy in central Australia – the camel team.

Social Darwinism

In 1859 Charles Darwin published *On the Origin of Species*, setting out his theory of evolution – that animals and plants best adapted to their environment were the ones more likely to survive and to pass on their evolutionary advantages to their offspring. Some Christians saw this as a fundamental threat to their beliefs that their God created the world about 6000 years ago, as calculated from the Old Testament. Others had no problem maintaining their belief in a Creator while still accepting the scientific evidence that the process of creation took millions of years.

Scientists and thinkers applied Darwin's theory to humans and believed that there was good evidence the races were not equal, and that the superior ones would survive while the inferior would die out.

This was expressed in the book *South Australia: Its History, Resources, and Production*, published in 1876 under the authority of the Government of South Australia, and intended to attract British investment to the colony. The author William Harcus refers to the colonial process in which the 'feebler race bends before the stronger as the reeds bend to the sweep of the winds' due to the new colonists' supposedly superior civilisation replacing the Indigenous one.

Chartism

There were many British Chartists on the goldfields in the 1850s and their ideas were commonly expressed during the mass meetings at Eureka. The Chartists got their name from their support for the People's Charter of 1838, which called for six reforms of the existing political system to make it more democratic. These demands were for every man over the age of 21 to be able to vote, the introduction of the secret ballot, any adult male to be able to sit as a Member of Parliament without owning property, payment of Members of Parliament, equal population in electoral areas, and annual elections. Most of these became part of the different colonies' political systems during the second half of the 19th century.

Capitalism and socialism

Two contrasting economic and political ideas of the era were capitalism and socialism.

The basic idea of capitalism was that people used their capital (money) to set up a private business, which was not controlled by the government or state, and then customers or buyers chose what they wanted to buy from the variety on offer. If two or more businesses were offering the same goods, then buyers would choose who they would buy from. Those who supplied what the buyers wanted would succeed, and those who did not would fail. So under capitalism the 'free' market (free because it was independent of state control) would determine economic winners and losers. The capitalist economic system would work best in a political democracy.

Socialism was the economic opposite of capitalism. The key figures in the development of this ideology were the Germans Karl Marx and Friedrich Engels. In 1848 they published *The Communist Manifesto*, which became one of the most politically influential books of the

Opposite: An Australian family of 1895.

19th and 20th centuries. Socialism was based on the idea that the state or government, not the free market, should decide what was produced, and what it would cost. It would do this in a way that was fair to everybody. Those who had a lot would be expected to help those who did not. In this way, society would be even and fair. Socialism was often associated with the political idea of communism, where the state controlled all economic activity, though many of socialism's supporters believed that it could be introduced in a political democracy.

The main supporters of socialism were the colonial Labor parties of the 1890s. Although these parties developed out of organisations of shearers in Queensland, and trade unions in Sydney, all colonies had Labor parties of some sort by 1901.

The first Labor Party

In 1890, the colonies were in an economic depression. Employers wanted to reduce their expenses by cutting workers' wages. The unions resisted this, and there was a series of great strikes. The unions lost, and realised that they needed to work inside the political system if they were to make gains and protect their interests, hence the formation of the Labor Party in 1891. In 1899, the Queensland Labor Party became the world's first Labor Government and its leader Andrew Dawson the Premier – though only for one week.

Conflicting economic ideas

There were also conflicting economic ideas about protection and free trade. Under free trade, there would be no restrictions on people selling their goods. In the Australian colonies, this meant that if goods could be produced cheaply in one colony they could be sold in other colonies without any taxes or additional costs imposed on them by the other colonies to drive up their price.

Protection was the opposite: as it might be more expensive to make or grow goods in one colony, the price of the less expensive competitors' goods should be increased by a tax so that local buyers would buy the local goods, not the imported ones. This was done to protect the workers in the more expensive colony. If people did not buy the local goods, this could cause unemployment and hurt the whole colony economically. Those who supported protection believed it was better for goods to cost the customer a bit more, in order to keep people in the colony employed.

Imperialism

Colonial Australia was the result of British imperialism, as was the British colonisation of New Zealand, Canada, South Africa, India and many other countries. Imperialism is the practice of one nation extending its rule over other regions or nations. Britain had the world's largest empire, and many Australians took great pride in being part of that empire. They did not look as sympathetically on other imperial nations, especially Germany, which after 1880, tried to build an empire that would rival Britain's.

Most Australians saw no problem or contradiction in being both British and Australian, since Britain let the colonies govern themselves. In other parts of the British Empire, especially in India and parts of Africa, the political will to break away from the British Empire would gradually grow and result in decolonisation during the next century.

Colonial liberalism

Another significant political idea in late-19th century Australia was liberalism. This was the political movement of the emerging middle classes. Liberals believed in free trade and individual effort, but also that the power of the state should be used to help people, rather than letting them fail and suffer. Colonial liberal governments introduced laws to make lands available to selectors, create compulsory and free education, improve conditions in factories, and pay old-age pensions. New South Wales, Victoria, Queensland, South Australia and Tasmania all had influential liberal politicians at this time, and reforms made in the colonies would later be adopted by the Government of the Commonwealth of Australia (or the Commonwealth Government) after 1901. When Labor parties developed in the 1890s, they often worked with the Liberals to enable such reforms to be introduced.

INCREASING CONTACT WITH THE WORLD

Military aid

The colonies' main contact with the world was through seaborne trade. Every colony exported and imported through its major ports.

The colonies assisted in Britain's wars and conflicts. Small numbers of colonial volunteers went to the Maori wars in 1845 and the Waikato War between 1863 and 1864, both in New Zealand; to the Sudan campaign in northern Africa in 1885; and to the Boxer Rebellion in China in 1900.

Australia's most significant involvement was in the Boer War in South Africa between 1899 and 1902. In the south of Africa, British colonies and Dutch-Afrikaner settlers, known as 'Boers', had engaged in periodic territorial conflict since the 1850s. The discovery of gold and diamonds in Boer republics heightened tensions and the Boers attacked in an attempt to prevent British expansion. Australia supported Britain. Australia's troops in the Boer War included the first national force, the Australian Commonwealth Horse, which was formed after Federation in 1901. About 16,000 men and a few nurses served, with about 600 killed or dying of wounds or disease. The war began as a popular one, but its brutal nature led many people to oppose it.

Humanitarian aid

Colonial Australians also contributed generously to overseas humanitarian causes, supporting the Irish during the country's potato famine in the 1840s, helping fund Jews who were being persecuted under Ottoman (Turkish) rule in Palestine in 1854, as well as the Lancashire mill workers hit by the blockading of the cotton trade during the United States Civil War of the early 1860s. In 1877, receipts from a Carlton versus Melbourne football game in Victoria all went to the Indian famine relief fund. In 1889, money was sent to London dockworkers who had gone on strike.

There were also Australian missionaries active in New Guinea, New Hebrides, Fiji, Africa and China – these people were preachers, but also teachers, nurses and translators.

The first Labor premier

In 1899, Queensland Labor Party leader Andrew Dawson (born 1863; died 1910) became premier of the first Labor Government in the world. It was a minority government and lasted only a week.

Dawson had been brought up in an orphanage after his parents' deaths. He left school at 12 and became a manual worker in the gold town of Charters Towers. In 1886, he went off to the Kimberleys gold rush, returned and married.

Dawson taught himself to write and speak effectively, and joined a union. He stood for parliament and was elected in 1893 as part of the opposition group to the government.

In 1899 the government resigned. The Labor Party held the balance of power between the two main political groups of liberals and conservatives, and Dawson was invited by the governor to become premier. This had the effect of uniting enough members of the other two groups to reform their government, and after a week the Dawson Government was defeated in parliament, and a new premier appointed.

Later suffering from ill-health, Dawson had to retire from state parliament, but won a senate seat at the first Commonwealth election and became Minister for Defence in 1904.

He lost favour among his Labor Party colleagues and did not win a seat at the next election in 1906, when he stood as an independent.

Dawson retired from politics and died in 1910.

TOWARDS FEDERATION

The economic stimulation created by the gold rushes contributed to the development of trade unions, higher wages and better working conditions.

In 1856 the most skilled tradesmen were the stonemasons. There was heavy demand for stonemasons to build the great stone buildings that the wealthy and governments could now afford, thanks at least in part to gold.

The stonemasons in Victoria knew that they were in a position of great strength to win better wages and conditions – they had special skills, and there were plenty of people competing to employ them. They went on strike and demanded an eight-hour day (eight hours of work, eight hours of recreation, eight hours of rest), as opposed to the ten-hour day they were currently working. Unions in the other colonies followed suit, and gradually the eight-hour day for a six-day week (and then a five-and-a-half-day week) became accepted, even among unskilled workers. From the 1850s the living and working conditions of workers improved greatly.

Depression in the 1890s

The decades of development ended suddenly in the early 1890s. The international price for wool and minerals fell, the British loans that had financed the building of railways and roads dried up, and people began to queue at banks to withdraw their money so that they could pay off their debts. Many banks did not have enough funds to pay back depositors and, as a result, the banks collapsed. This meant that many depositors lost all their savings.

At the same time, both private and government loans from overseas had to be repaid. Governments cut back on spending – which included projects such as road and rail building, and installing sewerage and water pipes in cities – creating widespread unemployment. Many people lost their jobs, their houses and their savings. A number of wealthy people declared themselves bankrupt, had their debts written off, and were free to start all over again.

Australia had entered a depression, a period in which the country suffered a huge financial shortfall. The economic distress was compounded by a series of strikes in different colonies. There were strikes between 1890 and 1894 among the unionised workers in the shipping, mining and shearing industries. The unions tried to keep workers' wages high at a time when employers' profits were disappearing. If the unions could force the employers to hire union members only, then wages could be kept up. If the employers could break the union, they could hire workers from among the many unemployed people willing to accept lower wages. Men, women and children went hungry and relied on charity while the strikes dragged on.

Waltzing Matilda

In 1974, a national vote was held on an Australian national anthem. The results were:

'Advance Australia Fair'	2,940,854
'Waltzing Matilda'	1,918,206
'God Save the Queen'	1,257,341
'The Song of Australia'	652,858

While 'Advance Australia Fair' won the most votes to become the new national anthem, 'Waltzing Matilda' was declared Australia's national song.

'Waltzing Matilda' was written by Sydney solicitor Andrew Barton Paterson. Paterson wrote bush poetry for *The Bulletin* magazine under the name 'The Banjo', after a racehorse owned by his family.

In 1895, Paterson was staying at the Queensland pastoral station Dagworth, when family member Christina Macpherson played a tune called 'The Craigielee March', based on an older tune, 'Thou Bonnie Wood of Craigielee'. Paterson put words to it, and thus was born 'Waltzing Matilda', a song about a sheep thief who drowns himself rather than be caught.

Though Paterson never spoke publicly about the writing of 'Waltzing Matilda', historians see deeper messages in the song.

One interpretation is that the song is about the mysterious death of a shearer, Samuel Hoffmeister, whose body was found near a billabong.

Another view is that the song is a call for political action against the law during the union disputes of that time.

A third view is that it was a love song. Some historians believed that through the words of 'Waltzing Matilda', Paterson was actually flirting with Christina, who was also a friend of his fiancée's.

Soon the conflict between employers and unionised employees became violent, as the employers brought in non-unionised workers, supported by police. Men were shot and killed in clashes, and shearing sheds were burned down. In one episode, the *Rodney*, a Murray River paddle steamer carrying non-union labour, was set ablaze in the water.

The 'Federation drought' 1895–1902

A major drought spread across eastern Australia from 1895 to 1902. Pastoralists and agriculturalists had expanded in good years into marginal areas and had overstocked the land, not realising that the land could not carry the number of sheep and cattle they put on it. When rain fell, the livestock would eat the new vegetation down to the soil and this led to erosion, as well as starving animals. Whole areas of farmland shifted. Strong winds blew the exposed topsoil hundreds of kilometres away. The depression and the drought hit the colonies badly, but out of them came a renewed move during the 1890s to federate and to create an Australian nation.

The shearers' dispute at Hughenden Strike Camp in Queensland, 1891, between union and non-union workers of the wool industry, is one of the most important industrial strikes in Australian history. It was hugely influential in the growth of socialist sentiment and the formation of the Australian Labor Party in the late 19th century.

Milestones in Australian democracy

	NSW	TAS (Van Diemen's Land)	QLD
Colony established	1788	1825	1859
Upper house created (Legislative Council)	1823	1825	1860
Lower house created (Legislative Assembly)	1856	1856	1860
Manhood vote	1858	1900	1872
Female vote	1902	1904	1905
Female can be elected	1918	1922	1915
Payment of MPs	1889	1890	1886
Secret ballot	1858	1856	1859
Free and compulsory education	1880	1885	1875

	SA	VIC	WA
Colony established	1836	1851	1829
Upper house created (Legislative Council)	1836	1851	1832
Lower house created (Legislative Assembly)	1857	1856	1890
Manhood vote	1856	1857	1893
Female vote	1894	1909	1899
Female can be elected	1895	1924	1920
Payment of MPs	1887	1870	1900
Secret ballot	1856	1856	1877
Free and compulsory education	1875	1872	1895

5 Creating a Nation

On 1 January 1901 the 20-year process of federating Australia's six colonies culminated in the creation of a new nation.

Medallion presented to Bransby Beauchamp Cooper after he made the highest score in an England vs Victoria cricket tour match, 1873. The medallion features the Australian coat of arms, a significant symbol showing Australia's growing national identity.

AUSTRALIA BEFORE FEDERATION

By 1890, each of the six colonies had its own parliament. This meant that each colony could make its own laws about local defence and immigration, and have its own army. Each colony could decide what taxes people paid, what schools and hospitals would be built, even what size railway tracks the trains would run on.

Each colony was, however, still tied to Britain. Britain was responsible for the colonies' relations with other nations and provided each colony with a governor, who represented the British monarch. Each colony also had British courts as their main court of appeal.

This heavy British political presence did not worry most of the colonists, as many identified themselves as Britons. By 1900 a large majority of people living in the Australian colonies had been born there and considered the colony their homeland, but most of the population still had British heritage and culture. Virtually the whole non-Indigenous population spoke English and were Christian. Great Britain was the world's richest nation, was the leading industrial and manufacturing nation, and had the strongest navy and the greatest empire. The people of the Australian colonies were proud of this connection.

But at the same time there was another force developing, a sense of being Australian as well as being British.

A home being carved out of the bush. Australia's popular image was clearly linked to 'the bush', even though most people lived in cities and towns.

A developing identity

People were becoming more aware and proud that the Australian continent was different from other places. 'Australianness', and a feeling of identification with the country, was developed in the work of writers and painters in the late 19th century, as some artists focused on themes and settings unique to Australia, rather than mimicking British or European ones (though there were still many who presented European themes). Henry Lawson, for example, was a very popular writer whose work revolved around the Australian bush. Tom Roberts was known for painting images of Australian rural life, such as *Shearing the Rams* (1890), which shows a shearing scene inside an outback woolshed. One art reviewer in the magazine *Table Talk* called it 'a distinctly Australian picture . . . representative of the life of the country'.

Organisations began to use Australian animals and plants – such as kangaroos, koalas, wattle, waratahs and banksias – as symbols in their advertising, indicating the colonists' growing appreciation of the land and its animals. Even though most people lived in towns and cities, they saw the Australian 'bush' as part of their lives.

A developing sense of national identity can be seen in these symbols on the Klondike flag, used by Australians when they went to Alaska for a gold rush in 1898.

Defence

The Australian colonies were defended by British troops until 1870. After that each colony had its own army, and some also had a navy, all backed by the Royal Navy.

During the 1880s, the colonists became concerned about the influence of the Germans in New Guinea, and the French in New Caledonia and New Hebrides (now Vanuatu) in the Pacific Ocean. Many people were worried that a European colony in the region might be used as a base in an attack against Australia or its shipping if there was a war in which that country and Britain were involved.

In 1889, British Major-General James Bevan Edwards was sent by the British Government to inspect the Australian colonies' defences and report on what he had seen. He suggested that the colonies should combine their separate small armies and navies into a much larger and stronger one. In order to achieve this, the colonies would have to cooperate and put their forces under a new national military authority.

Race fears

The gold rush attracted a large number of gold-seekers from China between the 1850s and the 1870s, which led to most colonies passing laws to limit Chinese immigration. Once the gold rushes had stopped, the colonies scrapped these laws. But when the numbers of immigrants started to rise again, colonial politicians met in 1888 to pass uniform laws. They realised that if the laws were not the same, then immigrants could land in one colony and move overland to others. The politicians met again in 1896 to agree on even stricter laws, which this time would restrict all non-European immigrants.

A British Doulton porcelain kangaroo umbrella stand, 1885. The increasing decorative use of unique native animals showed a growing awareness of an Australian identity.

Contact between the colonies

People from the different colonies started to meet more frequently and cooperate as Australians, rather than as Victorians or Queenslanders or Western Australians. Improvements in transportation and communication, and increasing economic activity between the colonies meant that individuals and organisations had much more intercolonial contact.

Unions, businesses and common interest groups held many intercolonial meetings during the 1880s and 1890s. There were discussions about unifying the management of lighthouses, statistics, weather records and postage, all of which could be done better if the colonies cooperated.

Henry Lawson

Henry Lawson (born 1867; died 1922) was one of Australia's most popular writers. He had a lonely and hard childhood, was poorly educated, and lost much of his hearing at an early age.

As a young man he travelled by foot through drought-ravaged western New South Wales, and it was these journeys that influenced his writing. Lawson's stories and poems were usually about the struggle of ordinary, decent people against hardship and loneliness. They also emphasised political egalitarianism, unionism and republicanism. Even though the majority of people in Australia lived in cities or towns, they identified with Lawson's bleak and realistic view of the bush.

Louisa Lawson

Henry's mother, Louisa Lawson (born 1848; died 1920), also helped to shape a sense of Australian national identity.

Louisa was a writer, newspaper owner and feminist. She founded the *Dawn* newspaper in 1888, and the Dawn Club in 1889 to promote improvements to women's lives and rights. She campaigned for the vote for women, publicised failures of the law to protect women, urged parents to educate their daughters to become more than domestic workers, argued for opening up professions such as law and medicine to women, urged governments to appoint women as prison warders and factory inspectors, and advised on health care for children.

Louisa was the original hard-working, resourceful, kindly and long-suffering bushwoman who featured in her son's stories.

Setting the clocks

Before 1884 there was no universally accepted standard time – that is, no one agreed place from which all time was measured.

This changed in 1884 during the International Meridian Conference. Greenwich, near London, England, was agreed upon as the international 'prime meridian' or 0 degrees longitude, from which time would be measured. The world was divided into 24 time zones: any places that were within the same time zone would have the same time difference from Greenwich.

In 1892, a meeting of chief surveyors from each of the colonies argued that all places within a colony should have the same time, and that the colonies as a whole should be on a standard time compared to the rest of the world. Before this meeting, every town in Australia could set its own time, called local mean time, and time in neighbouring towns often differed by several minutes.

In 1895, the colonies were placed in three time zones – a western zone for Western Australia, a central zone for South Australia, and an eastern zone that included Queensland, New South Wales, Victoria and Tasmania.

Technology and communication

The colonies were also being linked to each other and to the world by technology, in the form of the telegraph system.

A customer in Perth could write out a message on a special form at the post office. A telegraph operator would tap out the message in morse code, which was a set 'alphabet' of dots and dashes corresponding to letters. The message would travel through telegraph wires as electrical impulses to a repeater station, where an operator would

Sir John Forrest's carriage clock

Sir John Forrest became the first Premier of Western Australia in 1890, and attended all Federation meetings. This clock was designed so that the internal working was not damaged by the swaying of travel on a train.

Sir John Forrest's carriage clock reminds us that great distances separated people in the colonies, but also that they needed to work together as Australians to set common policies such as time zones.

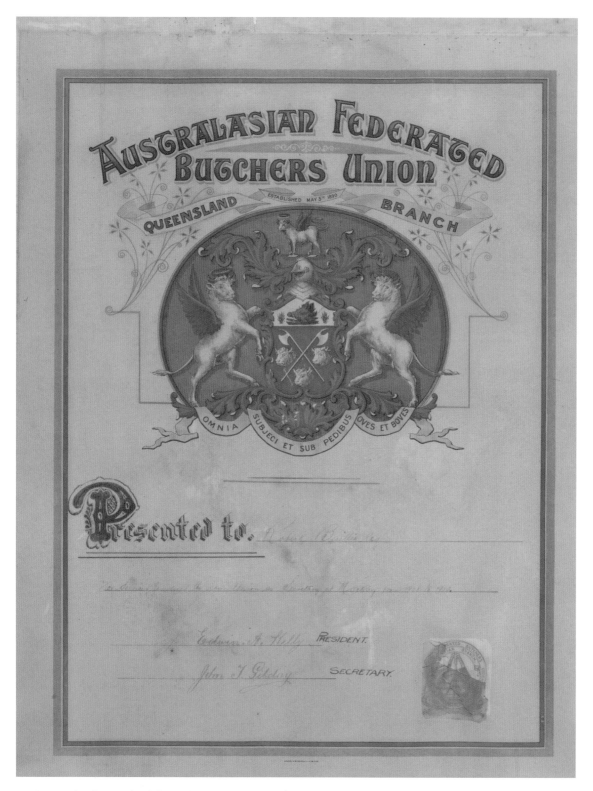

AUSTRALASIAN FEDERATED BUTCHERS UNION

ESTABLISHED MAY 5TH 1890

QUEENSLAND BRANCH

OMNIA SUBJECI ET SUB PEDIBUS OVES ET BOVES

Presented to

Edwin A. Kelly PRESIDENT.

John J. Golding SECRETARY.

Increasing intercolonial meetings, contacts and organisation, such as the joining of colonial butchers' unions into a unified Australian one, helped bring Australians together and promote Federation. This certificate was presented to Robert Baillie Esq, 'for Services Rendered the above Union as Secretary at Mackay from 1908 to 1910'.

receive the message and resend it to the next station, hundreds of kilometres away. Once the coded message was received at its final destination, it would be translated and written out by a clerk, and a telegram boy would deliver it to the customer's home address.

In 1872 this went further when the Overland Telegraph Line from Adelaide was run to Darwin, and linked into the international cable on the seabed. This meant that news from Europe could be sent directly to all the colonies through their linked telegraph line system.

Travel

Railway networks were expanded within and between the colonies. Victoria's and New South Wales' rail lines linked at Albury in 1883. However, the width (or gauge) of the lines was different in the two colonies, because each had sourced steam engines from different countries and so travellers had to swap trains at the border to continue their trip. New South Wales and Queensland were linked by rail in 1888. Victoria linked with South Australia in 1887. The only gap left was between Perth and South Australia, with Western Australia demanding a rail link before they would join in Federation. Poet and journalist Henry Lawson described the significance of this great nation-building movement in his poem *The Roaring Days*:

> *The flaunting flag of progress*
> *Is in the West unfurled,*
> *The mighty bush with iron rails*
> *Is tethered to the world.*

OPPOSITION TO FEDERATION

The last decade of the 19th century saw many forces pushing Australia towards Federation. But there were differences that continued to divide the colonists.

Some people had a strong loyalty to their specific colony. They saw themselves as Tasmanians or Western Australians first, and as Australians second, or even third (after their British heritage).

Referendums held in 1898 and 1899 in most colonies, and 1900 in Western Australia, asked the public to vote either 'Yes' or 'No' to the proposed constitution, as a step towards a federated Australia. This was a world-first, as never before had people been allowed to vote and approve the national constitution that would govern their country. But in 1898, less than 50 per cent of eligible voters bothered to participate in the non-compulsory referendum, and in 1899 less than 60 per cent, perhaps indicating a lack of interest in the issue.

Other factors complicated the establishment of Federation, including political differences, colonial competition and varying loyalties.

Free trade versus protection

One of the major differences that had to be resolved was the question of free trade or protection. 'Free trade' meant that goods could be sent from or brought into a colony without any extra tax being put on them. 'Protection' meant that a tax was put on the product to raise its selling price. This was done so that local makers of the same goods, who might be paying higher wages to their workers and therefore forced to sell the product at a greater price, could still compete against their rivals. The main aim was to protect jobs.

New South Wales was the largest colony in favour of free trade, while Victoria was the chief supporter of protection. The issue was solved when delegates agreed that under the new constitution trade between the states would be 'absolutely free', but that it was up to the new Commonwealth Parliament to decide what tariff or tax, if any, would be placed on goods imported into Australia from overseas. Until the Parliament made a decision, the existing trade policies of the states would stay in place. The Parliament introduced a uniform tariff on imports on 8 October 1901, and on that date free trade existed between the states.

Rivalry and competition

During the debates over the drafting of the Constitution, rivalry between colonies intensified. New South Wales politicians thought Sydney should be the new national capital city, and those in Victoria thought it should be Melbourne. Meanwhile, other colonies believed it should be neither!

The colonies with smaller populations (Queensland, Western Australia, Tasmania and South Australia) were also worried that if the colonies united, the larger colonies would dominate. They feared that they would work together to put their interests ahead of the smaller ones. For example, if New South Wales and Victoria joined and made laws about the water in the Murray River, they could reduce its quality and flow to South Australia, which depended on the river for its water supply.

Such rivalry meant that the balance of political power in the new parliament had to be worked out before there could be a new nation.

THE TEN BEST CITIZENS OF VICTORIA
As Voted for by "The Herald" Readers

The 2nd Professor Adams

No. 9.—HON. ALFRED DEAKIN

A postcard featuring a cartoon depiction of the Hon. Alfred Deakin, who was voted one of the top ten best citizens of Victoria by *The Herald* readers. Date unknown.

Political differences

The growing labour movement was a substantial source of difference. Unions had been growing in size during the 1880s, but began to shrink again in the 1890s. During the economic depression of the early 1890s, unions had been involved in a number of strikes to try to protect their members' wages and conditions. These strikes were unsuccessful due to the large number of unemployed people who were prepared to work for lower wages.

Union leaders decided that in order to have their policies and beliefs implemented as law, they needed to work inside parliaments. So they created Labor parties and stood for elections, with some candidates being elected in colonial parliaments after 1891.

These Labor members often supported more radical policies about Federation than did most other politicians. In particular, they opposed the idea that the Senate would have equal numbers of representatives from each colony, regardless of the size of the population (for example, the largest colony, New South Wales, would have the same number of senators as the smallest colony, Tasmania). They saw this as undemocratic. So while these Labor members did not oppose Federation, they were against the specific sort of federation that was being proposed in the draft constitution.

There was also some republican opposition to the proposed constitution. These people believed that Australia should break away from Britain and be totally independent.

International sport as a symbol of Federation. A cartoon that shows us the power of the colonies uniting against a sporting enemy. The text in the cartoon reads 'COMBINE AUSTRALIA: Umpire Punch "YOU'VE DONE JOLLY WELL BY COMBINATION IN THE CRICKET FIELD, AND NOW YOU'RE GOING TO FEDERATE AT HOME. BRAVO BOY!".'

Most Australians rejected republicanism, both because they were proud to be British, and also because ties to Britain guaranteed Australian trade and defence in a way that would not be possible if Australia were independent.

Pacific Islands labour

In Queensland, many political leaders and land owners believed Europeans could not work effectively as labourers in the intense tropical heat. Between the 1860s and 1890s, large numbers of people from the nearby Pacific Islands were brought in to become contracted workers on the colony's sugar plantations, which were a major contributor to the Queensland economy. Other colonies did not want non-European workers as it did not suit their vision of a 'White Australia', a nation peopled by the 'European race', which at that time referred predominantly to British people. Queenslanders would have to agree to cease their use of Pacific Islander labour if they wanted to be part of the new Australia.

HOW WAS FEDERATION ACHIEVED?

How did the colonies of Australia in the late 19th century overcome the issues that divided them? It took the supporters of Federation ten years of campaigning and many meetings and compromises to achieve their goal.

1880s: The first Australasian Federation Conference

During the 1880s, the colonies formed a Federal Council to try to make common laws and policies. The council consisted of representatives from the different colonies. Although Tasmania, Victoria, South Australia, Queensland, Western Australia and Fiji participated in these meetings, the largest colony, New South Wales, refused to take part. Therefore the council was not a true national body, and not very effective.

1889: Henry Parkes' call for Federation

Henry Parkes called for Federation on 24 October 1889 at a meeting in Tenterfield in New South Wales. His speech stoked a nationalist sentiment that focused on the unification of the colonies. He argued that Australians shared a 'crimson thread of kinship', and should be one nation. It was this speech, along with his later political work, that would earn Parkes the title 'Father of the Australian Federation'.

In 1890, a group of political leaders of the six Australian colonies and New Zealand (which was considering being part of the Federation) met to try to create this nation. They agreed that it was time to start working to achieve Federation.

1891: The first Australian Constitutional Convention

Once the colonial leaders had agreed that they wanted to federate, someone had to work out how to do it. A federal constitution was needed – that is, a set of rules about what laws a new national parliament could make, and what laws existing colonial parliaments could continue to make.

A key group comprising Sir Samuel Griffith (Queensland), Andrew Inglis Clark (Tasmania), Alfred Deakin (Victoria) and Charles Kingston (South Australia) drafted a constitution. Under this constitution, the national parliament would make laws about national issues (such as defence and printing money), and the colonial parliaments would make laws for their own colony alone (such as railways and factory laws). The colonies were to examine this constitution carefully and then decide if they were happy to go ahead with Federation. If there were parts of the constitution they did not agree with or that did not suit their colony, they would not proceed.

1892: Economic depression and severe drought

Before the colonial parliaments could debate this constitution, Australia was struck by a double disaster: the economic depression of the1890s and the severe drought that lasted from 1893 to 1902.

In the short term, the political leaders stopped thinking about Federation and focused on trying to balance their budgets to help their colonies survive economically.

In the long term, however, the depression of the 1890s might have helped Federation. Some leaders realised that the colonies may have been able to tackle their problems more effectively if they had worked together as a single economy, rather than as six separate ones. The discovery of gold in Western Australia at that time also helped offset the economic depression in the east coast of the country.

1893: Corowa Conference

While political leaders might have put Federation aside, many people in the Australian colonies still wanted it. A public conference was called for 31 July and 1 August at Corowa, in New South Wales, near the border with Victoria. This was a meeting organised by ordinary

Sir Samuel Griffith

Sir Samuel Griffith (born 1845; died 1920) was born in Merthyr Tydfil, Wales. He came to Queensland in 1853 and became a lawyer and politician, and then a judge. His extensive legal experience was valuable in his role of shaping the Australian Constitution. After Federation, he became the first Chief Justice of the new High Court of Australia.

people: local shopkeepers, businessmen and tradesmen who believed that Federation was important. For the first time, individual supporters and pro-Federation organisations were involved in the process. They would provide the drive to make Federation happen, even if the politicians had lost focus on the issue.

Two important new ideas were put forward at the Corowa Conference by a lawyer, Dr John Quick. The first was that the people would be able to vote for representatives from their colony to discuss the proposed Australian Constitution. This meant that the public could decide who would consider the proposed constitution. The second was that the people themselves would be able to vote for or against the drafted constitution. It was no longer a decision that only the politicians would make.

1894: Meeting of Federation Leagues in Melbourne

After Corowa, more supporters began to tell political leaders that they wanted Federation. One significant meeting occurred in Melbourne in 1894, when interest groups, called Federation Leagues, came together to lobby. These gatherings were further evidence of ordinary people working towards a federated country.

1895: Premiers' meeting in Hobart

In 1895, the premiers of the six colonies met in Hobart to debate the points raised at Corowa two years earlier. They agreed that the public would be able to vote for representatives to consider the Australian Constitution, and that they would also be able to vote on whether or not to accept that constitution (and therefore federate).

The movement towards Federation was starting to gather pace.

Alfred Deakin

Alfred Deakin (born 1856; died 1919) was a lawyer, journalist and politician first in Victorian state politics and later in Commonwealth politics, where he helped decide what would be in the new Australian Constitution. Deakin was a great believer in organisations such as the Australian Natives' Association (of Australian-born Europeans), which rallied public interest in Federation. He became Australia's second prime minister in 1903. Deakin passed away in 1919, and a British flag was draped over his coffin.

1897: The National Australasian Convention

On 4 March 1987, the colonies voted on their representatives to debate Federation at the National Australasian Convention. The only exceptions were Queensland, which could not decide whether to be involved in the voting, and New Zealand, which had decided it would not be part of the new Federation. At this convention the elected representatives finalised the new Australian Constitution. One South Australian woman, author Catherine Helen Spence, put herself forward as a candidate, but she did not get enough votes to be elected. It was not until 1921 that the first woman was elected to parliament, when Edith Cowan was voted in as a member of the Western Australian Legislative Assembly.

1898: People vote on the Constitution

Once the convention had agreed to a constitution, it was time for the public to vote on it. All males aged 21 and over could vote, as well as women of the same age range in South Australia and (in 1900) in Western Australia. In 1898 the electors of New South Wales, Victoria, South Australia and Tasmania voted on the Constitution, and all voted in favour of it.

Western Australia and Queensland did not vote, and New South Wales did not get the minimum number of Yes votes (80,000) that its parliament had decided were required in that colony for the Constitution to be accepted. It was clear that something had to be done to gain support from New South Wales and Queensland – if these two colonies refused to participate, there could be no real federation.

Charles Kingston

Charles Cameron Kingston (born 1850; died 1908) was a lawyer and politician in South Australia, serving under the Protectionist Party. He was socially progressive and brought in many reforms, including votes for women, better arbitration systems for solving industrial disputes, the reduction of powers in the upper house (the Legislative Council) and better factory conditions. A fiery character, he was once arrested while on his way to a duel with pistols. Kingston was a great reformer in the South Australian Parliament and was popular with many, but had a reputation as a bully towards his political enemies.

Catherine Helen Spence

Catherine Helen Spence (born 1825; died 1910) was a writer, preacher, reformer and feminist. She was born in Scotland, and came to Australia in 1839. Spence quickly became involved in reform activities, helping orphaned and destitute children and fighting for equal rights for women. Spence was Australia's first female political candidate when she ran unsuccessfully for election as a delegate to the 1897 Federal Convention. She never married but raised three families of orphaned children.

1899: The draft constitution is changed

The political leaders of the colonies met in 1899 and made seven changes to satisfy New South Wales and Queensland. These included an agreement that the new capital city, which was to be in New South Wales, must also be at least 100 miles (160 kilometres) from Sydney. They also agreed that the Commonwealth Government could make special financial grants to the states for specific purposes. These are called 'tied grants', and they have given the Commonwealth Government power in areas such as education and health – areas over which the makers of the Constitution never anticipated the Commonwealth having power.

On 20 June 1899, the people of all colonies except Western Australia voted on this revised constitution and the majority of voters supported Federation. The government of Western Australia still did not believe that its interests were being met in the Constitution, but the other colonies were ready to create the new nation.

1900: Political leaders take the Constitution to London

Federation of Australia could not go ahead without the approval of the British Government. A small group of people were dissatisfied with this and wanted a republican nation – that is, one that was totally politically separated from Britain.

In order to gain Britain's support, delegates Edmund Barton (New South Wales), Alfred Deakin (Victoria), Charles Kingston (South Australia) and Sir Phillip Fysh (Tasmania) took the proposed Australian Constitution to Britain for the parliament in London to pass it. The trip took six weeks on a steam-powered ship.

The British Government made some amendments to the Constitution. In particular, they changed it so that the highest court of appeal in some legal cases was the British Privy Council

Referendum results

Results of the 1898 referendum

1898	Yes	No
New South Wales	71,595	66,228
South Australia	35,800	17,320
Tasmania	11,797	2716
Victoria	100,520	22,090

Results of the 1899 referendum

1899	Yes	No
New South Wales	107,420	82,741
Queensland	38,488	30,996
South Australia	65,990	17,053
Tasmania	13,437	791
Victoria	152,653	9805
1900	**Yes**	**No**
Western Australia	44,800	19,691

Australian Electoral Commission Federation Fact Sheet 1 The Referendums 1898–1900
http://www.aec.gov.au/About_AEC/Publications/Fact_Sheets/factsheet1.htm

and not the Australian High Court. This action was taken to protect the interests of British companies in Australia.

Following these changes, the British Parliament approved the Australian Constitution, and therefore Federation itself. However, Western Australia had not yet said it would be part of the new nation.

The people of Western Australia voted in a Federation referendum on 31 July 1900. The economy of Western Australia had been transformed by the discovery of gold in the 1890s and the population had soared from 50,000 in 1890 to 200,000 in 1900. Nearly all of the new residents came from the eastern colonies. The Western Australian political representatives were mainly from the 'old' or pre-gold-rush population, and they had opposed Federation to protect local producers from cheaper competition. However, the new residents brought their 'eastern' attitudes and values with them, and tipped the vote in

favour of Federation. After the result, a telegraph message was immediately sent to Britain – 'Western Australia is IN'.

Western Australia was now part of the agreement, and Australia would become a nation of six states.

THE AUSTRALIAN CONSTITUTION OF 1901

The makers of the Australian Constitution worked primarily from two existing constitutions: the Constitution of the United States of America (created in 1789) and the British Constitution. There is no single written British Constitution document, but its accepted elements have developed over nearly 1000 years, dating as far back as some of the principles in the Magna Carta of 1215.

The Constitution as a rule book

The Australian Constitution is in essence a rule book. It sets out the roles and rights of the Australian Parliament and the states, including in which areas the Australian Parliament can make laws for the nation.

The main areas set aside for the Australian Parliament were defence, immigration, currency, posts and telegraphs, marriage, some pensions, customs and foreign affairs. Most of these were set out in one part of the Constitution, section 51, where 39 specific areas were listed. These areas could be expanded if people voted in favour of a change at a national referendum.

The states kept the power to make laws about any areas not specifically listed in section 51 – such as transport, health, education, police, agriculture, water, forests, land – and anything else not given to the Commonwealth.

The states could also make laws in some of the areas given to the Commonwealth, such as marriage and immigration, but if the Commonwealth made a law in the area then it had priority over the comparable state law.

There was one other major complication. The Commonwealth could give money to the states for a specific purpose. However, if the state did not agree to this purpose, it would not receive the money. This has meant a great increase in the power of the Australian Government over people's lives since Federation, as the Commonwealth can tell the states what laws to make in areas that were supposed to be only for the states, such as education and health.

THE NATION ON DISPLAY

On 1 January 1901, the first day of a new century, Australia became a nation. The country celebrated by holding a large official ceremony in Sydney. There were many British soldiers in the procession, to symbolise Great Britain's continuing connection to Australia and its promise to defend Australia in times of war.

Colonial troops who had recently returned from the Boer War, in support of Britain, also marched. There were also a thousand British troops from famous regiments, and brilliantly dressed mounted Indian soldiers.

The procession passed under arches built by and symbolising different Australian industries and groups: the wool industry, the wheat industry and the coal industry. There were also arches representing each of the other British colonies and the American Government. These impressive structures highlighted the new nation's economic strengths, its political unity, and its ties to other countries.

Many workers marched under trade union banners, including shearers, timber-getters, miners, wharf labourers and sailors. These groups were headed by the Eight-Hour Banner, which represented the concept of eight hours' work, eight hours' rest, and eight hours' recreation per day.

A commemorative mug for the Federation of Australia, featuring Henry Parkes and Lord Hopetoun.

Invitation to the Commonwealth of Australia

This invitation to attend the ceremony celebrating the Commonwealth of Australia uses plenty of symbolism to convey how people saw the country at the time of Federation.

The six women in the boat represent the fresh, young Australian states (formerly colonies). They are voyaging together, beneath a flag that represents a unified Australia (the Southern Cross) with ties to Britain (the Union Jack). A bright sun is dawning, and all is good and right with this new and pure nation.

Absences also tell us about Australia. All the marchers in the procession were male. The only women present were there in costume, as Britannia or Boadicea – legendary figures of British history. No Aboriginal people were in the march. There were no Chinese marchers either, but some did celebrate the day with arches and a traditional dragon.

The march finished at a specially built rotunda in Centennial Park near Randwick.

John Hopetoun, the Earl of Hopetoun and the first Governor-General of Australia and Queen Victoria's representative in Australia, formally announced the birth of the new nation, to be known as the Commonwealth of Australia.

The British national anthem, 'God Save the Queen', was performed and the British flag was unfurled, as there was no official Australian flag yet. The members of the official party drank toasts

1901 Australian Federation celebration.

to 'The Queen'. Lord Hopetoun swore in Prime Minister Barton and the nine interim ministers who would serve until the first election was held.

In 1901 Australia became the world's newest nation. It was the only nation that occupied a whole continent, and did not share a land border with another country.

The colony of Queensland becomes the State of Queensland on Federation. The shield of Queensland has the Latin motto *Audax et Fidelis* (Bold and Faithful). On the back reads 'In Unity Is Strength' – the meaning of Federation.

Comparison of constitutions

This table shows some of the main aspects that needed to be included in the Australian Constitution and how the constitutions of the United States and Great Britain dealt with these matters in 1901. It also shows how the Australian Constitution was influenced by other ideas and processes.

Aspects of a constitution	The United States Constitution	The British Constitution	The Australian Constitution
The names of the two houses in the legislature	House of Representatives, Senate	House of Commons, House of Lords	House of Representatives, Senate
How members are determined	*House of Representatives:* Electorates that are equal in population, organised in states – the largest states will elect the largest number of representatives. *Senate:* Two senators for each of the 50 states, regardless of the size of the state's population so as to ensure balance of power across all states.	*House of Commons:* Members of Parliament are elected from the whole population, divided into electorates. *House of Lords:* Some members are there because of hereditary succession; most are now appointed by the government.	*House of Representatives:* Electorates that are equal in population, organised in states – the largest states will elect the largest number of representatives. *Senate:* Six senators (now 12) for each of the six states, regardless of the size of the state's population.
The balance of power between federal and state parliaments	The national parliament has specific and limited powers. It can only make laws in those areas that are specifically listed in the Constitution. The state parliaments can make laws in all other areas.	There are no state parliaments, only the national parliament and local councils. The national parliament can make laws in all areas.	The Australian Parliament has specific and limited powers. It can only make laws in those areas that are specifically listed in the Constitution. The state parliaments can make laws in all other areas.
The head of state	The president	The British monarch	The Governor-General representing the British monarch
The head of government	*The president:* Is not in the parliament (Congress), makes treaties, sets foreign policy, appoints ambassadors, can veto (reject) legislation.	*The prime minister:* leader of the party in power but has no individual powers.	*The prime minister:* (even though this position is not specifically mentioned in the Constitution) leader of the party in power but has no individual powers.

Aspects of a constitution	The United States Constitution	The British Constitution	The Australian Constitution
The balance of power between the legislature*, the executive** and the judiciary***	Legislature – two houses of parliament Executive – the president and the people he or she appoints as ministers Judiciary – the Supreme Court, with judges who are not part of the parliament or ministers	Legislature – two houses of parliament Executive – Prime Minister and ministers who are selected from within parliament Judiciary – the High Court, with judges who are not part of the parliament or ministers	Legislature – two houses of parliament Executive – Prime Minister and ministers who are selected from within parliament Judiciary – the High Court, with judges who are not part of the parliament or ministers
The franchise (Those with the right to vote)	Adult males Free black men (no black slaves) No women	Adult males No women	All adult males and females who had the right to vote in states in 1901
Changing the Constitution	Vote of Congress plus a vote by ¾ of the state congresses (parliaments)	By act of parliament	By referendum of the voters
Ministers in charge of making sure the laws are put into operation	Appointed by the president and are not members of the parliament	Must be members of parliament	Must be members of parliament
The court that will interpret the Constitution if there are any disputes	Supreme Court given specific power	No court has specific power	High Court given specific power
The balance between the powers of the two houses	Both are equal	They are almost equal, but the upper house cannot originate or amend appropriation bills – those that authorise the spending of public funds	They are almost equal, but the upper house cannot originate or amend appropriation bills – those that authorise the spending of public funds

* those who make the laws – the two houses of parliament

** those who carry out the laws – the ministers and the various public service departments

*** those who enforce the laws and settle disputes about the Constitution – the judges of the federal courts

The New Nation: 1901 to 1914

As the country progressed economically, so did its social policies, improving the lives of its citizens. Australia continued to look towards Britain for its defence and trade, but recognised new threats and potential friends elsewhere.

The opening of the first Australian or Commonwealth Parliament in Melbourne in May 1901.

ELECTING THE FIRST PARLIAMENT

The new nation of Australia came into existence on 1 January 1901, and the first national election (or Commonwealth parliamentary election) was held on 29 and 30 March that year. Most voters were men; South Australian and Western Australian women had gained the right to vote in state elections (in 1894 and 1899), and so could also vote in the Commonwealth election, but women in the other states could not. This would soon change.

The Protectionist Party won the most seats in the House of Representatives (where the government is formed). Its leader, Edmund Barton, who had been appointed prime minister of the new federal government from 1 January 1901 until the election could be held, continued as the first prime minister.

The parliament first met on 9 May 1901 to begin the task of drafting laws for the whole nation, guided by the Australian Constitution. Hundreds of dignitaries gathered at the Royal Exhibition Building in Melbourne to hear the Duke of Cornwall and York declare open the first Australian Parliament.

The new nation was self-governing, but was still subject to British policy in international decisions, and to the highest British courts in some legal appeals. Greater independence from Britain would come later in the century.

The 1901 Election Result

	Protectionists	Free Traders	Labor Party/ Independent
House of Representatives	31	28	16
Senate	11	17	8

NATIONAL SYMBOLS

The Australian Parliament had to create a set of symbols for the new nation, which included designing a flag, a coat of arms, a type of currency and postal stamps. The parliament also needed to make a decision about the location of the national capital.

A national flag

On 14 May 1901, every state school in the country raised a national flag to celebrate the new Federation. However, the flag raised was not one representing Australia – it was Britain's Union Jack.

It was another four months before Australia gained its own national flag, after a competition supported by the Australian Government. The competition's only rule was that the Union Jack had to be part of the design. There were over 32,000 entries and five winners, all of whom entered largely the same design and shared the £200 prize. This was at a time when the minimum wage in Australia was about £2 a week.

The winning design was much like the current Australian flag, except that the large Federation or Commonwealth Star contained six points to represent the states (rather than the seven points now featured), and the Southern Cross stars ranged from five to nine points to represent their relative brightness in the sky.

The flag was flown for the first time on 3 September 1901 in Melbourne, the home of the first Australian Parliament. Australia finally had its own national symbol. A slightly varied design was officially approved and formally recognised as the Australian national flag by Britain in 1903.

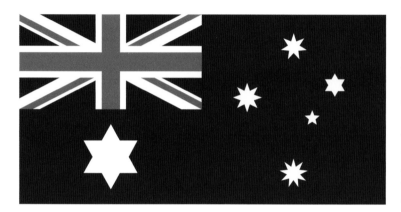

This is the winning design of the Australian flag competition. It has been modified three times since 1901. The Commonwealth Star and all stars but one of the Southern Cross now contain seven points.

Edmund Barton

Edmund Barton (born 1840; died 1920) was a lawyer and politician from New South Wales. He supported Federation and became one of the key political leaders who helped create the new Australian Constitution. Barton was a dedicated advocate of Federation. During Federation campaigns, he would go by train and then ride in a buggy at night, in order to arrive on time at the next place to speak.

Barton became the first prime minister of Australia, and then a judge of the High Court.

Coat of arms, stamps and currency

The Australian coat of arms was first approved by King Edward VII in 1908. It was changed slightly in 1912 and remains the same to this day. It is used to show the authenticity of government documents, including Australian passports.

The first Commonwealth Coat of Arms (1908)

1912 Commonwealth Coat of Arms

The symbols of the current Australian coat of arms include:
- a kangaroo and emu (native animals that can't easily move backwards), which some believe symbolises Australia always going forward
- a shield that contains the six state badges
- a background spray of golden wattle (a native Australian flower)
- a seven-pointed gold star on a blue and gold wreath, representing the unity of the six states and the territories of the Commonwealth of Australia
- the word 'Australia'.

In 1912, Australian national stamps were introduced to replace state stamps. The first of these showed a red kangaroo standing on a map of Australia.

Progress on a distinctive Australian currency was much slower. Up until 1913 several different legal currencies were used in Australia – British money, gold coins minted in Sydney and Melbourne from the 1870s, the notes provided by major private banks and, from 1893, notes printed by the Queensland Government.

The first national Australian currency notes were printed in 1913. (The very first Australian banknote ever printed, a ten-shilling note number M000001, recently sold for over $3 million.) The designs of the notes reflected aspects of the Australian economy, such as the gold and wheat industries. Australian coins were introduced to replace British ones in 1910.

The first national Australian stamps were introduced in 1913. The twopence stamp featured a kangaroo standing on a map of Australia. Others, such as this 1½ pence stamp, featured King George V, indicating Australia's ongoing connection to Great Britain.

Denominations

The decimal dollar we use today was introduced on 14 February 1966. At Federation, Australia's primary currency was the pound, which had the following denominations:

Denomination	Symbol	Value
Farthing	¼d	One quarter of a penny
Halfpenny	½d	Half a penny
Penny	d	
Threepence	3d	Three pennies
Sixpence	6d	Six pennies
Shilling	1/-	12 pence (pennies)
Half crown	2/6	Two shillings and sixpence
Crown	5/-	Five shillings
Pound	£	20 shillings
Guinea	£1/1/-	21 shillings, or one pound and one shilling

Goods that cost five pounds three shillings and twopence halfpenny would be written £5/3/2½.

The capital city

The Australian Constitution did not specify the site of the capital, but set certain conditions: the city had to be in New South Wales, and at least 160 kilometres from Sydney. This had been decided because of fierce Sydney–Melbourne rivalry surrounding the issue, which might otherwise have delayed Federation. Many places

Lithograph titled 'Cycloramic view of Canberra site looking from Mount Vernon'. 1911.

were considered, including Dalgety and Tumut, but the Yass–Canberra area was selected by the Parliament in 1908.

More than 700 different names were suggested for the new capital before 'Canberra' was chosen by a vote of the Members of the Australian Parliament. The name was believed to mean 'meeting place' in the language of the local Ngunawal people, and was also used by white settlers in the area. Today some Ngunawal people say the word means 'cleavage' as a description of land between two mountains. The Parliament also held an international competition for a design for the new capital. The American architects Walter Burley Griffin and his wife Marion Mahony Griffin were selected from the 130 entries. The future city was officially named Canberra on 12 March 1913.

Commemorative days

Although symbols were being created to represent the new Federation of Australia, there was no consensus on the national day of commemoration for many years.

In New South Wales, and particularly in Sydney, 26 January was celebrated as Foundation Day. Meanwhile, other states had their own Foundation days stemming from their date of separation from New South Wales and the beginnings of self-government.

Other national celebrations included Empire Day on 24 May (which was Queen Victoria's birthday) and Wattle Day on 1 September, which marked the coming of spring. Some in the labour movement preferred Labour Day or May Day (usually 1 May), or even Eight-Hour Day (celebrated on a variety of days in different states). Irish people of the Roman Catholic faith had St Patrick's Day (17 March) as a day of celebration.

The new nation still celebrated its links to the British Empire. An Empire Day gathering, 1907.

WHITE AUSTRALIA

The first major laws created by the new national parliament included the *Immigration Restriction Act* and the *Pacific Island Labourers Act*, which were passed in December 1901. These Acts were intended to restrict immigration by people from outside Great Britain and a few European countries, to ensure a 'White Australia'.

White Australia badge, proclaiming a commonly held view of the time. 1906.

Many people, including many Australians, considered the technology, economy, culture and government of the 'White European race' to be more advanced than those of other cultures, and this was used to justify laws and policies that reflected racial inequality. The United States, Canada, South Africa and New Zealand had enacted laws against 'coloured' immigration, as had the Australian colonies at various times during the second half of the 19th century to control Chinese and then Japanese migration to the country.

But not everyone agreed that some races were superior to others. Former prime minister Alfred Deakin and Commonwealth judge Henry Higgins believed in racial equality, but did believe in cultural superiority – that the races had distinct and different cultures, and that the cultures should not mix. They wanted to limit non-European immigration to Australia, not because they believed people were inferior, but because they believed the values and culture of the less industrialised and technologically developed nations could not co-exist with those of British Australia.

Non-British immigration

Although there were many Italian, Greek, Maltese and Jewish Russian immigrants in Australia between 1901 and 1914, they were certainly far fewer than the 400,000 British migrants who arrived in this period.

By 1901, around 30,000 Chinese migrants lived in Australia. Some were merchants in the major cities and many had market gardens, worked as laundrymen or were carpenters in factories in the major cities of Sydney and Melbourne. Chinese people also worked as cooks and itinerant grocers in country areas. Although they weren't necessarily viewed as equals by white or European settlers, Chinese people were accepted as part of local communities.

Immigration Restriction Act 1901

The *Immigration Restriction Act* was the basis of the White Australia policy, which continued in Australia until the 1960s. The Act stated that any potential immigrant could be asked to sit a 50-word dictation test to assess their standard of education.

In practice, the test was chiefly used to exclude Chinese immigrants. Immigrants could be tested in English or any other European language, so that even English-speaking Chinese could be excluded. It was a racial test disguised as an education test so as not to offend the Japanese.

Japan had a treaty with Britain, which legally gave its people the same rights as Britons to migrate to Australia. By making the entry condition one of education, Australia would not be violating the treaty, because – in theory, at least – the test would be standardised.

Government officials chose those who had to sit the test. The test was successful in excluding most non-Europeans while at the same time allowing businessmen, officials and

Aboriginal prisoners in Darwin, 1905. In 1911 the Northern Territory of South Australia was transferred to Commonwealth control as the Northern Territory.

others whom the government wanted into Australia. On average, between 3000 and 4000 Asian were exempted from the test in each year between 1902 and 1914.

Though the main arguments in favour of the *Immigration Restriction Act* were racially based, they were also economically driven. It was argued that the cheaper labour provided by Asian workers could undermine existing wage levels and lead to the unemployment of white workers and social distress for their families.

Immigrants already living in Australia were not expected to sit the test, although if they left Australia and wished to return, they might have had difficulty re-entering the country. Immigrants who had naturalisation papers could come and go. Regardless of their ethnic heritage, children born in Australia were classed as citizens and were therefore not covered by the Act. Under the Act, non-European residents could only bring their families to Australia temporarily. Exemptions were made for Japanese and Indian students and businessmen, who did not have to pass the dictation test if they didn't intend to settle in Australia permanently. Japanese pearl divers were also exempt because their skills were needed.

Pacific Island Labourers Act 1901

The *Pacific Island Labourers Act* of 1901 was created to stop the immigration of labourers from Melanesian and Polynesian islands (mainly Vanuatu and the Solomon Islands) after 1904, and to deport by 1906 most of those who were already in Australia.

Between 1863 and 1891, over 46,000 Melanesian and Polynesian labourers (usually called 'Pacific Islanders') had been brought to Queensland to work on sugar cane plantations. In 1901, there were about 10,000 Pacific Islanders in the country, most of whom were vital to the sugar industry in Queensland. Initially, only about 700 of these labourers would be exempt from deportation, based on their long period of residence in the country.

Pacific Islanders and their Australian supporters (including church leaders who saw it as unjust and the planters who wanted the cheap labour) opposed the Act and won some exemptions, with an estimated 2500 people avoiding deportation. However, over 7000 labourers had to leave, resulting in many workers being separated from their Australian-born families.

The Australian Government overcame the planters' concerns by paying an incentive of £3 per tonne on sugar cane grown from 1905 on the condition that white people were employed for labour. This allowed planters to pay higher wages to labourers and still make a good profit.

Other restrictive Acts

The *Immigration Restriction Act* and the *Pacific Island Labourers Act* were not the only discriminatory laws of the period. In 1903, the Western Australian Government forbade Chinese people from owning new factories. In 1904, the Queensland Government excluded Asians from government funding for agricultural industry. No mines in the Northern Territory could be owned by Chinese people. The Australian Government excluded non-European-grown sugar from a government subsidy in 1903. It also refused to grant mail contracts to ships with non-European crews.

The restrictive immigration laws stopped most non-European immigration but slowed the development of tropical northern Australia, where many non-European labourers would have lived if they had been allowed to enter, preventing it from developing in any significant way for the next 50 years.

A sugar cane cutting knife.

DEMOCRACY IN THE NEW NATION

The emphasis on racial inequality in the new nation suggests that Australia was an unfair and unequal place, but in many regards it was one of the most democratic countries in the world during the early 20th century. Most adult males had a vote, and from 1902 most adult females were able to vote. Internationally, only three other nations – New Zealand in 1893, Finland in 1906 and Norway in 1913 – had given women the right to vote.

Australia had a representative government, meaning that it was elected by and accountable to the voters. It was also a responsible government, in that it was formed from and accountable to the Australian Parliament.

Women's role in society and the right to vote

Women's role in society mainly revolved around domestic duties and providing stability for their families. The common view in the early 20th century was that women had a civilising influence on society, as they focused on mothering and moulding their children into good and useful citizens for the country.

Some people challenged this very limiting view. Organisations such as the Women's Christian Temperance Union and the Australian Women's Franchise Society campaigned for female suffrage, or the right to vote. Notable individuals such as Mary Lee, Vida Goldstein, Henrietta Dugdale, Rose Scott, Louisa Lawson and Edith Cowan were all determined that women should gain full citizenship. They organised protests, wrote letters, published articles in newspapers, addressed crowds and lobbied politicians. The activists were not one single group – there were differences among them on many social issues – but they all agreed on a greater recognition of women's rights.

The Australian Constitution did not specify whether women could vote, but it did give the new national parliament power to decide who could vote for it, including women.

In 1902, the Australian Parliament introduced the *Commonwealth Franchise Bill*, which proposed to give a vote to all resident citizens, male or female, aged 21 or over. This law would only apply to Commonwealth elections, which meant that if it passed, women still might not be able to vote in state elections. However, since women already had the vote in New Zealand, South Australia and Western Australia, and there were active and popular campaigns in other states, it was clear that the Act reflected public opinion and would be passed.

Opponents argued that women were inferior to men intellectually. They also argued that allowing women to vote would lead to a change in social values as women would not be able to carry out their domestic roles properly.

Most parliamentarians supported the right of women to vote in Commonwealth elections for several reasons. It was about fairness, they argued, and it was unjust for women not to have a say in the society they lived in. It was also about civic benefit – women would be able to contribute more to society by being involved in making decisions about how their country was governed.

Aboriginal and Torres Strait Islander people

During the debates on the *Commonwealth Franchise Act*, the question of Aboriginal voting was raised.

Most Aboriginal people lived in one of four situations during the early 20th century: in traditional communities mainly in northern and western Australia; as fringe dwellers in country towns; in slum areas of major cities; in religious missions or protectorates (defined areas where the Indigenous inhabitants were controlled by a government official, a Protector). A fifth situation was also developing – Aboriginal men were becoming vitally important workers as stockmen in the northern cattle industry.

Every state except Tasmania had a system of Protection Acts to provide safe and secure areas where Aboriginal people could live, but the cost of this was the almost total restriction

Female activists

Mary Lee (born 1821; died 1909) was born in Ireland and migrated to Adelaide in 1879 to nurse her dying son. A widow with seven children, she was a leader in the female suffrage movement.

Mary Lee

Catherine Helen Spence (born 1825; died 1910) was a writer, Christian preacher, reformer and women's suffrage campaigner. She worked to improve the treatment of orphaned, destitute and delinquent children. She also worked tirelessly for electoral reform and women's rights.

Henrietta Dugdale (born 1826; died 1918) was a social reformer. Born in London, she arrived in Melbourne with her husband in 1852. She was responsible for the first society that campaigned for women's voting rights in Australia.

Rose Scott (born 1847; died 1925) was a wealthy Sydney socialite who worked for women's suffrage, prostitution law reform, prison reform, pacifism and fought for the rights of single mothers.

Edith Cowan (born 1861; died 1932) was a women's rights campaigner who helped found the first women's club in Australia (the Karakatta Club) aimed at educating women to further their prospects. She stood as a Nationalist candidate in the 1920 federal election, and became the first woman to be elected to an Australian parliament.

Vida Goldstein (born 1869; died 1949) was a prominent supporter of women's suffrage. She helped her mother with social reform causes and soon became leader of the women's radical and reform movement in Victoria. She campaigned for women's suffrage, pacifism and socialism.

Vida Goldstein

Voting

Voting rights varied by state. The Australian Constitution allowed all who had the vote in their state on 1 January 1901 to vote in Commonwealth elections. This included all adult non-Indigenous males, all women in South Australia, and all non-Indigenous women in Western Australia. Adult Indigenous men could vote in the colonies (states) before 1901 unless they were specifically excluded (as in Queensland and Western Australia), but in practice this was not encouraged, and was even hindered. The 1902 *Commonwealth Franchise Act* restricted the vote to only those Indigenous men and women who were already on the state electoral rolls in 1902.

	NSW	TAS	WA	SA	VIC	QLD	CWLTH
Adult male franchise	1858	1896	1893	1856	1857	1872	1901
Adult female franchise	1902	1903	1899	1894	1908	1905	1902
Adult women able to stand for election	1918	1921	1920	1895	1923	1915	1902
Adult Aboriginal men can vote	1858	1896	1962	1856	1857	1965	1962
Adult aboriginal women can vote	1912	1903	1962	1895	1908	1965	1962

of their rights and freedom. European expansion in Australia had led to the dispossession of Aboriginal people, and the destruction of much of their culture. Frontier conflict and disease had greatly reduced the Aboriginal population. Contact with Europeans had led to much racial mixing. To most people in Australia at that time, it appeared that the Aboriginal people were a dying race. It seemed the best that could be done was to provide safe and secure lives for the survivors.

Governments set aside special areas for Aboriginal people, but every aspect of their lives was strictly controlled by the European protectors or missionaries – health, education, work, care of their children, finances, even who they could marry and where and when they could travel.

Believing that the Aboriginal race would soon disappear, anthropologists rushed to study Aboriginal societies, and this led to some of the greatest works documenting

Daisy Bates

Daisy Bates (born 1863; died 1951) is a controversial figure in Australian history. She was born in Ireland, and migrated to Australia as a 21-year-old. She married and left Harry 'Breaker' Morant, who was later executed in South Africa for killing enemy prisoners during the Boer War.

Bates moved to Broome to investigate stories of atrocities against Aboriginal people. She increasingly turned her attention to the welfare of remote Aboriginal people who were at the border between traditional life and European influences. For the next 30 years she lived alone in harsh, isolated bush camps on the Nullarbor Plain where she helped local Aboriginal people.

Bates wrote newspaper articles about Aboriginal life and culture. These were often sensitive and perceptive accounts of cultural differences, but were mixed with occasional and suspect claims of cannibalism and

arguments in favour of keeping Aboriginal people separate, and allowing them to die out as a race.

languages and culture. Many missionaries devoted their lives to protecting and improving the lives of Aboriginal people, while also converting them to Christianity. This often involved forbidding the people to speak their language or continue cultural practices. So while Europeans tried to protect Aboriginal people and record their culture, they also played a role in its destruction.

Most members of parliament did not support Aboriginal and Torres Strait Islander suffrage. A typical attitude was that of Sir Edward Braddon, former premier of Tasmania, who said during the debates on women's votes in 1902 that *'the Aboriginal native is [not] a person of very high intelligence, [or] who would cast his vote with a proper sense of the responsibility that rests upon him.'* (*Commonwealth Parliamentary Debates,* 24 April 1902, page 1197)

Others argued differently. Senator Richard O'Connor, a minister in Barton's government, said during the same debate, *'It would be a monstrous thing, an unheard of piece of savagery on our part, to treat the Aboriginals, whose land we are occupying, in such a manner as to deprive them absolutely of any right to vote in their own country simply on the ground of their colour.'* (*Commonwealth Parliamentary Debates*, 9 April 1902, pages 11,450 and 11,453)

The *Commonwealth Franchise Act* was passed by a majority of both Houses of the Australian Parliament in June 1902, and became law when it was signed by the governor-general. Most women aged 21 and over were now able to vote on a national level. The exceptions were Aboriginal, Asian, African and Pacific Islander women and men who did not already have a vote in their own state – and most did not.

Exclusion

While some policies were aimed at aiding or protecting Aboriginal and Torres Strait Islander people, several Commonwealth laws sought to deliberately exclude Indigenous and other 'non-white' people.

In 1903, the *Naturalization Act* confirmed that all people not born in Australia who had been naturalised (made citizens) in a state or colony were now citizens of the Commonwealth, but specifically excluded 'aboriginal natives of Asia, Africa or the Islands of the Pacific, excepting New Zealand'.

In 1910, the *Emigration Act* stated that a person could not take an 'Aboriginal native' out of Australia without special permission. This was a measure designed to protect Aboriginal and Torres Strait Islander people from being taken overseas for exploitative theatrical performances, but which also reduced their legal status to that of a child. In other words, decisions were being made on behalf of Aboriginal and Torres Strait Islander people, who had no say over how they were being treated.

Influential Australians

These Australians had a significant impact in the early 20th century but have been virtually forgotten today.

William Knox Darcy (born 1849; died 1917) was a mining entrepreneur who established the very rich Mount Morgan gold mine in Queensland. He used his wealth to retire to Britain, then to invest in the search for oil in Persia (modern Iran). On the brink of failure, his team found oil, and Darcy created what would eventually become British Petroleum (BP), one of the largest companies in the world.

Anthony George Michell (born 1870; died 1959) was an engineer and inventor who developed super-efficient bearings that allowed the use of larger propellers and engines in ships, and thus the development of much larger and more powerful ships. In 1913 the German armaments manufacturer Krupps started using Michell bearings in its great battleships, prompting the British to do the same.

Henry Sutton (born 1856; died 1912) was the most brilliant but probably least recognised of all. He worked alone in the country town of Ballarat, and is now believed to have independently developed or invented telephones, light bulbs, photo printing, a version of television, wireless telegraphy, and the first radio broadcast. He was the Australian Thomas Edison.

Aboriginal and Torres Strait Islander men and women were excluded from the benefits of the 1908 *Invalid and Old Age Pensions Act*, and women from the 1912 *Maternity Allowance Act*. Aboriginal males were excluded from the compulsory training obligations of the 1909 *Defence Act*. There were also many state Labour or Factory Acts that favoured the employment of people from a European background over workers from non-European cultures.

ECONOMIC PROTECTION

The Australian economy in the early 20th century was still dominated by wool, wheat, meat and minerals, especially gold. There was a growing industrial sector, but the wealth of the nation was from its primary exports.

Development

By 1900, the Australian farming environment was in poor shape. Too many animals (primarily sheep and cattle) were grazing on pastoral land, and too many crops were being grown on

Smelting – the extraction of metals from ores – played a huge role in the expansion of the manufacturing industry in the early 20th century. This postcard features a colourised photograph of the smelter and grain silos in Port Pirie. Circa 1907.

agricultural land that could not sustain them. The population of rabbits had exploded and their distribution expanded, which greatly reduced the grass available for livestock. The seven-year 'Federation drought' from 1895 to 1902 had also affected the industry badly.

By the time the drought ended, new developments were introduced that helped the agricultural capacity of the land.

The spread of cattle into the Northern Territory and in the Queensland gulf was helped by the railway system in the 1880s, which allowed for cattle to be moved efficiently to coastal meatworks.

The Canning Stock Route in the Kimberley area of Western Australia was developed between 1908 and 1910 to help with cattle transportation. Alfred Canning surveyed the route, which included the creation of 48 water wells for the cattle at various points along the track. This destroyed many traditional Aboriginal wells. For the first 20 years the route was largely unused. From 1931 to 1959 there was droving activity on the route but it was never as heavily used as had been hoped. The greatest and most lasting impact of the route was on the Aboriginal people through whose Country it was built, causing unprecedented dispersal of these people.

The agricultural economic recovery was also helped by the development of the Australian sheepdog and cattle dog breeds (these canines were as effective at rounding up livestock as several men), the growth of the sugar industry due to government subsidies, the great expansion of the wheat trade, and the continuing richness of the Western Australian goldfields.

While farming was vital to Australia's economy, the majority of the population continued to live in cities or towns, with 70 per cent of jobs concentrated in factories and workshops, or providing commercial or business services. This led to a problem: Australia's economic advantage was from its primary industries (those involving growing, grazing or mining), which employed relatively few people, while the majority of its workers were in industries that could not compete against those of other countries. This meant that a majority of Australian workers were vulnerable to unemployment and so a decline in their living conditions.

The country had to find a way to help its uncompetitive industries survive against cheaper international competitors. Prime Minister Alfred Deakin found a solution through 'New Protection'.

New protection

By 1906, the Australian Parliament comprised three roughly equal parties: Free Traders, Liberals (formerly the Protection Party) and the Australian Labor Party. This created a problem for whichever party was in government – it had to convince one of the other two parties in order to get a majority in the Parliament to pass laws. The government also had to balance this negotiation with its own political vision of what it wanted to achieve for Australia. Some commentators at the time likened it to trying to play a cricket game with three teams.

The Liberal Government headed by Prime Minister Alfred Deakin favoured 'protection'. To give local industries a chance to become established, Deakin wanted to raise the tariff (import tax) on goods coming into Australia. This would increase their selling price in the local market, and allow the Australian competitors to build up their own sales. This, in turn, would lead to higher employment and improved living standards for all.

The Free Trade Party would never accept this, so Deakin needed the support of the Australian Labor Party to increase the tariff (or protection) rate on imported goods. As the Labor Party was divided on the issue, it could not guarantee Deakin a majority.

Deakin devised a way to overcome this problem: he would introduce higher tariffs as a direct benefit to working people, thereby guaranteeing Labor Party support. He did this by increasing tariffs only for those industries that were paying fair wages to their employees. So, where farm machinery made by a local manufacturer cost more than its imported competition, if the local manufacturer was paying a fair wage to the employees, the government would add a tax to the import to make it more expensive.

As a result, the local producer would win because of increased sales, while workers would also do well because they were receiving a good wage. Australia would benefit because there would be continued employment and social spending. And although farmers would be paying a higher price for their new machinery, such technology would increase productivity and therefore their profits.

This policy led to a series of *Customs Tariff* and *Excise Tariff* Acts of Parliament, which were passed between 1905 and 1908.

Harvester case

In 1906, the government passed a *Customs Tariff (Agricultural Machinery) Act*, which placed a tax of £12 on imported stripper-harvester machines. At the same time, the *Excise Tariff (Agricultural Machinery) Act* imposed a £6 tax on locally produced stripper-harvesters, which would be dropped if the local manufacturer paid his workers a 'fair and reasonable' wage.

Employers began applying for exemption from the excise tax. Among them, in 1907, was Hugh McKay, owner of the Sunshine Harvester Company. This was the country's largest agricultural machinery plant, employing over 500 workers at Sunshine, an industrial suburb in Melbourne. McKay wanted to get labour at the cheapest possible price, but still be a fair employer. The company discouraged trade unionism, which pushed for higher wages, but helped employees to build houses nearby to reduce financial pressure on their families.

Was McKay paying a 'fair and reasonable' wage? Justice Henry Higgins was the High Court justice who would decide this in the Conciliation and Arbitration Court. He set about gathering evidence of the living conditions of working people in Victoria to help determine just what was meant by a 'fair and reasonable' wage.

Higgins collated evidence from the Sunshine Harvester workers regarding their wages, the hours they worked, and what they spent their money on. He looked at the cost of rent, food, education, clothing and luxuries.

The Sunshine factory manufactured the stripper-harvester, which improved agriculture production, while the owner's wage policy led to the setting of a basic wage in 1907.

Higgins decided that a fair and reasonable wage was seven shillings a day or £2 and 2 shillings a week. Because McKay was paying six shillings a day to his employees, Higgins decided that McKay was paying his workers less than the minimum wage that was required for 'the normal needs of the average employee regarded as a human being living in a civilised community'. So Higgins refused to exempt him from the excise tariff.

McKay appealed to the High Court on the grounds that the New Protection legislation was unconstitutional and therefore invalid, and won his case. But the idea of a minimum or basic wage remained in force as a legal principle and the system continued for the next 60 years.

The living wage

The basic wage only applied to males. It was assumed that working women were part of a family group headed by a male 'breadwinner', and so did not need to earn the same as a man.

In 1912, Justice Higgins heard a case brought by South Australian rural workers' unions arguing for equal pay for women. Higgins was unable to recognise the importance of women's labour: *'fortunately for society, the greater number of breadwinners are men. The women are not all dragged from the homes to work while the men loaf at home.'*

Higgins assumed that working women were either single (and had no dependants) or were part of a larger family unit and making a supplementary contribution to the family income. He decided that in women's traditional areas of employment such as shoe factories, clothing factories and as maids and cooks, they should only receive 54 per cent of a male wage. This decision continued to control women's pay until the 1950s. Only in a few occupations where women worked alongside men, such as fruit picking, were they awarded the same wage.

Price of food, 1907

Basic wage: £2/2/-
- Bread: 2½ pence per 2-pound loaf (about 1 kilo)
- Flour: 2½ pence per kilo
- Milk: 2 pence per pint (approx. half a litre)
- Butter: 3 pence per 100 grams
- Sugar: ½ pence per 100 grams
- Tea: 3½ pence per 100 grams
- Coffee: 4 pence per 100 grams

Waltzing Matilda and the Sunshine Harvester Factory: The early history of the Arbitration Court, the Australian minimum wage, working hours and paid leave, Fair Work Australia, RS Hamilton (ed).

SOCIETY AND SOCIAL PROTECTION

Between 1901 and 1914, two seemingly conflicting ideas dominated Australian politics: individual freedom of people to make their own decisions and be responsible for their own lives (liberalism), versus government intervention in people's lives for the good of the whole society (socialism).

Justice Higgins explains his ideas

'If A lets B have the use of his horses, on the terms that he give them fair and reasonable treatment, I have no doubt that it is B's duty to give them proper food and water, and such shelter and rest as they need; and, as wages are the means of obtaining commodities, surely the State, in stipulating for fair and reasonable remuneration for the employees, means that the wages shall be sufficient to provide these things, and clothing, and a condition of frugal comfort estimated by current human standards. This, then, is the primary test, the test which I shall apply in ascertaining the minimum wage that can be treated as "fair and reasonable" in the case of unskilled labourers. Those who have acquired a skilled handicraft have to be paid more than the unskilled labourer's minimum.'

From Ex parte Hugh McKay, *Commonwealth Arbitration Reports*, Vol II, 1907–1908

Australia's laws and culture had elements of both ideas. The majority of people, including most members of parliament, saw it as right and proper for individuals to do what they wanted, but also for the government to intervene in people's lives when necessary. It was freedom, but with protection, to ensure a 'fair go' for all. The Australian and state governments began to pass laws that influenced people's lives more and more, in order to protect those who were most vulnerable in society.

Pensions

In 1901, most help for the needy came from private charity, not from governments. Governments had not traditionally seen this as their role. Voluntary and religious organisations provided money, food, clothing or temporary accommodation. In the years after Federation, state governments of South Australia, New South Wales, Victoria and Queensland began offering support in some areas, especially in old age pensions.

In 1908, the Australian Government passed the *Invalid and Old-Age Pensions Act*, to come into effect from 1 July 1909 for old age pensions, and 15 December 1910 for invalid pensions. These pensions were an acknowledgement that many people had contributed greatly to society during their lives, and that the state owed them assistance at a time when they could no longer fully support themselves. The state was thus accepting new responsibilities for its citizens.

Baby bonus

In 1912, the Australian Government established a maternity allowance payment. This involved a one-off payment that was intended to help with the sudden new expenses of caring for a child and for medical care to improve mother–child survival rates. (In 1912, the death rate of infants was 71.74 deaths per thousand live births, compared with our present rate of about 4 deaths per thousand births.)

The government awarded a payment of £5 to a mother on the birth of her child, and this was not subject to any means test. This payment seems to have been generous, bearing in mind that the 1907 minimum wage had been fixed at £2 and 2 shillings a week.

The policy was progressive, but had its restrictions. As with most beneficial Acts of Parliament of this period, Aboriginal, Asian and Pacific Islander people were excluded from receiving the payment. These people were not considered to be full citizens, so were not felt to be entitled to the full benefits of citizenship.

Factory safety

The 1912 *Workmen's Compensation Act* broke new ground by introducing a system of compensation for industrial accidents and disease for all Commonwealth employees – and therefore set a standard for other non-government or private employers to follow.

There was also an increasing number of Factory Acts – laws that set minimum safety and health standards for factory workers. Most workers had to complete a 70-hour week, and

"CALL AGAIN, OLD MAN — THANKS FOR A MILLION!"

A 1950s cartoon celebrating the child welfare or 'baby bonus' payment.

factories could be dangerous and unsanitary places with unprotected machinery and bad ventilation. These factory laws were passed by states rather than the Commonwealth.

The factory laws and regulations were an advanced measure for their day, but they did not prevent all workplace hazards – especially for female workers who were employed to produce clothing at their own homes or small workshops where the laws did not apply.

Commonwealth Bank

During the 19th century, all banks operated privately. The great financial crash of the early 1890s sent many of these banks broke, and thousands of people lost their savings. In 1911, the Australian Government set up the Commonwealth Bank, which was guaranteed by the government, so people could never lose their savings again.

PROTECTING THE NATION

On top of economic and social protection, Australia also began focusing on national defence against possible enemies.

Defending Australia

In 1909, the Australian Parliament invited British military hero Lord Kitchener to advise on Australia's defence needs. Kitchener reported that Australia needed a large and well organised citizen army of 80,000 men, and a navy. The Australian Government passed the *Defence Act*, which authorised a system of conscripting boys and men for compulsory training and for military service in Australia. This would come into effect from 1 January 1911.

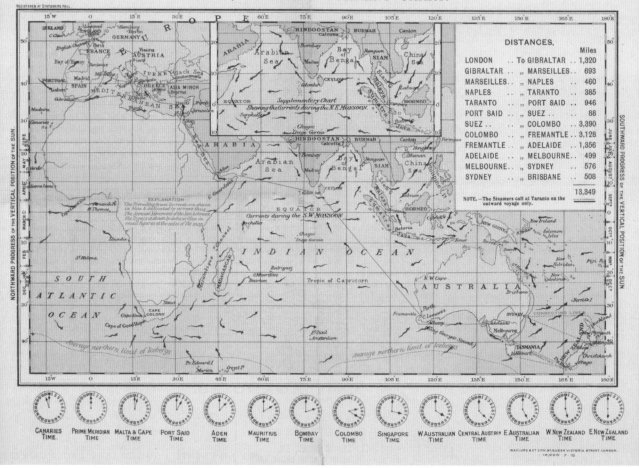

The Orient Steam Navigation Company (Orient Line) shared an Australian Government contract with the Peninsular & Oriental Steam Navigation Company (P&O) to deliver mail between Britain and Australia. During the First World War, all of the Orient Line ships were commandeered for war service.

Naval defence

In the days before aircraft and long-range missiles, if another country were to attack Australia, it would need a strong naval fleet. Germany had a very sturdy fleet and colonies in nearby New Guinea and the Pacific. Many Australians also feared Japan's growing naval power. In 1905, Japan defeated Russia in the Russo–Japanese War, a naval victory made possible because Japan had powerful, modern warships. This was the first time an Asian nation had defeated a European one, and Japan became a growing power in the Pacific. Japan signed a military alliance with Britain in 1902 and renewed it in 1905 and 1911. Australia was concerned that Japan might use this British alliance to overturn Australia's discriminatory White Australia immigration policies.

Australia therefore took steps to secure greater naval protection. From 1903, the Australian Government had been paying the British Government part of the cost of keeping some British warships in the Pacific Ocean. It was assumed that this fleet would be able to protect Australia against a foreign naval threat.

In 1908, Prime Minister Alfred Deakin did an extraordinary thing: he invited an American fleet to visit Australia. It was called the 'Great White Fleet' because the Americans painted their ships white to show their peacefulness, rather than the usual black or grey. The British were outraged, believing that they should have been responsible for Australia's

A postcard featuring the American flagship *Connecticut*. The two hands holding one another symbolise Australia welcoming the US fleet. Circa 1908.

international relations. But the American fleet came and Australians took the message that in times of trouble, perhaps they could look to the United States as well as Britain for help.

In 1909, the Australian Government ordered a fleet of new ships to be built in Britain, as the technology and expertise was not available in Australia. Some of these ships were to be crewed by British sailors as well as the Australian Navy. The first ships of this new Australian fleet sailed into Sydney Harbour in 1913.

Military training

In addition to developing a navy, the 1909 *Defence Act* stated that Australia was to have a small permanent army, plus a civilian army – a large body of trained civilians to call on in time of need.

To achieve this vision, young men aged 12 to 26 would have to train periodically. Boys between 12 and 14 had to register for the junior cadets and carry out 90 hours of training in drill and other military activities; those between 14 and 18 had to carry out 64 hours in the senior cadets; and those between 18 and 26 had to train in the citizen militia.

There were exemptions for those who were physically isolated in remote country areas, or who lived in a community that was too small to support a training system. Those who were 'not substantially of European descent' were not deemed part of the core citizenship community, and were not required to train.

There was some allowance for objection – if a young man had a conscientious belief that prohibited him from bearing arms he could carry out non-military training. If war broke out these men were expected to carry out clerical duties, or be stretcher bearers.

The few who actively opposed compulsory military training (or 'boy conscription' as many called it) had a variety of reasons: the inequity of the system (they argued that wealthy young men were able to complete their obligation at school, while the working poor had to use up their own leisure time); religious and pacifist beliefs; and the suspicion that the military trainees might be used to break strikes and attack workers. Most Australians accepted the conscription system even if they did not particularly support it.

AUSTRALIA AND THE WORLD

Australia's engagement with the world was overwhelmingly influenced by its relationship with Britain and its geographical place as an island close to Asia and the Pacific and Indian oceans.

At the start of the 20th century, Britain was Australia's main trading partner (accounting for 60 per cent of Australia's imports and 44 per cent of its exports), and the source of security for its vital shipping lanes. The United States was seen as a potential new ally.

Meanwhile, Japan was seen as a threat in Asia; Germany and, to a much lesser extent, France were seen as military adversaries in the Pacific. Germany had controlled German New Guinea and the Bismarck Archipelago (a group of islands off New Guinea) since 1884.

Papua and Antarctica

In 1902, Australia took control of Papua (the south-eastern portion of the island of New Guinea) as a protectorate. One of the least developed places in the world, Papua had no sealed roads or bridges, and a population that spoke hundreds of quite distinct languages.

In 1904, Hubert Murray was sent to Port Moresby as Chief Judicial Officer. He was appointed Administrator of Papua in 1908 and remained there for 31 years. Murray supported the white settlers while remaining friendly with the indigenous people, whom he defended and encouraged. Rather than developing or exploiting Papua, Murray's objective was to ensure it continued to offer security to Australia.

Australia also laid claim by occupation to much of Antarctica. By 1911 Britain, France, Germany, Japan, Sweden, Belgium and Norway had all

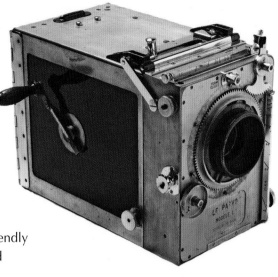

A camera purchased by Australian photographer Frank Hurley for the British, Australian and New Zealand Antarctic Research Expedition in 1929.

Antarctica became an area of Australian interest in the early 20th century.

sent expeditions to Antarctica to explore parts of that last great unknown continent. With the support of the government, Australian explorer Douglas Mawson organised a scientific research expedition to investigate the geology, glaciology and biology of the region in 1911. Mawson and his party remained there until the end of 1913, and established bases that provided the legal claim that Australia made to a large part of Antarctica.

Douglas Mawson

Sir Douglas Mawson (born 1882; died 1958) was important in establishing Australia's scientific 'footprint' in Antarctica.

Men of Stamina — **Sir Douglas Mawson**

He was born in Britain, came to Australia with his family in 1884, and became a geologist at the University of Adelaide.

In 1908 he was part of the British Antarctic Expedition to Antarctica, studying glaciation and its geological features. He nearly died on that expedition when he fell into a crevasse, but was seen and rescued.

In 1911 he organised and led the Australasian Antarctic Expedition. The expedition established three bases, which still operate today.

In 1912 disaster struck the Australasian expedition. Mawson and two others were on a trip when one of the men and the dog sled of provisions disappeared into a crevasse. Mawson and his companion, Xavier Mertz, struggled on and were forced to eat some of the dogs. They did not know that dogs' livers are very rich in Vitamin A and potentially poisonous.

Both men became increasingly exhausted and ill, and Mertz died. Mawson abandoned most of his equipment, used a pocket saw to cut his sledge in half, and dragged it the last 160 kilometres to the base. He arrived to see the supply and rescue ship *Aurora*, which had been involved in a search for him, leaving. However, a small party had been left behind to continue searching for him. They nursed Mawson back to health and were all rescued in 1913.

The data that the whole expedition had collected was vast. Mawson took on the mammoth task of editing the Australasian Antarctic Expedition *Scientific Reports*, and the final and 22nd volume was published in 1947.

Mawson returned to his academic career, was knighted, and helped create the Australian Antarctic Division that runs the Australian Government's research activities in Antarctica.

1914: ON THE EVE OF THE FIRST WORLD WAR

A snapshot of Australia in 1913 can show the many ways in which the young country was developing before it was affected by the great war the year after.

Transport

Australia was nation-building. In 1913, work started on the transcontinental railway that would link Perth to the rest of Australia.

In the main cities, streets were shared by horsedrawn coaches and wagons, bicycles (a cheap and popular form of transport), motorbikes, small cars (relatively cheap but still beyond most people), grand touring cars, and lorries.

Adelaide Electric Trams, Opened March 9, 1909.

First Car Driven by Mrs. Price.

Celebration at the opening of Adelaide's electric tramway system, 1909.

Living conditions

There were unhealthy slums in the capital cities. Families were crammed in old, decaying houses with poor ventilation and unsanitary conditions that promoted sickness – including plague. There were 12 major plague outbreaks in Australia between 1900 and 1925, as ships imported wave after wave of infection. Sydney was hit hardest. In 1900, more than 44,000 rats were caught and killed, and 103 people died. The disease also spread to northern Queensland, Melbourne, Adelaide and Fremantle.

Culture

Although a third of Australians lived near beaches, a beach culture had yet to thrive. It was only since 1902 that sea bathing had been allowed in New South Wales between the times of 6 am and 8 pm. By 1913, there was mixed bathing in modest costumes.

Australia had a strong sporting culture. Some sports were common nationwide, such as tennis and cricket, while others were specific to certain states: Australian Rules was popular in the southern states and Western Australia, and rugby in New South Wales and Queensland.

Society

Strict gender roles governed almost all aspects of society, as demonstrated in the divisions in the workplace, but there were signs of change – the typewriter was mostly used by males in 1913, but would soon open new areas of employment to women.

Part of the agreement on Federation was to link Western Australia to the rest of Australia by a transcontinental railway.

Continuing urbanisation. The inner Sydney suburb of Newtown, date unknown.

Australia was often described in this period as 'a working man's paradise'. It may seem an extreme description to us today, aware as we are of the existence of poverty, crime, racial and gender inequalities of that time, but by the standards of the world it was undoubtedly true for most people. In general, Australians were better off: healthier, more democratic and more equal and free than in any other country.

But this promising society was about to be placed under the strain of war.

NSW Postal Service postbox, circa 1875.

7 Australia and the First World War

On 4 August 1914, Australia became part of the First World War. People faced economic and political pressures, and social divisions emerged. When the war ended, Australia was a different society, one whose unity and sense of identity was strongly influenced by its military experiences.

Postcard featuring King George V of Britain surrounded by the leaders of France, Serbia, Russia and Belgium to denote the Allied countries, circa 1914.

AUSTRALIA IN 1914

In August 1914 the great European powers – Britain, France, Germany, Russia and Austria-Hungary – went to war. At the time, many called it the Great War, because of the enormous scale of the conflict and the casualties, while today it is known as World War I or the First World War. Even though Australia was 16,000 kilometres from Britain, it immediately became involved in the war due to its strong social, political, economic and military links to Great Britain.

A British nation

After Federation, Australia was self-governing but its international affairs were controlled by the British Government. News from overseas came from British sources, and contained British points of view. There were about five million people in Australia in 1914. About 80 per cent were Australian-born, but 95 per cent of the population was of British background and heritage.

A First World War Army recruiting poster.

As Australia is an isolated country in the Pacific, any military or political challenge could only arrive by sea. Australia had created a large 'citizen' army and its own navy, on the understanding that the navy would be placed under British control in time of war. It made sense to Australians to look to Britain for their defence, and to be prepared to 'pay' for that security by supporting Britain.

In the early 20th century, Australia's only likely enemies were Germany and Japan. Germany was a great imperial and naval rival of Britain, and occupied German New Guinea just to the north of Australia. Japan, the strongest Asian nation, was seen as a potential threat to 'White Australia'.

This picture of a pro-British Australia does not tell the whole story. There had been a strand of republican nationalism in Australia during the 1880s and 1890s, which stressed the unique Australian bush as its source of Australian identity. There were differences of religion, wealth, class, politics, race, economic interest, local and regional loyalties, and urban and rural attitudes and values. The war had the potential to unify the nation or force dividing lines open. It did both.

THE CAUSES OF THE FIRST WORLD WAR

At the beginning of the 20th century, Europe and the world were divided between rival empires. This sparked a series of events that would soon lead to the First World War.

The events leading to war

On 28 June 1914 Archduke Franz Ferdinand, heir to the Austro-Hungarian throne, was on an official visit to the Bosnian city of Sarajevo. Bosnia had recently been added to the Austro-Hungarian Empire, but wanted to unite with Serbia instead.

A group of young Bosnian students, encouraged and supported by a secret militant Serbian organisation called the 'Black Hand', shot and killed the Archduke and his wife.

7 July–25 July

Austria-Hungary wanted to take this opportunity to crush Serbia, but needed its ally, Germany, to guarantee help in any war against Serbia. Germany was a new nation looking for opportunities to expand, and so it agreed. Russia also saw the possibility of expanding its influence and empire, and promised to support its fellow Slavs in Serbia. Russia was an ally of France, so if Russia went to war against Austria-Hungary and Germany, France would also be involved.

France was stronger than Russia, and the Russians would take longer to be ready to fight, so the German plan was to defeat France quickly in the west, then move east to meet and defeat the Russians.

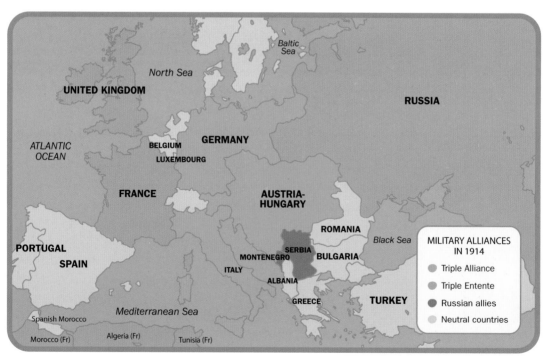

Europe in 1914. The colour coding shows which territories had been claimed by various military alliances.

GERMAN "KULTUR" – RETRIBUTION

A pro-Allies postcard using popular symbolism of the time. A British bulldog and French poodle, with their respective flags, defend a child representing Belgium from attack by a German eagle with imperial iron cross. The Japanese and Russian flags fly behind the flags of their allies.

However, France had strongly fortified borders with Germany, so Germany planned to move through Luxembourg and Belgium, neutral countries that did not have strong borders with either Germany or France. Germany's plan was to move quickly into France, seize Paris and force the French to surrender, and then send the majority of German troops against Russia in the east. This was called the Schlieffen Plan, after the German general who created it.

This now brought Great Britain in. Britain warned Germany not to invade Belgium. Britain had an 1839 treaty to help Belgium, but a stronger motive to defend Belgium was the fear of Germany occupying a port in Holland, Belgium or France, and being in a position to challenge Britain's greatest strength, its naval fleet.

On 4 August, Germany invaded Belgium to attack France. At 11 pm British time (9 am in Melbourne, the temporary Australian capital between 1901 and 1927), Britain declared war on Germany.

Eventually the 'Allies', as they became known, included France, Britain, Russia (to 1917), Italy (from 1915), Britain's dominions and colonies of Australia, Canada, New Zealand, Newfoundland, South Africa and India, and the United States (from 1917). Opposed to the Allies were the Central Powers: the Austro-Hungarian Empire, Germany, the Ottoman Empire and Bulgaria (from 1915).

The war would last four years, and be fought in Europe, Egypt, Africa, Asia, the Middle East and the Pacific.

Australian soldiers in uniform posing for a photo with rifles in their hands.

Australia enters the war

On 5 August 1914, Governor-General Sir Ronald Craufurd Munro Ferguson issued a proclamation that Australia was at war against Germany. It was at war because all the British dominion nations were automatically, legally included in Britain's declaration.

Australia did not have to actively support Britain, but both major political parties and the public wanted to. Crowds came into the streets, singing and cheering. Newspaper editorials supported and praised the decision. Church leaders preached sermons in support of the decision to go to war against what it described as a brutal enemy. Women's organisations immediately began raising money to support the troops who would soon be sent overseas.

Some religious leaders and groups opposed the war, especially the Quakers, who opposed all violence. There were small pacifist groups of men and women, such as the Australian Freedom League and the Women's Political Association, who spoke out against the war. Some radical elements of the labour movement, such as the Industrial Workers of the World and the Victorian Socialist Party, opposed it, calling it a war for the capitalists to become rich while working men and women would suffer and die.

German New Guinea

The first Australian involvement was not in Europe but in the islands north of Australia.

When war was proclaimed, Australian naval ships and a military force were sent to seize control of New Guinea, which had been colonised by Germany in 1884. The Australian

First shot of the war

The British Empire's first shot of the war was fired from an artillery gun at Fort Nepean, overlooking the entrance to Port Phillip at Point Nepean in Victoria.

Australian authorities received a telegram that Britain had declared war against Germany on 4 August 1914 at 11 pm London time, which was 5 August, 9 am Melbourne time. At 10.45 am, a German merchant ship, the *Pfalz*, was stopped from leaving Port Phillip Bay when a gun fired a warning shot at it. The ship stopped, was taken back to port, and seized by the Australian Government.

It was re-named the *Boorara* and used to transport Australian troops to the war. The German crew was interned for the remainder of the war in Berrima prison in New South Wales.

In a great coincidence, the same artillery gun at Fort Nepean that was used to stop the *Pfalz* was also used to stop a ship leaving Port Phillip on the first day of the Second World War in 1939. This was Australia's first shot and probably the first hostile Allied shot of that war.

force landed on 11 September in the capital, Rabaul, and quickly overcame a small number of German and New Guinean troops, with six Australian deaths. A few days later there was a far greater loss of the 32 sailors in the Australian submarine *AE1*, which accidentally sank in the area.

The Matrosen Division of the Kaiserliche Marine, German Navy.

Creating and training an army

In 1914, Australia had a navy of about 3400 sailors (around half of whom were on loan from Britain) and an army of about 2000 permanent soldiers. The *Defence Act* prohibited conscripts being sent overseas to fight, so Australia had to create a volunteer army.

The government quickly organised an army of 20,000 volunteers to be sent to support Britain's war effort. Men from all states rushed to enlist for a variety of reasons: adventure, a belief in the moral rightness of the war against German militarism, duty, to be with their mates, loyalty to the Empire, loyalty to Australia, because of the good pay, and because of social pressures.

To qualify, men needed to be aged between 18 and 35 (though men as young as 14 and as old as 70 slipped in), be a minimum of 168 centimetres in height, have a minimum chest measurement of 86 centimetres, and be in perfect health (though many were accepted despite their bad teeth).

Although many Aboriginal and Torres Strait Islander volunteers were rejected because of their race, at least 1000 Aboriginal and Torres Strait Islander soldiers served during the war. Most Aboriginal people didn't have voting rights or were not counted in the census, but in the army they were treated as equals, and were paid the same amount as the rest of the soldiers. Reginald Rawlings and Henry Thorpe were awarded the Military Medal and Cyril Rigney was awarded the British War Medal.

Others, especially men of Chinese heritage, were also rejected as being 'not substantially European', though many still joined.

The first convoy

On 1 November 1914 the newly formed volunteer army, called the Australian Imperial Force (AIF), set off to war.

A convoy of 38 transport ships gathered at Albany, Western Australia. They were carrying 20,000 soldiers and nurses, 8000 horses, and food, equipment, tents, ammunition – everything needed for an army. The convoy steamed out of King George Sound at Albany, escorted by four warships, two of them Australian, and one each provided by Britain and its ally, Japan.

Postcard depicting Australia ready to advance to Europe, with an angel looking on.

During the voyage the convoy came close to a German raider, SMS *Emden*. HMAS *Sydney* was ordered to leave the convoy and hunt for the *Emden*, and later found and destroyed it near Cocos Island.

The fleet arrived in the Egyptian port of Alexandria. The troops went to Cairo by train and camped beside the pyramids. By then the plans had been changed – they were not to go to Britain for training as they had expected, but were to defend the Suez Canal from attack by the Ottoman Empire (Turkey), which had entered the war on 28 October.

In a foreign land

This was the first time most of the men and women of the AIF had travelled outside Australia. Many were overcome with wonder at a world they had learned about in school, history books and the

White china cup commemorating the sinking of SMS *Emden* by HMAS *Sydney* at Keeling Cocos Island on 9 November 1914.

Bible. They rode camels and donkeys, clambered up the pyramids, bought souvenirs in the markets to send back home, and posed with locals. They were tourists in an ancient biblical land, as well as soldiers training for war.

They were also in contact with an unfamiliar culture, which sometimes led to conflict. Most of the soldiers believed themselves to be racially superior to the Egyptians, and some were thoughtless, undisciplined, disorderly and treated the local people cruelly. Over 300 soldiers were sent home in disgrace in January 1915, later to be discharged from the army.

When not in Cairo, the soldiers trained in the sand and the heat and the blistering wind, preparing themselves for their first action. Strict military life annoyed many, who saw

ANZAC or Anzac?

Anzac is an acronym – a word created from the initial letters of words in a phrase. It stands for Australian and New Zealand Army Corps. It originated in early 1915 when clerks needed a shorter term with which to refer to the Australian and New Zealand forces in Egypt. It started first as A.&N.Z., Army Corps, and became A.N.Z.A.C., and then ANZAC, and in 1915 Anzac.

Australia, New Zealand and the United Kingdom passed laws protecting the word – it could not be used for commercial purposes without permission.

The Australian War Memorial, the Returned and Services League, State and Commonwealth legislation and the Department of Veterans' Affairs now use Anzac generally (so, for example, in Anzac Day), and ANZAC only if they are specifically referring to the army formation.

Postcard showing an unnamed soldier, woman and child. Many of the soldiers who enlisted left behind families.

themselves as civilians who were fighting a war, not as professional soldiers. All were keen to test themselves against the enemy, to see if Australians were worthy members of the British Empire.

The Gallipoli plan

Before dawn on 25 April 1915, a huge fleet gathered in the silent darkness off the coast of Turkey. The Australians and New Zealanders were to be part of an invasion of the Gallipoli peninsula. The Turks knew that they would attack, although not where and when.

The aim was to force Germany's ally, Turkey, out of the war, and provide support to Britain's ally, Russia. Turkey controlled the Dardanelles Strait, the only entry to the Black Sea. This meant that no supplies could reach Russia through its Black Sea ports and its grain could not be sent back to feed Britain.

If the Allies could take Constantinople (Istanbul) they believed Turkey would quickly surrender, and this would open up the sea route from the Mediterranean Sea to the Black Sea. This would free Russian troops who were fighting Turkey on the Caucasus Front to be sent to fight the Germans. But the British and French had failed at their attempts to force their way through the Dardanelles Strait.

The alternative way to open the Strait was by a land attack. Allied troops would have to land on the Gallipoli Peninsula and fight their way to the coast to destroy the artillery and forts defending the narrow waterway.

Or so the theory went.

The plan was to land at several points simultaneously, one of which, Z Beach (soon renamed Anzac Beach or Anzac Cove), would be the responsibility of the Australian and New Zealand Army Corps. Four thousand men would land as a covering force to secure the beach and the cliffs. They would go in two waves, landing in the dark from small boats. Once they were ashore, thousands more troops would be landed to move inland.

The Anzacs (as the soldiers quickly became known) were to capture the high ground in the middle of the peninsula. By controlling this country, Turkish movement of fresh troops and supplies between the north and south of the peninsula would be cut, and as a result the Turks would be less able to resist the main British and French invasion force landing at its southern point.

Myth – Australia the only volunteer army?

Many Australian history books claim that the Australian Army was the only volunteer army in the First World War. This is not quite true. Australia had only volunteers and no conscripts, but so too did several other countries. Forces from South Africa, Newfoundland, the West Indies and India, which by 1918 numbered over two million soldiers, were all volunteers.

The landing

Before dawn on Sunday 25 April 1915, men with packs and rifles clambered silently from troopships into large rowboats carrying about 38 soldiers each. Steamboats towed these boats towards shore.

Suddenly, there was gunfire. The invaders had been seen. The Turks, few in number but on the high ground, fired down onto the invaders.

A few soldiers were killed in the boats, while some leaped out too far from shore and, weighed down by their heavy packs and equipment, drowned. The remaining men charged in a disorganised mass, scrambling up the steep hills. Many soldiers would later write in letters or diaries that the scent of thyme always brought back this first day, as they hurled themselves into the scrubby wild thyme and rosemary bushes on the cliffs to take shelter from Turkish rifle fire.

While the Anzacs were scrambling up the cliffs, the Turkish defenders had sent an urgent message for reinforcements. Ottoman forces, led by senior Turkish officers Lieutenant Colonel

Private Simpson

One of the most iconic images associated with Gallipoli is Private Simpson and his donkey bringing the wounded to safety, under fire. Simpson became a symbol of bravery and compassion.

Simpson's story is more complicated.

His name was not John Simpson, but John (Simpson) Kirkpatrick. He was a British-born migrant. He had worked at many jobs and was a bit of a larrikin. The most famous painting of Simpson, showing him leading his donkey and bringing back a wounded soldier, does not show Simpson but a New Zealander who did the same thing at Gallipoli.

On Gallipoli, he preferred to work with the Indian mule drivers rather than his Western Australian mates. Most of the men he helped were lightly wounded and were not in mortal danger, but Simpson was – he was killed on 19 May 1915. In 2013, a government inquiry rejected the claim that Simpson should be awarded a Victoria Cross.

A bronze maquette of Private Simpson and his donkey. © Peter Corlett, *AWM 044154*

Mustafa Kemal and Lieutenant Colonel Mehmet Sefik, rushed to two vital points and pushed back the attackers. Those Australian troops who had advanced the furthest were cut off, and killed or taken prisoner.

At the end of the first day, the Anzacs had an established hold of the beach and the surrounding ridges, but they had failed to advance inland and secure the strategic high ridge. The invasion had failed. After some hesitation, the commanders ordered the men to dig in.

This decision would lead to eight months of bitter trench warfare, sometimes in terrible heat with infestations of flies, sometimes in terrible cold and snow and sickness, and always with shortages of food and water, and inadequate sanitation.

Stalemate

One of the worst encounters during the eight months of the Gallipoli campaign was at The Nek – made famous in Australian popular culture in the 1981 film *Gallipoli*.

The Light Horsemen, who were trained as mounted infantry troops but were fighting on Gallipoli without their horses, attacked in four successive waves across an area about 200 metres wide and 100 metres deep. The Turks had at least three machine guns there. The Australian troops charged into a volume of fire of at least 5000 bullets per minute, nearly 100 for every second.

In early 1919, when the official Australian war correspondent and later official war historian Charles Bean returned to Gallipoli, the remains of 200–300 men who had died in the 7 August charge were found. These unidentified soldiers now lie under the grass at The Nek.

Withdrawal

In December 1915, the Allies admitted defeat and all troops at Anzac were secretly withdrawn in stages.

The Anzacs destroyed much equipment. Some soldiers booby-trapped food and supplies, and left them for the Turks, who would soon move into the abandoned Allied lines. Also left behind were the bodies of nearly 50,000 Allied soldiers, some of them in marked graves, some in unknown graves, and others never found.

The first Australian VC

The Victoria Cross was the British Empire's highest award for bravery. The first Australian VC of the First World War was awarded to Lance-Corporal Albert Jacka, for his actions on the night of 19–20 May 1915 at Gallipoli. The citation said: 'Lance Corporal Jacka, while holding a portion of our trench with four men, was heavily attacked. When all except himself were killed or wounded, the trench was rushed and occupied by seven Turks. Lance Corporal Jacka at once most gallantly attacked them single-handed and killed the whole party, five by rifle fire and two with the bayonet.' (*London Gazette*, 24 July 1915)

Memorial

About 8000 of the 50,000 Australians who served on Gallipoli were killed. Out of the 9000 New Zealand troops, 2000–3000 soldiers were estimated to have perished. The British lost over 21,000, the French 10,000, the Ottoman Empire an estimated 86,000.

On the Gallipoli Peninsula today, there are 31 war cemeteries, 21 of which are in the Anzac area. There are several memorials to the missing, the largest of which are the Helles Memorial and the Lone Pine Memorial. On Chunuk Bair there is also the New Zealand National Memorial, which remembers the New Zealand soldiers who died on Gallipoli.

The Gallipoli cemeteries contain 22,000 graves, but only 9000 of them are identified. Many men died in battle but could not be buried, while other graves were lost when Turkish soldiers used grave markers as firewood.

Fob medallion awarded to Corporal O'Toole on his return from service.

The Anzac spirit

Gallipoli was a defeat, but from the first report by British journalist Ellis Ashmead-Bartlett Australians believed that their troops had behaved magnificently. What was called the 'Anzac legend' became a key part of Australia's national identity. The basis of this identity was the commonly held belief that when the Australians were 'tested' for the first time in war on Gallipoli they showed qualities that the nation was proud of, including courage, mateship, determination, and a certain irreverence towards any authority that had not proven it deserved respect.

A newspaper editorial commemorating the first anniversary of the landing at Gallipoli explained that –

Before the Anzacs astonished the watching nations, our national sentiment was of a flabby and sprawling character. We were Australian in name, and we had a flag, but we were nothing better than a joint in the tail of a great Empire . . . Anzac Day has changed all that . . . we are at last a nation, with one heart, one soul, and one thrilling aspiration. (*Freeman's Journal*, Sydney, 27 April 1916)

The *ANZAC Book*, published in 1916, also contributed to the growing notion of the Anzac spirit. This was a collection of stories, poems, drawings, sketches, jokes and articles written by some of the men on Gallipoli, and collected and edited by the official war correspondent Charles Bean.

For the rest of the war, the qualities and spirit and achievements of the AIF were reported and celebrated. Letters sent home by soldiers were often printed in local newspapers, and the writers often expressed their pride as Australian soldiers – Anzacs.

Jim Martin

Jim Martin arrived at Gallipoli in 1915. Only 14 years of age, he had told the recruiting officer that he was 18. In his file is a sheet of paper signed by his parents allowing Jim to enlist. His family later explained that Jim was determined to join the army, and that if they did not give their permission, he would have run away and enlisted elsewhere.

Private Martin landed on 8 September after his troop ship had been torpedoed by a German submarine. He went into the trenches but contracted typhoid fever and was evacuated to a hospital ship on 25 October. He died that night and was buried at sea. Martin was one of over 20 other Australian soldiers under the age of 18 known to have died during the war.

AUSTRALIANS ON THE WESTERN FRONT

By 1917 five Australian infantry divisions, each of about 15,000 men, were serving on the Western Front. After the defeat on Gallipoli, Australian troops returned to Egypt to rest and re-organise. Most were sent to the Western Front, in France and Belgium. Soon, far more Australian soldiers would serve there than had served on Gallipoli (nearly 300,000 compared to 50,000), and they would suffer far greater casualties (46,000 deaths compared to 8000).

The Western Front was a continuous line of trenches running from the English Channel to the French–Swiss border, a distance of about 760 kilometres. The AIF divisions were mostly engaged around Ypres in Belgian Flanders, in northern France and also in the valley of the River Somme. This was a largely static trench war, as each side tried to push the other back, and achieve a breakthrough that would bring about victory.

The Australians were involved as part of the British forces in four key phases of the war between 1916 and 1918:

- Somme offensive, 1916
- German withdrawal to and Allied attack on the Hindenburg Line, 1917
- German spring offensive, March–April 1918
- the Allied counter-offensive, August–November 1918.

Trench warfare

Trench warfare was industrial warfare on a mass scale. It involved large numbers of men, artillery, machine guns, aeroplanes, barbed wire, poison gas and, later in the war, tanks.

The front line of troops faced each other in their trenches. The exposed open area between the trenches was known as 'no man's land'. Each side tried to destroy the enemy's troops and capture their territory. Trenches often were just long holes in the soil or clay, waterlogged and turning to mud in winter, and infested with rats. The trenches were built in a zigzag style, so that if the enemy fought their way into one they could not simply fire along the trench and kill a long line of soldiers all in a row.

A typical attack started at dawn. In the days before an attack, masses of soldiers would arrive and assemble a few kilometres behind the front trenches under the cover of darkness. Soldiers would write what might be their last letters to their families, check and arm their weapons, file in to the front trench, and wait for the order to advance. The enemy often knew an attack was coming because there was usually a massive bombardment by artillery to destroy the defending front line troops to make it easier for the attackers to advance.

Being in an artillery bombardment was a horrific experience. The men being attacked in this way pressed themselves into whatever shelter they could find. The shells that rocked the earth could bury men alive, and blasted their eardrums, even making them bleed. Shrapnel rained down: small pieces of jagged metal or tiny balls, designed to shred flesh. Men could be reduced to trembling wrecks, sobbing uncontrollably. All they could do was try to stay under some cover, make themselves as small a target as possible, and wait for what would come next – the attack.

There might also be gas – chlorine, phosgene and mustard gas – a new weapon of war. They were all designed to blind or poison the troops by attacking their lungs and other internal organs, making them unable to fight. The only protection was to quickly put on a gas mask, or to hope the wind changed and blew the gas back on the attackers. Small numbers of soldiers were killed immediately by gas, but many carried the painful and harmful effects for years after the war as the gas continued to eat away their lungs.

Officers would check their watches, and at the agreed time would blow whistles to signal the men to climb over the trench-top and start walking towards the enemy. At the same time,

Making the war into a game. 'Trencho' was a board game created by an English company for an Australian market. The game revolved around trench warfare, which was heavily linked to the Australian soldier experience.

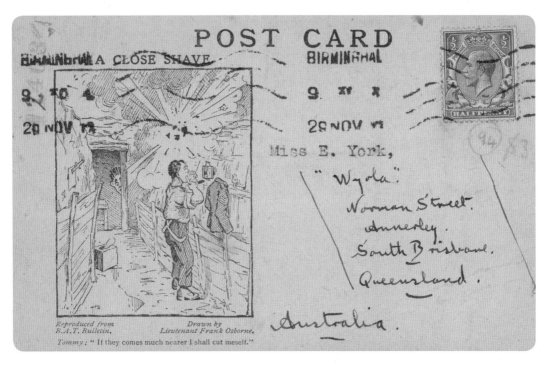

A postcard making light of the frightening conditions faced by soldiers on the Western Front. Postmarked 29 November 1914.

Main military engagements

These were the Australian troops' main engagements in France. They appear on unit banners in Anzac Day marches, indicating the battles that unit was engaged in.

1916
Somme
Fromelles
Pozières
Mouquet Farm
Flers

1917
Bullecourt
Lagnicourt
Messines
Menin Road
Polygon Wood
Broodseinde
Poelcappelle
Passchendaele

1918
Dernancourt
Morlancourt
Villers-Bretonneux
Hangard Wood
Hazebrouck
Le Hamel
Mont St Quentin
Montbrehain

the artillery would stop or, later in the war, would 'walk' the falling shells forward, trying to provide a moving curtain of shells to protect the advancing troops while still pulverising the enemy.

The attackers would usually only advance a few metres before the enemy, having survived the artillery barrage, scramble back into their front trench, point their rifles and, most ominously, their machine guns forward to where they knew the enemy would advance through the smoke and the breaking light and any uncut barbed wire.

Then came the terrible chattering of the machine guns, and the broken drum roll of the rifles firing. Men advanced over rough and, in winter, muddy ground gouged out by shell holes. The battlefield became a mix of bullets, blood, screams of pain, screams of bloodlust, smoke, the acrid smell of gunpowder, ear-splitting artillery noise, adrenalin, fear, excitement, yells, curses, selfless heroism and selfish self-protection.

Then, if they reached the enemy, the fierce and barbaric fighting would begin – with bullets, bayonets, rifles swung as clubs, fists, feet, teeth, anything. And then perhaps advancing, screaming, shooting at the retreating enemy, capturing some, killing others, rushing forward to the designated halting place, and digging in to hold it against the almost inevitable enemy response, when the attacker would now become the defender, the hunter the hunted.

If they failed to reach the enemy trench, the attacking troops would make a panicked retreat, scrambling back, praying not to be shot before returning to friendly lines, jumping into shell holes to shelter from the gunfire, perhaps helping wounded mates back, perhaps leaving them.

During the attack, stretcher bearers would gather the wounded and bring them back on stretchers. These men would often be fired on and cut down in their acts of mercy. Often the wounded could not be brought back, and the soldiers might have to listen to the moans and pleading of their wounded mates, whom it was too dangerous to rescue.

Most attackers were not killed or wounded during a battle – though some attacks did have that effect, and the more attacks a man took part in, the greater the chance was that he would be killed

A collection of badges showing patriotic activities that were encouraged during the war – including a call to vote 'Yes' for conscription. Some causes could unite society, but conscription divided it.

or wounded some time. Men in combat had to see, do and suffer things that might scar and damage them forever.

This did not happen all the time. Major battles were relatively rare. Soldiers were in the front lines for perhaps 15 per cent of the time, in rear trenches about 40 per cent of the time, and out of the fighting – kilometres away, resting in a village, flirting with the local women, enjoying a drink, playing cards with their mates, fussing over village children, on leave in Britain – about 45 per cent of the time. And not all troops were front line infantry – there were engineers, cooks, medical orderlies, clerks, laundrymen, bakers, signallers, drivers. But most soldiers were infantrymen near the front, and most experienced at least one attack.

Victory at last

The Bolshevik Revolution of 1917 overthrew the Russian Tsar (or emperor) and Russia abandoned the war. This released large numbers of German troops fighting Russia on the Eastern Front. They moved to the Western Front to fight the Allies.

John Monash

General Sir John Monash (born 1865; died 1931) was a Melbourne engineer and citizen (part time) soldier before he enlisted. He served (though without distinction) on Gallipoli, and then far more successfully on the Western Front.

In 1918 he was appointed commander of the Australian Corps – all Australian troops on the Western Front.

Monash was one of the earliest generals in the Allied forces to develop new and effective tactics in the battles of 1918. Some of his strategies included attacking in darkness, creating dummy installations to confuse the enemy, and using bomber planes to mask the noise from supporting tanks. These were first used at the Battle of Hamel in July 1918.

Monash made sure all his officers were clear about the plans at Hamel and he had large-scale models of the area made to illustrate the tactics.

All the preparations worked perfectly and the successful attack, planned to take 90 minutes, took 93. Monash wrote:

'A perfect modern battle plan is like nothing so much as a score for an orchestral composition, where the various arms and units are the instruments, and the tasks they perform are their respective musical phrases.'

Villers-Bretonneux today

The town of Villers-Bretonneux, France, was captured by German forces on 24 April 1918. It was recaptured by two brigades of the AIF, with 1200 Australian lives lost. The town remembers Australia to this day. It has streets named Rue de Kangourou (kangaroo), and Rue de Melbourne.

In the 1920s, Victorian school children donated money to rebuild the town's school. A notice on the wall today says that '1200 Australian soldiers, the fathers and brothers of these children, gave their lives in the heroic recapture of this town from the invader on 24 April and are buried near this spot.' Above every blackboard in the school are the words

'N'oublions jamais l'Australie' – never forget Australia.

Villers-Bretonneux is also the site of the Australian National Memorial for Australians killed in France. After the war, many nations selected one soldier killed in the war and whose identity was unknown to stand as a symbol for all the dead of that nation. Australia did not do this until 1993, when the remains of an unknown Australian soldier were taken from a grave in the Adelaide Cemetery and re-interred on 11 November 1993 at the Australian War Memorial. He became the Unknown Australian Soldier, who represents all the Australian dead of all wars.

The Allied naval blockade of German ports was bringing Germany close to starvation, and the submarine warfare that Germany had used to attack Allied and neutral supply ships had failed when the Allies developed the convoy system to protect merchant ships. The German policy of attacking neutral ships brought the United States into the war against them in 1917. The Germans planned one last push, the 'Spring Offensive' of 1918, to defeat the enemy before the American troops arrived and Germans starved.

For a time, it seemed that the German offensive might at least break through, separate the defending British and French armies and threaten Paris itself. But the German advance was stopped, partly by the British and French reacting to halt them and partly because the Germans became exhausted. Australian troops played a notable part in halting the offensive.

On 8 August, the great Allied push to break through the Hindenburg Line began, aided by American troops. The Hindenburg Line was Germany's final strong line of defences. This was the offensive that finally broke the Germans. Australian troops in the front of the advance gained 10,000 metres in a day, and the Allies a total of 64 kilometres.

When the war stopped, on 11 November 1918, there were no Australians in the front line. They had been exhausted by their last successful attack at Montbrehain on 5 October, and were resting in rear lines. At last the troops could actually believe that they would survive and see Australia again.

AUSTRALIAN TROOPS IN PALESTINE

Not all Australian soldiers were sent to the Western Front after Gallipoli. Thousands of men, mainly Light Horsemen, continued to be involved in the war against Turkish forces in Egypt, the Sinai Peninsula, Palestine and Syria, as part of the Egyptian Expeditionary Force (EEF). The EEF had British infantry, but included cavalry from India, camel corps, Mounted Rifles from New Zealand and Light Horsemen from Australia.

The Ottomans tried to take the Suez Canal again in 1916, but the EEF stopped the force at Romani, and started to push them back across the Sinai Desert and into Palestine.

Desert warfare had three main features that influenced battle plans: there were very few roads or rail lines, an army had to carry its own supplies, and water was very limited. This made the mounted infantry of the Australian Light Horse, on their sturdy walers (cattle horses), a key element in the campaigns.

The Light Horse's greatest moment came at Beersheba, a town at the far end of the Turkish line in Palestine in October 1917. After a long and waterless march into position over several days, the subsequent attack on Beersheba was failing. If it was not taken before the end of the day the army would have to retreat to find water. At the end of the day the Light Horsemen were ordered to charge the defences outside the town. Instead of their usual tactic of dismounting when close to the enemy, the horsemen kept charging, leapt over the Turkish trenches, and continued into Beersheba town. The Ottoman and German defenders surrendered, and the town's wells were taken before they could be destroyed. This success helped the British army to advance northwards to Jerusalem, which fell in December 1917.

The Ottoman Empire in the Middle East had collapsed after 600 years. The commander of the British army in the Middle East, General Edmund Allenby, later praised the Anzacs, saying 'the Australian light horseman has proved himself equal to the best. He has earned the gratitude of the Empire and the admiration of the world.'

OTHER AUSTRALIAN FORCES

The Australian Flying Corps

The Australian Flying Corps (AFC) was part of the AIF. Its first involvement in Mesopotamia, around the modern Iraq–Iran border, was in 1915. This was mainly reconnaissance work, flying over enemy lines to gather information about enemy forces and defences. Several pilots were captured and made prisoners-of-war by the Turkish forces.

The AFC was much more successful in Palestine, where it carried out reconnaissance, bombing, mapping and artillery observation tasks. Most AFC pilots, observers and ground crew served on the Western Front.

The AFC suffered 178 deaths among its total force of approximately 3000 pilots, observers and ground crew.

The Royal Australian Navy

Australia had a navy of 37 ships of various types and sizes, crewed by about 5000 men. Australian ships were involved in all five key aspects of the naval war: eliminating German raiders from the Indian and Pacific oceans, trying to take Constantinople, blockading German ports to cause starvation, keeping the German navy bottled up; and escorting food and troop convoys against submarines.

Walers

The Australian Light Horse rode mounts called 'walers'. The mounts were called that because during the 19th century they had originally been supplied to the Indian cavalry from New South Wales – though the horses supplied to the Light Horse during the First World War could have come from almost any state in Australia.

Walers were cattle horses, smaller and lighter than traditional cavalry horses, but faster and more agile. They were also able to carry a heavy weight for a long distance, and required less food and water than cavalry horses.

The typical waler was 14–16 hands or 140–160 centimetres high. (A 'hand' is about 10 centimetres, and the height of a horse is measured to the top of its shoulder.) When not on active service the horses were groomed three times daily, watered twice, fed three times and exercised twice. With many Light Horsemen spending almost the entire day with their walers, it comes as no surprise that they became very close.

At the end of the war, the Australian Government decided that the estimated 13,000 walers of the Light Horse could not be brought back to Australia. It would have been expensive to do so, as all the room on ships were taken up by the returning soldiers. There were also concerns that the horses might bring back parasites or diseases that could have devastated Australia's livestock or crops.

The walers in the higher classifications were sold to the Indian cavalry, or locally. Walers in the lowest classification were killed, and their manes, tails, skin and horse shoes were sold.

The only horse that was returned from the Middle East was 'Sandy', who had belonged to Major General Bridges, the commander of the Australian forces. Bridges was killed at Gallipoli in 1915.

RAN ships served in the Pacific, Atlantic and Indian oceans, and in the Mediterranean, Adriatic and North seas. About half the sailors were British, and the ships were usually part of a Royal Navy force.

The RAN suffered 171 deaths, including the entire crew of 32 on the *AE1* submarine off New Guinea.

The Australian Army Nursing Service

The soldiers who went to the Western Front in 1916 were not the first Australians to serve there – in August 1914 an Australian Volunteer Hospital had been formed from Australian nurses living in Britain, and they worked in France soon after. More than 3000 civilian nurses volunteered to join the Australian Army Nursing Service (AANS).

More than 2000 Australian nurses served overseas. Most served on the Western Front or in hospitals in Britain, but there were also nurses in Egypt, Salonika, Lemnos and India. There were also Red Cross volunteers called 'Voluntary Aid Detachments', who served in hospitals, at home and overseas. Red Cross nurses, known as 'Bluebirds', served in French frontline hospitals.

Some Australian nurses and women doctors paid their own way to be involved in medical service during the war. There were also masseuses (physical therapists), those who focused on blood transfusions, and other support medical occupations who served with the British Queen Alexandra's Imperial Military Nursing Service. Some New Zealanders also enlisted in the AANS, as the country did not send its own nursing force overseas until 1915. More than 400 AANS nurses served in hospitals in Australia.

Entry requirements

Nurses in the AANS were expected to be single or widowed. Some married women got through the recruiting checks, and some married during their period of service, though they had to resign immediately on their marriage. Of those who served overseas, seven were aged under 21 (though the official minimum age for enlistment was 21), 1184 were aged 21–30, 947 were aged 31–40, and 91 were 41 years or older.

Working conditions

Nurses served in three types of hospitals: at casualty clearing stations, where they were sometimes hit by artillery shelling; at general hospitals, nursing the wounded and preparing them for transfer to Britain; and in British hospitals or convalescent homes (where sick people received medical treatment).

Conditions for nurses were sometimes as bad as for troops – freezing in winter, baking hot in summer, with poor food and excessive workloads. But the worst feature was the constant procession of the suffering men, who were damaged physically, mentally, or both. The nurses treated hundreds of badly wounded men. They also often contacted families and let them know what had happened to their men. Eight women received the Military Medal for bravery under fire, and 25 died of wounds or disease.

The nurses' experiences

The quotes below give insight into the fraught and traumatic experiences nurses experienced during the First World War.

'I was alone in a ward of 22 beds all pneumonia, mostly mad, and had about 3 deaths in every 24 hours. I was there [in that ward] 3 weeks without relief for one hour. The depression which settled on one watching these men die in spite of all you did for them was awful.'
Sister Mabel Brown, 1918–1919

'We are getting more stumps every day and now have about 300 without legs and arms.

I have about 30 leg stumps to dress every morning and about 40 beds to make.'
Sister Queenie Avenell, 1917

'One realises what the horrors of war must be like to reduce such fine men to this state. One aged 26 is just like a child, learning to talk again. He's very bright, you can't exactly call him mental but his condition never improves.'
Sister Evelyn Davies, 1917

'Blood! Blood! I am very tired. Oh dear God, how dreadfully tired, and broken-hearted too.' *Sister Gertrude Moberley,*
at the end of the war, 1918

The Red Cross

In Egypt in 1915 Vera Deakin, youngest daughter of former prime minister Alfred Deakin, set up the Red Cross Missing and Wounded Enquiry Bureau. The bureau was instrumental in ascertaining information for families of the circumstances of 32,000 men who were missing through death, wounding or capture. Women such as Rania McPhillamy and Alice Chisholm set up canteens in Egypt, providing facilities for soldiers on leave.

Australian Service deaths – First World War

(Exclusive of non-battle deaths of 6371)

Location	Dates	Total Deaths
German New Guinea	September 1914	6
Gallipoli	25 April – 20 December 1915	7841
Egypt and Palestine	March 1916 – October 1918	973
Western Front	March 1916 – November 1918	45,033
Other		5

Wray Vamplew (ed), *Australians. Historical Statistics.* Fairfax, Syme & Weldon Associates, 1987.

THE WAR AT HOME

After the initial public enthusiasm for the war, divisions and differences began to appear in Australia.

The significance of Gallipoli

Even though the Gallipoli campaign was a military defeat, it helped to provide Australians with a new sense of national identity and their place in the world. One reason for this was because the landing was a separate action in the war – it was not swallowed up in the general war news. People in Australia knew their 'boys' were training for their 'baptism of fire', and when it came the Australian landing at Gallipoli was reported on separately from the British and French ones.

The way the landing was reported also influenced how Australians viewed their country. The first report by British journalist Ellis Ashmead-Bartlett is now known to be inaccurate and even fanciful, but its impact on readers at the time was powerful, and heightened a sense of national pride among readers.

Another reason for Australia's growing national pride was that most people had some connection with the 50,000 men of the first AIF who had served on Gallipoli in 1915, or with the 400,000 who had served by the end of the war. Commemorative notices in newspapers on the first anniversary of the landing of 25 April were placed not only by family members, but by friends and other social circles. The ripples of those directly affected by the campaign spread throughout much of Australian society.

Australians had been brought up on stories about the glories of British military exploits. They were now part of that picture, and despite their exposure to the horror, savagery and suffering of war, many of the soldiers' diaries show that they felt that they had been tested as a nation, and not found wanting. In this way Gallipoli was seen by many soldiers and civilians as an affirmation of national worth.

Anzac Day quickly became a special commemorative day in Australia.

The changing role of women

The war did not greatly change the role of most women in Australia. Women tended to work in lower paid occupations or, when they were in similar occupations to men, they received about 54 per cent of the male wage.

Between 1914 and 1918, the female workforce rose from 24 per cent of the total to 37 per cent, but the increase tended to be in what were already traditional areas of women's work, such as the clothing and footwear, food and printing sectors. There was also a rise of female workers in the clerical, shop assistant and teaching areas. Unions were unwilling to let more women work in traditional male areas as they feared that this would lower men's wages.

A few women tried to become more involved in war-related positions such as cooks, stretcher bearers, motor car drivers, interpreters and munitions workers, but the government did not encourage this as it didn't believe it to be necessary or desirable.

Women's organisations

Red Cross badge, 1918.

Women's main role in the war was as volunteers in fund-raising, and sending comforts to the troops overseas. A number of women's organisations became very active during the war, including the Australian Women's National League, and the Australian Red Cross. One of the most active groups was the Women's Christian Temperance Union, which succeeded in having hotel hours restricted in several states, arguing that this would help the war effort by stopping men from wasting money on alcohol, and making them more productive in war efforts.

Women volunteers carried out a huge range of war-related activities. Red Cross and other volunteers packed billies for soldiers at Christmas time, greeted troop trains with sandwiches and tea for the travelling soldiers, and made cakes for local training camps and hospitals. School girls were encouraged to raise money for patriotic funds, including raffling geese, knitting, and selling various things such as pet lambs, homegrown vegetables and baked goods.

It was often the non-working, middle-class women in cities who had the time to be most involved in these activities, creating an image of patriotic commitment to the war that time-poor, working women could not match. In country areas there was a stronger tradition of all classes helping out with voluntary community activities, which continued during the war.

Internment

During the war, the phrase 'the enemy within' was often used to describe 'enemy aliens': non-naturalised residents (people who weren't citizens) of Australia who had been born in countries that were fighting against the Allies. Government policy was to intern many of these people – to put them into what, in effect, were prisons.

According to the 1911 census, there were about 33,400 German-born residents in Australia, with the majority living in South Australia and Queensland. Australia interned almost 7000 people during the First World War, of whom about 4500 were enemy aliens and British nationals of German ancestry who were already residents of Australia.

Even those who were not interned might suffer in different ways – many 'Germans' lost their jobs; many had to report periodically to local police; some were harassed by locals who would claim that the Germans were behaving 'suspiciously'. German schools and churches were closed by state governments, and 42 locations with German place names were renamed with British ones. (For example, Blumberg in South Australia became Birdwood, and German Creek in New South Wales became Empire Bay.) German language classes were banned.

Government powers

Internment without legal charge or trial was just one of the unprecedented powers that the Australian Government created during the war.

The Australian Government needed extra powers for issues such as censorship, trade and the prices of food and goods. The government also needed to raise a lot more money to pay all the extra costs of the war.

Using its extraordinary powers, the Australian Government ended its commercial contracts with firms in enemy countries. In 1915, it took on the power to tax incomes, which previously only the state governments could do. It also fixed the selling price of many goods, compulsorily bought farmers' wheat and wool crops, censored publications and letters, seized enemy ships and then used them to send the wool and wheat crops to Britain, banned organisations such as the Industrial Workers of the World (IWW) for alleged treason, and interned people associated with those organisations.

Economy

The increased powers of the Australian Government, and the nature of the war, affected the Australian economy. While some Australians benefited financially, others suffered economic loss. Some businesses were able to take over contracts that had previously been held by German firms in Australia. Local companies took over steel-making and the manufacture of pharmaceuticals. By the end of the war more than 400 products not previously made in Australia were being produced, and without international competition.

Farmers also benefited. The government compulsorily acquired all wheat, wool and meat grown for export and sent them to Britain – so the farmers had guaranteed sales of all their produce at a very good price.

However, the shortage of goods meant that prices rose, so ordinary people could not afford them, and their standard of living fell. There were also people who 'profiteered' – took advantage of shortages to sell scarce goods at a very high price. This created resentment in the community.

Another way that the government raised the money to pay for its wartime commitments, such as soldiers' wages, equipment, training, accommodation and food, was by receiving war loans from the public. Australians could lend their money to the government with a guarantee that they would get it back with a fixed rate of interest after the war. This meant that people who could afford to lend the money to the government would get that money back with interest, and so would profit from the war. Those who could not afford to lend the money would be hurt by the rising prices. Clearly, some were now profiting from the war, while others were suffering because of it. There was no equality of sacrifice.

Patriotism and loyalty

During the war, there were two conflicting ideas about patriotism (support for one's country) and loyalty, which divided Australian society.

One view was that as the nation was at war, the war was more important than anything else.

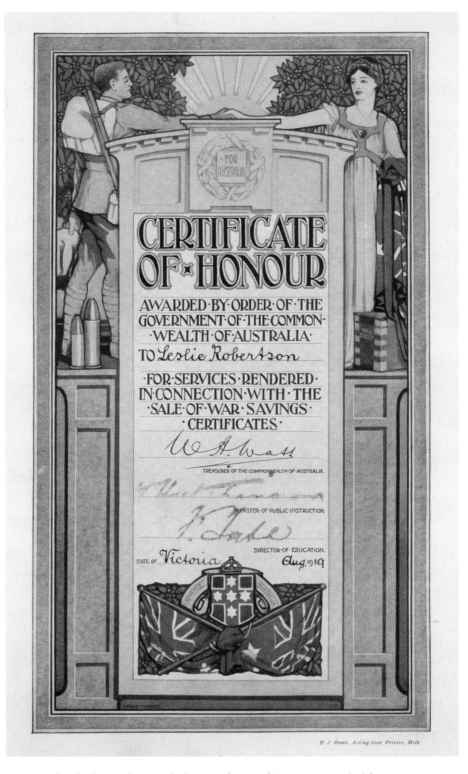

A way for the home front to help. Certificate of Honour awarded for assisting with the sale of war savings certificates, 1919.

The other view was the opposite – that life must continue regardless, that working and living conditions had to be protected, that those who had chosen to give all to the war had made that decision voluntarily.

Minority groups who opposed the war began to cluster together. These included those who were against the war on economic grounds, those who opposed Britain and supported Ireland, those who were pacifists, and those who felt their families needed them at home.

There were many calls in newspapers for sports and other entertainment to be abandoned. This was mainly because patriots believed that sport – rugby, football or racing – distracted people's attention from the serious business of the war. Competitive sport also seemed to flaunt that fit young men had not volunteered to fight, and therefore went against Australia's war commitment. Amateur sports did tend to stop for the duration, but the semi-professional football competitions continued.

I will help until the war is won. One view of patriotism, but not all agreed that winning the war had to be the first priority in Australia.

Strikes

As a result of these conflicting social beliefs and changing economic pressures, employees began to fight to keep their working conditions. In 1917, there was a series of major strikes among coal miners, railway workers and wharf labourers, mostly in New South Wales. The largest strike was caused by an attempt to bring in a system of checking on NSW railway workers, which some believed would make them have to work more quickly. The strike lasted five weeks and involved 100,000 workers across the nation. Trams and trains were stopped, there was no coal for fires and cooking, and street lights were out. Families had no food or no money to pay for rent. Non-union workers took over some of the jobs during the strike until it finally ended unsuccessfully.

Politics

In 1914, the Australian Labor Party had been fully in support of the war, and was elected to government.

In 1915, Prime Minister Andrew Fisher retired and was replaced by William Morris Hughes. Hughes believed that he and the nation had to give everything possible to support the Australian troops. However, other members of the Labor Party argued that the war was damaging working conditions in Australia, which caused strikes, and that this instead should be the government's main focus. As a result, the Labor Government began to split in two. A decrease in military volunteers from late 1915 increased the division in attitudes, as the government encouraged more men to fight in the war.

Recruitment and propaganda

The initial rush of volunteers was sustained for the first 18 months of the war. The original 20,000 was reinforced by an additional 30,000, who were sent to Gallipoli, and later more volunteers joined up as reinforcements for the campaign. After Gallipoli, most recruits went to the Western Front.

Nearly three-quarters of all those who volunteered for the AIF had done so before the casualties of the Western Front started to mount. From 1916, most Australian troops served in the trench warfare on the Western Front. In July that year, there was a huge British–French offensive to overwhelm the Germans. The offensive resulted in large casualty figures, which meant that more reinforcements were needed, just at the time when fewer men were volunteering. Australia was one of the very few Allied nations not using conscripted men as soldiers, and so the government had to appeal to young men to volunteer.

The Australian Government produced thousands of copies of propaganda posters. They were designed mainly to encourage men to enlist and used themes such as patriotism, nationalism, loyalty, duty, honour, guilt and hate.

Some posters asked what men's children would say to them about the part they had played in the war. Other posters asked why men were playing sport while their mates were dying in the trenches. Meanwhile, others encouraged men to enlist with a group of mates to join the adventure and see the world. Many more posters showed the enemy as brutal murderers, 'the beastly Hun'.

Winnie O'Sullivan's mourning locket containing a photograph of her fiance, boxer Les Darcy, and a lock of his hair. Darcy was accused of shirking the war, and seeking to advance his career in the USA. He died there in 1917.

Women were also targeted by propaganda – not to join and fight, as this was not allowed by the government at the time – but to apply moral pressure to men to enlist. They were encouraged to shun and shame eligible young men and only go out with soldiers.

But the recruitment campaign failed. This led to the most divisive events of the war – the conscription referenda campaigns.

Conscription

Prime Minister Hughes had visited Britain and the Western Front in 1916, and he believed in the necessity of pouring everything the nation could into winning the war. Voluntary recruiting was not bringing in enough new troops, so Hughes wanted conscription to force eligible men to join. The Australian Government had the power to introduce conscription for service inside Australia but not to send these conscripts overseas.

The first referendum (1916)

Hughes adopted the tactic of holding a referendum on the issue – a national vote. It was not really a referendum – a referendum is held to change part of the Constitution. Hughes did not have to change the Australian Constitution – he already had the legal power to introduce conscription for overseas service – but he did not have enough supporters in parliament to pass the amendment to the existing law, the *Defence Act*. So he held a 'plebiscite', which is, in essence, a national public opinion poll. He expected the 'Yes' vote to win, and that this would put moral pressure on some of the opposing senators and force them to support the amendments to the *Defence Act*.

Supporters versus opponents

Supporters and opponents campaigned hard on the issue. Pro-conscriptionists emphasised the desperate need for more men and the fact that volunteering was not providing enough reinforcements. They argued that more Australian soldiers would die without these reinforcements. It was a question of loyalty, of patriotism, of justice, and of morality.

Meanwhile, others opposed conscription for a range of reasons. Some said that so many volunteers were not needed; others said that conscription was wrong in principle. There was also a strong belief that it was more important to keep men working in Australia and not send them overseas. Another argument was that a man who had not already volunteered would not necessarily make a good soldier, so conscripts would harm, not help, the soldiers who were fighting.

The 1916 referendum results

In the end, the vote was very close. Conscription was rejected 51 to 49 per cent. The states that were least in favour were New South Wales and South Australia, while Western Australia was the state most in favour of conscription. Many commentators asked why conscription was rejected, but a better question was, why was the vote so close?

One explanation for the majority 'No' vote was that it was backed by a lot of people who

The cost of war – a Mothers and Widows badge issued to the mother of 9956 Driver Alison Hope Oliver, AIF, who died in England in 1918.

Industrial Workers of the World

The most extreme opponents of the war were the Industrial Workers of the World (IWW), who were nicknamed the 'Wobblies'.

They were a small, radical international group who believed the war was for the benefit of a few international capitalists, and was harming the ordinary working man. They opposed involvement in the war, and matched their words with actions. In Australia, no organisation opposed the outbreak of the First World War as promptly and vociferously as the IWW. The front page of the IWW newspaper *Direct Action* for 10 August 1914 declared:

War! What for? For the workers and their dependants: death, starvation, poverty and untold misery. For the capitalist class: gold, stained with the blood of millions, riotous luxury, banquets of jubilation over the graves of their dupes and slaves. War is hell! Send the capitalists to hell and wars are impossible.

During the war IWW members destroyed machines in industries that helped the war effort, encouraged strikes, and tried to sabotage the war effort by opposing recruitment. Some members were almost certainly involved in burning down businesses in Sydney, though others were probably wrongly convicted of these attacks through fabricated police evidence.

were opposed to or were disillusioned with the war for different reasons. While some were completely anti-war, others did support the war but were against conscription as a principle. Some people said that they did not oppose conscription, but were being hurt by Australia's economic situation of that time, which focused on funding money for the war. Others voted 'No' to protect unionism; and some Irish-Australians protested at the British treatment of the rebels fighting for Home Rule in Ireland.

The second referendum (1917)

After the defeat of the first conscription referendum in 1916, Hughes and a number of other politicians left the Australian Labor Party. They joined with the Liberals to form a new Nationalist Party, which became the government for the rest of the war.

In 1917, Hughes held another plebiscite on conscription. This time he had a majority in both Houses of Parliament and did not need the vote. He wanted, however, to give the people another chance to overcome what he saw as their great mistake in rejecting conscription the previous year. The campaign was bitter and divisive, and conscription was, again, defeated, this time by a slightly larger margin.

THE END OF THE WAR

In 1917 and 1918 people became war-weary. The deaths and casualties continued to mount, there seemed to be no substantial victories, and the war appeared to be at a stalemate.

Jubilation in Sydney on learning the war was over, November 1918.

The economic burdens of the war continued to affect many in the community, and military recruits now only trickled in, whereas they had flowed in 1915 and early 1916. When fighting finally ended on 11 November 1918, there was a great sense of relief.

Paris Peace Conference 1919

The final act of the war was to create a series of peace treaties between the Allies and the enemy nations. There were five separate treaties, all signed in France – at Versailles between the Allies and Germany at Trianon (with Hungary), at Neuilly (with Bulgaria), at Saint Germain (with Austria), at Sèvres (with the Ottoman Empire).

Four key issues were to be resolved in the treaties: the issue of war guilt (all the Allied powers blamed Germany for the war, and Germany had to accept this blame); a decision on the extent of reparations (compensation payments to the victors by the defeated nations); a re-allocation of German colonies in Africa and the Pacific to other nations; and the creation of a way of securing lasting peace in the future through disarmament (reducing armies and fleets) and an international dispute-settling body.

The main meeting was the Paris Peace Conference, held at the French royal Palace of Versailles in 1919. All the Allied nations had representatives there to express their national interests, and to vote on the final suggested peace terms.

One sign that the world had changed after the First World War was that Australia, as well as some of the other former colonies of Great Britain, now called Dominions, were each separately represented in the peace talks. Previously, Great Britain had spoken for them all. Now Australia, Canada, South Africa and New Zealand had their own representatives. Australia was represented by Prime Minister Hughes, Deputy Prime Minister Joseph Cook and Lieutenant Commander John Latham.

The defeated nations, Germany, Austria-Hungary and the Ottoman Empire, did not have any say in the peace treaties. They could only accept or reject them. If they had rejected them, the fighting might have started again.

The war cost the European nations and the Dominions heavily – both in dead and wounded soldiers, nurses and civilians, and financially. The Australian Government claimed that the war cost Australia £464 million (the Versailles settlement awarded £100 million, of which Australia received £5.6 million from Germany). It is difficult to give equivalent amounts in today's money, but multiplying the amounts by 200 gives an idea of their value in today's dollars. There would also be continuing expenses after the war in pensions and medical treatment for wounded veterans and their families.

The nation most actively seeking a less harsh peace with Germany was the United States. The United States wanted to avoid the question of who was to blame for the war. It also wanted Germany to be economically viable but not militarily strong, and it wanted the creation of a new body, the League of Nations, to solve international disputes.

Peace hat worn during celebrations in 1918.

League of Nations

Australia supported the formation of an international body to settle disputes but it opposed the introduction of a 'racial equality' clause in the League of Nations Charter, or statement of principles. This racial equality clause was supported by Japan, which saw itself as a superior Asian nation just as worthy as any European one. Japan wanted to assert this equality in a racially divided world.

Hughes feared such a clause would have meant the White Australia policy could be challenged in an international court, so he strongly opposed it. Many of the other nations were equally unhappy with the idea, including the United States, which also had many racially based policies, but they kept their opposition quiet. At one stage in the negotiations, the American President Woodrow Wilson asked Hughes if he was aware that he was standing out against the world in opposing the racial equality clause. Hughes replied, 'That's about the size of it'. The clause was defeated.

In the end the United States, which had proposed the formation of the League of Nations, did not support the new body because the majority of the American politicians wanted to isolate the United States from European affairs.

Colonies

The Treaty of Versailles gave Australia control of the former German colony of New Guinea. Hughes saw this as essential, as Japan had gained many former German colonies in the Pacific, and he was certain that at some time in the future a strong Japan would expand its influence and threaten Australia. Control of New Guinea gave Australia a northern frontier from which to defend the mainland.

Sectarianism

Hostility or division between religious groups is called 'sectarianism'. In Australia there was much underlying dislike between some Protestants and Roman Catholics. It was made worse by the division between those who believed that the British were suppressing Irish national separation from Britain. These racial and religious tensions were particularly obvious during the conscription referendums.

In 1916, a group of Irish nationalists in Dublin had tried to start a revolution against the British Government, which had promised but then failed to deliver Home Rule (or independence) to Ireland. The rebels were captured, and their leaders tried and executed.

The Irish-born coadjutor (a bishop who assists and often succeeds a diocesan bishop) Archbishop of Melbourne, Dr Daniel Mannix, did not support the rebellion, but was particularly strong in his condemnation of the brutal British suppression of it. He spoke out against the impacts of the war on social conditions in Australia, and against conscription, and influenced many of his followers to do the same. Not all Roman Catholic leaders opposed conscription: Sydney's Archbishop Michael Kelly supported it. But where Irish Catholics opposed conscription, they were accused of disloyalty and of being motivated by anti-British sentiment.

AFTER THE WAR

The greatest cost to Australia of the First World War war was its 60,000 dead. An Imperial (later Commonwealth) War Graves Commission created cemeteries and memorials for the dead and missing of all British Empire countries in the areas where they had been killed. Relatives could nominate what they wanted engraved on the headstones of their deceased loved ones in the war cemeteries.

At the time, few people could afford to travel to visit the last resting place of their loved ones, and so local memorials became especially important to Australian communities. Most suburbs and towns had their own memorials, built in prominent places, sometimes to the dead only, more often to those who had served as well. There were usually just names, not rank or awards, signalling that all were equal in memory.

However, what might be seen as a symbol of unity could also highlight old divisions long after the war ended. The memorials symbolised two parts of the community – those who had chosen to serve, and those who had chosen not to.

After the war ended, Australian society had to adjust to peace and confront a range of challenges. More than 250,000 returning soldiers and nurses would need jobs and houses. Many thousands would require hospital and medical care. These men and women would have to readjust to ordinary civilian life after years of military regimentation. Families would be reunited with their fathers and sons, who were certain to have changed from their experiences of war. Many women, who had become used to running the home and working, would suddenly find themselves back in a domestic role only.

The 1920s and 1930s would see Australia facing these new social and economic problems.

·WHEN THE BOYS COME HOME.

This postcard shows how the returning soldiers may have seen their return.

THE GREAT WAR

SERG'T G.H. SINCLAIR.
P'VTE J⁰ˢ SERVICE.
P'VTE J^{no} SERVICE.
SERG'T A.F. SOUTHAM.
P'VTE R.H. EYRE. — *Died of Wounds. Oct. 1916.*
P'VTE J. PRICE.
CORP'L M.H. SIMPKINS.
P'VTE H.M. COPPEN.
P'VTE T. SEDDON.
P'VTE C.S. STARK.
P'VTE L.S. McCLENAHAN
P'VTE W.J. BOOKER. — *Killed in Action. Apr. 1917*
D'VR G. BROCKWAY.
DVR G. HEMMINGSEN. — *Died of Illness. Oct. 1918*
P'VTE A.E. TOMBS.
SAP T.H. TOMBS.
DVR C.M. LAMB.
P'VTE W.N. MATTERSON.
SAP C.R. PARKIN.
SERGT A.A. MOSELEY.
SERG'T B.E.H. WADDELL.
SAP L.C. BOUSTEAD.
W.K.C. AUSTIN — (R.N.T.)

DID THEIR DUTY.

CARRINGTON LODGE. N⁰ 75.

P.A.F.S. OF A.

ROLL OF HONOUR

CORP'L T.F. BURGESS.
L'CE CORP'L G. COOPER. — *Killed in Action. Aug 1915*
LIEUT R. CRAWFORD. — D.C.M
CORP'L C. KELLY.
CORP'L H.C. MACKAY.
P'VTE A.J. SEARLE.
P'VTE W. MARTIN.
P'VTE J.N. JORDAN.
A.B. DVR A.G. MOSELEY. — M.M.
P'VTE C.R. MATTERSON.
P'VTE E.C. PEVERELL. — *Died of Wounds Dec 1917*
P'VTE F.R. PARDEY.
LIEUT W.G. DEVITT. — *Killed in Action Nov 1916*
P'VTE J.W. HUDSON. — *Killed in Action. Aug 1916*
SAP J. ROBERTSON.
SAP J.J. MANSON.
LIEUT W.W. VICK. — (R.A.F)
SERGT H.K. LAWSON.
P'VTE F.M. SEARLE. — *Killed in Action. Oct 1917*
P'VTE A.G. SEARLE.
P'VTE S.J. SAUNDERS.
P'VTE H. McAULAY. — *Killed in Action July 1916*

DID THEIR DUTY.

The cost of war – an honour board recording the service and deaths of members of a Protestant Friendly Society (a support and social group).

8

The Roaring Twenties and the Great Depression

The 1920s and 1930s were decades of huge change and adjustment. There were greater social freedoms and enjoyment for some, but unemployment was high, especially when the Great Depression of the 1930s hit, creating social inequality and political divisions.

The new national day as a focus for the community. Anzac Day in Bundaberg (Queensland) 1923.

BRINGING THE SOLDIERS AND NURSES HOME

The world of the 1920s was shaped by the consequences of the First World War, which ended in 1918. At the end of the war, 167,000 Australian soldiers and nurses were overseas. There were not only servicemen and nurses to bring home; more than 13,000 Australian soldiers had married during the war, mainly in Britain. Their war brides and children also had to be brought to Australia. The process of returning all these people took 13 months and 176 separate trips by ship.

Back to civilian life

For many soldiers and nurses, reuniting with their loved ones was joyous, and their lives, interrupted by war, could now return to normality. Many men quickly resumed their old civilian jobs and re-established family life.

But problems remained for others. Some servicemen suffered severe physical wounds and psychological trauma, preventing them from continuing their lives as they were before the war. These included men who were blinded, whose nerves were wrecked by 'shell shock', whose lungs were corroded by poison gas, and who were missing limbs and had to be fitted with artificial ones, and whose faces were horribly disfigured.

The nation accepted the obligation to care for the returned servicemen. Governments offered training and education schemes, low-interest loans for war service homes, a system of settling soldiers on new farms, and preference in employment in the public service.

The influenza pandemic

The returning troops brought back a terrible influenza, which killed more than 12,000 people in Australia – more than the number of Australians killed during the whole Gallipoli campaign. Most deaths occurred between April and September 1919.

Called the 'Spanish flu', even though it probably began in a military base and hospital in northern France, the disease struck with great speed. It caused uncontrollable haemorrhaging that filled the lungs, resulting in the victim drowning in his or her own body fluids. It struck healthy adults rather than the very young or very old, who were usually most vulnerable to other forms of influenza. A person who woke up healthy might be dead by the end of the day.

Authorities began vaccination programs, quarantined affected houses, and banned large groups of people from gathering, such as in churches, theatres and race meetings. Schools were closed and many people wore masks to reduce the chance of being infected.

As terrible as that was, Australia was in fact relatively unscathed by the epidemic. Australian authorities knew the influenza was coming and had time to prepare. Worldwide more than eight million soldiers had been killed during the war, but double that number of civilians died postwar as a result of the influenza.

Dedicated government-run repatriation hospitals were created to provide specialised treatment, and the Australian Government established a system of pension payments to help the soldiers and their families.

During the 1920s the single biggest element of government spending was on repatriation and war service pensions, which accounted for about 20 per cent of all spending. In 1920, 90,000 men received disability pensions for injuries sustained in the war, and 49,000 of their dependants also received pension payments. By 1938 there were still 77,000 incapacitated soldiers, and 180,000 dependants on pensions.

Nurses

Wartime experience also had a lasting impact on the thousands of nurses who had served during the war. Nearly 20 per cent were declared medically unfit on discharge. Nurses were eligible for pensions but received a lower rate than the returned servicemen. Like the soldiers, some nurses found it very difficult to settle back into civilian life. They remained single at a higher rate than other Australian women of their own age groups and continued to earn less than their male equivalents, even though they were often supporting dependent relatives and many had married soldiers they had cared for.

Families

The pension offered to soldiers did not allow for the hire of full-time carers, so the task invariably fell on the families of the men, especially their mothers, their sisters and, if they had married, their wives.

Women who had looked after families by themselves during the war, who had perhaps worked and gained new skills and independence, found themselves living in the greatest intimacy with men who were vastly different from the ones they had married, and from whom they had grown apart. The divorce rate jumped during the 1920s, but for most people divorce was not an affordable option. Many soldiers had been absent for years of their children's lives, and these children had to adjust to having their fathers back.

The RSL

The Returned Sailors' and Soldiers' Imperial League of Australia, later shortened to the Returned and Services League or RSL, was formed in 1916. The organisation's aim was to provide practical assistance to soldiers who returned to Australia due to injury, and to protect the soldiers' rights and interests. The RSL provided companionship for soldiers through its clubs and events, and promoted the importance of Anzac Day as a special day of commemoration. However, returned Indigenous servicemen were not welcomed by some RSL clubs.

The RSL was very effective in advocating for the returned soldiers and influencing government policies, particularly in the area of giving preference to returned servicemen in Commonwealth public service jobs. The RSL's success contributed to the belief held by some that returned soldiers were using their war service as a way to gain privilege over other members of society.

Young Australians of the 1920s. Grade 5 class, Epping (New South Wales), 1921.

Attitudes towards the soldiers

The returning soldiers had shared a common experience that crossed boundaries of class, wealth, occupation, education, politics, religion and even race. Some felt resentment towards those in society who seemed to have prospered at home during the war. One expressed it this way in a letter to the Victorian newspaper the *Age* on 7 February 1922:

> *I am a soldier teacher who spent four years on active service, and now suffer from an eye injury, received 'over there.' I receive a pension, which is gradually being cut down . . . Must I compete with slackers, &c., who are sound in body and limb? . . . I have a wife and two children to support, and hope that our country will not forget the promises made to the diggers, whose motto was at all times – 'Country first, self last'.*

In turn, some, especially the young, felt resentment towards these diggers, believing that the returned servicemen were trading on their special status and their misery. Writing in a NSW newspaper, *Labor Daily*, on 25 November 1931 one young man said:

> *I was born in 1913 and some of my boy and girl friends are thoroughly sick of war pictures, and especially sick of anything relating to Australian soldiers.*
> *We see nothing to interest us in these plays and talkies. What we actually see every day till they have got on our nerves are crippled, blind and battered wrecks, with brass badges on,*

243

The last original Anzac

Of the approximately 16,000 Australians who landed on the first day at Gallipoli, there were perhaps 7000 still alive at the end of the war. The last surviving Australian who landed on the first day of the Gallipoli campaign, Albert Edward 'Ted' Matthews, died in 1997 aged 101. He was also among the last to be evacuated on the night of 19 December and morning of 20 December.

Born in Leichhardt, New South Wales, Matthews was one of six children. A carpenter when war broke out, he had been in the Cadets and knew how to handle a rifle. He joined the engineers as a signaller because he knew morse code. He turned 19 on Gallipoli, and went on to fight in France and Belgium.

After the war, Matthews returned to carpentry, married, and had two daughters. During the Depression he set up a travelling library from a motorbike with sidecar, and later made soft drinks. He tried to enlist for the Second World War but was rejected because of his age.

begging in the streets, howling about pension reductions, while their women and children are in dire straits . . . the general opinion among fellows like myself is that Australians were very foolish to let themselves be lured into going . . . none of my friends like returned soldiers.

These comments reflected a truth of 1920s and 1930s Australian society, that not all Australians shared the same attitude towards the returned soldiers and the claim that the nation owed them a special responsibility. Returned Indigenous servicemen were legally entitled to the same repatriation benefits and pensions paid to others, but they were not allocated soldier settler blocks, and in some states the Native Welfare Departments kept back their wages and pensions.

POLITICAL AND INDUSTRIAL UNREST

Fear of Bolshevism and communism

The fall in value of wages during the First World War caused industrial and political unrest in the years that followed. Over six million working days were lost to strikes in 1919, and nearly two million in 1920. This was about the same number of days lost to strikes for the next seven years combined.

The unrest was also partly due to the influence on Australia of the communist revolution in Russia. In 1917 the radical political group known as the Bolsheviks had seized power in a bloody revolution. They believed the state should own all the means of production (factories and farms and shops), and redistribute wealth from the rich to the poor. But they were political communists, people who believed that there could only be one political party that completely ran the country. There could be no democracy and no opposition to them.

Many people in Australia, including the Australian Labor Party, supported the idea of socialism – that the functions of society are organised and regulated to take into account the community as a whole – but they wanted it to be introduced peacefully and democratically, not through force or a single dominant party. A few people, however, went further, and also wanted the sort of political change that the Bolsheviks had achieved: communism, or one-party rule. Most who wanted change in Australia did not want bloodshed, but they wanted the existing system to collapse and be replaced. There were three possible ways to do this: by direct action (such as strikes), by exercising influence through the Australian Labor Party, and by taking leadership positions in key unions. The Bolshevik supporters believed that strikes by workers would lead to such social and economic unrest that the people would demand a political change, and that they would be able to step in and take control like the Bolsheviks had done.

In 1919, a group of communists and unionists, including some politically radical returned soldiers, held a march in Brisbane. They flew the red flag of revolution and marched to show their determination to challenge the political system. A large group of politically conservative former soldiers broke up the march and attacked the marchers. The communists decided not to use protest marches after this. In 1920 they formed their own political party, the Communist Party of Australia. The political party only ever had one Member of Parliament, Fred Paterson,

A national parliament in a sheep paddock. The opening of the national parliament in the new capital city, Canberra, 1927.

who was elected to the Queensland Parliament in 1944, but communist leaders were very influential in several major unions and, for the first few years, in the ALP.

The Australian Labor Party

In 1921, the ALP adopted its own radical 'socialisation objective' whereby members pledged to the socialisation of industry, production, distribution and exchange. The Labor Party leaders quickly watered this down to make it less threatening, and they never actually tried to implement it. However the objective stayed as part of the ALP's official policy and provided a focus for much hostility from more conservative Australians.

Conservative Organisations

Some returned servicemen, worried about the rise of radical political influences, formed a number of groups, including the King and Empire Alliance (1920), the White Guard (1923), and the Old Guard (possibly from as early as 1917). Their collective aim was expressed by the King and Empire Alliance: '[we] view with grave concern the development in our midst of an element of disloyalty and disunion which is foreign to the true spirit of the Australian people' (*Sydney Morning Herald*, 24 January 1921). Their idea was to be available as fighters who could be called on during a crisis if needed to protect the nation against radical groups that threatened the existing democratic order.

THE 'ROARING TWENTIES'

As the 1920s progressed, huge social changes developed in Australia and other parts of the world. Often referred to as the 'Roaring Twenties', this decade was a time of 'fast' living by young people, notable for the Charleston dance, jazz music, short skirts, parties, drinking and the infiltration of American culture through the movies – silent at first, and then the 'talkies' from 1929. The attitude was that war was over, and it was time for greater social freedom, especially among young women.

The Roaring Twenties was a time of technological advancement in transport and communications – radios, planes, cars – and the creation of cheaper labour-saving household devices. It was also a time of economic growth, though unemployment remained high after the war. These developments were enjoyed far more by wealthy people in cities than the working class or those in remote rural communities.

Entertainment

Cinema

Going to the cinema became a mass entertainment activity in both cities and country towns. The cinema became a weekly treat for many families. There were a few Australian-made films but the vast majority came from the United States, which produced more films and could sell them overseas cheaply.

Film production companies in the United States virtually forced Australian cinemas to show only American films, leaving locally made films without audiences. Some Australian

Dandenong Town Improvement Pictures.

TUESDAY, JUNE 19th, 1923.

DOUG FAIRBANKS   *   in "One of the Blood".
"KING OF THE FOREST". Drama.   One horse Town. Comedy.
✳✳

SATURDAY, JUNE 23rd, 1923

WALLACE REID   *   in "Nice People".
M. MAY   *   in The Greatest Truth.
J. HINES   *   in Crowning Torchy.
    BURTON HOLMES Parisienne Faces and Figures.
✳✳

Thursday, June 28th, "MANSLAUGHTER".

Claude A. Quist, Printer, Potter Street, Dandenong.

A cinema program for Dandenong Town Improvement Pictures shows the screenings for American films in June 1923.

film-makers countered this by bribing cinema owners to show locally made films. By 1923, over 90 per cent of all films shown in Australia were from the United States. This influenced popular culture – what people saw and did and how they entertained themselves.

Radio

The number of radio broadcasting stations increased during the 1920s in capital cities and regional areas. Unlike the cinema, with its weekly American feature films, people could listen to their radio sets from home every day. Programs included news, serial dramas and comedies, music and community events such as singalongs. The government charged a licence fee for every radio purchased, but many people could easily build their own cheap crystal sets and tap into the radio broadcast waves for free.

In 1932, radio went national when the Australian Broadcasting Corporation (ABC) opened 12 stations – in Sydney, Melbourne, Brisbane, Adelaide, Perth, Hobart, Newcastle, Corowa, Rockhampton and Crystal Brook (South Australia).

News and media

Before the advent of regular television broadcasting later on in the 1950s, many Australians saw news footage at the cinema. Between 1913 and 1932, the Australian weekly news film *Australian Gazette* presented people with a view of the world, as well as of other parts of Australia.

Newspapers, popular since the 1850s, remained a major source of information and local culture, and continued expanding in numbers and circulation throughout the 1920s.

"THE VOICE OF AUSTRALIA"

Power - - 20 Kilowatts
Wave-Length 31.28 Metres

A.W.A. Owns and Operates

VK2ME

DARWIN

BRISBANE

SYDNEY

PERTH

ADELAIDE

CANBERRA
MELBOURNE

HOBART

The laughing notes of the Kookaburra open and close the A.W.A. World-wide Broadcasting Service.

Beam Wireless Services to Great Britain, The Continent of Europe and North and South America.

Beam Wireless Picturegram Service for the transmission of Pictures between Australia and Great Britain and North America

Wireless Telephone Services to Great Britain, The Continent of Europe, North and South America, Java and New Zealand.

Coastal Radio Stations in Australia, Papua, New Guinea and Fiji.

Wireless Services on ships of the Australian Mercantile Marine.

Radio-Electric Works for the manufacture of every type of transmitting equipment and Radiola broadcast receivers.

Research and experimental laboratories.

WORLD - WIDE BROADCASTING SERVICE

AMALGAMATED WIRELESS (A/SIA) LTD.
AUSTRALIA'S NATIONAL WIRELESS ORGANISATION

A used postcard promoting the AWA radio station VK2ME with the slogan 'The Voice of Australia'. Circa 1936.

One of the most popular icons of the time was the cartoon character Ginger Meggs. Tens of thousands of Australians followed the doings of the cheeky young ginger-headed boy and his pet monkey in the comic strip section of the newspapers. Through Ginger Meggs, Australians were being presented with an endearing self-image. Ginger was a lovable rogue, a 'battler' and a 'dinkum' Aussie.

A modern reader looking at Ginger Meggs today would be appalled by some of his behaviour and values – his rude attitude towards the Italian ice-cream man, his harassment of the more refined kids Cuthbert and Wentworth, and the casual violence between him and his archenemy, the bully Tiger Kelly. But to the 1920s audience, Meggs represented Australian innocence and goodness, though with a rough and sometimes crude edge.

Pin decorated with the cheeky popular cartoon character Ginger Meggs.

Transport

Cars

Car ownership grew during the 1920s. In 1921, there were about 100,000 motor vehicles and 37,500 motorcycles in Australia. By 1939 this had increased to 560,000 cars and 258,000 motorcycles. Only about one in five families had a car, but Australia had the sixth largest total number of automobiles in the world.

The first serious attempt to make an Australian car was the 'Australian Six', partly assembled and partly made in Sydney between 1918 and 1925. It boasted of being 'Made in Australia, by Australians, for Australians.' The Australian Six cost £495, and claimed to be £200–300 cheaper than the equivalent American or British import. Even at this price, cars were still only affordable for wealthier people. In 1919, a worker on the average wage would have to work 132 weeks to earn the cost of the 'Australian Six'. (A new car can be bought for 20 weeks' work at the average wage today.)

Cars had a great impact on Australia. They helped the spread of suburbs as people could live further from the city centre and drive themselves into work without relying upon public transport. Cars influenced the design of houses, as garages became necessary both to house the car and to store the spare petrol needed in case fuel ran out between the relatively few petrol stations. This also meant that property frontages became wider, to allow for the garage and driveway.

The car encouraged local tourism as people could now travel further on weekends. State governments spent about 25 per cent of all the money they borrowed on developing roads, creating thousands of jobs. Dirt roads were gradually covered with bitumen, making car travel safer and more comfortable.

Cars also influenced local industry, with commercial motor car assembly plants being set up by Ford and Holden in South Australia and Victoria. More cars meant fewer horses in city streets and improved health as there was less manure in the streets to attract blowflies.

A traffic survey

Figures prepared by the traffic control branch of the Victorian police force, as a result of a check of traffic passing over the intersection of Flinders and Swanston streets on Wednesday, January 23, show that 2391 vehicles travelled over the intersection between 5 o'clock and 6 o'clock in the evening. Of this number 1103 were motor-cars, 559 horse-drawn vehicles, 420 bicycles, and 309 cable trams. Wednesday was chosen because it is the quietest day of the week at this busy intersection.

The figures show that the average traffic on ordinary days during the busy hours moves at the rate of 40 vehicles a minute over the intersection of Flinders and Swanston streets.

Argus, Melbourne, 9 February 1923.

A similar survey today would show more than 13,000 motor vehicles per hour at major Melbourne city intersections.

Two new developments characterised the 1920s–1930s – mobility through the development of motor cars, and the increasing social freedom of women.

Aerial services

Aerial services also boomed in the 1920s. Many men had gained flying and mechanical experience in the Australian Flying Corps (AFC) during the war and brought these skills, and some planes, back to Australia.

This was the period of great aerial heroes such as Ross and Keith Smith, both pilots in the AFC during the war, who made the first flight from England to Australia in 1919. Long-distance and speed records were constantly being broken. Bert Hinkler halved the Smiths' time for an England to Australia flight in 15 days in 1928. He was given a government prize of £2000, six times what an average worker would make in a year. In 1927, Millicent Bryant was the first woman to gain a pilot's licence. In 1928, Charles Kingsford Smith and Charles Ulm made the first aerial crossing of the Pacific Ocean from the United States to Australia, and in 1930 Kingsford Smith flew solo from London to Australia in 10 days.

Aeroplanes helped to bridge the gap between remote rural areas and the urban centres. The first commercial airmail service between capital cities started in 1924, between Adelaide and Sydney, and internationally, between Australia and Britain, in 1934.

Aeroplanes also brought medical help to the outback. Presbyterian Minister John Flynn opened the Australian Inland Mission Aerial Medical Service in Queensland in 1928 to provide medical assistance to country people in isolated places over an area of almost two million square kilometres. It later became known as the Royal Flying Doctor Service.

A model of the popular aviator Charles Kingsford Smith's plane, *Southern Cross*.

Consumer goods

The production of electric consumer goods increased hugely in the 1920s. These included items we take for granted today, such as radiators, stoves, toasters, irons, vacuum cleaners and refrigerators. Many of these goods were still only available to the wealthy and the middle class – an electric vacuum cleaner, for example, cost between £9 and £10, about three weeks worth of wages.

The development of a time payment system helped more people afford such goods. Under this system, a person would pay for goods over a period of time and be able to use them while they were paying them off. As occurs today, interest payments were added to the overall cost, so that while people could access luxury goods, they were paying more for them, and if they failed to meet the payments the goods were repossessed.

A black metal 'Winner' brand hand-operated sewing machine.

Telephones also became more common in the 1920s. In 1921, there were fewer than five per thousand Australians. By 1928, there were just under eight per thousand people. It was all part of the speeding up of life and the greater ability of people to move and communicate postwar.

Changes to women's roles

The war led to great social changes to women's roles in some countries, including Australia.

Organisations such as the League of Women Voters and the Australian Women's National League, originally formed to win the vote for women, now pushed for the right of women to be elected to parliaments. The first woman to be elected was Edith Cowan in the West Australian state seat of West Perth in 1921. During the whole of the 1920s, only four women were elected to parliaments in Australia.

In 1923 in Queensland, women became jurors for the first time. Most other states did not allow women jurors until the 1950s and 1960s. In 1911, 22 per cent of university students were women. By 1921, this had risen to 29 per cent. Women were also moving into areas previously dominated by men, especially clerical work. They were also moving out of the traditional area of paid domestic service. Most women, however, still only earned about 54 per cent of the male rate of pay for the same work. Many of these changes were more noticeable in the city than in country areas and affected mostly younger women.

At the same time, organisations that promoted and protected traditional values of women in the home also grew. These included the Country Women's Association and temperance societies, which agitated to reduce alcohol usage and to maintain the limited hotel opening hours set during the war.

Image and culture

One symbol of the Roaring Twenties was the 'flapper', the young woman freed from traditional social values by her access to education, employment, consumer goods and entertainment. American women were the first to experience the era of the 'flapper' and the trend came to urban Australia through the cinema.

As in the United States, Australian women's dresses became shorter and less restrictive, reaching just below the knee (they had reached just above the ankle during the war) to reveal bare calves. Women wore more comfortable and practical shoes. Women's dress and behaviour reflected changes in independence and more relaxed social attitudes. Some people condemned aspects of the changes, such as women smoking in public, as a lowering of moral standards. A rhyme from a Sydney magazine, *Triad*, in March 1925 included the humorous but moralistic poem:

'Half an inch, half an inch, half an inch shorter,
The skirts are the same for mother and daughter,
When the wind blows each of them shows,
Half an inch, half an inch, more than she oughter.'

Women were also more able to be active outdoors. Mixed bathing, or swimming, had caused public disapproval up until the end of the war, but gradually became commonplace at popular beaches. Women played tennis and golf and went cycling – there were even women's football teams. The restrictions of the Victorian age were slowly being cast aside.

The 1920s saw greater social freedom for women, including the increasing popularity of sea bathing.

A hidden world

But there was a hidden world in Australia, a world of urban slums, of high unemployment, of a low basic wage and of destitute people. Houses in working class areas of the capital cities were often old, crowded, dilapidated, poorly ventilated and rat-infested, with poor water supplies and no electricity. They had outdoor toilets with waste pans buzzing with blowflies. Children were malnourished and filthy from playing in rubbish-strewn lanes and streets full of horse manure and dog poo. Diseases thrived in these conditions. Many factories were nearly as bad. The Roaring Twenties were certainly not glamorous and liberating for everyone.

A kerosene tin and kerosene lamp. Electricity was available only to some communities in the 1920s. Kerosene was the main fuel used for lamps in many inner city houses and in the country.

ECONOMIC POLICY AND CHANGES

The period from Federation in 1901 to the outbreak of the First World War in 1914 had generally been a time of economic growth. Australia was sometimes called the 'working man's paradise', until the war caused wages to fall and the cost of living to rise. The 1920s and early 1930s were decades of stagnation and even economic decline. In terms of buying power, wages did not return to pre-1915 levels until the late 1930s. The unemployment rate had averaged 5 to 6 per cent for most years between 1901 and 1920. It was never below 7 per cent and was usually at least 9 per cent during the 1920s.

Men, money, markets

The economic policies that governments pursued in the 1920s to try to bring Australia out of its postwar stagnation are often described by the phrase 'men, money, and markets', a slogan created in 1923 by Nationalist Party Prime Minister Stanley Melbourne Bruce.

Australia's Commonwealth and state governments believed that the nation needed to increase its population. This could be by natural births but also by planned immigration. The governments preferred that immigration to be British, in keeping with Australia's cultural heritage and social composition. They set about working with the British Government to establish schemes that assisted immigrants to come to Australia.

The states would tell the Commonwealth how many immigrants they could take, and the Commonwealth would pay the cost of bringing the migrants out. Under the *Empire Settlement Act 1922*, the British Government would also help subsidise the cost of this immigration. The states would then take responsibility for finding the immigrants work or settling them on the land, on farms, which were bought with money loaned by the Commonwealth.

The expected result was an increase in both primary production and the export of these products, mainly to Britain. This in turn would create wealth within Australia as the immigrant families spent the export income locally. Whole new productive rural communities would develop around these farms and contribute to the population, wealth and national development of Australia.

Among the immigrants brought from Britain were thousands of children – supposedly orphans being sent to a better life and future, but in many cases the children of single mothers who were pressured to give them up, or who did not know that their children had been sent to Australia. Many of these children were sent to special working farms in Western Australia and New South Wales, where they were made to work without pay. Many were also abused by the people in whose care they were placed. Most of these orphans were denied affection and love, and suffered emotionally. In 2009 Australian Prime Minister Kevin Rudd included these children in his formal apology to the 'Forgotten Australians' – children who were placed in institutions as a result of government policies.

Immigration was an expensive process – the immigrants needed to be sent to Australia by ship and then have farmland made available to them through loans. Other loan money was used to develop rural infrastructure – roads, railways, dams and electricity lines. This sort

Promotional poster for the Better Farming Train, an agricultural demonstration train that toured Victoria to promote better farming practices. Designed by Percy Trompf around 1935.

Poster designed by Frederick Herrick for the Empire Marketing Board. The board was established by the British Government to promote the products of the British Empire within the United Kingdom. 1929.

of development had great social benefits but did not bring in immediate income that could be used to repay the loans.

By the end of the 1920s, Australia seemed to be certain about how it wanted to develop economically. The 1920s was a decade of increased economic growth, from 1 per cent in the 1910s to 3.3 per cent in the 1920s. However, the 'men, money and markets' description of economic policies at this time was not the real cause of this growth.

There was a fourth element in government policies that resulted in the greatest growth: the widespread protection of Australian industries, especially manufacturing industries. Under 'protection' policies, internationally produced goods that competed against local manufactures had a tariff (or tax) placed on them to make them more expensive. This made the goods manufactured in Australia more competitive and therefore more likely to be bought by local people. This would help to keep Australian factories profitable and able to employ local workers. This is where the growth in the economy was occurring, but it was an area that was about to come crashing down as the world started to enter a huge depression.

THE COMING OF THE GREAT DEPRESSION

The Wall Street stock exchange crash

The worldwide economic depression of the early 1930s is usually thought to have started with the New York Wall Street stock market crash on 24 October 1929.

On that day, the value of shares suddenly started to fall and panic selling began. After only a few hours of trading, many share owners had suffered catastrophic losses. These losses then spread through the rest of the developed world like ripples from a stone thrown in a pond.

People had borrowed money to invest in shares; in effect to buy a part of a company, in the expectation that the company would produce them wealth through profits. By 1929, the value of the shares exceeded the real value of what many of the companies could produce.

When this was realised, people started trying to sell their shares, which pushed the prices of the shares down until many became virtually worthless. People and companies who had borrowed money to buy the shares still had to repay their loans, even though the shares were no longer earning income. Those who still had money to invest stopped doing so, as they could not get profit from their investment. Australia was hit hard by this stopping of investment and erosion of the value of capital investment.

Weaknesses in the Australian economy

In Australia, the economy had shown itself to be in a vulnerable state from as early as 1927. Australian export prices for its main primary products (wool and wheat) had been falling, largely because the new European nations created after the Treaty of Versailles were now growing their own food and no longer needed to import as much from Australia. Added to this was the failure of the rural migrant settlement and soldier settlement schemes.

Rural migrant settlement and soldier settlement schemes

Most of the new British immigrants arriving under the 'men, money and markets' scheme implemented from 1925 were from cities, and were not familiar with farming practices. Many of those on the soldier settlement blocks, established after the First World War to benefit returning servicemen, also knew nothing about farming – some were even physically incapable of doing it due to their war wounds.

The settlers and their families had to start from scratch. Often there were no homes on the land, and the land itself had to be cleared of timber, which was difficult, time-consuming work. As a result, the settlers' lives were primitive, hard and demoralising.

The farms were generally too small to be economically viable – the farmers could not grow enough to pay off their debts. The interest payments on the original loans were

Soldier settlers had to make do. A rough stool made by Harry Newman for his soldier-settler farm at Narrogin, Western Australia, in 1922.

higher than the farmers' income, so people could not acquire sufficient capital to spend on improving the land and to get themselves out of debt.

By 1929, about one third of the settlers had given up and simply walked off their farms with nothing. Eventually, this meant that some of those who remained could take over the abandoned blocks to try to create an economically viable unit, but the schemes as a whole were expensive and crushing financial failures – for the individual and for the government.

Agriculture and manufacturing

During this era, many established and successful Australian farmers also had reduced incomes because they were selling less overseas, but still had to repay loans taken out from banks to help them build up their farms.

Manufacturing had also depended heavily upon borrowed investment funds, as well as large tariffs on imports to make the goods competitive. Local manufacturers couldn't export their goods because they were too expensive to produce and their prices weren't competitive overseas. When the governments started sacking people from public works programs, the unemployed people stopped buying the manufactured goods, which in turn led to private manufacturers cutting down on staff numbers. As a result, there was less government income from taxation but the government still had to pay a substantial amount of its revenue back to the overseas lenders. This meant it had little money to use within Australia.

Public works and infrastructure

State and Commonwealth governments had also borrowed heavily from overseas to fund public works programs. These building projects were valuable socially, but they did not themselves generate income back to the governments, which still had to repay the loan money that had gone into creating them. The governments had to stop the programs and sack the workers.

Wool remained a major economic resource, but the adoption of new transportation technology took time.

This vicious spiral of economic depression started in 1929 and reached its worst in 1932, before the situation slowly started to improve. Hundreds of thousands of Australians were hit extremely hard during this period.

THE DEPRESSION EXPERIENCE

Unemployment

The social effects of the Great Depression were catastrophic for many Australians.

At the peak of the Depression in 1932, about 30 per cent of workers were unemployed. In 1933, more than half of all breadwinners were earning less than the basic wage (£3 per week):12 per cent of family breadwinners earned no money, about 25 per cent earned less than £1 per week and 17 per cent earned £2 per week. A minority of the unemployed were out of work for long periods of time, though most were unemployed for relatively short periods.

Young adults were more likely to be unemployed, as the last ones to start work were usually the first to be sacked, but they also tended to have fewer dependants than older people, and so were usually better able to deal with the experience. Because women were paid slightly more than half the male rate in most jobs, they were less likely to be made unemployed during the Depression period. However, if women did become unemployed, they were not eligible to receive sustenance payments from the government.

The manufacturing states of South Australia, New South Wales and Victoria were hit harder by the Depression than the others, all of which had a greater percentage of people in rural occupations. Unemployment was higher among the unskilled industrial workers in inner suburbs in building, furniture-making and engineering jobs, and lower in most country areas. However, mining was very hard hit during the period.

Initially, there were no government schemes to help the unemployed (except in Queensland), so people had to rely on charity and assistance from their communities, such as family, neighbours or their church.

Many families had trouble buying sufficient food or clothing, or enough fuel to heat their houses. Most people, whether in the city or the country, and whether they owned or rented their home, had small vegetable patches. Many kept chickens for eggs and had fruit trees in their backyards.

Some families fell behind on their rent or mortgage repayments and found themselves in debt and evicted onto the streets. These destitute families might then go to a 'shanty town', a place in a park or wasteland of the major cities where unemployed and homeless people lived in tents or huts made from scrap items.

Sometimes a family's father or eldest son would go 'on the wallaby' – that is, take to bush roads as swagmen, wandering from town to town, trying to find work or handouts from farmers along the way. They could claim a food voucher if they had travelled a certain distance, thus making sure they kept moving. Up to 30,000 men did this. Families were put under great strain as men struggled to fulfil their role as breadwinners, and women had to try to help both the husband and the children to survive.

Unemployment had been high for most of the 1920s, so it was common for poorer people to suffer periodic bouts of job loss in that time. Because many people had some experience of unemployment leading up to the Depression, they had developed strategies for survival that they could draw on as the economy grew worse. These strategies involved depending on a supportive network of family members, neighbours, friends or fellow church-goers who were able to help during the tough times. For some there was also support available through trade union assistance. Therefore, when the Depression hit, people who had periodical experience of unemployment were initially more ready for it and better able to persevere through it than those for whom unemployment was a totally new experience.

Opposite and on following page: This dress was made by Patricia Worthington's parents for her to wear at a local fancy dress party in Heidelberg, Victoria, when Patricia was about eight years old. The prize for the best costume was cash, and Patricia's parents planned to buy shoes for her if she won. Her mother made the dress out of an old curtain, and her father decorated it with leftover oil-based household paints. Patricia explained that the dress was not just decorative, but to act as an advertisement for her father and his fellow unemployed: 'The dress was my father's hope not only for himself but for all his friends and people that were needing work. If he could in some way help others as well as himself, it was all he wanted. I think by painting this dress he was more or less putting himself in the place of all of these jobs, thinking that he could do it or someone close by could do them, and hopefully that somebody might see it as an advertisement to work if they needed it.'

The majority of those who lost their jobs were working class, but the middle and upper classes were also affected. For some, it was a matter of reassessing budgets and lifestyles and sacrificing luxuries. Others found their investments failing or formerly thriving businesses barely surviving.

One cartoon in the New South Wales *The Bulletin* newspaper in 1932 put it simply, showing a shopkeeper standing in front of shelves empty of food, talking to a customer. The customer asks: 'How's business?' The shopkeeper replies: 'Crook! Even the people who never pay have stopped buying!' In these cases, people who had once lived very comfortably suddenly found themselves without an income and vulnerable to the same hardships as others around them.

Assistance for the unemployed

Those most affected by unemployment could get relief in three ways: through charity, government support, and group and individual action.

Charity

At the start of the Depression, only Queensland had a government scheme to support the unemployed, so in most areas of Australia early relief measures were undertaken by private charities. Large organisations such as the Salvation Army provided assistance, as did civic-minded individuals.

Often a moralistic judgement was applied to determine whether an individual was worthy of relief: to receive assistance, a person needed to be sober, industrious, clean and not suffering unemployment from any fault of their own. Those who were judged to have contributed to their own distress by their drinking, gambling, laziness or moral slackness would not be given help.

Charities tried hard but were quickly overwhelmed by the sheer number of people asking for support. Often their systems failed – charities generally only handed out food parcels, clothing or vouchers for food and supplies, and did not cover such things as rent or mortgage payments. Given the hardships of that time, it came as no surprise that these relief systems were open to exploitation – unemployed people might move from charity to charity, gathering something from each; shopkeepers might short-weigh the amount of food given for a voucher.

There was also private charity provided by individual philanthropists who might set up soup kitchens, make deliveries of firewood to houses, or hold Christmas parties for the unemployed.

Government relief schemes

Governments were forced to take over basic relief once unemployment started to soar in 1930. One approach was to provide food relief parcels, which later took the form of coupons. Food rations were often demeaning to people, providing them, for example, with the very cheapest cuts of meat. In January 1931, there was a large food riot in Adelaide with the unemployed demanding beef rather than mutton as part of the food ration. The government did not provide coupons for rent, heating and lighting, debts, mortgage, shoes or clothing.

Sport and the Depression

Sport was an important part of Australian identity. The 1930s were the period of the incomparable batsman Don Bradman, and the champion racehorse Phar Lap. Both were Australian favourites and provided people with the thrill of being winners despite the melancholy and hardship of the Depression. Many Australians mourned the apparently suspicious death of Phar Lap in the United States. The unsportsmanlike 'bodyline' bowling of the visiting England test cricket team between 2 December 1932 and 28 February 1933, designed to defeat Bradman's brilliance by bludgeoning him with head and body blows, created passionate hostility towards the English team among spectators.

The controversy peaked during the third Test at the Adelaide Oval. Australian captain

Legendary Australian cricketer Don Bradman.

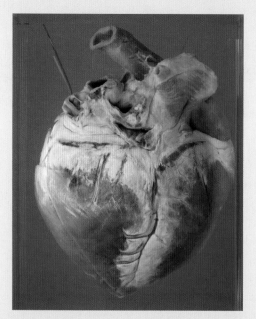

Phar Lap's heart, which is kept in the National Museum of Australia. Phar Lap's heart weighs 6.35 kilograms, which is significantly larger than an average horse heart of three to four kilograms.

Bill Woodfull was felled by a blow to the heart, almost provoking a riot. After Woodfull was dismissed, the English team manager came to privately express his sympathy. Woodfull refused to speak to him, saying 'There are two teams out there. One is playing cricket and the other is not.'

After another Australian player suffered a fractured skull, the Australian Cricket Board formally complained to the English cricket administrators. This led to threats of a trade boycott and a tour cancellation, so the Australian board had to retract its criticism. The sporting public did not have to diplomatically withdraw – one wit in the crowd at a cricket test, watching the English captain Douglas Jardine brushing away flies as he fielded, yelled out, 'You leave our bloody flies alone, Jardine!'

Dole and 'susso'

Governments provided relief in the form of dole payments, which were coupons that could be exchanged for food and other necessities. State governments also introduced sustenance payments known as the 'susso', which offered very little income. These were in return for work on public projects, such as building new roads, railway tracks and public buildings. Men were selected for this work according to need; married men with children got the most work. However, each job was usually for only a short period, often less than a week.

Work camps

Unemployment or underemployment meant that there were many young men who simply didn't have enough to do to fill their days, and felt that there was little hope of improving their situation in the near future. Some of these men were sent to camps in remote country areas, where the men worked as timber cutters. Others were given opportunities to become gold seekers. From the government's point of view, these policies removed potentially troublesome or disruptive young men from cities, where they might cause trouble or be recruited by political radicals who saw the Depression as a chance to promote their revolutionary ideas.

Group strategies

The unemployed also fought for the improvement of their living and working conditions, particularly in regards to government relief works. There were strikes in Western Australia, riots in Cairns and in Adelaide, a rent strike in Sydney, demonstrations in Darwin, and deputations (delegates appointed to communicate the needs of a group) in multiple locations.

Such protests were often supported by the Unemployed Workers' Union, a political group that formed to help the unemployed, and that hoped to gain their support in challenging and changing the capitalist system of the economy. In many cases the Communist Party also helped organise the unrest, as they saw the Depression as a way to recruit large numbers of disaffected and suffering people to their cause. As part of this strategy, they supported and assisted people who were resisting eviction.

Individual action

Unemployed people developed their own ways of coping with the Depression. Those who could not pay their rent often did 'a midnight flit': they would pack up and leave during the night, and move into a new place. One joke claimed that every time the members of a constantly unemployed family walked into their backyard, their chooks lay on their backs and stuck their legs up to be roped, indicating they were ready to be taken to their next house. Some property owners were happy to let tenants stay on without paying rent, as this meant the property was not empty and would not be invaded by 'squatters'.

The unemployed often helped themselves by making things to sell, growing vegetables, doing odd jobs for money or food, or breaking into railway yards to steal coal for fires. Some people resorted to begging or stealing. All these were ways by which the unemployed tried to ease their situation and, wherever possible, assert their independence and retain some dignity.

ECONOMIC PLANS

Many different economic policies were put forward to help solve the problem of the Depression. Governments (state and federal), political parties, businesses, unions, economists and ordinary individuals all tried to come up with plans that they believed could ease the financial burden and pressure it caused.

Government options

At the beginning of the Depression, the task of creating an economic solution fell to the Australian Labor Party Government, which had been elected in September 1929 and was led by Prime Minister James Scullin and Treasurer Edward Granville Theodore.

The Labor Government wanted to continue funding policies that created employment and that helped the victims of unemployment, but as unemployment started to grow and the prices of exports continued to fall, there was less money available for them to use in these ways.

The government tried to increase wealth by cutting imports and encouraging farmers to grow more, thereby making more produce available for export and reducing Australia's dependence on imports. But, as other countries were also struggling with the Depression, the export price of primary products continued to fall. Even though Australia was exporting more, it was still earning less. The government faced an enormous problem: how to manage the economy with what was available. Three options stood out: the Niemeyer Plan, the Theodore Plan and the Lang Plan.

A political handbill, urging a vote against the Lang Labor Government and for former Labor Treasurer Joseph Lyons, leader of the United Australia Party. The handbill stresses financial responsibility.

The Niemeyer Plan – spend less

Most economists of the day believed 'deflation' was the answer. Deflation meant reducing government costs and spending less in order to balance the government's budget.

The economists argued that Australia's standard of living was too high and that Australians were living beyond their means. The government therefore had to cut back on spending, which would lead to income (money coming in) and expenditure (money going out) becoming balanced over time. Ordinary life could resume, but at a lower and more affordable standard. The initial burden of these cuts would be borne by working people, whose wages and government support had to be reduced for this approach to work.

This plan was associated with the Bank of England's representative, Sir Otto Niemeyer, who came to Australia in 1930 to advise the state and federal governments on what they should do. Britain had provided most of the loan money that Australia relied on, so it was in the Bank of England's interest to influence how Australian governments solved the problem.

The Niemeyer Plan was put into effect in August 1930 through the Melbourne Agreement between the Commonwealth and the state premiers. Under this plan, governments would balance their budgets by reducing the amount of spending on public programs (leading to more unemployment), stop borrowing money from overseas (which had to be paid back with interest), and cut pay rates set by the Commonwealth Court of Conciliation and Arbitration. All this would cause pain, but once spending matched income, governments could start borrowing and spending again to create more jobs.

In June 1931, the states all agreed to continue these cuts through the Premiers' Plan. This involved reducing government spending, including workers' pay and pensions by 20 per cent, increasing taxation, reducing bank interest rates, and reducing interest on money already loaned to governments. This was supposed to share the burden of dealing with the Depression among all classes.

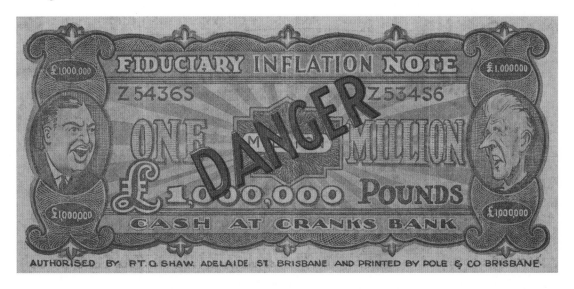

Although the state governments had agreed to this, many politicians soon changed their minds and started calling for an increase in spending, not a decrease. In New South Wales, the Australian Labor Party under Jack Lang gained power in 1931. Lang had initially agreed with the Premiers' Plan, but then refused to implement it in New South Wales.

The Theodore Plan – spend more

The Niemeyer Plan also worried the Commonwealth Labor Government Treasurer, Edward (Ted) Theodore. He had been forced to stand down as treasurer while he was investigated for his possible involvement in a mining scandal in the 1920s when he had been premier of Queensland. As soon as he was reinstated as treasurer, Theodore immediately proposed an alternative plan – one of inflation rather than deflation.

Theodore believed the government should spend more money so as to stimulate the economy and create jobs. The Commonwealth would obtain this money by lowering the value of the Australian pound against the British pound. The British pound would therefore be able to buy more for the same cost, which would lead to higher demand for Australia's now-cheaper primary products. This would result in a rise in sales, meaning that manufacturers could employ people to make more goods to meet overseas demand. Theodore also wanted the Commonwealth Bank to print and issue more money, which would be available as loans to producers, who could expand and employ a higher number of people.

But Theodore was not able to implement his plan. The Labor Government did not have the support of enough senators to pass the Act of Parliament needed to create a change in the rate of exchange. It was also opposed by the Commonwealth Bank, which was independent of the Australian Government and which also supported the deflationary approach of Niemeyer. The bank refused to print the additional money to be made available to lenders.

The Theodore plan split the Labor Government: five Labor members who supported the deflationary approach, led by Joseph Lyons, resigned and joined with the opposition Nationalist Party to form a new party, the United Australia Party. This party would defeat the Labor Government in December 1931.

Another group of members of the Commonwealth Labor Government also split from the main group. They were known as the Lang Labor group and were the supporters of the third plan of the time, which was put forward by the Labor Premier of New South Wales, Jack Lang.

The Lang Plan – put local people first

Lang supported the inflationary approach of Theodore, namely to spend more money, not less. However, Lang's plan differed from Theodore's as he wanted to spend all the money in the Australian economy on Australians first. His NSW Government would only repay its overseas loans to Britain once the Australian economy had improved. The cost of recovery would be borne by the British money-lenders rather than Australian workers and pensioners. Lang also believed that the British should lower their interest rates on the loans, just as the United States had reduced the interest rates Britain had to pay that country.

Lang's policies appealed to many people, but his many critics believed it was extremely dangerous. They argued that because overseas lenders would not get their money back, nobody would ever loan money to Australia again. Lang's plan created both passionate opposition and passionate support, and on occasions led to extreme reactions.

POLITICAL REACTIONS TO THE DEPRESSION

Premier Lang and the New Guard

The Depression worldwide saw the rise of fascist political groups – extreme anti-democratic nationalists who believed in a strong central government with no opposing political parties. Fascists usually supported capitalism and opposed communism. The fascist movement was especially powerful in Italy, where Benito Mussolini was dictator from 1925, and in Germany, where the Nazis (National Socialist German Workers' Party) under Adolf Hitler was to come to power in 1933. There was also a strong fascist movement in Britain led by Sir Oswald Mosley, but it did not gain political power.

Metal matchbox holder titled 'Two Champions'. It shows the much-loved and much-hated NSW Premier Jack Lang on one side. The other side shows a jockey on a racehorse.

A form of extremism that was close to or sympathetic to fascism was also present in Australia, where several political groups formed to oppose Labor governments. These included the All For Australia League in New South Wales and the Vigilantes in Queensland. Political action by these groups was mostly peaceful and democratic. However, one group known as the New Guard did seem to be ready to overthrow the government if it felt it had to.

The New Guard

The New Guard began in New South Wales in 1932, in response to Lang's political victory in 1931 and his economic plan. While Lang's supporters believed that his policies focused on protecting the working people's interest, his opponents, including the New Guard, saw them as a threat to good government, order, stability and what they saw as the Australian way.

The New Guard consisted of about 40,000 members. It was composed of former First World War servicemen and led by a businessman, lawyer and decorated former army officer, Eric Campbell. Campbell believed that Premier Lang's repudiation of debts – that is, his unwillingness to repay the government's debts on overseas loans until the local economy was stable – would result in the rest of the world losing confidence in Australia and refusing to loan more money. Campbell called on old friends to gather and drill with weapons, ready to take over if the Lang Government continued to behave in what they believed was an irresponsible manner.

Between 1931 and 1932, the New Guard sent members to public meetings held by communists and left-wing supporters of Lang, broke up the meetings and attacked the speakers and their supporters. They even had a plan to kidnap Premier Lang and other cabinet ministers while at the same time taking control of radio stations, electricity supply stations, telephone exchanges, public transport and banks, and holding them until their vision of a new and legitimate government could be established or elected.

Opening the Sydney Harbour Bridge

The most public moment for the New Guard was at the opening of the Sydney Harbour Bridge on 19 March 1932. A New Guard member and former First World War soldier, Francis de Groot, slipped into the official party. Uniformed and mounted on a horse, de Groot charged up and sliced the ribbon for the iconic new symbol with his military sword, declaring the bridge opened in the name of 'all the decent and respectable people of New South Wales'. De Groot was dragged from his horse and taken to a nearby police station. He was found guilty of behaving in an offensive manner, and fined £5 with £4 costs. Meanwhile, officials knotted the ribbon together and Premier Lang used special commemorative scissors to cut the ribbon and open the bridge.

A memento of the opening of the Sydney Harbour Bridge.

Defeat of Lang

As was his promise, Premier Lang started defaulting on loan payments to Britain in 1931 and 1932. The Australian Government stepped in and made those payments and then demanded the money back from the NSW Government. But Lang refused, and in doing so broke the law. He was dismissed from office in May 1932 by the Governor of New South Wales, Sir Philip Game.

At the election a month later, the Labor Government suffered a huge and widespread swing of votes against it, losing 15 per cent of its previous votes, and 31 of its 55 seats in parliament. The new conservative United Australia Party–Country Party coalition government resumed paying the state's international debt obligations. The New Guard lost its main purpose for existing and quickly faded away, taking with it the threat of violent revolution or even civil war in Australia.

Unrest in country areas

There was also deep dissatisfaction in northern Queensland and the northern and Riverina areas of New South Wales with the way the economic crisis of the Depression was being handled.

Many communities and business leaders in these areas believed that they could be more prosperous if they separated from the rest of the existing state and formed their own states.

New Guard member Francis de Groot beating Premier Lang to cut the ribbon to open the Sydney Harbour Bridge.

They were not threatening to do this by force, but by legal means under the Australian Constitution.

Western Australia went even further, and in 1933 two-thirds of the state's electors voted to secede from the rest of Australia and form their own nation. This would have required the British Parliament to alter the Australian Constitution, which it would never do without the Australian Parliament's approval. The Australian Parliament would, in turn, never put such a request, so secession was never a realistic possibility. However, the dissatisfaction expressed by these areas showed their sense of alienation from the eastern states. Eventually the secession movements faded away as the economic recovery continued from 1933.

RECOVERY

By 1933, the economy slowly began to recover as businesses started to employ more people, and governments were able to balance their budgets and start spending again.

Manufacturing

Every plan put forward to solve the problems of the Depression assumed that Australia would be brought out of economic decline when primary exports increased and their prices recovered.

The Australian Government tried to help this by immediately adopting the Ottawa Agreement of 1932, under which Australia and the other Commonwealth countries of Britain, Canada, South Africa and New Zealand agreed to reduce import tariffs on British manufactured goods in return for Britain not imposing the tariffs on primary products from those countries. Tariffs would be imposed on goods imported from other countries. This attempt by Commonwealth countries to preference each other's trade at the cost of other nations' trade did not help much as primary prices remained low. In fact, it led to a reaction by European countries, the United States and especially Japan, who objected to the policy and found other suppliers for their wheat and wool.

The real generator of recovery was manufacturing. The Premiers' Plan of 1931 cut wages, which made businesses more profitable and so allowed employers in manufacturing industries to re-employ workers. This meant more Australians had money to spend, which provided stimulus and growth. As money started to circulate, overseas lenders regained some confidence and saw the possibility of profits. As a result, loan monies began to flow into Australia again. Governments could start spending more as their income taxation revenue from workers increased.

One example of this resumption by the government of public works was the building of the Hume Dam in Victoria. Completed in 1936, the dam opened up new areas to irrigation and therefore increased crop yields and sales, and spending in the area.

Governments also started restoring the wage cuts of 1931, enabling wages to rise, which allowed people to spend more money. As Australians spent more, production increased, more jobs were available, and income started to go up rather than down as in the worst years of the Depression. However, despite the great economic improvement in 1933, the rate of unemployment remained at about 10 per cent for the rest of the decade. Indeed, the event that would restore full employment did not come until 1939 – the start of another world war.

AUSTRALIA IN 1938

150th anniversary celebrations

The 26th of January 1938 marked the 150th anniversary, or sesquicentenary, of Australia's foundation as a British colony. All the states celebrated this, but the main focus and greatest enthusiasm was in Sydney.

There, the celebrations started with a re-enactment of the landing of Governor Arthur Phillip at Sydney Cove. The landing was shown as being peaceful: 26 Aboriginal re-enactors brought in from western New South Wales followed the official script and meekly accepted the invasion – even though that was not really the way it happened in 1788.

There was then a procession of 120 floats depicting aspects of the theme 'March to Nationhood'. The floats showed such historical events as the crossing of the Blue Mountains and the discovery of gold. Floats also represented major industries: wool, wheat, dairy. The floats were all motorised, symbolising the increasing place of the car in Australian society. The procession was filmed and later shown in cinemas across the nation.

Part of the celebration included a London to Melbourne air race. The first to arrive were the British aviators Charles Scott and Tom Black (with a flying time of 71 hours), but the winner on

Parade float in the sesquicentenary celebrations in Sydney, 26 January 1938.

handicap – taking into account the different sizes of the planes – was a Dutch team with a flying time of 90 hours. They had become lost near the Victorian–New South Wales border town of Albury. A quick-thinking engineer switched the town street lights on and off to signal the name of the city in Morse code to the crew. A fleet of local cars rushed to the race grounds, and lined up with their headlights on to illuminate an emergency landing strip. The plane landed, was bogged in mud but eventually recovered to fly the last leg of the victorious flight to Melbourne.

There were also omissions from the celebrations. These were as significant as the inclusions. There was no convict float – Australia's convict past was considered a 'stain' to be hidden rather than acknowledged. There were no interstate floats included – 26 January was not widely celebrated in the other states, although all the state premiers attended. There was no float for the Labour movement – its celebrations were kept for May Day rather than Australia Day. Catholics joined in official prayers, but they preferred to focus on their own celebratory St Patrick's Day events in March. Though there were Aboriginal people on the first float, depicting life before European contact, there were no acknowledgements of the second-class citizenship that was the reality for most Aboriginal and Torres Strait Islander people in 1938. The 26th of January 1938 marked the first 'day of mourning' for Aboriginal and Torres Strait Islander peoples.

Aboriginal and Torres Strait Islander Australians

The position of Aboriginal and Torres Strait Islander people had not improved during the 1920s and 1930s. Many were under the rigid control of Protection Boards, who saw it as their responsibility to oversee the way Indigenous people lived their lives. Men who were able to find jobs mostly worked as unskilled and seasonal labourers, while women usually worked as low-paid domestic servants.

A group of Indigenous women and children at the Hermannsburg Mission, Northern Territory. 1923. Photograph taken by Herbert Basedow.

Educational opportunities were limited. Aboriginal and Torres Strait Islander people stayed largely isolated on the fringes of country towns, or in a few slum areas of the main cities. Some people in remote Queensland, Western Australia, Northern Territory and South Australia retained their traditional culture and were largely unaffected by European influences. However, many were starting to be influenced by missionaries, who provided food, medical care and even some education to the residents, as well as providing them with Christian teaching.

Violent conflict and even massacres still occurred: there may have been a mass killing in the Kimberley in Western Australia in 1926, though the evidence for this is not certain. At least 26 Aboriginal men, women and children were killed near Coniston Station in the Northern Territory by a returned Anzac, Constable George Murray, and his reprisal party of local settlers. The number of deaths was almost certainly far higher than Murray admitted, but there were no independent witnesses to establish the full facts. A special inquiry cleared Murray, finding that he acted in self-defence against attacks and that he was justified in trying to apprehend people who were resisting arrest. Critics remained unconvinced and believed that a massacre was being officially covered up, and even supported, by the government.

In 1927, when the Australian Parliament moved from Melbourne to Canberra, two Aboriginal men, Jimmy Clements and John Noble, were present at the outdoor ceremony. Clements, also known as 'King Billy', was initially told to move on by police because of his scruffy appearance, but members of the crowd objected and both Clements and Noble stayed. They were the first Indigenous Australians to enter Parliament House and to be in the presence of the Duke and Duchess of York (later King George VI and Queen Elizabeth, parents of Queen Elizabeth II).

By 1938, when the sesquicentenary celebration floats processed through Sydney's streets, there was little evidence of the original Australians to be seen. However, as the floats passed near Australian Hall, about 100 people were engaged in a highly significant and alternative symbolic act. This was the Aboriginal Conference for a Day of Mourning and Protest, the start of a call for equal citizenship rights for Aboriginal and Torres Strait Islander people. A resolution was passed unanimously by the predominantly Aboriginal representatives there:

'We, representing the Aborigines of Australia, assembled in conference at the Australian Hall, Sydney, on the 26th day of January, 1938, this being the 150th Anniversary of the Whiteman's seizure of our country, hereby make protest against the callous treatment of our people by the whitemen during the past 150 years, and we appeal to the Australian nation of today to make new laws for the education and care of Aborigines, we ask for a new policy which will raise our people to full citizen status and equality within the community.'

President of the Aborigines Progressive Association Jack Patten, as quoted in the *Abo Call*, April 1938

The representatives produced a statement, 'Aboriginal Claim Citizenship Rights', which was presented to Prime Minister Joseph Lyons.

Anzac Day

There was much criticism that there was only one Anzac float in the sesquicentenary procession on 26 January 1938, and an unimpressive one at that. However, 25 April, Anzac Day, was chosen as the end of the official sesquicentenary celebrations. On that date, the truly national 'Australia Day' became obvious as the whole nation commemorated the sacrifices and achievements of the soldiers and nurses in the war that had ended only 20 years earlier.

In 1938, approximately one in every ten living Australian adult males was an ex-serviceman, and together with over 1800 ex-nurses they numbered around 227,380 people. Communities all over the country commemorated that dawn landing at Gallipoli in 1915, usually at their local war memorial. Then the soldiers and nurses marched. Fifteen hundred marched in Hobart; over 3000 in Perth; nearly 4000 in Brisbane; in Adelaide 6650 bemedalled veterans marched through heavy rain; in Melbourne over 22,000. The largest march was in Sydney, where 43,000 men and women marched.

The number of Sydney and Melbourne marchers together was only slightly more than the number of Australian men who had died in the war – which would soon be swelled by those of another generation who were about to face the challenge and tragedy of the Second World War.

Australia and the Second World War

Australia's participation in the Second World War was an 'all in' effort on the war front and the home front. Thirty thousand men and women were killed or died during their service. The nation developed industrially, women's roles and status improved dramatically, and Australia was set for a postwar boom.

One of the midget Japanese submarines destroyed during their attack on ships in Sydney Harbour, 1942.

CAUSES OF THE WAR

In 1919 the victors of the First World War imposed a punitive peace treaty on Germany, known as the Treaty of Versailles. The treaty compelled Germany to reduce its army and navy, pay reparations to other countries affected by the war and give up control of many colonies and territories. This damaged Germany's economy, creating a sense of injustice and resentment among the German people.

During the 1930s, Germany worked to overturn the treaty. Its new leader, Adolf Hitler, re-introduced conscription and rebuilt the German air force from 1935 onwards. In March 1938, Hitler's troops peacefully entered Austria after the Austrian Government had been forced by the German Government to invite them. Austria became part of Germany. Then in September 1938, Hitler forced the Czechoslovakian Government to hand over German-speaking areas, under threat of invasion.

Isolationism and appeasement

Germany's actions were not immediately challenged by the rest of the world. The

FUND FOR THE RELIEF OF POLISH VICTIMS OF THE WAR.

HON. MR. T. A. WELCH, IMPL. RUSSIAN CONSUL
TREAS.: SIR THOMAS HUGHES, M.L.C.
HON. GEORGE EARP, M.L.C.
8 SPRING ST., SYDNEY.

The Homeless Women and Children of Poland are Far........ but need they be Far from Your Hearts? PRAY HELP US TO HELP THEM!

PRESIDENT:
THE CHIEF JUSTICE, HON. SIR WM. CULLEN, K.C.M.G.
HON. SECRETARIES: MRS. GEORGE EARP. MR. C. G. DERKENNE.

A postcard created to promote funding for the homeless women and children of Poland. There were many home front organisations formed to help victims of the war.

United States had become isolationist, meaning it avoided participating in international affairs. Britain and France were too weak to stop Germany. Many political leaders also believed that Germany was justified in breaking some of the harsh elements of the Treaty of Versailles. British Prime Minister Neville Chamberlain was prepared to do almost anything to avoid another war. Britain's policy was called appeasement – giving concessions to an aggressor in return for peace.

The German claim to Czechoslovakia finally provoked international action. In September 1938, the leaders of the four main European powers – Prime Minister Neville Chamberlain of Britain, President Édouard Daladier of France, Prime Minister Benito Mussolini of Italy and Chancellor Adolf Hitler of Germany – met in Munich, Germany. Germany was given the right to occupy the Sudetenland in Czechoslovakia, an area with a mostly German population. Prime Minister Chamberlain returned to Britain declaring that he had achieved 'peace with honour . . . peace in our time'.

Many people in Australia, and the Australian Government, supported the policy of appeasement. They remembered very clearly the devastation of the previous war, which had finished only 20 years earlier. Chamberlain was momentarily a hero.

Invasion of Poland and declaration of war

The peace was short-lived. In March 1939 Germany forced the government to hand over the remainder of Czechoslovakia, or be invaded. Germany invaded Poland on 1 September 1939 and Britain threatened to declare war if the troops were not withdrawn. The German troops remained and Britain declared war on 3 September.

The USSR

Germany was not the only country attempting to expand its territories. Following the Bolshevik Revolution of 1917, Russia and its remaining territories had formed the Union of Soviet Socialist Republics (known as the USSR or Soviet Union). In August 1939, the Soviet Union and Germany had secretly drawn up a non-aggression pact, an agreement that they would not fight each other or aid one another's enemies. The Soviet Union invaded Poland on 17 September and attacked Finland on 30 November 1939. The United States, still committed to neutrality, took no action.

AUSTRALIA ENTERS THE WAR

The Australian Government had also followed the developing European crisis, and was willing to participate. On Sunday night, 3 September 1939, Prime Minister Robert Gordon Menzies broadcast to his fellow Australians on radio stations across the country that it was his 'melancholy duty to inform you officially, that in consequence of a persistence by Germany in her invasion of Poland, Great Britain has declared war upon her and that, as a result, Australia is also at war.'

Australia's reaction

Australians were overwhelmingly in support of the country's involvement in the war, though without the celebrations that had been present at the outbreak of the First World War in 1914. The daily newspapers, the churches and most of the labour movement agreed that it was a just war against a dictator who was illegally invading sovereign nations.

The support was in large part due to Australia's ties with Britain. In 1939 Australia's culture was still substantially a British one. Australia's trade was mostly with Britain and this trade was seaborne. As Australia did not have a substantial navy of its own, the country's trade and security depended on British control of the seas. If Britain was defeated, Australia's international trade would be unprotected against attack by a victorious German navy.

There was also unease about Japan. Japan had invaded China in 1931, and was believed to be looking to expand into other areas of Asia and the Pacific. It already had colonies in

Two of the 20 boys aged from nine to 14 who toured the world from December 1938 to September 1939 as the Vienna Mozart Boys Choir. Having toured throughout the United States, the Pacific and Australia they became stranded in Perth when the ship on which they were to return to Austria was requisitioned. Germany had just invaded Poland and Australia had entered the Second World War. Dr Daniel Mannix, then the archbishop of Melbourne, offered that his parishioners would provide foster care in return for the boys forming a choir at St Patrick's Cathedral, Melbourne. Remaining in Australia likely saved their lives, as they came of age during the war and would have been conscripted into the German army. Only one returned to live in Vienna after the war.

the Pacific, and had a strong fleet. Australia's only security against a Japanese threat was the British navy and the 'Singapore strategy', which was Britain's plan for defending its colonial interests in the Asia-Pacific region by sending a strong fleet to Singapore to deter Japanese aggression.

The Australian Labor Party was the Opposition in 1939 and supported involvement, though with many reservations. The ALP believed that Australia's war effort should not harm working conditions as had happened during the previous war, and that there should be no compulsory overseas service.

Opposition

Not all Australians supported the war. Fighting was against the fundamental beliefs of pacifists and members of some minority religions, such as Quakers and Jehovah's Witnesses. But this opposition was small – during the whole of the war only 2791 people claimed exemption from military service on the grounds of a conscientious belief against war.

The Communist Party of Australia was specifically against Australian participation in this conflict, due to the party's commitment to and domination by the Soviet Union, which had signed a non-aggression pact with Germany. Australian communists denounced the war and

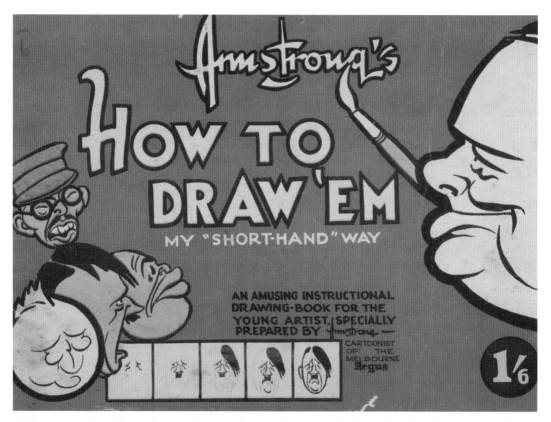

An instruction booklet that shows how to draw caricatures of political leaders of the Second World War (e.g. Adolf Hitler, Benito Mussolini and Hideki Tojo). It was created by cartoonist Harold B. Armstrong for the *Argus*, 1944.

some worked against the Australian war effort over the next two years, especially through strikes in factories that produced war supplies, and on the wharves where communist-influenced workers deliberately disrupted the loading and unloading of military goods.

In 1940 the Menzies Government declared the Communist Party an illegal organisation. The party's policy of opposition to the war only changed in 1941 after Germany invaded the Soviet Union.

Defence preparations and enlistment

Australia was not ready for war in 1939. Australian governments had cut defence spending to the bone during the Great Depression of the 1930s, and had sunk some of Australia's ships as part of the peace settlements after the First World War. Governments believed Australia could rely on the British 'Singapore Solution' for their safety.

Thousands of men and many women quickly volunteered. People's

As part of political propaganda, images of family were used to encourage men to enter the war. In this example, a wife and mother is shown carrying a newborn child, indicating that one's love and care for the family should also translate to military participation.

reasons for enlisting were varied: loyalty, duty, mateship, adventure, peer pressure, family expectations, and the promise of good pay. The prospect of pay was important to many as the unemployment rate was still about 10 per cent in 1939.

There were about 600,000 men aged between 20 and 29 in Australia in 1940 and therefore eligible for military service. About one in six of these had volunteered after only a few months.

Initially women were able to join the army only as nurses. Many wanted to do more and formed their own semi-military organisations and started training in a variety of jobs: as drivers, motorbike dispatch riders, and in communications. Many of these organisations would be called on later, but early in the war the main role for women was voluntary fundraising through local councils and organisations such as the Red Cross.

The government planned its recruiting in a more orderly fashion than it had for the First World War, and made sure that key civilian workers needed for vital war production were not scooped up in the first rush to enlist.

In a few months, Australia raised the 6th, 7th and 8th Divisions (about 60,000 men), of the volunteer 2nd Australian Imperial Forces (AIF), as well as enlisting thousands of Royal Australian Air Force (RAAF) recruits who were mainly sent to Canada for training. The Royal Australian Navy was placed under British control.

Government powers

On 9 September 1939 the Australian Government passed the *National Security Act*. This allowed the government to exercise extraordinary powers and to intervene in areas of life that it normally did not have the constitutional power to do. The key limitation to its power was that it could not introduce conscription for overseas service without amending the *Defence Act*. This would become an issue later in the war.

Internment camps

The presence of potential enemy aliens during wartime presents a challenge to any country's democratic principles. Like many countries during the war, Australia imposed travel and movement restrictions on 'enemy aliens'. These were people who were citizens of the countries with which Australia was now at war, and who might therefore be a security risk. Those considered the greatest risk were interned – placed in prison camps – even though these people had committed no offence and were not given any trial to prove their harmlessness or loyalty.

The *Dunera* Internees

During the war, both Australia and Canada agreed to accept some foreign internees from Britain to reduce a popular outcry against what were seen as enemy sympathisers. In July 1940, Australia accepted 2542 'enemy aliens' on the ship *Dunera*. There were 200 Italian and 251 German prisoners of war, and several dozen Nazi sympathisers, but there were over 2000 anti-Nazi civilians, most of them Jewish. However, in one of the great injustices of internment of the war, they were all mixed together and considered to be Nazi sympathisers.

The internees' possessions were looted by guards, the ship was overloaded, food and water were limited, and toilet facilities were poor. The guards physically and verbally abused detainees.

On arrival in Australia in September, the Australian authorities were horrified by the reports they heard and laid charges against the ship's military commander. The detainees were sent to Hay, New South Wales, where they proceeded to set up a small city, complete with concerts, a 'university', and an administration system.

Most internees were released in 1941. Many returned to Britain to fight against the Nazis. Others joined the Australian military forces. About a thousand stayed, and many became leaders in industry, the arts, commerce, science and education after the war. One of the internees, Franz Stampfl, coached Roger Bannister to become the first runner to break the four-minute mile.

NATIONAL SECURITY (ALIENS CONTROL) REGULATIONS.

LOCAL PERMIT under ALIENS CONTROL REGULATION 17.

Adelaide _____ Police Station, South Australia, 18th September 1945

Permission to travel given to_____ Ilario CAPPELLUTI

of_____ Italian _____ nationality, Certificate No. 0864

residing at 318 Wakefield Street, Adelaide

to travel to_____ British Tube Mills, Kilburn.

subject to the following conditions :—

The person to whom this permit is issued is permitted to travel to the British Tube Mills each day Mondays to Fridays from 7 a.m. until 6 p.m. each day and from 7 a.m. until 1 p.m. on Saturdays. He will be employed on Fricker Bros Job at the Tube Mills.

This permission is valid until_____ 20th October _____ 194 5 on which date this Permit MUST be returned to the issuing A.R.O. or to the A.R.O. where the holder then is. The person to whom this Permit is issued MUST carry the Permit whilst travelling in accordance with the Permit, and produce it to an officer on demand.

I. Cappelluti.

Signature of Alien.

J W O'Kely

Signature of A.R.O.

SPECIAL NOTE.—Enemy aliens are NOT permitted to travel other than by train, tramcar, or other public conveyance, unless the holder of this Permit has been granted a Permit to possess or use a motor vehicle under Aliens Control (Prohibited Possessions) Order.

5M—10.43 16344

K. M. STEVENSON, GOVERNMENT PRINTER, ADELAIDE.

A travel document issued to Ilario Cappelluti that allowed him to travel to his place of work. Because Cappelluti was originally from Italy, he was considered an 'enemy alien' and required official paperwork in order to be able to leave the internment camp.

The internment camps were run well and according to accepted international conventions. There were cases of Australians intimidating aliens and attacking their property, but these were not typical of most people's reactions.

From November 1940, public protests against what were seen as harsh restrictions against many people who were not enemy sympathisers led to the creation of an appeals system.

As the war progressed, the government interned citizens of each Nazi-conquered European country whose government sided with Hitler, as well as Italian-born and Japanese-born Australian residents. More than 16,000 people, mostly men but including some women and children, were interned during the war.

After the war ended, most internees were given the choice to stay in Australia or be returned to their homes. The exception was the Japanese, virtually all of whom were sent back to Japan.

FROM 'PHONEY WAR' TO 'ALL-IN WAR'

After the initial invasions of Poland and Finland the fighting virtually stopped. The period was known as the 'phoney war', and life in Australia and most other countries went on fairly normally. The Germans were waiting for spring when they would unleash their full might against Europe.

Germany launched their *blitzkrieg*, or 'lightning war', against Western Europe on 9 May 1940. Germany attacked and invaded Denmark, Holland, Norway, Belgium, Luxembourg and France. All surrendered within months and were occupied. The northern half of France was occupied by German troops, while the southern half set up a German-friendly government based in the town of Vichy. This Vichy Government promised not to fight Germany in exchange for southern France not being occupied by German troops.

In June 1940, Germany started aerial attacks on Britain. The aim was to bomb manufacturing centres and industrial areas, and to destroy the British Royal Air Force, leaving Britain vulnerable to a planned seaborne German invasion. The invasion could only succeed if Germany destroyed Britain's aerial defences. Germany failed to gain control of the skies above Britain and had to postpone, and then abandon, the invasion by sea. More than 30 Australians were involved as aircrew in this campaign, which is known as the 'Battle of Britain'.

The Axis powers

On 27 September 1940 Germany, Italy and Japan signed an agreement to cooperate with each other and became known as the Axis powers. Their opponents – including Britain and the Commonwealth nations, China, and later the United States and the USSR – were known as the Allies.

Australian engagement in Libya and Syria, 1941

When Italy entered the war, fighting spread to the Mediterranean and North Africa. Royal Australian Air Force aeroplanes and Royal Australian Navy ships were sent into action there. In July 1941, HMAS *Sydney* sank the Italian cruiser *Bartolomeo Colleoni*. This was Australia's most significant naval success of the war.

Australian troops of the 6th, 7th and 9th Divisions joined a British force in defeating Italian troops at Bardia, Benghazi and Tobruk (all in Libya), and against Vichy French troops in Syria. The combined forces in Tobruk were in turn besieged by German forces. This was a war of rapid movement, of great sweeping attacks, of desert sand and wind, of speeding tanks and roaring artillery. The Allied troops finally defeated the advancing German Afrika Korps of General Erwin Rommel at the two battles of El Alamein, Egypt, in July and November 1942.

Australian naval ships served in the Mediterranean against the Italian navy and supported Australian troops at Tobruk. The ships would run supplies in to the besieged troops by night, frequently while under heavy attack from the German Air Force. The Australian ships

Waterhen and *Parramatta* were sunk at Tobruk, the latter with only 23 survivors from a crew of 160. More than 800 Australian troops were killed in Tobruk and 900 were captured.

Rats of Tobruk

In a propaganda broadcast, the British traitor William Joyce, nicknamed Lord Haw-Haw, contemptuously referred to the Allied defenders of Tobruk as being caught like rats in a trap. The Australian and British troops took on this title with pride, calling themselves the 'Rats of Tobruk'.

Australian troops in Greece and Crete, 1941

Some of the Allied defenders of Tobruk were sent to Greece as part of a British force opposing a German invasion through Yugoslavia. There were heavy casualties among the Australians and the British, and over 2000 Australian soldiers were taken prisoner.

The survivors retreated to Crete, where the same thing happened – defeat, more dead, and over 3000 Australian prisoners taken. Australian ships helped in both evacuations but many soldiers could not be taken off Crete.

Reg Saunders

One of those left on Crete was Aboriginal soldier Reg Saunders. He and a small group took to the hills and hid by day in olive groves, coming out at night to forage for food. Village people often helped them but this was at great risk to themselves. In one instance, Saunders watched as two local people, screaming their defiance of and hatred for the invaders, were grabbed by German troops, tied to chairs, shot and handed back to the village for burial.

Saunders was among a group of 75 men who survived on Crete for months, and were finally shepherded down to a quiet beach by the local resistance to be picked up by a British boat. They were told to strip naked before going on the boat as their clothes were filthy and infested with lice.

Reg Saunders went on to become the second Aboriginal person commissioned as an officer during the war. It has long been

AWM 003967

believed that he was the first Aboriginal soldier ever to be commissioned, but recent research suggests that honour belongs to Alfred John Hearps from Tasmania, who was commissioned a Second Lieutenant shortly before his death in action in 1916.

PEARL HARBOR AND THE START OF THE PACIFIC WAR

Japanese expansionism

On 7 December 1941, Japan dramatically entered the war by making a surprise attack on the United States naval base at Pearl Harbor in Hawaii and on British possessions in Malaya.

During the 1920s and 1930s the Japanese Government had been increasingly focused on expanding Japan's industry and military strength. Japan lacked the natural resources needed for its industrial expansion, especially rubber and oil, and so invaded neighbouring regions in an attempt to increase its empire and gain access to these resources.

In 1931, Japan invaded Manchuria (in north-east China). In 1933, it withdrew from the League of Nations, thereby declaring its intention not to be ruled by world opinion. In 1937, Japan invaded China itself. Western countries punished Japan for this unprovoked aggression by placing a ban on the provision of vital raw materials, oil and rubber, to Japan from other Western nations.

In 1940 Japan formally announced its vision of a Greater East Asia Co-Prosperity Sphere, which included most of Asia, and which Japan would invade and liberate from the western colonial powers. Any invasion to achieve this would ordinarily have been resisted by the Western countries that had colonies in the region, but by 1941, these Western powers were tied up in the war in Europe.

The attack on Pearl Harbor

The United States was the only power with aircraft carriers and warships in the Pacific that would be capable of defeating Japan's fleet of aircraft carriers, warships and fighter planes.

The attack on Pearl Harbor was a calculated gamble. Japan expected to find the United States Pacific Fleet in port and virtually unprotected. The attack sank or damaged several battleships and killed 2403 service people, but the prize targets – the aircraft carriers *Lexington* and *Enterprise* – were unexpectedly at sea. The raid was a strategic blunder as it provoked a fierce determination in the American people to crush Japan and avenge what was seen as a cowardly attack.

In effect, Japan lost the war at Pearl Harbor, though this was not to be realised for several years. The attack brought the United States into the war against both Japan and Germany.

Attacks against Asian colonies

About an hour before the attack on Pearl Harbor, Japan launched invasions of Malaya, Thailand and the Philippines. Japanese forces swept through the Netherlands East Indies (modern-day Indonesia) and the southern and western Pacific, including much of New Guinea. The period from Japan's entry into the war until the end of 1942 was the most serious of the conflict for Australia. War came to Australian soil and Australian sea lanes, and Japan was expected to launch an invasion of Australia, a fear which did not realistically disappear until mid-1942.

A push towards independence

The closeness of the Pacific War pushed Australia towards greater national independence from Britain than before, though into a closer dependence on the United States. This can be seen in four important decisions in 1942 and 1943.

1. Australia declares war

Australia declared war against Japan as soon as news spread of the attack on Pearl Harbor and of the Malaya and Thailand invasions; the Australian Government did not wait for Britain's declaration. Australia was asserting its right to act in its national interest. The threat posed by the Japanese led to the Military Board fully accepting the enlistment of Aboriginal and Torres Strait Islander men.

2. Australia looks to the United States

Secondly, war had come to Australia's region when the country's main ally, Britain, was desperately fighting for survival in Europe. The United States was a colonial power in the Pacific region and so could be expected to wage a full war effort against the Japanese, whereas

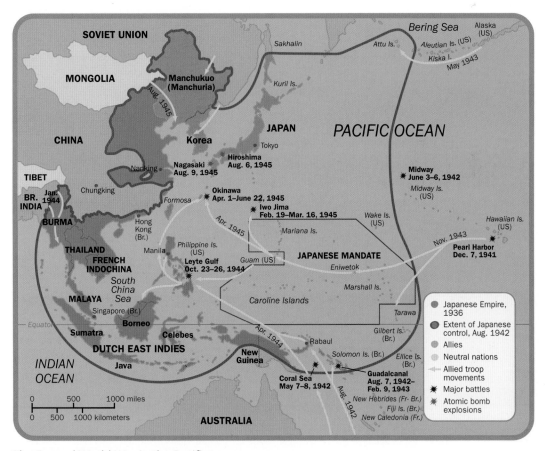

The Second World War in the Pacific.

Britain could not. In late December 1941, Prime Minister Curtin wrote a newspaper article in which he said that 'Australia looks to America for help, free of any pangs as to our traditional links or kinship with the United Kingdom.'

3. Bringing troops home

In February 1942, Australian troops had been sent by British Prime Minister Winston Churchill from the Middle East to fight against the Japanese. A dispute arose between Churchill and Australian Prime Minister Curtin over where the troops should be sent. Curtin wanted the troops to go to Australia and New Guinea. Churchill ordered the troops to Burma to prevent Japanese forces seizing the strategically important port of Rangoon, which would have disrupted Allied supply lines to Chinese forces fighting the Japanese. Curtin protested vigorously and Churchill gave way. The troops returned to Australia, but a great rift had appeared between what Britain and Australia each saw as important.

4. A break from British control

Since Australia's Federation in 1901, Britain had maintained control over key areas of law-making, especially laws related to foreign affairs and international shipping. Australia could remove this legal dependence on Britain by adopting the *Statute of Westminster,* a British Act passed in 1931 specifically to allow Dominion countries (Canada, South Africa, Australia and New Zealand) to cut such legal ties. By adopting the statute, the Australian Government could remove Britain's power to make laws that affected Australia without Australia's approval. This action had been available since 1931, but was not adopted until October 1942, and made retrospective to 3 September 1939 to ensure that all actions by Australians during the war were subject to Australian and not British law.

Handing control to MacArthur

Although the Australian Government was making assertions of independence, it still sought the support of a larger power to defend Australia. In April 1942, the government handed control of Australia's forces in the Pacific to the United States military commander in the region, General Douglas MacArthur. MacArthur had come to Australia in March 1942 to organise the United States' fight against the Japanese in the Pacific after the Japanese had invaded the Philippines in December 1941. Prime Minister Curtin allowed him, rather than an Australian general, to set the policy for where Australian forces would be used. Australian commanders, especially General Blamey, who was the commander of all Australian troops, resented this effective transfer of power from Australia to the United States.

WAR COMES TO AUSTRALIA

Japan's entry into a Pacific War in December 1941 threw Australia's war strategy into chaos. Most trained RAAF personnel were in Europe and most soldiers were in North Africa, leaving Australia virtually undefended. Australia depended on British warships at Singapore to deter any enemy invasion.

The Malayan Campaign and the Fall of Singapore

The Japanese invasion of Malaya started on 8 December 1941. Britain had sent two warships, the *Prince of Wales* and the *Repulse*, to fight any Japanese naval fleet, but both ships were destroyed by Japanese aircraft.

Australia had committed a quarter of its AIF, the 8th Division, to defend Malaya and Singapore. Australian, British and Indian troops resisted the Japanese invasion but were defeated. The Japanese were outnumbered by the Allied forces, but they were battle veterans and used the terrain much more effectively. Heavy fighting resulted in the greatest number of Australian combat deaths of any single campaign in the war, but there was also much retreating, confusion and, in some cases, panic.

The Allied troops retreated to Singapore at the end of the Malayan peninsula. The Japanese invaded the island and, faced with the certainty that their water supply would be cut off, the Allied troops surrendered. On 15 February 1942, Singapore fell, and with it any remaining belief that Britain could protect Australia.

The Malaya/Singapore campaign was Australia's greatest disaster of the war. These ten weeks accounted for 25 per cent of all battle deaths against the Japanese during the whole Pacific War, including some who were murdered when they surrendered. Fifteen thousand soldiers of the 8th Division, plus airmen, sailors, nurses and civilians, were made prisoners of war. More than one third of these would die over the next three years from murder, beatings, starvation and medical neglect.

After the fall of Singapore, Japanese forces continued to sweep all before them, taking Sumatra, Borneo, Java, north-east New Guinea, the Philippines, and many Pacific islands, including the Solomons, Guam, Wake Island, and the Gilbert and Marshall islands.

A prisoner-of-war banknote issued by the Japanese Government to be used in the countries Japan conquered.

Colour jigsaw puzzle featuring portraits of American President Franklin Roosevelt and Australian Prime Minister John Curtin, indicating the alliance between Australia and the USA during the Second World War.

Ambon, Timor and Rabaul

Three Australian battalions (of about 1000 men each) were sent to islands north of Australia: Gull Force went to Ambon, Sparrow Force to Timor and Lark Force to New Britain. The men were poorly trained and equipped, and were outnumbered by the vastly superior Japanese forces. They could not hope to hold the islands, but were sent to slow down the Japanese advance. The Australians resisted briefly but were either killed in battle, captured or fled into the jungle. Many of the Australians taken prisoner died as a result of their brutal treatment or were murdered. So, too, were local people who helped the Australians against the invading enemy.

The Bombing of Darwin

From February 1942, Japan launched nearly 100 air raids on Australia, covering territory from Onslow on the north-west coast of Western Australia to Townsville on the north-east coast of Queensland. Sixty-four of the raids were on the city of Darwin, and the first of these was on 19 February. This was not part of an invasion of Australia but was designed to destroy Allied opposition to Japan's invasion of Timor, which was about to commence. A formation of 188 Japanese fighters and bombers launched from aircraft carriers in the Timor Sea swept over Darwin in the morning, taking the defenders by surprise.

A coastwatcher on Melville Island and a missionary on Bathurst Island had seen the planes and radioed warnings to Darwin, but a series of misunderstandings and poor communication meant that the warnings were ignored. The 40 minutes' warning would probably have saved the lives of at least some of the victims, who would have had time to seek shelter.

At least 243 people were killed, 188 of them United States sailors, and civilian and military buildings were destroyed during the 42-minute attack. Ten ships were sunk in the harbour. Ten United States Kittyhawk fighters were approaching the airfield to re-fuel, and nine of them were destroyed before they could respond. Only one plane stayed in the air to engage the enemy. Anti-aircraft batteries brought down only two enemy planes. An hour later a second raid by 54 land-based bombers from Ambon destroyed what remained of Darwin's airfield.

Soon after the raid there was a rush to evacuate the town by civilians and some military. Shops and business premises had been locked, but that night some servicemen began looting – many expected that there would be an invasion, and the food and goods would be no use to anyone then. Servicemen also deserted the air force station in great numbers.

Defending the Australian coast

Around the Australian coast, and especially on the east coast, the government set up gun emplacements and strung barbed wire along beaches that were possible enemy invasion landing points.

The threat to merchant ships increased as Japanese submarines prowled coastal waters for targets. Between 1942 and 1943, 19 Australian merchant ships were sunk, with 503 people killed. Shells fired from submarines hit Sydney and Newcastle without causing real damage.

On 31 May 1942, three Japanese midget submarines sneaked into Sydney Harbour to seek out the United States warship *Chicago*. Two were sunk before they could fire their torpedoes, but one hit a floating barracks, HMAS *Kuttabul*, killing 19 sailors.

Teddy Sheean

During a mission to take 66 troops to help the guerrillas in Timor, HMAS *Armidale* came under attack from Japanese aircraft on 1 December 1942. When the enemy started machine-gunning the sailors in the water, Ordinary Seaman Edward 'Teddy' Sheean helped some mates into a life raft, then went back and strapped himself alone to the three-man deck gun and fired at the enemy planes. He was wounded, but kept firing, shooting down one plane, and trying to keep others away from the exposed sailors. Forty-nine of the ship's crew of 149 survived.

Teddy Sheean (right) and his brother, Mick Sheean. *AWM 044154*

Sheean was last seen still firing as the ship sank. He was 18 when he died. The Victoria Cross and the Mentioned in Despatches (the lowest bravery award) were the only two awards that could be given posthumously at the time. In 1999, one of the Royal Australian Navy's Collins-class submarines was named the HMAS *Sheean* after him.

Lieutenant Kieu Matsuo

The submarine that sank the *Kuttabul* was commanded by Lieutenant Kieu Matsuo. He and his crewman both shot themselves when their submarine was damaged. Their bodies were recovered, and they were cremated with full military honours. Their ashes were returned to Japan with the returning Japanese Ambassador to Australia, Tatsuo Kawai. In 1968 Kieu Matsuo's mother, Mrs Matsue Matsuo, travelled to Australia and presented gifts to the Australian War Memorial, including this handwritten poem:

I nurtured my son just as I grew precious flowers
So that he could dedicate himself to the Emperor.
Now that the storm has passed
And all the cherry blossoms have blown away,
The garden looks very deserted.

The worst event was the torpedoing of the hospital ship *Centaur* off the coast of Brisbane. The ship had been brightly lit and clearly marked as a hospital ship. Of the 332 merchant seamen crew and medical personnel aboard, only 64 survived. Despite these attacks the Australian coast was not a focus for sustained Japanese aggression.

PAPUA NEW GUINEA, 1942

Part of Japan's strategy to control Asia was to isolate Australia as a base for military opposition. As Japanese forces moved on from Singapore, Port Moresby became the key to the control of Papua New Guinea and potentially to the control of the seas around Australia. If Japan could control Port Moresby it could launch attacks against the Australian mainland, disrupt supplies coming to Australia from the United States to be used against the Japanese, and protect any forces gathering to invade Australia, if such an invasion was to become a goal at a later stage.

The Battles of the Coral Sea, Midway and Milne Bay

Three battles had a great influence on Japanese attempts to reduce Australian and United States resistance.

Battle of the Coral Sea

In May 1942, Japan sent an invasion force from Rabaul towards Port Moresby. However, United States commanders knew the plan. They had broken the Japanese secret naval codes and were able to oppose the move.

The Allied force, including some Australian ships and planes, attacked the Japanese warships. The Allies suffered greater damage than the Japanese, but succeeded in forcing the Japanese to divert. As a result, Japanese troops had to try to take Port Moresby by a much harder overland route along the Kokoda Track.

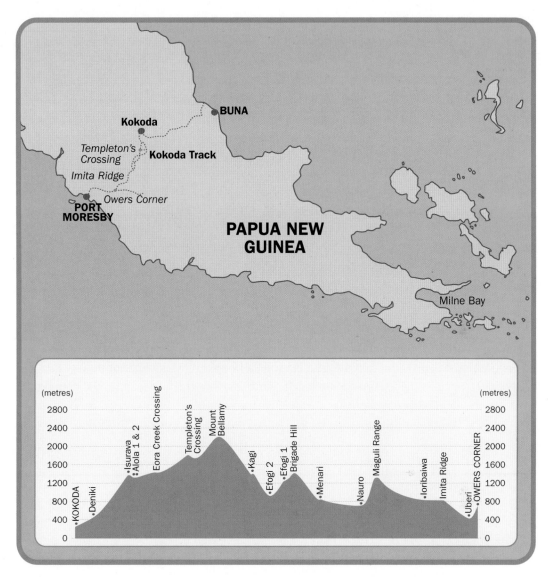

The land map (top) shows the geographical placement of the Kokoda Track in Papua New Guinea. The terrain map (below) shows the heights in metres of the different sites on the track.

Battle of Midway

Despite the setback in the Coral Sea, the Japanese planned to use their fleet to destroy the American fleet. The Japanese set a trap for the United States fleet: they attacked the island of Midway on 4 June 1942 knowing that the United States forces would respond despite being unprepared.

However, the United States commanders knew of the trap from their interception of the secret Japanese codes. Both sides suffered heavily but the Japanese fleet's aircraft carriers were effectively destroyed. There was no longer any practical possibility that Australia could be invaded by Japanese forces.

Battle of Milne Bay

The Japanese still wanted to take Port Moresby as a base for launching air attacks against the Allies.

On the night of 25/26 August, a Japanese force of about 2000 soldiers landed to seize the Australian airbase at Milne Bay. However, for the first time in the war, the Allies had control of the air, and RAAF fighter planes were able to disrupt the landing, while Australian ground troops forced the Japanese to withdraw after fierce fighting.

Milne Bay was the first defeat of Japanese land forces in the war and provided great morale value, as well as protecting Port Moresby from attack from the east. This meant that Allied forces could focus on resisting the Japanese land forces now pushing along the Kokoda Track to take Port Moresby from inland.

Kokoda Track

In July 1942, a well equipped Japanese invasion force of about 7000 men had started to move through the jungle towards Port Moresby. Another 10,000 combat troops followed over the next few months.

Two weeks before the Japanese landing, about 1000 Australian troops of the 39th Militia Battalion, poorly trained and under-equipped, had set out from Port Moresby to cross the Owen Stanley Range. Conscripted Australian militia troops could not be sent overseas to fight, but New Guinea and Papua were legally Australian territory at the time. The battalion's goal was to secure Kokoda and act as a protective force for United States engineers building an airstrip at Dobodura. This airstrip would have allowed the supply of Allied troops in the campaign.

The 39th were not equipped for the task. They had insufficient clothing for the wet, freezing nights, and their khaki-coloured uniforms stood out in the jungle. They carried quinine as protection against malaria but the main problem was dysentery, for which they had very few medical supplies.

On 23 July 1942 about 30 Australian troops, together with Papuan Infantry Battalion members, faced the advancing Japanese force near Kokoda. After bloody clashes the Australians fell back.

After more clashes and retreats, the 39th was ordered to hold at all costs. They had lived for weeks without a change of clothing or proper food: their boots were holey and torn; their clothes were constantly wet; they slept without shelter or blankets; most were weakened by dysentery; and ammunition was desperately short.

Experienced AIF reinforcements, men who had fought at Tobruk, Greece and Crete, arrived to relieve the weary 39th, but there were not enough men to hold the area, so the 39th stayed on with them. For the first time the volunteer Australian Imperial Force (AIF) and the conscript Citizen Military Force (CMF or Militia) fought together.

The battle raged for four days. On the fourth day, 29 August, the Japanese were threatening to break through until Private Bruce Kingsbury bravely charged the enemy with a Bren gun and cleared the area. Kingsbury was then killed by a sniper's bullet. He was posthumously

Jungle warfare

Jungle warfare was a horrific experience. Men had to cope with the heat, tropical rain, stinging and biting insects, and the terror of not knowing where the enemy was – perhaps even only metres away in the thick jungle.

The ground was steep and often muddy and men felt as though their legs were being torn from their bodies as they climbed and crawled up steep mountainsides, always mentally alert for the hidden enemy. The sounds of the enemy were everywhere but they were often not seen until the woodpecker noise of the Japanese machine-gun suddenly ripped into the foliage. Fighting was often hand-to-hand and savage, and because there was no way to look after prisoners none were taken by either side.

Diseases racked the soldiers' bodies, and hunger and thirst had to be endured as getting supplies to the men was extremely difficult. Supplies could only be brought some of the way by motor vehicle, then were transferred to mules or porters. Eventually the tracks of the Kokoda grew too steep even for mules and supplies had to be carried in by men. Most of the carriers were conscripted local Papuans, who carried wounded troops out on stretchers. The work of these men was profoundly appreciated by the wounded soldiers, and the carriers were affectionately nicknamed 'fuzzy wuzzy angels' in war propaganda.

awarded the Victoria Cross, the first Australian soldier to be awarded such a recognition of bravery on Australian soil.

By 25 September, the Japanese were less than 50 kilometres from Port Moresby. But then the Japanese high command ordered the Japanese troops to withdraw. Now it was the Australian troops who were advancing, and the Japanese retreating. On 2 November 1942 Australian troops retook Kokoda. The campaign had taken four months and the Australians had suffered 607 killed and 1015 wounded. For every man killed or wounded, another two or three had been hospitalised for sickness. No overall casualty figures for the estimated 6000 Japanese soldiers on the Track are known.

The Japanese were pushed back towards Buna, on the coast. Much savage and bloody fighting was needed at Buna, Gona and Sanananda before the Japanese were finally defeated. The Papua campaign finished in January 1943 with a total of 2165 Australians, 1300 Americans and more than 6000 Japanese dead. The few Japanese prisoners who were taken were sent to a POW camp in Australia.

Coastwatchers

A little-recognised group that helped win the Pacific War were the Coastwatchers. These were mostly young men, often plantation managers and patrol officers, who remained behind as the Japanese conquered the islands of the south-west Pacific. The Coastwatchers bravely provided information to Allied headquarters of Japanese movements. If found, the Coastwatchers and the local helpers were certain to be tortured and killed.

Australian involvement outside the Pacific, 1942

Australians were active in many areas other than Papua New Guinea.

RAAF

Royal Australian Air Force (RAAF) airmen remained active in the air war over Europe. RAAF airmen took part in the defence of Malta and several thousand RAAF and Army personnel served in Burma, India, Cyprus, Ceylon (Sri Lanka) and even in China, where 'Tulip Force' helped train Chinese guerrillas to fight the Japanese.

RAN

Australian naval ships helped with convoy protection in the Atlantic and Indian oceans. Many naval ships were also engaged in action in the Pacific and Atlantic oceans. They were subject to torpedo attacks from submarines, strafing and bombing from enemy aircraft, and late in the war the new threat presented by Japanese *kamikaze* pilots, who were ready to die for their country by deliberately flying their planes into ships.

Merchant Navy

The Merchant Navy is the term used to describe commercial shipping and crews during wartime. Ships of the civilian merchant navy carried vital cargo – food, supplies, ammunition, guns, oil, wool, grain – all of which were vital for Australia's economy and war effort. The crews were not trained for war, their ships were not armoured or protected against mines, submarines, warships or planes. The death rate among merchant ship crews was as high as it was in the fighting services.

ON THE HOME FRONT

After April 1940, life at home reflected the dramatically changed war situation. Prime Minister Menzies called in a radio broadcast for an 'all-in effort'. *'Every good thing that we have is now at stake . . . our own freedom, the safety and independence of the mother country, and the continued existence of the British Empire.'* (*Argus*, 16 June 1941)

Cowra

In August 1944, over 1100 Japanese prisoners of war were being held at Cowra in New South Wales.

According to the Japanese warrior code of *bushidō*, surrender was inexcusable. Many of the prisoners could see the pointlessness of this and quietly wanted to survive and go home, but some officers urged them not to be 'shamed' by accepting imprisonment.

On 5 August they staged a mass escape. Four Australians were killed, as were 234 Japanese, many of them in a suicidal rush into machine-gun fire. Others died from shooting each other or from lying down on railway tracks. Three hundred and thirty-four of the prisoners were recaptured and returned to Cowra. The last prisoners were repatriated in 1947.

The government had fixed the price of many goods (to prevent retailers from selling essential items at exorbitant prices and claiming it was because the war had made those goods scarce) and banned the Communist Party, which was actively opposing the war against Germany (the ban was lifted six months after the Soviet Union attacked Germany in June 1941). It also appointed a Director-General of Information with wide powers to make newspapers include government information, increased income taxation, took control of shipping, and rationed petrol.

One hundred thousand more men were accepted as volunteers for the Australian Army. There was also increased conscription of men aged between 18 and 60 for compulsory home service in the Militia.

Political change

In 1941 the disunited United Australia Party–Country Party Coalition Government of Prime Minister Menzies lost the support of two independents, Arthur Coles and Alex Wilson, which

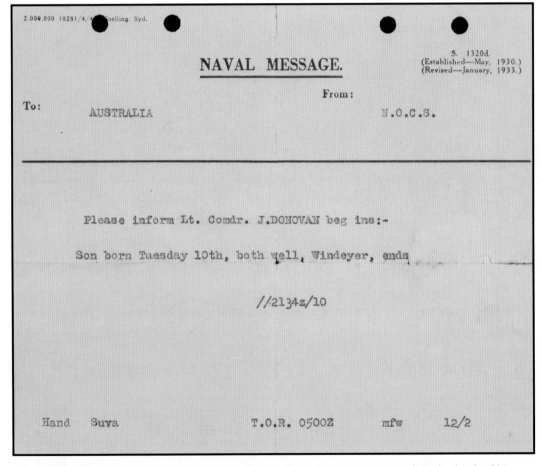

A naval message telegram to Lieutenant Commander Jack Donovan regarding the birth of his son. 1942.

An initiative established by the Commonwealth of Australia to encourage Australians to buy war savings stamps, the profits of which would go towards the war effort. Circa 1942.

meant the government lost its majority. The independents promised Labor their support and John Curtin became the prime minister of a Labor Government on 7 October 1941. He was about to be sorely tested as the war reached its lowest point for Australia.

Government controls and 'total war'

The Curtin Government responded to the Japanese threat by gearing Australia towards a total war effort. For every man fighting the enemy, there were dozens of men and women working to support him.

The government took control of the nation's economy and activities as it had never done before, creating major changes to normal Australian life. It imposed limits and restrictions on profits, prices and wages. It cut the Christmas–New Year holiday period to three days. It imposed restrictions on weekday sporting events, and non-essential travel. It introduced daylight saving. Every person had to have an identity card. Letters to and from soldiers were censored so that useful information was not given to the enemy.

Directed labour

The government took on the power to direct people to areas of employment that best suited the requirements of the war effort, such as fruit-picking during the harvest season. In effect, this was civilian conscription. Nearly 80,000 engineers and labourers were employed in a Civil Constructional Corps to build roads, airfields, barracks and gun emplacements to improve Australia's defences and create a supply line to the northern front at Darwin. About a third of all these workers were conscripted into the Corps.

Industry

The war transformed Australian industry. Imports of manufactured goods were severely reduced, and this forced Australian industry to produce many goods that it had previously imported – guns, planes, ships, high-precision machine tools, chemicals and high-quality glass. These developments set Australia up for a postwar industrial and economic boom.

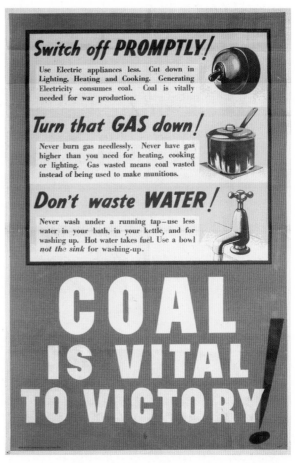

Australians were encouraged to be conservative with their coal usage (which powered general lighting, heating, cooking and electricity) to help bolster the supply of coal for military purposes.

National Security (Man Power) Regulations

Notice to be posted in YOUR ESTABLISHMENT

ADVICE has been received from the Director-General of Man Power that as from 11th August 194

GEORGE HENRY FEALY. 74 GEORGETOWN ROAD. GEORGETOWN

EXTENT OF PROTECTION = IN RESPECT OF BAKING AND DELIVERY OF BREAD ONLY

have been declared as " protected " under National Security (Man Power) Regulations.

This declaration brings into operation the provisions of Regulation 14 of Regulation No. 34 1942, which is as follows the above Regulations as amended which is as follows:-

" 14. (1) An employer carrying on a protected undertaking shall not, except with the permission in writing of the Director-General or of a person authorised by him—

    (a) terminate the employment in the undertaking of any person employed therein;

    (b) without terminating his employment, cause or permit any such person to give his services in some other undertaking (except, in case of emergency, for a period not exceeding fourteen days); or

    (c) except in pursuance of an award, order or determination of an industrial tribunal, or of an industrial agreement, alter any customs or usages observed in the undertaking.

    (2) A person employed in a protected undertaking shall not, except with the permission in writing of the Director-General or of a person authorised by him, change his employment.

    (3) Notwithstanding any permission given by the Director-General, or by a person authorised by him, under this Regulation, the terms of any award, order or determination of any industrial tribunal, or of any contract or other instrument, shall insofar as they relate to the giving by either party of notice to terminate the employment of any person, or the length of such notice, remain in force, but where any such award, order, determination, contract or other instrument provides for the giving of less than one week's notice to terminate the employment, not less than one week's notice shall, if the Director-General so requires, be given.

    (4) No person employed in a protected undertaking shall be appointed to or enlisted in the Defence Force without the permission in writing of the Director-General."

If any employees were in other employment at the time of lodgment of military enrolment forms, it is necessary to notify National Service Officers or the Military Area Officer in the districts in which they reside, of change of employment, in order that enrolment forms might be corrected. Any such cases should be reported to the Manager.

Man Power authorities have pointed out that the protection afforded cannot be regarded as of a permanent nature, and that in view of the absolute necessity for meeting the requirements of the armed forces it is essential that everything possible should be done to release men for military service, by the replacement of men in military age groups with other types of employees, or by re-organisation, etc.

Employers should immediately notify the National Service Officers in the Area concerned of any employees leaving the establishment without authority.

34934 10.42   A. H. Pettifer, Acting Govt. Printer.

An example of the exercise of extensive powers given to the Commonwealth Government under the *War Precautions Act*.

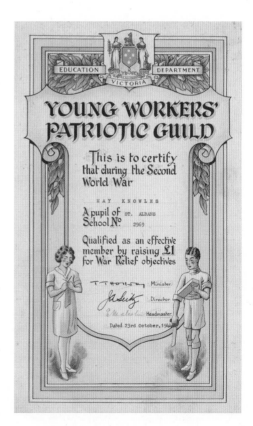

This unused clothing ration card belonged to Zena Marjorie Hansen. Clothes rationing was introduced in 1942 and continued till 1949, four years after the end of the Second World War. Rationing greatly reduced the consumption of clothes and allowed resources to be diverted into support for the armed services. People like Mrs Hansen further helped the home war effort by not using their allocated ration.

Rationing

As workers and resources were directed towards the war effort, severe shortages of some consumer goods emerged. The government rationed clothing, footwear, meat, tea, butter and sugar.

Voluntary efforts

As in the First World War there was a huge voluntary effort, led by women, to raise funds for war victims and to provide comforts for soldiers both in Australia and overseas. The Red Cross was the most active group again, providing welfare services for soldiers and their families, helping in homes, driving trucks and ambulances, raising funds, knitting socks and jumpers, packing and sending comforts parcels, and providing recreational services for soldiers on leave. More than 450,000 Australians were members, most of them women and girls –

One way children could help the war effort was through fundraising.

making it the largest civilian organisation in Australian history. School children also contributed again, raising money, planting vegetable gardens and collecting scrap metal and rubber for reprocessing into war materials. They were even urged to gather old aluminium pans to be melted down and turned into fighter planes!

Ready for invasion

In 1942, Australians prepared for an invasion that did not occur. In the capital cities, buildings were surrounded by sandbags to absorb some of the flying debris that would come from a bombed building. Windows were taped to stop glass shards from flying into the streets. Cities were subject to brownouts (reduced public lighting) and blackouts (a total power cut to street lights). Air Raid Precaution wardens would walk the streets and call out to people who had chinks of light shining through windows not properly curtained. Steps and gutters were painted white so that people would not fall over them in the dark.

Some families built bomb shelters in their backyards, and local councils dug trenches in public parks to provide people with protection during air raids. In cities and towns around the country, people practised evacuation procedures.

Some people prepared for guerrilla warfare by reading manuals on how to create simple weapons such as 'molotov cocktails' (petrol bombs), how to live off the land and how to

Clothing shortages and rationing during the war meant that people had to improvise – here a bride has made her wedding dress out of mosquito netting!

implement a 'scorched earth policy' – burning all crops, buildings and equipment so that the advancing enemy could not use them.

Many men who were unable to enlist because of their age or their essential war occupations joined home defence organisations. Members of the Volunteer Defence Corps and the Volunteer Air Observers' Corps helped to erect and patrol coastal defences or look out for enemy aircraft, warships and submarines.

Some men joined the Naval Auxiliary Patrol, a volunteer organisation of the Royal Australian Navy. Many of the volunteers provided their own vessels – from dinghies to luxury yachts – to patrol the coasts.

Women in the services

By early 1941, women's involvement in the war had started to go well beyond traditional tasks such as sending food and homemade goods to the troops. The military services needed as many men as possible in combat and direct support roles. As a result, the services started to replace men in non-combat roles with women.

For the first time, women were allowed to join the armed services: the Women's Australian Auxiliary Air Force (WAAAF) was formed in February 1941, the Women's Royal Australian Naval Service (WRANS) in April 1941, and the Australian Women's Army Service (AWAS) in July 1941. Women served as signallers, drivers, cooks, searchlight operators and cryptographers. About 43,600 women would serve with Australian forces during the war; however, it was mainly only nurses who served overseas in areas where there was any combat.

Women's role on the home front

The 'Total War' period saw a great increase in the number of working women, as well as women joining the Auxiliary Services. In 1939, 644,000 women worked; in 1944 it had increased to 855,000. A more significant figure was the number who transferred from domestic service to manufacturing – from 149,000 in 1939, to 516,000 by 1944.

Women also took on work in many occupations that had traditionally been done by men only: as letter deliverers, train, tram and bus conductors, bread carters, ice deliverers, bus drivers, railway porters, security guards, meter readers, taxi drivers and many others. Most of these women received about 90 per cent of the male wage. While the number of working women increased during the war, those in traditionally female jobs often still received about half the male wage.

Australians helped Britons who were facing food shortages during the war by sending them food parcels, which included things like beef dripping.

Changing values

Women's magazines stressed the glamour of women's roles. *Australian Women's Weekly* journalist Dorothy Drain wrote of 'Miss Munitioneer': 'surrounded by a whirr of machinery, her pretty face set in intense concentration (her hair and complexion just so) and her deft fingers capably, ceaselessly engaged on some small part of the enormous and complex job of munitions making' (*Australian Women's Weekly*, 31 May 1941).

Other observers recorded what was probably a more balanced and realistic picture. In 1941 and 1943, a team of researchers from Melbourne University carried out a survey of why more women in Footscray, an industrial suburb of Melbourne, were working. The increase in the number of women workers was in part a direct result of the enlistment of their menfolk. One said she 'got sick of being at home'. One 60-year-old woman took a job as a cleaner 'in order to help the labour shortage . . . Didn't really need the money but was bored with nothing to do'. The most common motive was undoubtedly a desire to add to the household income, often under the pressure of necessity.

The increased numbers of women in paid work brought some tensions to society. Male union leaders worried that women would continue to work after the war ended, leaving fewer jobs for returning servicemen. The Roman Catholic Archbishop of Melbourne, Dr Daniel Mannix, worried that 'working women who placed their children in care while they worked might destroy the family' [*Tribune* (Melbourne), 23 July 1942]. The place of children, he said, was in the home with their mother, not in an institution under the care of strangers.

Most women's war experience was still a domestic one, as home maker. This job was made much harder by the absence of men from many families, and the blackouts, rationing, shortages and difficulties of wartime life. This was acknowledged as a war role in itself: at a time of rationing, shortages and austerity, a mother who could run the home efficiently and sustainably was contributing to the war effort. As one advertisement for Uncle Toby's oats claimed these women were working 'on the kitchen front'.

Farms and the AWLA

About 100,000 men had left their farms to enlist in the war. The Australian Women's Land Army (AWLA) was formed to provide a few thousand young women as farm labourers, although the majority of the farm work was taken on by existing farm women – mothers, wives, daughters and sisters. There were also about 18,000 Italian prisoners of war who were sent to Australia after their capture and who worked as farm labourers from 1941 onwards.

Americans in Australia

The arrival of United States troops brought changes to many Australians' lives. The first contingent of troops arrived in Brisbane on 22 December 1941, but it was several months before newspapers were allowed to mention their presence. An estimated one million United States servicemen and women spent some time in Australia between December 1941 and 1945. They were camped or billeted in major cities as they trained or prepared to be sent to the Pacific front. Many were stationed in northern Australia – in Townsville, Cairns, Brisbane,

A postcard featuring US marines passing by The Exhange, Sydney. Photo by Walter Davies.

Rockhampton – and others returned from the front for rest and recreation, or to convalesce in Australia.

The United States servicemen, known as 'GIs' (referring to the 'galvanised iron' military equipment was made from), were better dressed, much better paid, and had access to luxuries denied to Australians. Some diggers resented the attractiveness of the Americans to Australian women. This sometimes led to brawls between United States and Australian servicemen on leave in the cities. The Australians said they had only three complaints about the Yanks – that they were overpaid, oversexed and over here!

More than 12,000 Australian women married United States servicemen. Many went back to the United States after the war with their new husbands but some were later dumped by the soldiers. The law had to be changed to allow an Australian woman to get a divorce from an American in an Australian court, but there was no possibility of forcing the men to pay maintenance to the deserted wives.

The presence of so many United States troops caused a huge boost in rural production as industries rushed to keep up with the increased demand for food supplies. The troops needed entertainment as well as food, and in towns and cities, opening hours of hotels, clubs and restaurants became more liberal to accommodate them.

African Americans
The United States forces were racially segregated, and about 10 per cent of all United States forces to move through Australia were African American. Most were in labour units and, after a protest by the Australian Government, which still maintained the White Australia policy, African-American troops were sent to regional areas where possible rather than the capital

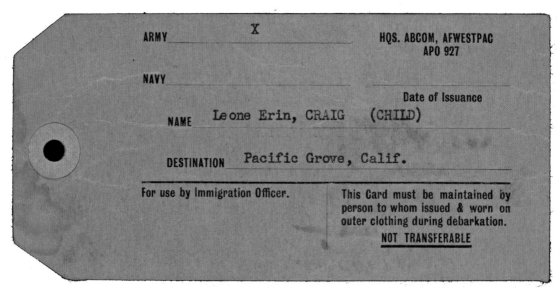

ARMY _____X_____ HQS. ABCOM, AFWESTPAC
APO 927

NAVY _____

Date of Issuance

NAME Leone Erin, CRAIG (CHILD)

DESTINATION Pacific Grove, Calif.

For use by Immigration Officer.

This Card must be maintained by person to whom issued & worn on outer clothing during debarkation.

NOT TRANSFERABLE

Erin Craig's disembarkation tag at the end of her voyage to the United States. Erin was the daughter of Australian war bride Iris Adams and James Craig, who was a master sergeant in the US Army in Australia during the Second World War.

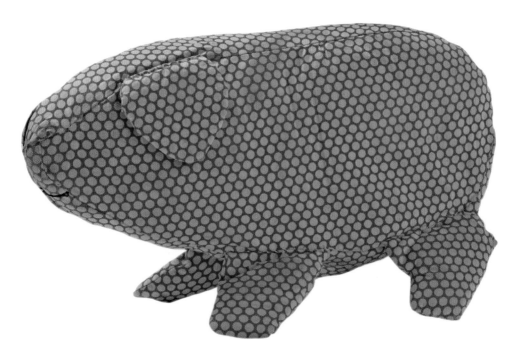

The toy pig awarded to young Erin on the voyage for 'having the reddest hair'.

cities. The Australian Government told the press to avoid any reference to a United States soldier's colour, as it was detrimental to national security. However, Australians could see what the newspapers could not say: that there were black Americans in Australia and that, although there was still racial tension within the United States military, the African-American troops were well paid, skilled and confident. This had a great impact on many Aboriginal and Torres Strait Islander Australians who mixed readily with the black American troops, helping them to realise that they, too, could demand greater social and economic equality.

Conscription

In late 1942, the issue that had divided Australia in 1916 and 1917 re-emerged: conscription for overseas service.

By 1942, Australian Military Forces was made up of two parts: the volunteer AIF (Australian Imperial Force), which could be sent to fight anywhere; and the mainly conscripted CMF (Citizen Military Force), which could be compelled to serve only on Australian territory. In 1939, the *Defence Act* had been amended to include Papua New Guinea as Australian territory, leading to some CMF troops fighting in New Guinea side by side with the AIF and, towards the end of the year, with United States conscripts.

In late 1942, Prime Minister Curtin led his party to support the proposal to extend the boundaries of where conscripts could be sent. (The boundaries were, essentially, the islands around New Guinea.) The government and the public supported the amendment to the *Defence Act* due to the state of the war, the fact that foreign and Australian conscripts were already fighting and dying in the area, and the limit put on where conscripts could be sent.

Propaganda

After the Japanese entry into the war, government propaganda flooded the Australian consciousness, from radio programs, newspaper advertisements, films, newsreels, cartoons and posters. The propaganda emphasised fear, hate and duty and the Japanese were crudely portrayed in various negative ways.

TOWARDS VICTORY, 1943-1945

From 1943 the Australian Government started releasing men from the armed forces so that they could return to Australia to help with what was now seen as a more significant contribution: manufacturing war supplies such as guns and vehicles, and growing food. However, there was still hard fighting to be done by Australians and Allies.

Strategic bombing of Germany

By 1943, German forces were in retreat on two fronts: in the east, by the Soviet Union, and in the west, by the Allies.

Large numbers of RAAF volunteers were in Britain, mostly serving in Bomber Command. Some were ground crews, but most were aircrew in the huge and powerful bomber planes, which flew from bases in Britain over enemy-occupied territory in France and Germany.

Bombing missions were a terrible experience for both the crews and the people who lived and worked in the cities, factories and infrastructure the missions destroyed.

The planes were cold, the trips were long, conditions were cramped, many of the men were very inexperienced pilots, and accident rates were high. The planes were frequently attacked by enemy fighters and shot at from the ground by anti-aircraft guns. Air crews were required to fly 30 missions before being taken out of the fighting, though the average life span for a crew was only 14 missions.

The Allies continued to bomb and destroy cities in Germany and occupied countries while gearing up for the great seaborne invasion of Europe from the west, known as the Normandy Landings on D-Day, 6 June 1944. Allied ground troops took on the German ground forces and fought their way towards Berlin from the west. RAAF airmen took part in the Allied drive through France, Italy and Sicily. RAAF squadrons also participated in anti-submarine patrols, and attacks on shipping in the Atlantic Ocean and the North Sea.

Allied POWs in Europe

When the Allied armies invaded Europe and started to push into Germany and occupied European countries, they eventually liberated thousands of prisoners of the Germans. Many of these were Australians.

Australian soldiers who had been captured in fighting in Greece, Crete and North Africa, and hundreds of airmen who had been shot down had been kept in prisoner of war (POW) camps in Italy, Germany, France, Poland and other European countries.

For the most part, the captors treated these men according to the accepted rules of warfare: they fed, housed and clothed them adequately. There were exceptions where prisoners were tortured, beaten or virtually starved, and cases where men who tried to escape were murdered by their captors, but these were relatively rare. At the end of the war, prisoners were sometimes forced to march to new camps, where conditions were severe.

Most Australian captives received mail and Red Cross parcels and this helped the men to survive. A few spent much of their time planning escapes, which rarely worked, and trying to keep themselves occupied. Some POWs were forced to work in German farms and factories. Of the 22,000 Australian military and civilian prisoners of war held by the Germans and Italians, all but 265 survived. At least 12 Indigenous Australians are known to have been kept in POW camps during the Second World War.

The Holocaust

As the Allied armies liberated Europe from German control, and as they pushed into Germany and Poland, they made horrifying discoveries: not German prisoner of war camps, but German concentration and extermination camps. These were camps set up specifically to murder people, or to work them to death.

Part of the Nazi philosophy against which Australians fought was 'racial purity', which for the Nazis included eliminating Jews, gypsies, homosexuals, radicals, Slavs and the physically or mentally handicapped. As the Allies liberated places such as Belsen and Dachau in Germany, and especially Auschwitz-Birkenau in Poland, they saw the results of this Nazi attempt to destroy, in particular, the Jews of Europe.

Special discriminatory laws had been passed against Jewish people as soon as the Nazis had seized power in Germany in 1933. By the start of the war, however, Jewish people were being taken from their homes and either executed by roving execution squads, or sent to camps to be worked or starved to death, or gassed. There was resistance by some victims, but most were simply unable to do anything other than submit to the well organised and ruthlessly efficient process.

Whole families were wiped out. There are survivors living in Australian cities today who can name dozens of close family members and friends who simply disappeared in these camps. A commonly accepted estimate says about six million Jews died in this holocaust.

Civilian deaths

At least 45 million civilians lost their lives in the war, not just to battles and bombings, but to enemy troops moving through their countries, and due to war-related diseases and famines. Millions in Eastern Europe, in particular Russians, were killed by German troops. Millions of German troops were also killed by the Russians. Tens of thousands of German civilians were slaughtered by Russian troops during their push to Berlin, and then far more as Russia expelled Germans from occupied countries. The greatest civilian casualties were probably in China, where the number of deaths may have been 20 million, but could also have been as many as 50 million.

The final stages in Pacific and Asia

By early 1943, the Japanese had been defeated in Papua, but they still held most of New Guinea. During 1943, 1944 and 1945, Australian troops were involved in a series of operations in New Guinea, New Britain and Borneo.

The New Guinea offensives of 1943 to 1944 involved mainly Australian troops, with Australian naval and United States and Australian air support. The offensives were the single largest series of connected operations Australia had ever mounted. They involved the Militia, the AIF, United States forces, and thousands of New Guineans, and included some of the fiercest fighting of the war.

The terrain was rugged, the climate appalling and more men suffered from disease than enemy bullets. The offensives involved the dirty, dangerous and distasteful task of isolating Japanese troops – cut off now from their main forces – and either killing them all, or killing them until the remaining ones surrendered.

The places these men fought are now virtually forgotten to Australians other than to that declining number of old men who gather once a year under their unit banners bearing those names.

Island-hopping

From late 1943, United States forces, supported by the Australian navy and air force, began a strategy known as 'island-hopping'. This was to isolate and starve out the Japanese garrisons in Dutch New Guinea and the Netherlands East Indies (Indonesia) as part of the move to retake the Philippines. The Allies would attack a Japanese stronghold, secure the beach for the landing of supplies, drive the Japanese into an isolated area, then leave troops to 'mop up' the enemy using firepower while the next island was taken.

The RAAF played a significant part in the Battle of the Bismarck Sea (2–4 March 1943), which destroyed a Japanese convoy heading for Lae, New Guinea. The large Japanese force at Rabaul was cut off from supplies and 100,000 Japanese soldiers were made ineffective by the American blockade. HMAS *Australia* became the first Allied ship to be hit by a *kamikaze* (suicide attack) aircraft on 21 October 1944, in the Allied invasion at Leyte Gulf in the Philippines, although it was not sunk.

Germany defeated

On 7 May 1945, Germany surrendered and Australians celebrated VE (Victory in Europe) Day on 8 May. The Pacific war continued and Australian soldiers were tasked with their final battles in 1945. These included helping to take the Solomon Islands, especially Bougainville, and retaking Tarakan, Brunei Bay and Balikpapan in Borneo.

Japan's surrender

From early 1945 United States forces were able to set up airfields in islands near the Japanese home islands and to start a campaign of bombing Japan's major cities. The final act was to drop atomic bombs on Hiroshima on 6 August 1945, and Nagasaki on 9 August 1945. The bombings remain controversial even today. Many countries have developed and tested nuclear technology, but no nuclear weapons have been used in conflict since the Second World War.

Japan surrendered six days after the bombs, but a major contributing factor was the entry of the Soviet Union into the war against Japan on 8 August. The Soviets swept through Japanese-occupied Manchuria, and threatened to invade the Japanese home islands from the north. Japan's final defence strategy was to hold out against the American invasion from the south, and the north was virtually unprotected. The prospect of a successful invasion of their home soil added to the pressure to surrender.

Hiroshima ended the war, and also became a symbol of hope for no future wars.

The liberation of POWs of the Japanese

After Japan surrendered, VP (Victory in the Pacific) Day was celebrated across Australia.

Australians only then began to learn of the appalling experiences of the prisoners of war, civilian internees and local people held by Japanese forces. Of the more than 21,000 Australian military and civilian prisoners of the Japanese, over 8000 died.

The largest number of Australians was kept in Changi prison, in Singapore. Conditions were terrible and prisoners suffered from overcrowding, poor food and inadequate medical treatment.

Other prisoners were selected to work as slave labour in Japanese coal mines and factories, and some Australian POWs were witness to the dropping of the atomic bombs at Hiroshima and Nagasaki.

Thousands of prisoners were transported from Singapore to Thailand and Burma to build a railway supply line to aid Japan's expansion. Conditions on the Thai–Burma Railway were harsh. Allied prisoners were bashed, starved, tortured and given poor medical treatment, as too were Asian labourers conscripted to join them. More than 90,000 people died building the 415-kilometre track.

Most Australian soldiers and officers endured their conditions and helped each other as much as possible. Great bravery was shown by some, including the inspirational doctors Lieutenant Colonel Edward 'Weary' Dunlop and Lieutenant Colonel Albert Coates. They endured beatings to protect the men under their command, while providing medical and surgical treatment in appalling conditions.

This, as well as the countless examples of mateship, fortitude and skill in military behaviour indicates just how much of the Anzac tradition was still alive in the values of the Second World War service men and women. In fact, a common theme in cartoons at the start of the war was the handing on of the flame from the first AIF of the First World War to their sons in the second AIF in the Second World War, thus suggesting a continuation of the important Anzac tradition in Australian life.

Aboriginal and Torres Strait Islander servicemen and women

Aboriginal and Torres Strait Islander men found it fairly easy to enlist in the first year of the war, but from late 1940 the government toughened the rules of enlistment to exclude many non-Europeans and some volunteers were turned away. Many men managed to get around this ban. An estimated 3000 Aboriginal and Torres Strait Islander men served in the armed forces in the Second World War.

Indigenous Australians served in the Militia, the AIF, the RAAF (where one fighter pilot, Leonard Waters, flew 90 sorties against the Japanese) and the RAN. They received equal pay, could expect promotion on merit, and forged friendships with their comrades. For many white Australians this was their first contact with Aboriginal and Torres Strait Islander people. Both benefited from it. There were, however, examples where Indigenous Australians, even in uniform, were refused service in pubs or endured racial taunts from other soldiers, usually men they had not served closely with.

Many served in a specially raised unit, the Torres Strait Light Infantry Battalion, which was formed in 1941. The experience of the troops in this unit differed from those in the regular military forces. They were paid less than other troops (roughly half pay) and generally did not have access to many veterans' benefits. Some Aboriginal and Torres Straits Islander people in northern Australia joined the units that patrolled the extensive coastline

ROYAL AUSTRALIAN AIR FORCE
Certificate of Service and Discharge

Number 14194   Rank Acting Sergeant

Full Name PARSONS, John William

Date of Birth 3/12/1910   Date of Enlistment 18/3/1940   Date of Discharge 5/12/1945

Occupation in Civil Life Labourer

Reason for Discharge under the provisions of A.F.R. 115 (t)

"On Demobilisation"

Character on Discharge Exemplary

R.A.A.F. Mustering or Trade Driver Motor Transport

Degree of Trade Proficiency: A   B.SUPR   C.SUPR

DESCRIPTION
(On enlistment)

Height 5'9"   Colour of Hair Fair   Colour of Eyes Blue   Complexion Fair

Marks and Scars or Wounds   Nil

Qualifications and Special Courses R53 R.D. Cse 11.4.40. 2 R.D. 1/40

PROMOTIONS, REMUSTERINGS, Etc.

Rank	Date	Mustering or Trade	Decorations, Medals, etc.
Aircraftman Class 1	18. 3.1940	Guard	1939-43 Star
Leading Aircraftman	1. 7.1940	Guard	Canberra 32/44
Aircraftman Class 1	1.11.1940	Driver Motor Transport	Pacific Star
Leading Aircraftman	16.10.1941	Driver Motor Transport	82 W/Hq 14/45
Corporal	1.10.1942	Driver Motor Transport	
Acting Sergeant	25. 9.1943	Driver Motor Transport	

Remarks: Qualified for a Returned from Active Service Badge

Office of issue and date stamp. Royal Australian Air Force Headquarters, Melbourne 5th January, 1946

_____
Air Member for Personnel

R.A.A.F. PRINTING UNIT   FOR NOTES SEE OVER.   R.A.A.F. FORM P/P.83A, REVISED SEPTEMBER, 1945

and searched for crashed Allied and enemy airmen. Men in these units were not formally enlisted and often missed out on pay and benefits. Indigenous women also enlisted in the auxiliary services.

An estimated 3000 Aboriginal and Torres Strait Islander civilians were employed as labourers, mainly in Western Australia and the Northern Territory performing vital tasks for the military. They salvaged crashed aircraft, located unexploded bombs, helped build roads and airfields, and assisted in the delivery of civilian and military supplies. They stacked ammunition and timber, maintained gardens and slaughtered cattle. Aboriginal women were employed in domestic duties or as hospital orderlies and cleaners.

The army eventually employed about 20 per cent of the Northern Territory's Aboriginal population. In Port Hedland in Western Australia many local Aboriginal people were conscripted into work on cattle stations and in the pastoral industries. Others became members of the voluntary defence corps and operated coastal defences, searchlights and anti-aircraft batteries in emergencies.

After the war

Manpower controls were quickly eased, as was censorship. Some rationing remained (until 1949 for petrol), but most goods were soon available again. Many war workers were dismissed from their factories but other peacetime industries began to spring up and absorb the dismissed workers. Rehabilitation and reconstruction began quickly.

In December 1945, the final casualty figures could be published, with over 35,000 Australians dead. Many more had been wounded physically or mentally. Many of these men and women, and their dependants, would need support from the Australian Government for a long time to come. The families of the servicemen and nurses had endured painful years of worry about the safety or even the whereabouts of their loved ones. Some never found out how and why they died.

Second World War battle-related deaths by services

(Exclusive of 10,137 deaths by other causes)

Service	Deaths by all causes
Royal Australian Navy	1900
Australian Military Forces	18,713
Royal Australian Air Force	6460

John Robertson, *Australia Goes to War 1939–1945*, Doubleday, 1984

Opposite: The war is over. A services discharge certificate.

POW stories

Sister Vivian Bullwinkel

Sister Vivian Bullwinkel was a South Australian nurse who had joined the Australian Army Nursing Service in 1941 and been sent to Singapore.

On 12 February 1942, Bullwinkel and 65 other nurses boarded the transport ship *Vyner Brooke* to escape the Japanese invasion of Singapore. Two days later the ship was sunk by Japanese aircraft. Bullwinkel, 21 other nurses, and a large group of men, women and children made it ashore at Banka Island. They were joined the next day by about 100 British soldiers. The group decided to surrender, and while the civilian women and children went to search for someone in charge, the nurses, soldiers and wounded waited. Japanese soldiers appeared and executed the men. They told the nurses to wade into the sea and then machine-gunned them. Bullwinkel was struck by a bullet and pretended to be dead until the Japanese soldiers left. She hid with a wounded British soldier for 12 days before they decided once again to surrender.

They were taken captive but the soldier died soon after. Bullwinkel spent the next three and a half years in captivity. She was one of just 24 of the 65 nurses who had been on the *Vyner Brooke* to survive the war.

AWM P03960.001

Charles Hughes Cousins

Charles Hughes Cousins was a captain in the AIF. He was captured at the Fall of Singapore. The Japanese found out that he had been a radio announcer and demanded he broadcast propaganda at Changi prison camp, which he refused. He was then taken to Tokyo at the end of July 1942. There he wrote propaganda scripts, coached English-speaking Japanese announcers and made shortwave broadcasts over Radio Tokyo. He maintained that he did so under threat of torture and death, and that the broadcasts were of little use to the Japanese. He claimed that he deliberately sabotaged the broadcasts by using subtle ridicule and by putting in information useful to the Allies.

At the end of the war Cousins was sent back to Sydney under arrest. To some he was a traitor while to others, including members who served with him, he behaved in a justified and sensible way. The AIF decided not to put Cousins on trial. Three months later the men of his battalion elected Cousins to lead them on the Anzac Day march through Sydney.

The war had cost Australians the equivalent of about $74 billion in today's terms. Many industries had, however, prospered and developed far more quickly than would otherwise have been the case. There were great shortages of civilian materials, especially building materials to meet the demand of returning soldiers eager to set up their new lives. Jobs were needed for the returning soldiers and servicewomen. Educational opportunities had been cut off for many and they would now look to complete courses and training.

Australia itself had changed: people had been exposed to new ideas, experiences and influences. Millions of people throughout the war-torn countries were destitute or refugees and looked to make a new life in a better place: could Australia help them? Could Australians revert to their prewar lives and standards, or would they have to create a new society in Australia which reflected postwar values and needs?

Spanish refugees in Toulouse, circa 1940s. The war had left millions of people in need of a safe home.

10 Postwar Australia

An economic boom sparked by postwar conditions and new waves of immigrants allowed Australia to grow socially and culturally. The country became more active in international politics and affairs. There was movement towards greater Indigenous equality. Improved technology gave rise to a consumerist culture that attracted the teenage generation.

The first Holden car, launched by Prime Minister Chifley in 1948, was evidence of the growing significance of secondary industry in Australia.

IMMIGRATION

After the Second World War, the Australian Government decided the country needed a larger population both for military defence and to create wealth through economic development. The larger the population, the more demand there would be for goods and services, and therefore employment. In 1945, the population was seven million. The government wanted 2 per cent growth or 140,000 more people each year. The birth rate was only producing 70,000, so the other 70,000 would have to come from immigration.

'Ten pound poms'

The Minister for Immigration, Arthur Calwell, initially looked to the traditional source of Australia's immigration: Britain. The Australian Government paid the fare of British ex-servicemen and their families to Australia. The government also subsidised tickets for other British migrants. They only had to pay £10 for an adult fare and £5 for a child aged 14–18 for passage by ship to Australia. At the time a full fare cost about £120.

A 1949 poster designed to project a vibrant image of Australia in order to attract migrants.

The scheme was offered on the condition that migrants remain in Australia for a minimum of two years. More than one million Britons took this chance to change their lives. There are many famous Australians whose family immigrated this way, such as Kylie Minogue and Hugh Jackman, whose parents were 'ten pound poms'. Prime ministers Julia Gillard and Tony Abbott also came to Australia as children under the assisted passage migration scheme.

Displaced persons

As British immigration wasn't high enough, Calwell looked to the displaced persons of Europe. Millions of people in Europe had lost everything during the war. Homes were destroyed during bombing raids, civilians fled approaching armies or were taken as forced labour, countries were invaded and the populations pushed out or thrown into prison or concentration camps.

In 1947, approximately 1.6 million people still remained in displaced persons' camps in Europe. Calwell visited some of the camps and agreed that Australia would take an annual minimum of 12,000 refugees between 1947 and 1953. The refugees would be bound to work for two years wherever they were sent, but would be given accommodation, care and a job. Calwell selected healthy people whom he believed would work and assimilate easily into the Australian community due to their appearance, culture and religion being similar to those of the majority of Britons and Australians.

The 'Beautiful Balts'

The first boatload of 844 of these refugees arrived in Fremantle on the *General Stuart Heintzelman* in 1947. Calwell knew that he had to 'sell' this new source of immigration to Australians and government photographers were there to take propaganda shots of the new arrivals. The photos showed beautiful young women and smiling strong men from Estonia, Latvia and Lithuania, waving and cheering as they arrived. The images worked, and newspapers reported favourably on the new immigrants, who were nicknamed Calwell's 'Beautiful Balts'.

Within two years, ships were regularly travelling between Naples and Australia bringing migrants under the Displaced Persons Scheme. When the scheme ceased in 1953, it had delivered 170,000 refugees to Australia.

Migrant reception camps

At first, the refugees were housed in former army camps. The biggest and best known camp was at Bonegilla, near Wodonga, in Victoria. About 300,000 displaced persons and other sponsored immigrants went through Bonegilla between 1947 and 1971.

Country of birth of settler arrivals

Top sources of immigration in 1945–1949 and in 1970–1975

Country	1945–1949	Country	1970–1975
UK and Ireland	51.5%	UK and Ireland	50.4%
Germany	18.6%	Yugoslavia	10.6%
New Zealand	5.7%	Greece	5%
India	4.7%	Italy	4.4%
Italy	4.5%	United States	4.3%
United States	3.8%	New Zealand	3.6%
China	2.3%	Lebanon	2.8%
Poland	2.2%	Turkey	2.7%
Total: 167,546		**Total: 501,201**	

They're a Weird Mob

One of the most popular books of the 1950s and 1960s was *They're a Weird Mob*, by Nino Culotta (pseudonym of author John O'Grady). It is the story of Italian migrant Giovanni, known as Nino, a journalist who wants to tell Italians about Australia. Nino speaks fluent formal English, but is introduced to working class Australian slang when he takes a job as a brickie's labourer. The humour is in Nino's confused attempts to understand the strange language.

The book was actually written by John O'Grady, an Australian writer. It can be seen as sexist, centred towards the attitudes of men and patronising towards migrants, but it also reflects the qualities that were in the ideal Australia – humour, acceptance, enterprise, hard work, enjoyment of life, love of family, mateship and a 'fair go' for all.

The conditions were basic. People lived 26 to a tin hut, dormitory style, with little furniture and no heating. Men and women were in separate huts, even if they were married, though this changed later. The camp provided meals, a hospital and cleaners, while the government worked out where to send the migrants to work. The migrants were also provided with English language classes, and training in 'Australianness'. Most stayed in the centres for four to six weeks, but some up to six months.

Directable migrants

Between 1951 and 1959 the Australian Government negotiated agreements with individual countries to bring out migrants. These migrants would be directed into particular jobs for two years. Agreements were made with the Netherlands, Italy, West Germany, Belgium, Austria, Greece, Spain, the United States, Switzerland, Denmark, Norway, Sweden and Finland. About 500,000 migrants were sponsored in this way.

Smaller numbers of refugees arrived from China in 1949, and from Czechoslovakia and Hungary in the 1950s, when the Soviet Union took control of those countries.

An example of a passenger transit card, which allowed migrants to leave the ship at various ports.

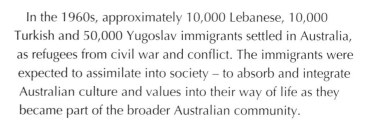

In the 1960s, approximately 10,000 Lebanese, 10,000 Turkish and 50,000 Yugoslav immigrants settled in Australia, as refugees from civil war and conflict. The immigrants were expected to assimilate into society – to absorb and integrate Australian culture and values into their way of life as they became part of the broader Australian community.

Assimilation

The slang term 'DP' (displaced person) for all non-British migrants was changed officially in 1951 to 'New Australians'.

The postwar immigration program provided Australia with many benefits. It brought in hard-working people who wanted to succeed, weakened the idea of 'White Australia' as a part of national identity, and introduced greater cultural variety. There were tensions and prejudices among some people on both sides, but governments, along with organisations such as the Good Neighbour Council, churches, community groups and many individuals worked to welcome and integrate migrants into the Australian community.

Many migrant groups clustered in particular areas, drawn by the need or comfort of a familiar language and culture, so suburbs became associated with specific ethnic groups. Usually the young people in these migrant groups married into the host population and became identified to themselves and to others as, for example, Italian-Australians or Greek-Australians, and not just Italians or Greeks.

Migrants brought their old culture with them to the new society. Guna Kinne made this outfit over a period of 30 years – starting work on it as a sewing project while a schoolgirl in Riga in 1942, completing the jacket as she fled Latvia at the end of the Second World War, with final touches made to the costume after she migrated to Australia. As she fled her homeland, she took the unfinished costume with her, together with some clothes and photographs. She later wore the costume at a dance in a displaced persons camp in Germany, the day she met her future husband.

SNOWY MOUNTAINS SCHEME

Many of the migrants contributed to one of Australia's greatest building achievements. In 1944 the Commonwealth, New South Wales and Victorian governments agreed to create the country's largest ever engineering project: the Snowy Mountains Hydro-Electric Scheme. Work started on the project in the Great Dividing Range in 1949.

The Snowy Mountains were particularly suitable for the scheme because they are the highest peaks in Australia, where rain and snow is easily collected. Water from the headwaters of the Snowy River and its tributaries naturally flows east to the sea. Under the scheme, that water is captured and diverted through huge tunnels to the western side of the mountain range to generate electricity and to provide water for irrigation on the western plains. The steep drop down the western slopes allows the water to gather sufficient force to rotate the turbines and create electricity.

This was a massive engineering job in a beautiful but harsh area. It involved creating a series of huge reservoirs, dam walls, tunnels, power stations, roads, supply depots, settlements and electricity towers and cables – in a virtually uninhabited area, in all seasons.

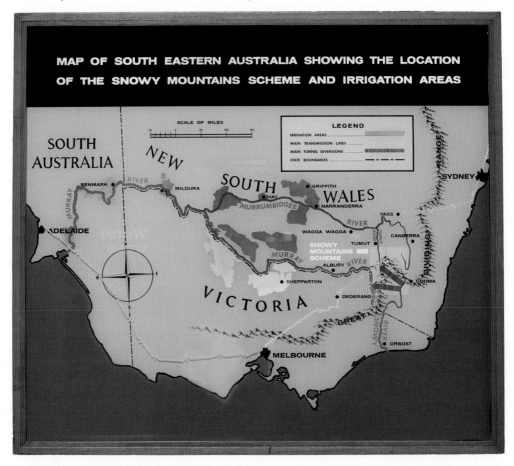

A lightbox showing details of the Snowy Mountains Scheme, which employed thousands of new migrants.

The scheme was completed in 1974. It now covers an area of approximately 8000 square kilometres, and includes 16 major dams, 145 kilometres of connecting tunnels and 80 kilometres of aqueducts.

As well as generating hydroelectricity, the waters diverted to the west irrigate the Murrumbidgee Valley and the Murray-Lower Darling Valley, both in New South Wales and the Murray-Goulburn Valley in Victoria. The water is used to grow rice, crops for pasture of animals, cereals, vegetables and fruit. It stimulated population growth and employment in these regions. The scheme also increased access to the Snowy Mountains for tourism and winter sports.

Pride and achievement in work were powerful forces in uniting people from different backgrounds on the Snowy scheme. World tunnelling records were made and broken during construction of the scheme. This medal was awarded to worker A. S. Novikov when a tunnelling team advanced 474 feet (144 metres) in a week.

There were costs other than the huge monetary price of the scheme. The engineering destroyed some natural areas and historic settlements, and reduced the flow of the Snowy River – the river made iconic by Banjo Paterson, who imagined his Man from Snowy River chasing wild brumbies down steep mountain slopes.

A snapshot of migrant lives

Werner Hessling was unable to secure a home for his young family in postwar Germany. He was brought to Australia on a government assistance scheme in 1954, and spent some time in the Bonegilla migrant camp before getting a permanent job with the Commonwealth Railways.

Petronella and Michael Wensing left the Netherlands in 1953. They had two small children with another on the way. Petronella's skills as a dressmaker and craftswoman were widely admired and helped her feel accepted in the community.

In 1944 **Lilija Brakmanis** fled Latvia after the Russian invasion, bringing her dentistry equipment with her. She responded to an Australian advertisement for skilled labour, but her qualifications were not recognised here, and she worked as a housekeeper and cleaner. Eventually she qualified to work again as a dentist.

Triantafylia Stamatiou (Rose Pappas) grew up on the small Greek island of Castellorizo. During the Second World War the island was bombed, and the population fled to Cyprus, before coming to Australia in 1949, with her precious Castellorizian costume.

The people

The scheme was a triumph of engineering, and a triumph of multiculturalism and assimilation. More than 100,000 people worked on it, at least 70 per cent of whom were migrants from more than 30 countries.

A large part of the workforce was made up of displaced persons from Europe, whose lives had been disrupted by the Second World War. Some of the different European ethnic groups represented by the scheme's workers had long-standing traditional grievances, or had even been enemies during the recent war. All of the workers had to be fed, sheltered, equipped, and helped to become part of an effective and harmonious working group, within the broader Australian community.

Ilarione CAPPELLUTI

THE

GOOD NEIGHBOUR COUNCIL OF S.A.

extends congratulations and good wishes to you upon the occasion of your Naturalization and welcomes you to full citizenship in the national life of Australia.

47 Waymouth Street, Adelaide.

Paul Mc Guire
President

For migrants and for local support organisations, such as the Good Neighbour Council, naturalisation was evidence of successful integration into the Australia community.

There were occasional outbreaks of ethnic tension, but very few. In most cases people wanted to escape the past, not bring it with them, and were working to build a future. And in the hard and often dangerous conditions, it was necessary to work together.

Among the 'old Australians', there was some anti-foreign prejudice: jealousy over young foreign men meeting local girls, the reluctance to accept strange new food and customs, and irritation at not understanding foreign languages. Much of this was broken down by younger generations in the schoolyard, where kids swapped stories and joined together to play.

The Snowy Mountains Scheme reflected what was happening in Australia's cities: some migrants quickly adopted typical Australian habits, others chose to maintain strong elements of their birth culture; some learned English quickly, others spoke in their native language whenever they could; some mixed socially with others in the community, others kept to their own family and national group.

ECONOMIC DEVELOPMENT

The Second World War had forced Australia's industry to expand and modernise, leading to an economic boom that continued for the next 35 years. As countries rebuilt after the war they needed food as well as minerals for manufacturing – and Australia could supply both. Because the Korean War (1950–1953) was waged for part of the year in freezing landscapes, the United States Government needed to buy huge amounts of wool for its troops' uniforms. This combined with a return to prewar international demand to create a boom in Australian wool.

There was a postwar housing shortage as the soldiers returned, leading to many quickly built homes in new boom suburbs.

By the late 1940s, with massive support from the United States, Europe and Japan had started to re-industrialise, and imported large quantities of Australian coal and iron ore. By 1967, Japan had overtaken Britain as Australia's main export market. The demand led to increased exploration in Australia for minerals, and major deposits were found: iron ore and nickel in Western Australia, oil and gas in the Bass Strait, manganese and uranium in the Northern Territory, coal in the Bowen Basin in Queensland and bauxite for aluminium in Queensland and the Northern Territory.

Australia's rapid population growth in the 1950s and 1960s through immigration created a higher demand for food, locally manufactured goods, building materials and services such as education and health. The period between 1945 and 1965 is commonly referred to as the 'baby boom' era, as there was a large and sustained increase in births following the instability of the Second World War. Australia's protected manufacturing industries benefited from this postwar demand. Increased productivity led to full employment, high wages and profitability, and ever-improving working conditions. Governments and private industry continued to borrow heavily to finance developments, and this added to their debt repayment commitment.

The cost of this growth began to appear. By the end of the 1960s, Australian-manufactured goods were becoming too expensive to export, while locally they were too expensive to compete with foreign-made imports. As other countries, especially Japan, improved their productivity and the quality of their goods, their products started to outsell locally made ones. The United States and Japan would also in time become the major sources of Australia's imports, reflecting the development of Australia as a consumer society.

AUSTRALIA IN THE WORLD

After the Second World War, Australia played a more active role as a world citizen than it ever had before, particularly in the Asia-Pacific region. It also took its place clearly on one side of the Cold War, which began in 1945.

The United Nations

The United Nations (UN) was formed in 1945 to promote international cooperation and prevent another conflict as devastating as the Second World War.

Australia was one of the 51 founder members of the United Nations that met for the first time in London in 1946. Minister for External Affairs Dr Herbert Evatt was the President of the UN General Assembly when it passed the historic Universal Declaration of Human Rights in 1948.

Another Australian, Jessie Street, had been the only woman adviser to the Australian delegation involved in drafting the Declaration. She was responsible for including gender in the Declaration's vision, in recognition of the need for equal rights for women and men. This vision stated that *'Everyone is entitled to all the rights and freedoms set forth in this Declaration, without distinction of any kind, such as race, colour, sex, language, religion, political or other opinion'*.

ALP leader Dr Herbert Evatt was a key player in Australia's participation in the formation of the United Nations.

Turning towards Asia

The Second World War increased Australians' knowledge and experience of Asia and contacts with Asian people. Rather than depend on its traditional cultural links to Britain, Australia became more aware of greater global connections and opportunities. Australia was engaged in peacekeeping in Asian countries, economic aid and development in the Asia-Pacific region and promoting immigration and training of Asian students. The Cold War also caused new conflicts in Asia, in which Australia participated.

White Australia dismantled

After the war, attitudes to racial exclusion were changing and Australia gradually began dismantling the White Australia policy, which had excluded most Asians from Australia for the previous 50 years.

Published by the Commonwealth Office of Education, Grace Building, York St., Sydney—August 22, 1949

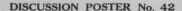

TRUSTEESHIP

U.N. stands guard over the rights of primitive people

The U.N. Trusteeship Council, formed in 1947, is standing guard over the rights of 15 million primitive people living mainly in the tropical areas of Africa and the Pacific Islands. By periodically visiting the territories involved, accepting petitions and examining reports submitted by administering nations, the Council aims to promote the political, economic, social and educational advancement of the native inhabitants. A long-range objective is for each territory to become either self-governing or independent.

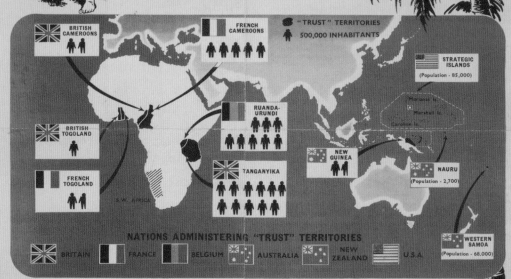

BRITISH CAMEROONS

FRENCH CAMEROONS

"TRUST" TERRITORIES
500,000 INHABITANTS

STRATEGIC ISLANDS
(Population - 85,000)

Marianas Is.
Marshall Is.
Caroline Is.

BRITISH TOGOLAND

RUANDA-URUNDI

NEW GUINEA

FRENCH TOGOLAND

TANGANYIKA

NAURU
(Population - 2,700)

S.W. AFRICA

NATIONS ADMINISTERING "TRUST" TERRITORIES

BRITAIN   FRANCE   BELGIUM   AUSTRALIA   NEW ZEALAND   U.S.A.

WESTERN SAMOA
(Population - 68,000)

How The System Works

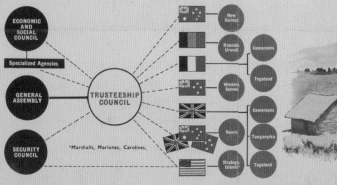

ECONOMIC AND SOCIAL COUNCIL

Specialized Agencies

GENERAL ASSEMBLY

TRUSTEESHIP COUNCIL

SECURITY COUNCIL

*Marshalls, Marianas, Carolines,

New Guinea

Ruanda-Urundi — Cameroons

Western Samoa — Togoland

Cameroons

Nauru — Tanganyika

Strategic Islands — Togoland

It has been suggested that, instead of being responsible merely for the mandates held under the old League of Nations, the Trusteeship Council should supervise the administration of ALL colonial territories. What arguments can you advance for and against this proposal? How can the interests of primitive native peoples and those of the administering authorities be most effectively combined?

SIMMONS LTD., GLEBE, SYDNEY

Australia had received 6000 Asian refugees during the Second World War. At the end of the war, Australia supported Indonesian independence from the Dutch. In 1947 Minister for Immigration Arthur Calwell fought unsuccessfully to allow Chinese residents who had been in Australia for at least 15 years to be naturalised. In 1949 the new Liberal-Country Party Government of Robert Menzies allowed 800 of the refugees to stay, and in 1957 changed the law to give citizenship to non-Europeans after 15 years of residence. The Menzies Government also made entry easier and abolished the immigration dictation test in 1958.

In 1965 the Liberal–Country Party Coalition Government and the Australian Labor Party opposition both dropped White Australia as part of their policies. A year later, the government abolished any reference to race in immigration and accepted applications on the basis of the applicants' professional qualifications, suitability as immigrants, their ability to integrate and their usefulness to Australia.

As a result non-European arrivals increased rapidly, though still in relatively small numbers. Between 1966 and 1970, an average of 6500 Asian people were allowed to settle each year.

Peacekeeping in Indonesia

Japan had replaced the Netherlands as the colonial power over Indonesia during the Second World War. After the war, the Netherlands wanted to resume its control. Indonesian nationalists wanted to establish their own independent nation and there were clashes between the Indonesian and Dutch forces. A truce was called, and the Australian embassy and military officers became part of the very first UN peacekeeping activity by acting as independent observers of the truce from 1947 to 1951. This role helped Indonesia gain national independence.

Helping Japan

Australian servicemen and servicewomen were called on to supervise Japan's disarmament and to help the nation rebuild and recover. The Occupation of Japan lasted from 13 February 1946 to the end of 1951, when the San Francisco Treaty was signed. About 16,000 Australians served in this British Commonwealth Occupation Force.

The Colombo Plan

From 1951, students from south-eastern and south Asia arrived in Australia through the Colombo Plan. The plan was developed as a scheme for Commonwealth countries to assist developing countries in south-eastern and south Asia, and to help counter communist movements. Australia played a leading role in the designing of the scheme – to help these countries by educating and training Asian students in Australia and as an attempt to defuse the continuing tensions of the White Australia policy. The students would then return and help to develop their own countries educationally, politically, socially and economically. A form of the plan continues today and provides practical help and personal contacts between Australia and Asia.

Opposite: A poster on 'Trusteeship' created by the Commonwealth Office of Education in 1945. Such posters and pamphlets focusing on the world and national events was an effort by the Chifley Government to explain and stimulate discussion regarding Australia's socio-economic and political situation postwar.

Jessie Street

Jessie Street (born 1889; died 1970) was one of Australia's greatest human rights advocates. Born in India, she moved to New South Wales with her parents in 1896.

Street was an activist for women's equality in politics and for equal pay. She advocated against the discrimination of women in the law and public office, such as being able to serve on juries. Her methods of advocacy were personal – letters to newspapers, meetings, conferences, radio talks, leading delegations to ministers. As a result of the Second World War she became a pacifist, and also a supporter and admirer of the Soviet Union, which seemed to treat women equally.

Street was the only woman on Australia's delegation to finalise the Charter of the United Nations in 1945, and was one of several women who were successful in getting gender equality included in the UN Declaration of Human Rights.

She worked with Douglas Nichols, Faith Bandler and others to bring about a referendum in 1967. This referendum removed some of the discrimination in the Australian Constitution against Aboriginal and Torres Strait Islander people, and enabled the Australian Government to start legislating to improve Indigenous people's lives.

Street was also a strong sports enthusiast. She enjoyed playing tennis and hockey and was one of the founders of the University Women's Sports Association.

THE COLD WAR

The Cold War (1945–1991) was a period of military and political tension between the Western Bloc (the United States and its allies) and the Eastern Bloc (the USSR and its allies). From 1949, communist China was also part of this rivalry and tension.

After the Second World War, the European allies of the United States formed a military alliance called NATO (North Atlantic Treaty Organisation), which favoured capitalism and democracy. The USSR and the eastern European nations it controlled formed the Warsaw Pact or Eastern Bloc, which favoured the USSR's single-party communist system.

For the next 46 years, the United States and the USSR each tried to expand its power and influence over the other. It was called a 'cold' war because the conflict was primarily political, with little large-scale fighting – at least between the United States and USSR. Australia supported the United States and its allies, with opposition to communist expansion and influence becoming a strong element in Australian politics.

Anti-communism

In Australia a Liberal-Country Party Government was elected in 1949. As prime minister, Robert Menzies was deeply suspicious of the power that the small Communist Party of Australia had within key unions. He believed that these unions used the disruption of strikes to harm the Australian economy.

In 1950, Menzies passed a law to ban the Communist Party. The law was challenged in the High Court and overturned, but in 1951 Menzies held a referendum to change the Australian Constitution to allow his anti-communist law to pass. The referendum was narrowly defeated as many Australians believed that freedom of association was an important democratic principle, despite their concerns about communism.

In 1954 a Soviet agent in Australia, Vladimir Petrov, defected and revealed that Soviet spies and agents were active in Australia, including some with strong links to the Australian Labor Party and the Australian public service. Menzies could not make public all the evidence as this would have revealed that the United States had cracked Soviet codes, and was secretly monitoring them. The Labor Party argued that Petrov's claims were not genuine but there is now no doubt that Soviet spies were operating successfully within Australia, and with help from some Australians.

Atomic tests in Australia

The fear of communism and the possibility of another war in which Australia would be attacked led the Australian Government to participate in British and United States atomic weapons testing.

In 1949 the British Government wished to develop its own weapons and needed a safe place to test them. It approached Australia for help.

Between 1952 and 1959, Britain tested 12 atomic bombs on Australian territory – on the uninhabited Montebello Islands off the coast of Western Australia, and at Emu Plains and Maralinga in South Australia. The South Australian sites were chosen because of their remoteness and the relatively small numbers of their permanent population, the Anangu people. However, Indigenous Australians did fall victims to radiation from the tests.

Another 200 tests in the Maralinga area between 1959 and 1963 studied elements of atomic weapons. These resulted in deadly plutonium contamination of a large area around the test sites.

In 1946, in a joint project with the British Government, Australia established a site at Woomera, South Australia, for testing rockets intended to deliver atomic weapons. One of these rockets was used to launch Australia's only satellite, WRESAT, from Woomera in 1967, making Australia only the eighth nation in the world to launch a satellite.

In the 1950s, the United States established a base at Nurrungar, near Woomera, as a tracking station for its own tests. The base was also an important part of the United States' global military surveillance (or spy) network until the late 1990s and was therefore a significant element in the Cold War, making Australia a potential Soviet nuclear weapons target.

Radiation and contamination

The details behind the Maralinga tests are top secret. One likely goal of the tests was to gauge how the bombs affected unprotected people. Australian and British troops at Maralinga were lined up to see the explosions. They were instructed to turn their backs to the bomb ten seconds before detonation, then cover their eyes and finally turn to observe the bomb about five seconds after detonation. Film from the time shows them obeying these orders, dressed in shirts and shorts and shading their eyes as the mushroom-shaped cloud forms near them.

Both Australians and Britons who observed the tests in this way have developed cancer at a greater rate than their peers in the community. British courts have rejected claims for compensation and the costs of treatment by victims, arguing that there is no conclusive proof of a connection between the tests and their illnesses.

When government authorities set up their test site at Maralinga in the mid-1950s they had failed to find and remove all the traditional owners, the estimated 1200 nomadic Anangu people, from the area. Some Anangu were caught in the 'black mist' of one of the atomic explosions. The people, their water and food sources were covered in contaminated dust. Many became ill, and some died. Nuclear testing stopped in 1963, but the site was contaminated with radioactive material. The British Government did not clean the area properly until an Australian inquiry in the 1980s forced them to do so.

On 11 October 1956 a bomb test caused drifts of radioactive fallout over Adelaide. From 1957 to 1978 the Australian Government ran a monitoring program to measure radioactive fallout over the entire continent. The program measured the radioactive isotopes caesium-137 and strontium-90. Bone samples were taken from deceased bodies far from the tests sites – Perth, Adelaide, Brisbane, Melbourne, Sydney, plus Adelaide – and then tested. Results showed an increase in strontium-90 during atmospheric nuclear explosions worldwide, but not in sufficient quantities to cause physical harm.

Australia participated in testing atomic weapons in the 1950s and 1960s. This tie given to members of the test team ironically includes Aboriginal symbols – though the local people were forced to leave the area.

By 1963 it was clear that nuclear fallout from atmospheric atomic tests was the cause of severe health problems in many people. Australia signed a treaty in that year to ban atmospheric atomic tests and most testing went underground. The last known atmospheric test was by China in 1980.

The traditional Aboriginal owners of the Maralinga lands were denied effective access to these lands for over 30 years as a result of the British test program. The land was finally declared clear of contamination and most of it handed back to the Anangu people in 2009. The final small parcel was returned in 2014.

COLD WAR CONFLICTS IN ASIA

After the Second World War, communist ideology became a prevalent force in East Asia. Communist practice sought to overthrow the capitalist system in favour of a community, in which each individual contributed to the running of the country and in turn received basic needs. In practice it had led to one-party states with governments closely controlling people's lives. Communism was particularly strong in China when the People's Army, led by Mao Zedong, defeated the Chinese Nationalist Party to govern the country in 1949. Australia feared the threat of communism and entered four armed conflicts to help prevent its spread throughout Asia: the Korean War (1950–1953), Malaya (1950–1960), Indonesian Confrontation of Malaysia (1965–1966), and the Vietnam War (1962–1972).

Korean War

Not long after the end of the Second World War, Korea was divided into two parts at the 38th parallel north (the circle of latitude north of the Earth's equatorial plane). The southern zone was controlled by United States forces; the northern zone came under the influence of the Soviet Union.

In June 1950, North Korean forces invaded South Korea. The United Nations sent a force to defend South Korea. The force was composed of contingents from 15 nations including Australia, Britain, the United States, Canada, Turkey, Greece, Colombia, New Zealand, the Philippines, France, the Netherlands, South Africa and Luxembourg, and medical units from Denmark, India, Italy, Norway and Sweden. The Australian Government believed national security would be at risk if communist aggression was not stopped in Korea. The government also wished to show its full support for the United Nations.

The United Nations force managed to push the North Koreans back towards the Chinese border but this brought China into the war. The United States commander of the UN forces, General Douglas MacArthur, wanted to use atomic weapons against China, but he was refused permission and was replaced.

After years of bloody fighting in extremes of heat and cold, the two opposing sides ended up at the original border and a truce was called. Australian casualties numbered more than 1500, of whom around 340 were killed. Almost half a million South Koreans died as a result of the war, and an unknown number of North Koreans and Chinese.

Malaya

In the 19th century, Britain had claimed Malaya and parts of Borneo as colonies. In 1941, Japan had seized control of both these countries. During the Second World War many local Malays and Malay Chinese fought as guerrillas against the Japanese.

At the end of the war, the British wanted non-communist Malays to take control. The Malay Chinese, some of whom were communists, wanted Malaya to be a communist country, so they fought the British.

The Malayan and British governments asked Australia for military support and the government agreed. It was keen to help stabilise a friendly government in the region; to maintain a traditional commitment to Britain; and to meet potential enemies in other countries, rather than in Australia. The communist forces in Malaya were defeated by 1960.

Indonesian Confrontation

In 1963, the new Federation of Malaysia was created by the union of Malaya, North Borneo, Sarawak and Singapore (until 1965). Indonesia's pro-communist President Sukarno believed that the creation of the Federation of Malaysia was an attempt by Britain to maintain colonial rule of its former colonial possessions in south-east Asia.

Indonesia used the word 'Konfrontasi' (Confrontation) to describe their efforts to destabilise the new federation between 1962 and 1966. Indonesia launched a series of cross-border raids into Malaysian territory in early 1963.

Australian forces mounted cross-border operations to obtain intelligence and force the Indonesians to remain on the defensive on their own side of the border.

Indonesia and Malaysia signed a peace treaty in Bangkok in August 1966. Twenty-three Australians were killed during Confrontation. Because of the sensitivity of the cross-border operations, which remained secret at the time, Confrontation received very little coverage in the Australian press.

THE VIETNAM WAR

The Vietnam War was Australia's largest military conflict in the period.

In the north of Vietnam, nationalists called the Viet Minh were led by communist leader Ho Chi Minh. The Viet Minh fought for independence from French colonial powers in Vietnam. They succeeded in 1945, declared the Democratic Republic of Vietnam (DRV or North Vietnam) and claimed that they were the legitimate government of all Vietnam.

The south of the country became the Republic of Vietnam (RVN – South Vietnam). Local Viet Minh in South Vietnam tried to destabilise the government. The United States supported South Vietnam, believing that if it became communist, other neighbouring countries – Thailand, Laos, Cambodia and Malaya – would follow. This was called the 'Domino' theory.

Australian forces in Vietnam

Australia provided military advisers and trainers to South Vietnam from 1962. During 1963 and 1964, the United States called on its allies, including Australia, for increased military help.

In 1965, Prime Minister Robert Menzies announced to parliament that Australia would send combat troops to South Vietnam. Menzies' aim was to stop the threat and spread of communism, to support democratic nations and to support its ally, the United States, from whom Australia required military support should there be conflict in the Asia-Pacific region.

The Australian forces consisted of combat troops, supply troops, RAAF transport and combat aircraft and helicopters. The navy transported soldiers and supplies to and from Australia. There were also service nurses and civilian medical volunteers and civil aid workers. Many Indigenous Australians served during the war.

Australian commanders applied the theory of counter-revolutionary warfare they had learned in Malaya: rather than depending on large-scale battles, as was typical in the Second World War, the enemy should be denied access to its areas of supply – the local villages – and so be forced to wither and die. The approach was successful, and Phuoc Tuy province became one of the safest in South Vietnam during the Australian operations there.

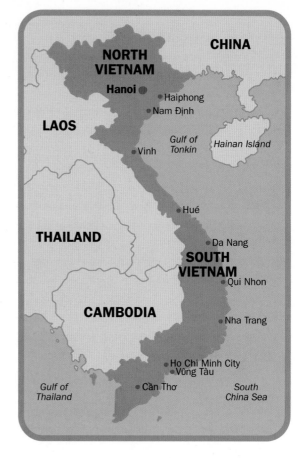

The end of the war

Between 1962 and 1975, 61,000 Australian troops and over 1600 civilians served in Vietnam. Most units were sent for 12-month tours.

By 1970 the growing unpopularity of Australian and US involvement in Vietnam led to increased public demonstrations against the war. Both governments claimed that they were confident the South Vietnamese were now able to defend themselves, and withdrew all combat troops. The last Australian combat troops left in 1971, and the last military trainers in 1972.

After the Allied troops left, the South Vietnamese forces struggled on but were overrun in 1975 when North Vietnamese tanks crashed through the gates of the Presidential Palace in Saigon.

OPPOSITION TO THE WAR

The Australian Government saw the conflict as a Chinese-supported communist invasion of the south by a dictatorial north. Some Australians saw it as a nationalist and anti-colonial movement and a civil war that foreign powers ought not to be involved in. Although most Australians supported the war at first, over time public opinion split dramatically. Different groups protested against the war for various reasons. Some people opposed the war itself, while others opposed the principle of conscription that operated during the war. The most vocal opposition came from student groups, who supported North Vietnam and targeted United States official premises or businesses in their protests.

National service (conscription)

Much of the eventual opposition to the war was due to the introduction of national service, or conscription for overseas service. A compulsory national service scheme was introduced in 1964 because of fears that Indonesia might turn communist and pose a military threat to Australia.

The system operated from November 1964 to December 1972. It was designed to add 4200 men to the army twice a year. All Australian men turning 20 that year had to register. Twice a year, marbles numbered to indicate birthdates were placed in a barrel. Those whose birthdates were drawn were called up for two years' military service – provided they passed the medical test and were not temporarily exempt (such as to complete university studies). Those whose birthdates were not drawn were exempt from the system. Once Australia committed to sending combat troops to Vietnam in 1965, it was clear that sooner or later conscripted soldiers would also be sent. The first conscripts were sent to Vietnam in 1966. Between 1966 and 1971 Australian infantry battalions were typically comprised of an even mix of regular soldiers and national servicemen.

The Whitlam Government ended the scheme in December 1972. During the scheme, 804,286 twenty-year-olds registered for national service; 63,735 national servicemen served in the army; and 15,381 served in Vietnam. Of the 500 Australians who died during their Vietnam service, 200 were national servicemen.

Regular public opinion surveys showed that most people supported the policy of conscription throughout the war, but they did not want the conscripts sent to Vietnam.

The television war

By 1970, the Vietnam War had become the longest conflict Australia had engaged in. Growing numbers of the public questioned whether the war could be won and, if not, whether Australian lives and resources should continue to be spent on it. News reports of inhumane behaviour by some United States troops, such as the massacre of 500 civilians in the village of My Lai in 1968, also added to public doubts about the war.

The Vietnam War has been called the 'television war', based on the idea that the public would watch nightly news broadcasts of events that had unfolded that day. This is only partly true for Australia. The government did not allow journalists and film crews to accompany the troops on combat missions. The time taken to get film back to Australia also meant that there was little 'current' combat footage. Most of what was shown on Australian TV was American footage of American battles. However, protests against the war could be filmed and then shown that same night. Student groups were particularly active, and their protests were at times provocative or aggressive, which garnered extra attention from the media.

In 1970 and 1971 a series of mass protests known as moratorium marches filled the streets of the capital cities – more than 200,000 Australians participated in these peaceful protests.

The soldiers' return

Many Vietnam War veterans who write about their experiences mention feeling a lack of appreciation or even rejection on their return to Australia. If they were part of an infantry battalion, they were brought back together by ship, and retained the camaraderie of the group with an official march through their capital city. Those who were not infantry, or who had arrived separately from the rest of their unit, were often simply flown back to Australia and

Australian participation in the Vietnam War divided the community. In 1970 a series of 'moratorium' demonstrations in cities and towns across the country saw hundreds of thousands gather in protest. This badge came from Wellington, New Zealand, where such anti-war sentiment was also prevalent.

discharged. Back home, some of these men knew nobody with whom they could share their experiences and struggled to readjust to their new lives.

The division the war created in Australian society meant that returning soldiers were not greeted as heroes. Some returned Vietnam servicemen felt they were not being included as part of the Anzac tradition, established during the first and second world wars, and which is so important in Australian identity. It was not until the 1987 Welcome Home parade for veterans of the Vietnam War that many finally felt thanked and accepted by their nation.

SOCIAL AND CIVIL RIGHTS

In 1946 the British Commonwealth nations agreed to stop referring to their citizens as 'British' citizens of their respective countries. In 1948 Australia passed the *Nationality and Citizenship Act*, and on 26 January 1949, the legal status of every person born in Australia, or born of Australian parents, or naturalised in Australia, changed from 'British subject' to 'Australian citizen'.

Citizenship involves three areas of rights: political, civil and social. Political rights include the right to form and join associations, and the right to stand for, and be an elector of, democratic legislatures. Civil rights are related to individual freedoms, such as freedom of speech and religion, the freedom of people to form contractual agreements with no government restrictions (freedom of contract), the right to own property, and the right to just treatment. Social rights include the right to security, ensured through welfare provisions, and the right to fair and equal economic opportunity.

While all Australians were now citizens, they did not all have equal rights, as there were limitations on the rights of many women, and of almost all Aboriginal and Torres Strait Islander people. The passing of the Universal Declaration of Human Rights by the United Nations in 1948, and Australia's acceptance of it, indicated a greater recognition of the need for all citizens in Australia to be treated equally.

Women's rights

In the years after the Second World War, most Australian women had equal political rights to men, but not civil and social equality. Developments during the next 25 years helped make progress towards equality.

A huge social change came with the invention of the contraceptive pill in 1961. The pill gave women greater control over their reproduction choices. This benefited the health of many women, and contributed to making some women less financially dependent on men.

Women had been expected – and in some cases legally compelled – to resign their jobs if they married. In 1966 the rule barring married women from being employed in the Commonwealth Public Service was abolished. All other government and private industries gradually followed the precedent.

This helped boost the number of women working, but not their wages. In 1969, the Commonwealth Court of Conciliation and Arbitration ruled that women were entitled to equal pay for equal work. This reversed the previous landmark decision of the court in the famous Harvester Case of 1907, which had condemned women to less than 60 per cent of the male wage.

On 21 October 1969, Melbourne woman Zelda D'Aprano chained herself to a door in the court to draw attention to women's wage inequality, gaining great publicity for the 1969 decision. Although the law demanded equal pay for equal work, it did not state that women's work was equal to men's. The law still said that when the work was usually undertaken by women, they did not have the right to equal pay with men doing that same work.

Uniform worn by Shirley Strickland at the 1956 Summer Olympics in Melbourne. Strickland won the 80 métres hurdles and with the 4x100 metres relay team.

In the broader social sense, attitudes towards women were also changing. In the Melbourne Olympics of 1956, the exceptional achievements of female Australian athletes, such as Betty Cuthbert, Dawn Fraser and Shirley Strickland boosted the respect for and prestige of women's sport. In 1965, Merle Thornton and Rosalie Bognor protested for their right to be served in the public bar of a pub, rather than in the separate 'ladies' lounge'. A month later, Thornton established the Equal Opportunities for Women Association.

In 1970, the Australian-born academic Germaine Greer published *The Female Eunuch*, in which she argued that women should not only have equal rights, but that they should throw off traditional male dominance of their lives and society. Greer urged women to assert themselves as independent and autonomous people freed from all gender restrictions and stereotypes. It was a controversial and enormously popular and influential book.

Aboriginal and Torres Strait Islander rights

In the first half of the 20th century, the states continued to make and enact laws about how Aboriginal and Torres Strait Islander people lived. There were restrictions on the ability to work, on rates of pay and how it was saved or spent, on freedom to travel, on owning property, on social service benefits and on the right to vote in the elections of some states. In some states, people needed permission to marry and could not buy alcohol. Many were not legal guardians of their own children.

After Federation, the Australian Constitution gave the right to vote in federal elections to those with the right to vote in state elections. However, the law was interpreted to mean that only Indigenous people who were already registered as state voters in 1902 could vote in federal elections. This was only a few hundred people.

While the Australian economy improved in the postwar years, and most Australians experienced a rise in the standard of living, the majority of Aboriginal and Torres Strait Islander people had a different experience.

Many Aboriginal and Torres Strait Islander people lived in cities, where their lives were similar to those of other Australians – superficially, at least. Many people hid their Aboriginality to avoid exposing themselves to racial prejudice and intolerance.

Others lived in slums or fringe areas of towns and cities, excluded from mainstream life because of prejudiced social attitudes, and the lack of skills that resulted from being denied a full education. Many locals would only employ Indigenous people for periodic unskilled work, and many communities banned them from clubs, swimming pools and cafes.

Many Indigenous people continued to live in missions or reserves, under the system that had begun in the 1830s. Government-funded missions had been established by churches as places of refuge from violence and exploitation, as well as to convert people to the Christian religion. Though usually well meaning, the missions often undermined traditional culture as people were removed from their land, different groups were placed together and cultural practices were, typically, discouraged or forbidden. Communication with family members outside the mission and with the world at large was often restricted. Government reserves had also originally been established to protect Aboriginal and Torres Strait Islander people from

'Warburton Mission: Leaving Time', 2011, by Judith Yinyika Chambers shows people leaving the United Aborigines Mission at Warburton, Victoria. The mission had grown crowded in the mid-1960s and many people left to go to new settlements in Laverton and Docker River.

abuse and exploitation, but they were places of strict control, governed by state laws that were applied only to Indigenous Australians and not to other Australians.

Some former residents recall their time on mission with affection because of the communal life. Many more recall feelings of dislocation, of being controlled, and the lack of basic civil rights. In the second half of the 20th century, these missions and reserves were dismantled as government policies turned to granting Indigenous people control of their own communities.

Moves towards Indigenous equality

There was little contact between the inhabitants of this world of second-class citizenship and the majority of Australians. Most Australians were ignorant of, or indifferent to, the difficulties faced by Aboriginal and Torres Strait Islander people.

During the Second World War, thousands of Aboriginal and Torres Strait Islander men and women joined the armed services or worked in industries. This was the first contact that many non-Indigenous Australians from the southern states had with Indigenous people, and it created greater awareness of their situation.

In 1945, the Australian Parliament amended the *Commonwealth Electoral Act* to give the vote in federal elections to Indigenous people who had fought overseas.

Nationality and Citizenship Act and assimilation

The *Nationality and Citizenship Act* had made all Australians citizens, but the power to make laws affecting Aboriginal and Torres Strait Islander people's lives remained with the states (and territories when they were created).

Aboriginal and Torres Strait Islander people could apply to be 'exempted' from the discriminatory state legislation but only at a great cost to their identity. Among other conditions, applicants had to pledge to abandon association with their Indigenous community. Their exemption certificate had to be carried at all times and produced on demand. Aboriginal people called them 'dog tags'.

In 1951, the Australian Government convened a Conference for Native Welfare with every state and territory represented except Victoria and Tasmania, which claimed to have no Aboriginal 'problem'. The conference officially adopted a policy of 'assimilation' for Aboriginal people. By assimilation the governments meant 'in practical terms that it is expected that all persons of Aboriginal birth or mixed blood in Australia will live like white Australians do.' This meant that there could be full social, economic and political equality and inclusion. The cost would be cultural separateness.

Social Services Act

In 1959, Commonwealth social services – such as old age pensions and unemployment benefits – were extended to include Aboriginal and Torres Strait Islander people. The change was evidence of improving attitudes towards Indigenous people, but its effect was limited at first. Nomadism (moving from place to place), a lack of proof of age and a lack of awareness of the right to access these services meant that many eligible people did not benefit.

Vote for all

In 1962, the *Commonwealth Electoral Act* was amended again so that all Aboriginal and Torres Strait Islander adults were able to vote in federal elections. The last two states that had continued to limit voting rights finally acknowledged this right in their own laws: Western Australia in 1962 and Queensland in 1965. Contrary to popular belief, the 1967 referendum did not recognise the right to vote. In 1962, the *Commonwealth Electoral Act* was amended again so that all Aboriginal and Torres Strait Islander adults were able to vote in federal elections, but there was no special campaign to inform people of this new right.

THE AUSTRALIAN ABORIGINES LEAGUE

THE ABORIGINE SPEAKS_
THE VOICE of THE ABORIGINE MUST BE HEARD

An example of increasing demands by Aboriginal leaders for the right to represent themselves in public life.

Developments in Indigenous rights were indicative of changing attitudes in the broad community and increased activism by Indigenous Australians. Indigenous activism in regards to land rights and social awareness created a greater understanding of Indigenous experiences and the need for Australian society to continue to explore these issues.

Mapoon

In the 1890s at Mapoon, on Cape York, missionaries had taken in the survivors of decades of warfare between cattlemen and explorers and the traditional owners, the Tjungundji, Yupungatti and Tanikutti. Over time the residents had adopted Christianity and traditional ways had weakened. By the 1950s, the mission was the only home that several generations had known.

In the late 1950s, large quantities of bauxite were discovered on land that had been leased to the missionaries. The residents were pressured by the Queensland Government and the new leaseholders, the mining company Comalco, to move to another site to allow the mining to proceed. This included the withdrawal of services such as building maintenance, the Royal Flying Doctor Service – which gave access to medical help – and the removal of the local school teacher. The residents physically resisted but were forced to leave. The mission was closed in 1964.

After continued lobbying by traditional owners of the land, the Queensland Government finally handed a deed of grant to the Mapoon people for part of the land in 1989. Trustees appointed by the Queensland Government, which included traditional owners, worked together with the Mapoon Aboriginal Council regarding land administration matters.

Yirrkala petition

In 1963, mining exploration was approved at Gove in the Northern Territory's Aboriginal Arnhem Land Reserve. In response there were two parliamentary 'firsts'. The people of Yirrkala presented a petition to the Australian Parliament protesting against the mining prospect. The petitions were framed with bark painted in traditional designs. This was the first time traditional Indigenous documents had been recognised by Parliament. As a result of the Yirrkala bark petition, Member of Parliament Kim Beazley senior presented a case for the creation of an Aboriginal land title.

Opposite: The Yirrkala bark petition of 1963 was one of the first calls for the Commonwealth Parliament to give Aboriginal land rights and control over land use.

TO THE HONOURABLE SPEAKER AND MEMBERS OF THE HOUSE OF REPRESENTATIVES
IN PARLIAMENT ASSEMBLED.

The Humble Petition of the Undersigned aboriginal people of Yirrkala,
being members of the Balamumu, Narrkala, Gaping and Miliwurrwurr people
and Djapu, Mangalili, Madarrpa, Magarrwanalmirri, Gumaitj, Djambarrpuyu,
Marrakulu, Galpu, Dhaluayu, Wangurri, Warramiri, Maymil, Miritjinu tribes,
respectfully sheweth.

1. That nearly 500 people of the above Tribes are residents of the land
   excised from the Aboriginal Reserve in Arnhem Land.
2. That the procedures of the excision of this land and the fate of the
   people on it were never explained to them beforehand, and were kept
   secret from them.
3. That when Welfare Officers and Government officials came to inform
   them of decisions taken without them and against them, they did not
   undertake to convey to the Government in Canberra the views and
   feelings of the Yirrkala aboriginal people.
4. That the land in question has been hunting and food gathering land
   for the Yirrkala tribes from time immemorial; we were all born here.
5. That places sacred to the Yirrkala people, as well as vital to their
   livelihood are in the excised land, especially Melville Bay.
6. That the people of this area fear that their needs and interests will
   be completely ignored as they have been ignored in the past, and they
   fear that the fate which has overtaken the Larrakeah tribe will
   overtake them.
7. And they humbly pray that the Honourable the House of Representatives
   will appoint a Committee, accompanied by competent interpreters, to
   hear the views of the Yirrkala people before permitting the excision
   of this land.
8. They humbly pray that no arrangements be entered into with any company
   which will destroy the livelihood and independence of the Yirrkala
   People.
And your petitioners as in duty bound will ever pray God to help you and us
   (English language translation)
===

Buludjulmi gonga'yurru napurrunha Yirrkalalili Yulnunha malanha
Balamumu, Narrkala, Gaping, Miluwurrwurr manapurru dhuwala mala, ga Djapu,
Mangalili, Madarrpa, Magarrwanalmirri, Djambarrpuyyu, Marrakulu, Gumaitj,
Galpu, Dhaluangu, Wangurri, Warramiri, Maymil, Miritjinu malanhabapan-
mirrudjal dhunapa.

1. Dhuwala yulnu mala yalki 500 nhina ga dhiyala wanganura. Dhuwala wanga
   Arnhem Land yurru djae'yunna napurrungala.
2. Dhuwala wanga djae'yunna ga nhaltjana yurru yulounundja dhiyala wanga
   nura nhaltjanna dhu dharrpanna yulnu walandja yakano lakarama
   nänayanguuna.
3. Dhuwala nunhi Welfare Officers ga Government bungawa lakarama yulnuwo
   nalanuwa nhaltjarra nhuwa gana wanganuuinha yaku nula napurrungu
   lakarama, walala yaku lakarama Governmentgala nunhala Canberra nhaltjan
   na napurru ga guyune yulnuyu Yirrkala.
4. Dhuwala wänga napurrungu balangu larrunarawu napurrungu näthawa,
   ruyawa, miyapunuwa, naymalnu nunhi napurru gana nhinana bitjarrayi
   nathillmirri, napurru dhawalguyamana dhiyala wänganura.
5. Dhuwala wänga yurru dharrpahha yurru yulnuwalandja malawala, ga
   dharrpalnha dhuwala bala wunuwuyundja nhinanharawu Melville Baydhurru
   wänga balandayu djae'yun wanguhanin.
6. Dhuwala yulnundja mala yurru nhänana balandawunu nha malkurru nhina
   yurru moma ga daranan yalalanuwirrinha nhaltjanna dhu napurru bitjanra
   nhakuna Larrakeahyu nomawa bialanguwuy wänga.
7. Buli dhu bungawayu House of Representatives djae'yun yulnuwala näthili
   yurru nha dhu lakarana Interpreteryu bungawawala yulnu natha, yurru
   nha dhu djae'yun dhuwala wänganudja.
8. Nunhiyina dhu wärrlayan marrawu'ndja nhinanharawu yulnuwa marrnawa-
   thinyarawu.

   Dhuwala napurri yulnu mala mala yurru liyawirriyama bitjan bili warr
   yurru napurrin nha gonga'yunna wandarr'wu.
   (Australian natha.) ========================
   _____

Milirrpum.

Djalalingba.   Manunu
Nuymbalipu.   Lanrahan
Djaykla   Wulangbuma
Dundiweny.   Wawuggmarra

Dhunggala   Nyabiliyu
Raiyini.

The Yirrkala people challenged the mining project in court in 1968 but the case was lost. The judge found that any rights the Yirrkala people may have had before colonisation had been invalidated by the Crown. (This decision would later be overturned by the Mabo decision of 1992.)

Almost a decade later, in 1978, the Yirrkala people gained title to their land under the *Aboriginal Land Rights (Northern Territory) Act*, but the mining leases were specifically excluded.

Freedom Ride

In 1965, Arrernte man and University of Sydney student Charles Perkins led a group of non-Indigenous students on a 'Freedom Ride' bus tour of western and coastal New South Wales towns. Perkins was one of the very few Aboriginal students at university during the 1960s and was the first Aboriginal man to graduate from an Australian university. The Freedom Ride's purpose was to draw media attention to racial discrimination and the poor state of Aboriginal health, education and housing in those places. The students had been inspired by similar civil rights protest tours in the United States. The route included visits to Walgett, Gulargambone, Kempsey, Bowraville and Moree.

A simple but powerful symbol of the racial discrimination that existed in most Australian towns where there was a significant Aboriginal population – wooden cinema seats for the Aboriginal patrons, comfortable padded ones for the non-Indigenous audience.

The students were shocked at the conditions in which Aboriginal people lived, usually on the outskirts of the local town. The people were routinely denied service in shops, or had to wait while white people were served. They were banned from clubs, swimming pools and some cafes. At Bowraville the local cinema was segregated: white people on plush seats up the back; Aboriginal patrons on wooden seats down the front. Aboriginal people had to enter the theatre via a special door after the film had started.

The students talked to local people and protested and demonstrated. In some places they were threatened with violence, and on one occasion their bus was run off the road by locals in their utes.

The publicity generated by the ride led to greater public awareness in the major cities, especially Sydney, of the condition of rural Indigenous people, and this led to the gradual elimination of the discriminatory local practices.

Bowraville theatre reopened in 2000, having been closed for more than three decades. Local Gumbaynggirr elders held a ceremony to cleanse the building of its unhappy past. Charles Perkins' son Adam delivered a speech at the opening. The year 2015 marked the Freedom Ride's 50th anniversary, and another Freedom Bus retraced the original 1965 journey. Events were held in the key towns of Walgett, Gulargambone, Kempsey, Bowraville and Moree to celebrate and promote Aboriginal affairs and stronger relationships between local communities.

Wave Hill

In August 1966, Vincent Lingiari, a stockman on Wave Hill station, went to the station manager and asked for higher wages for Aboriginal stockmen. When the manager refused, the Aboriginal stockmen went on strike, walked off the property, and set up a new camp at Wattie Creek, a place of significance to them. They called the new settlement 'Gurindji', their own name for themselves.

The wages strike changed to a movement for land rights. Lingiari was one of four signatories to a 1967 petition to the governor-general that argued that 'morally the land is ours and should be returned to us.'

The British owner, Lord Vestey, promised improved workers' conditions if the stockmen returned, but by then they wanted control of their land.

The Gurindji eventually gained part of the Wave Hill lease that included the land most important to them. In 1975, Prime Minister Gough Whitlam poured earth from Wave Hill (now called Kalkarindji) into Vincent Lingiari's hands to mark the return of Gurindji lands.

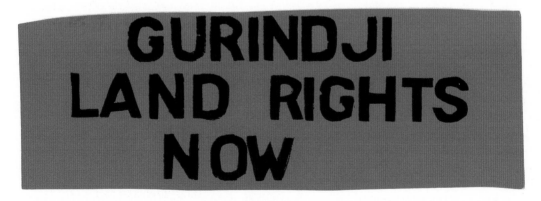

The strike for better conditions at the Vestey-leased Wave Hill Station changed to a call for full land rights for the Gurindji people.

Aboriginal workers and their families lived in primitive conditions on the pastoral stations of the Northern Territory.

Equal pay

In 1966 the Conciliation and Arbitration Commission ruled that 2500 Aboriginal workers in the pastoral industry in the Northern Territory were to be paid equal wages to non-Indigenous workers. Employers had paid their Aboriginal stockmen lower wages – in the case of drovers, one-fifth of the white wage. The employers argued that Aboriginal stockmen should not be paid a wage equal to that of non-Indigenous pastoral workers because they took much time off for traditional ceremonies, and because the families of the workers were allowed to camp on the property and were provided with food and clothing. The Commission decided that workers should be paid equal wages, but the victory was hollow for many. As predicted, employers hired a smaller number of non-Indigenous workers to replace the Aboriginal stockmen and forced them and their families to leave the properties.

1967 referendum

In the mid-1960s Aboriginal and Torres Strait Islander leaders and organisations, together with many non-Indigenous people, organised a petition campaign calling on the Australian Government to change those parts of the Australian Constitution that discriminated against

Aboriginal and Torres Strait Islander people. In 1967, this pressure led to a referendum that proposed two amendments.

One was to Section 51 (xxvi), which gave the Commonwealth power to make special laws for people of any race, other than the Aboriginal people. The referendum proposed to delete the words 'other than the Aboriginal people'. If passed, this would give the Commonwealth power to make laws nationally to improve the condition of Aboriginal and Torres Strait Islander people.

The second proposed change was to delete Section 127 from the Constitution. This section stopped the Commonwealth from counting Aboriginal and Torres Strait Islander people directly in the periodical census counts. The effect of this had been to reduce the number of seats in the House of Representatives of those states where there were large Aboriginal populations. If the change passed, all Australians would be counted and represented based on a more accurate knowledge of where people lived. It would also mean that the Commonwealth would have more detailed knowledge of the living conditions of Aboriginal and Torres Strait Islander people, and be able to use that knowledge to make new laws and provide assistance where it would help most.

The slogans used in the 'Yes' campaign showed how people saw the issues: 'Towards an Australia free and equal'; 'Vote "Yes" for Aborigines'; 'Let's be counted – Vote "Yes"', 'Remove discrimination – Vote "Yes"; 'Vote "Yes" for equality'.

Supporters campaigned tirelessly. Few people opposed the changes. Nearly 91 per cent of Australians voted 'Yes' to both proposed changes.

Many books make mistaken claims about the referendum. The result did not give Indigenous people the vote (they already had it from 1962), and it did not give them citizenship (established in 1949). It did not give Aboriginal and Torres Strait Islander people

1967 Referendum Voting Results

State	For %	Against %
New South Wales	91	9
Victoria	95	5
Queensland	89	11
South Australia	86	14
Western Australia	81	19
Tasmania	90	10
Total	91	9

Parliamentary Handbook of the Commonwealth of Australia 2008

any more rights (other than the right to be counted in the census), but it provided the Australian Government rather than the states with the power to make changes to the lives of Indigenous people and to provide assistance for self-management, and the overwhelming 'Yes' vote was a very significant symbol of a move towards inclusion and equality of Indigenous people into national life.

Aboriginal embassy

On 26 January 1972, Australia Day, Prime Minister William McMahon announced that there would be no Aboriginal title to the land at Gove/Yirrkala, but Aboriginal people were entitled to apply for leases as long as they could put the land to reasonable economic or social use.

Aboriginal activists in Canberra objected, and set up a tent in the large park opposite the provisional Parliament House, claiming that they were an independent nation and this was their embassy.

Police tried to pull down the tent and evict the residents. This increased the tension created by the protest. The legality of removing the tent was challenged and after several more attempts to remove it the government allowed the site to be used for the protest.

The Aboriginal Tent Embassy is still there, a visual reminder of the many issues that Aboriginal and Torres Strait Islander Australians continue to raise with governments in Australia.

The future

By 1972, the citizenship status of Aboriginal people and Torres Strait Islanders had been improved. The 1967 referendum had been passed with an unprecedented majority. In most states Indigenous people could now move freely. Legal discrimination had almost disappeared and exemption certificates had been abandoned. Aboriginal and Torres Strait Islander people and organisations were more prominent in public life. Indigenous people were no longer seen as 'dying out' and identity was to be celebrated, not denied.

But not everything had changed: the issue of land rights had to be further addressed, social inequalities were still deeply entrenched, and many people maintained racist attitudes. In 1980, the Chair of the Aboriginal Development Corporation, Charles Perkins, returned to the Walgett RSL Club he had picketed on the Freedom Ride in 1965. The doorman turned and said to him: 'You know, you boys aren't allowed in here'.

There was much still to be done.

SOCIAL AND CULTURAL CHANGE

The 25 years after the end of the Second World War saw many changes, but also some continuities, in Australian life and popular culture.

Royal visits

In 1954 the young Queen Elizabeth II toured Australia. Huge crowds turned out all over Australia to see the beautiful young monarch and her husband, Prince Philip. This continuing popularity of the royal family in Australia would be seen again at the marriage of Prince Charles and Diana Spencer in 1981, and then the marriage of Prince William and Catherine Middleton in 2011.

New heroes

In 1961 the Russian migrant Tania Verstak was crowned Miss Australia, and in 1962 Miss International. Her popularity showed the nature of postwar Australia, where 'new Australians' were taking their place and contributing to the nation.

In 1968 Aboriginal boxer Lionel Rose thrilled the nation when he won the world bantamweight title against Japanese Masahiko Harada aka 'Fighting Harada'. He was the first Indigenous Australian to win a world title, and in the same year became the first Indigenous person to be named Australian of the Year.

Baby boom

A key element in Australia's social and cultural change was the 'baby boom'. Returning soldiers were keen to settle back into family life, and the huge increase in the number of births between 1946 and 1964, together with high immigration numbers, led to higher demand for houses, cars, public transport, hospitals and schools. This all created jobs, which became increasingly well paid as the economy recovered. Australia was entering a period of prosperity.

Education

As the economy grew, Australia ploughed money into education. For the first time the Commonwealth Government began to provide funding to schools, which had been the states' responsibility in the past. Under Prime Minister Robert Menzies, the Australian Government built school libraries and science laboratories for state,

In 1954 the recently crowned Queen Elizabeth II and her husband Prince Philip, Duke of Edinburgh, toured Australia. Queen Elizabeth is the first reigning monarch to have visited Australia, and the royal couple were greeted by enormous and enthusiastic crowds.

In 1961 the winner of the Miss Australia Quest was the Chinese-born daughter of Russian immigrants, Tania Verstak, who also went on to win the Miss International award that year. She was the first naturalised Australian to win the quest.

independent and religious schools, provided scholarships to help poorer students to complete their last two years of secondary schooling, and then to go to university. The children of thousands of families became the first generation able to attend university. The result was that during the 1950s and 1960s education standards rose, and provided a skilled workforce that could improve productivity.

Urbanisation

The returning servicemen and women, their 'baby boomer' children, and the wave of immigrants who arrived during the next two decades added to the spread of urban areas. Buying a block of land and building a home was considered the 'Australian dream'. There was a greater dependence on cars, as the development of infrastructure did not keep pace with the growing population, and it was a more convenient form of transport for families. New suburbs developed, with room for cars in garages and big backyards.

State governments started to clear slum areas and build subsidised high-rise housing for families on welfare. New technology in building materials meant that the previous height limit of about 12 storeys could be extended.

In 1958, Australia's first skyscraper, ICI House, was built in Melbourne. It was 20 storeys high, with glass curtain walls, and was a symbol of modernity, new building technology, progress and internationalism.

Similar building booms took off in the other capital cities. Old buildings, many of them now considered to have been architectural treasures, were ruthlessly pulled down to make way for the new and modern.

Work

The nature of employment in Australia changed greatly between the 1950s and the 1970s. The percentage of women in the workforce increased from 19 per cent in 1949 to 27 per cent in 1971. Agricultural employment decreased significantly, from 21 per cent in 1949 to 6 per cent in 1972. This change particularly affected small country towns, whose services and population diminished as people drifted off to live in the cities. Manufacturing, which had grown during the war, continued to rise as a source of employment. In 1949 the manufacturing industry provided 26 per cent of jobs in the workforce, peaking to 29 per cent between 1958 and 1961. This percentage began to decline in 1972 due to several factors: the lowering of tariffs on imported competition, the continuing growth of wages increasing the cost of manufacturing, and the growth of cheap, quality imports from the lower-wage cost and more modern factories of Japan.

Technology and consumerism

The growing wealth of the Australian people, greater leisure time, and the rise in cheaper technology meant that Australians increasingly participated in a 'consumer culture'. This affected the way of life for many, as items and luxuries became more accessible and, therefore, disposable. Goods either were not made to be repaired, or were so cheap that people thought replacing them was more efficient.

Domestic consumer goods became more affordable and were of better quality as advances in technology allowed for mass production of these items and made them more reliable. Electrical appliances such as refrigerators, vacuum cleaners and washing machines became more accessible, and helped change the domestic lives of women in particular, as household tasks became less labour-intensive and time-consuming. Advertising created and fuelled consumer demand by using the new medium of television, as well as the more traditional radio, newspapers and magazines.

The development of jet engines gradually made air travel cheaper. As prices fell and competition increased in the 1960s, more and more Australians could afford to fly domestically and internationally.

In 1956, television came to Australia. Few could afford televisions to begin with; people saved or bought them on hire-purchase and crowds would collect outside shop windows to watch programs. People visited their wealthier relatives or neighbours just to watch favourite shows, or to make a Saturday night of it. As they became cheaper, televisions started to dominate the living room. As the United States was the biggest producer of English-language television shows, this also meant that US popular culture, and the values it reflected, became more influential in Australia. People saw depictions of how American families ate, lived, played, spoke and behaved, and this affected Australians' attitudes, values and expectations.

Not everyone had equal access to the changes. Change was much faster in cities and towns than in country areas, and not everyone had the money needed to take advantage of the new developments.

Technology was also made to serve the economy. The Commonwealth Scientific and Research Organisation, CSIR (later CSIRO), developed a new way of dealing with the rabbit

Australian inventions and innovations of the 1940s–1950s

1945
Hills hoist
Although the rotary clothes line had originally been patented by Gilbert Toyne in Adelaide in 1926, Lance Hill came up with the idea to include a winding mechanism that allows the frame to be easily raised and lowered.

1958
Black box flight recorder
A device that records flight data and cockpit conversations in a plane, enabling investigators to understand what went wrong in an accident. It was invented by Dave Warren, who was a research scientist at the Aeronautical Research Laboratory in Melbourne.

1960
Plastic spectacle lenses
Adelaide company Sola Optical innovated spectacle lenses that were safer, lighter, more durable and more scratch-resistant than glass lenses. Sola Optical was the first company in the world to develop plastic bifocal, trifocal and progressive focus lenses.

plague of the 1950s: myxomatosis. Rabbits were eating grass that could have been eaten by export-income earning sheep, and causing erosion. Scientists released the myxomatosis virus among rabbits, and reduced their population from 600 million to 100 million in two years. However, the remaining rabbits developed immunity to the virus, and would not be challenged again until the CSIRO introduced the calicivirus in 1995, killing 10 million rabbits in just eight weeks. But once again the survivors began to build resistance against it.

Music and the rise of teen culture

Record players and transistor radios became more affordable, which contributed to the influence of music in popular culture. Increasing disposable wealth among families and cheaper technology led advertisers to target teenagers. They were urged to buy new clothes, magazines, cosmetics, food, records, to listen to pop music on the radio, and to watch youth culture films and TV programs, such as the hit music shows *Bandstand* and *Six O'Clock Rock* with Australia's own 'wild one', the singer Johnny O'Keefe. Teenagers increasingly developed their own music, slang, fashion and pop heroes, and became more prominent in the media as companies attempted to cater to and form their tastes.

Traditional acoustic instruments, musical arrangements, song themes and singing styles were overwhelmed by new technology. In the 1940s the most popular music was community singing of old favourites. Radio stations broadcast gatherings, and people – mostly housewives and children at home – would often sing along. The electric guitar had been invented in the early 1930s but became most prominent with the rise of rock and roll music in the 1950s. Bill Haley & His Comets brought it to mainstream audiences with 'Rock Around The Clock', and Elvis Presley took over to galvanise the young and unsettle their parents.

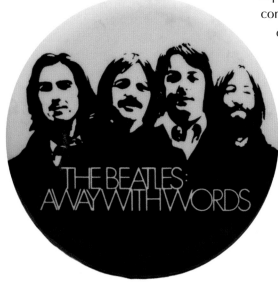

The Beatles were the most popular youth cultural phenomenon of the 1960s.

Popular music styles and movements of the 1960s continued to have their own associated clothing and culture. Surfie music fans had the Beach Boys, Kombi vans, sun, bikinis and the dance craze called 'The Stomp'. The Beatles' early style featured long hair and collarless suits and pop love songs. The Rolling Stones made harder, wilder music and were more dismissive of traditional values. The folkies were Peter Paul and Mary or Joan Baez; their image was of longer hair, earnestness, cheesecloth shirts and skirts, coffee shops and songs of protest, impending doom and destruction. The jazzers were all about Miles Davis and Theolonius Monk; they were a small and exclusive lot, serious and dressed in black. All these styles were represented by local individuals and groups who played at pubs and clubs, concerts and dance parties.

Fashion

Fashion changed greatly during the postwar period. During both world wars, people had been forced into 'austerity' fashion. Clothing was rationed; suits, shirts and dresses were restyled to eliminate excess material; and people had to 'mend and make do'.

From the 1950s changes in fashion developed alongside trends in popular music, and made teenage trends and tribalism more obvious. Fashion became less formal and modest for men and women, especially as the British 'Swinging Sixties' Carnaby Street styles of colourful clothes, fitted trousers for men or miniskirts, hot pants and boots for women. British model Jean 'The Shrimp' Shrimpton outraged conservative racegoers when she appeared at the 1965 Melbourne Cup in a dress that was then considered shockingly short (just above her knees), and without gloves, a hat or stockings!

New materials also influenced fashion, especially the development of synthetic materials that replaced cotton and wool, and made clothes both cheaper and easier to care for.

Harold Blair was a highly versatile Indigenous musical artist. His record, released in the early 1960s, relates to Blair's remarkable journey from Aboriginal mission orphan to internationally renowned singer. As a performer Blair ranged across a wide repertoire, from opera to music hall. As a politician and activist, he demonstrated an untiring devotion to Indigenous causes, becoming a leader of his generation. This collection of hymns displays not only his musical talent but his affinity with religious music, stemming from his early life in the Salvation Army.

Sport

The traditional sports remained popular: cricket, Rugby League and Australian Rules, tennis, athletics and swimming. Surfing rapidly grew popular in the 1960s, and developed a culture of its own as teenagers spent more time on the beach.

Internationally, Australia was one of the dominant nations in swimming, tennis, golf and cricket.

Australia's postwar prosperity meant that it could afford to host international sporting events. In 1956 the Olympic Games in Melbourne – Australia's first internationally renowned event – created new heroes: Dawn Fraser and Murray Rose in swimming, and Marjorie Jackson and Betty Cuthbert in athletics. In 1962, Perth started to put itself on the international map by hosting the British Empire and Commonwealth Games. These international events helped bring tourists to Australia, but the cost of international travel and the relatively long distance to reach Australia meant that international tourism was not a major industry yet.

Sport was a driving factor in the introduction of television into Australia in 1956. An outside broadcast van could take the required technical control room to any place for a live broadcast.

Attitudes and values

The world was rapidly changing. Australians were now more influenced by US culture through the popularity of American films, TV shows and music. Australians were also reaching out to the world in the 1960s, especially through the 'Oz invasion' of Britain – with satirist Barry Humphries (aka Dame Edna Everage), and writers Clive James, Germaine Greer and art historian Robert Hughes all achieving international success. Even while Australian writers and performers were making the 'Oz invasion' of Britain, Australia and Britain were loosening their traditional ties to one another. Britain turned away from Australia and towards the European Common Market as a major source of trade. In 1966, when Australia was switching to decimal currency, one new name suggested to replace the pound was the 'royal'. This was unsuccessful and the chosen name, 'dollar', symbolised Australia's swing towards the United States, before swinging again towards Asia in the 1970s.

Another great change had just started to reveal itself. On a night in early October 1957, people all over Australia wandered into their streets and looked up to see the tiny glowing dot of the Russian craft Sputnik 1 track slowly across the sky, the first satellite ever to be sent into space. They were seeing the start of the space age – an age that would see men land on the moon and the start of a technological revolution that would result in the development of internet and digital communication.

A piece of moon rock collected during the American Apollo space program in 1972, given to Australia by the US as a symbol of 'unity in diversity', and the Apollo program's desire for future world peace and harmony.

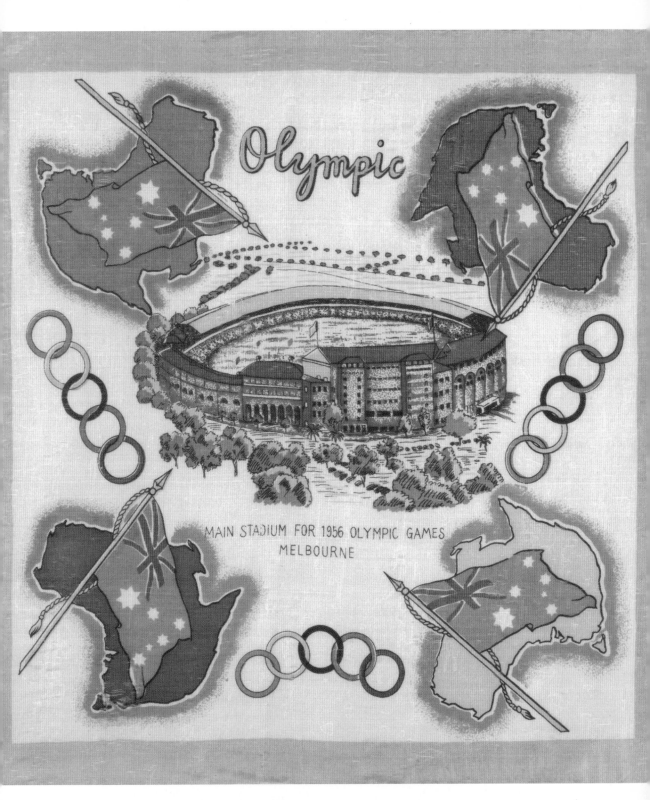

A souvenir silk scarf from the 1956 Melbourne Olympic Games.

Our Australia

In the late 20th and early 21st centuries, multiculturalism expanded, broadening the country's global outreach. Women continued to move towards greater economic and social equality, as did Indigenous Australians. Technology transformed communications, and scientific research helped people become more aware of the environment and the need to sustain it.

The Save the Franklin campaign was a major event in the development of an increasing environmental awareness movement in Australia.

A NEW ERA

In December 1972 the Australian Labor Party was elected to govern for the first time since 1949. The new prime minister was Gough Whitlam. It was seen as the start of a new modern era, the opportunity to bring in the social changes that had been building momentum during the 1960s.

The new government began a whirlwind period of law-making. It presented 118 bills (proposed new laws) to the parliament between February and April 1973, and had 103 of these passed. In contrast, the average number of laws passed between 1950 and 1972 was 53 per year.

Many of the reforms were socially progressive and seen as a step towards correcting injustices or prejudices, such as granting land rights to the Gurindji people in Wave Hill, proposing a race discrimination bill, introducing free health care and free university education for all students, legislating equal pay for women, replacing British honours with the Order of Australia system and abolishing the death penalty for federal crimes. Many reforms were overwhelmingly beneficial, while others created economic problems and social divisions.

Foreign policy changes

The Labor Government increased contact with China, weakening the hostility that had developed against the communist government during the Cold War. The new government also granted independence to Australian-administered New Guinea in 1975, though critics believed it had been rushed through and that the local people were not ready for it yet. The Whitlam Government chose not to intervene in the Indonesian takeover of East Timor in 1975, which led to many years of civil war before self-determination was granted in 1999, and nationhood in 2002.

The Labor Government ended the national service scheme and withdrew the last few remaining Australian troops from South Vietnam. The hostility of some Labor Government ministers towards United States foreign policy threatened intelligence-sharing arrangements between the two countries.

The dismissal

The Labor Government was re-elected in 1974, but economic and social scandals as well as deteriorating economic conditions made it increasingly unpopular. The government did not have a majority in the Senate, and the Liberal–Country Party coalition blocked the passage of supply bills – bills that gave the government the authority to spend money on government wages – until the government agreed to call an election. The government refused, and on 11 November 1975 Governor-General Sir John Kerr controversially sacked Gough Whitlam as prime minister, and authorised Opposition leader Malcolm Fraser to form a new government for the purpose of calling an election. Despite the passion and rage of the Labor Party supporters, the temporary Liberal Government was elected with a large majority.

GOUGH
A BIGGER MOUTH
THAN
'JAWS'

TIME'S UP!
WE'VE DONE
THREE YEARS
OF HARD
LABOUR!
VOTE
LIBERAL

Authorised by Peter J.Sanders, 9 Manor St., Brighton, 3186.
Printed by The Clarendon Press Pty. Ltd. 46 Boundary Street, South Melbourne, 3205

An anti-Whitlam election poster, 1975.

ECONOMIC DEVELOPMENTS

The immediate postwar period was a time of great economic growth in Australia and many other developed countries.

This was interrupted in 1973 when the Organisation of the Petroleum Exporting Countries (OPEC) cut oil production. The cut was in protest at Western support for Israel in the Yom Kippur War with Egypt and Syria. The decrease in production led to the price of oil rising up to 400 per cent by the end of the year. The price of many goods and services rose, as oil was required for their manufacture or transportation. These price hikes increased economic inflation in many countries, including Australia, meaning that the value of people's money was effectively lessened.

At the same time, the Labor Government introduced equal pay for women, and started reducing tariffs on imports. The combination of increased oil prices, economic inflation, higher wages for some employees and cheap international imports led to an increase in unemployment in Australia, from 1.4 per cent in 1970 to 6.2 per cent by 1980.

Recovery and crash in the 1980s

The local economy improved during the 1980s, aided by several significant changes introduced by the Labor Government of Prime Minister Bob Hawke.

In 1983, the government convinced the Australian Council of Trade Unions to agree to the Prices and Income Accord. Under the accord, the unions would keep wage demands down and provide more services, the government would bring inflation down, and the employers would create more jobs. This proved to be successful, and the rate of unemployment dropped and industrial unrest ceased.

The government 'floated' the dollar on the stock exchange in 1983. This meant that the value of the dollar was left to markets to decide rather than being fixed, by the government, against gold or the value of a stronger currency. When the economy was going well the value would rise, and when it was failing it would fall. In theory this meant that the dollar would always reflect the true worth of the Australian economy in comparison to other nations' economies.

Industrial legislation was changed to replace the basic wage with a minimum wage. Employers and employees could work out a wage between themselves, recognising productivity and flexibility, as long as it did not fall below a minimum level.

Banks were deregulated, which reduced controls over their lending policies. Banks started competing to lend money to borrowers, and many took risks with the people to whom they loaned the funds. The global stock market crashed in 1987 and led to a brief but severe recession. Unemployment and interest rates rose and many people who had borrowed beyond their means lost their businesses and even their homes, as they could no longer afford their debt repayments.

Globalisation and the shift from protection to free trade

By the 1990s, Australia seemed to have a 'miracle economy' – national productivity was increasing, inflation (which makes goods more expensive) was falling, as was unemployment, and wages and profits were both rising.

Australia was greatly influenced by globalisation – the growing economic interconnectedness of nations, which grew rapidly in the 1980s and 1990s. Australia participated in more global, regional and bilateral trade arrangements. Many of these involved a move towards free trade, where the trading nations agreed to reduce economic protections. Protections are government subsidies that help local industries, and tariffs (taxes) or quotas that restrict international competitors. During the 1980s the average Australian Government assistance to agriculture was 5 per cent, and to many industries 25 per cent. These dropped in the 1990s to 3.4 per cent and 18 per cent respectively.

While the reduction in protection benefited the consumer as a result of falling prices on imported goods, local industries stopped or reduced production, leaving many people without jobs.

The move towards free trade benefited producers who had a competitive advantage, especially in primary products such as meat, milk and other foods, which could now be exported in larger quantities. However, Australia's high wages in many industries, together with increasing mechanisation of work, meant that consumers were buying cheaper imported goods at the same time that there were fewer jobs available in manufacturing. The car, footwear, white goods (such as refrigerators and washing machines), and clothing manufacturers were hit worst. Manufacturing's contribution to the workforce fell from 25 per cent in 1970 to 9 per cent in 2010. In 1966 the most common occupations were tradesmen, production process workers and labourers (44 per cent), farmers, fishers and timber getters (12 per cent), and clerical workers (9 per cent). In 2011 the most common occupations revolved around specialised professions (22 per cent), clerical and administration (15 per cent), and skilled manual labour (14 per cent).

In 1997, several East Asian nations suffered a severe recession, and global financial crisis hit in 2001 and again in 2007 to 2008. Many nations had to cut back their spending savagely during these crises, which created unemployment and affected their imports and exports.

Australia avoided the worst of this, largely because of China's economic expansion. Under the leadership of Deng Xiaoping, China had industrialised rapidly from 1979 onwards. Australia began supplying huge quantities of coal and iron ore to the expanding manufacturing industries of China in 1973. This created a mining boom in Australia, at a time when Australia's own manufacturing industries were in decline. The development and export of resources including oil, gas, bauxite, iron ore, coal, aluminium, manganese, nickel and fertilisers carried Australia through the crises. The mining industry employed relatively few people, but contributed a large amount to Australia's export earnings.

Change and continuity

By the early years of the 21st century, the Australian economy had shifted significantly from its traditional nature. It remained a strong producer of primary products (crops, wool and minerals), but its manufacturing element had almost disappeared, replaced by high reliance on providing services (through shops, offices, health and education).

Australia continued its move towards increased urbanisation, but with more medium- and high-density living within capital cities, as well as the continuing low-density suburban sprawl.

Trade had shifted from Britain and Europe to the Asia-Pacific area. In 2013, six of the country's top trading partners were in Asia: Japan, China, India, Republic of Korea, Thailand and Singapore. The United States completes the list.

Agricultural products (such as wheat and wool) are no longer Australia's main export. In 2013, the top exports were iron ore, coal, education, natural gas, gold and tourism. The top imports were personal travel, petroleum, motor vehicles and freight transport.

CONTINUING MIGRATION

The Australian Bureau of Statistics estimated that the population of Australia had reached 23 million people on 23 April 2013, and is expected to reach 24 million during 2016. Much of this population is made up of immigrants or the descendants of immigrants, and the fact that it is growing at all is largely due to immigration.

Immigration and population growth

Immigration has contributed to Australia's prosperity, and it continues to profoundly affect the nation.

Until 1945, the great majority of migrants to Australia came from Britain and Ireland. The majority of Australia's immigrants continue to come from Britain and New Zealand. Since the 1970s, increasingly large numbers have also come from Asia, and to a lesser extent from Middle Eastern and African nations.

The 2011 census showed that 26 per cent of Australia's population was born overseas, and a further 30 per cent had at least one parent born in another country. The top ten countries of birth besides Australia were the UK, New Zealand, China, India, Italy, Vietnam, the Philippines, South Africa, Malaysia and Germany.

Immigration has also benefited the national economy, as it has allowed for greater links to overseas businesses and created import and export opportunities.

Migration streams

Australia's migration comes from three streams: permanent migration of people who have skills needed by Australian industry (about 62 per cent of the yearly total); family members of permanent residents (about 28 per cent); and humanitarian migration – refugees and asylum seekers (10 per cent). Australia sets a quota for all types of immigrants that it will take each year.

Under humanitarian migration, some people arrive in Australia by plane with a visa and seek asylum, some arrive without a visa (usually by boat) and seek asylum, while others are accepted directly from refugee camps overseas. Australia has an obligation as signatory to the United Nations Refugee Convention to protect the rights of refugees. However, if an asylum seeker is found not to be a refugee, there is no obligation to accept him or her.

Refugees

Australia has accepted over 700,000 refugees among the more than seven million permanent arrivals since 1945. A refugee is defined as one who has a well founded fear of persecution in their own country because of their race, religion, nationality, or membership of a particular social or political group. An asylum seeker is one who has not yet been categorised as a refugee.

Each decade has seen different groups of refugees coming to Australia.

In the 1970s, the majority of refugees were fleeing from a repressive government in Chile, civil war in Lebanon, or political persecution after the war in Vietnam.

In the 1980s, refugees came from Indochina (Vietnam, Laos and Cambodia), Latin America, Eastern Europe and the Middle East.

This Vietnamese musical instrument known as a *dàn tre* was built from a bamboo tube, an old olive oil tin and wire strings. It was handcrafted by Vietnamese refugee Minh Tam Nguyen, who brought the instrument with him to Australia in 1982.

In the 1990s, many refugees came from China. The majority were students who had been in Australia at the time of the Tiananmen Square massacre in Beijing in 1989, and who had spoken out in favour of democratic change and therefore feared persecution on their return. Other refugees came from Burma, Cambodia, the former Yugoslavia, Iran, Afghanistan and East Timor.

In the 2000s, many refugees arrived from Africa (particularly Sudan), the Middle East, Burma and Sri Lanka. Since the start of the Syrian Civil War in 2011, approximately nine million refugees have fled from Syria into its neighbouring countries in the Middle East and Europe. In 2015 the Australian Government, under the leadership of Prime Minister Tony Abbott, agreed to take in 12,000 Syrian refugees in a resettlement program estimated to take more than two years.

Vietnamese 'boat people'

After the fall of Saigon to North Vietnamese forces in 1975, supporters of the anti-communist forces in Vietnam were in danger. An estimated one to two million people were sent to 're-education' camps, where thousands died. Yet more thousands were killed or exiled by the new government.

An estimated one million South Vietnamese fled the newly unified Vietnam. They paid to board unseaworthy boats, bringing virtually no possessions. Refugees who survived this voyage had to stay in camps in Malaysia, Thailand, the Philippines, Hong Kong and Indonesia. Eventually several countries agreed to resettle as many of these refugees as possible: the United States took 823,000, Australia and Canada took 137,000 each, France took 96,000, and Germany and the United Kingdom took 19,000 refugees each.

The first of the Vietnamese refugees to reach Australia had arrived by sea without official visas or entry documentation, and were more

The steering wheel of one of the first boats to arrive in Darwin in 1978, bringing refugees from Vietnam.

commonly referred to as 'boat people'. They travelled aboard leaky fishing boats, directly from Vietnam or from refugee camps into Darwin Harbour. Only 56 boats from Vietnam holding about 2100 people reached Australia in this way, mostly arriving at Darwin. The first arrived in April 1976 and the last in August 1981. Most of the Vietnamese refugee resettlement between 1975 and 1985 was by air from the refugee camps in Asia, and was then followed by family reunion.

In 1981, 43,400 Vietnamese had been resettled in Australia. By 1991, there were 124,800 Vietnamese-born people in Australia, while in the 2001 census, 154,000 people declared themselves Vietnamese-born. Australia has accepted more Vietnamese refugees per head of population than any other nation.

The Tampa affair

Asylum seekers' arrival by boat, without visas, has been the subject of much controversy and political debate.

A cartoon commentary on the Tampa affair.

In 2001, the Liberal–National Coalition Government under Prime Minister John Howard was determined to stop the growing numbers of asylum seekers arriving via people smugglers' boats. In August 2001, a sinking Indonesian boat carrying 438 asylum seekers, mainly consisting of Hazara people of Afghanistan, was rescued in international waters by a passing cargo ship, the *Tampa*. The nearest port with appropriate medical facilities was the Indonesian port of Merak, about 12 hours away. Christmas Island was closer, but did not have the appropriate facilities, and its port could not handle a cargo ship the size of the *Tampa*.

The Indonesian authorities agreed to accept the rescued people, however a delegation of five asylum seekers threatened violence if the Norwegian captain did not take them to Christmas Island instead. The captain contacted the Australian authorities and reported that many of the passengers were becoming ill, and that his ship did not have the medical facilities nor enough lifeboats should they need to evacuate the ship. The captain declared an emergency and sailed towards Christmas Island.

Australian troops were sent to board the ship, and agreed that many passengers were unwell. The passengers were unloaded and sent to the Micronesian island of Nauru for processing. Eventually, about 150 of the asylum seekers were accepted by New Zealand as refugees. Most of the rest were accepted by Australia, other than 11 who were determined not to be genuine refugees and were returned to Iraq.

Most Australians supported the government's hard line on the *Tampa* refugees, and re-elected the Howard Government soon after. The strict policy had an immediate effect in halting the rapidly increasing number of asylum seeker boat arrivals. Boat arrivals increased

A refugee's story – Joyce Doru

In 1994, Joyce's village in southern Sudan was invaded by rebels. Her parents were beaten, and the rebels asked where Joyce was. She was at school and her uncle helped her to escape to a refugee camp in Uganda, but without her parents. The rebels occasionally came to the refugee camp and beat people – including her uncle, who was beaten to death in 1994. Joyce believed her parents were probably dead. In 1999 Joyce was shot by rebels, and had to be taken to hospital.

She applied and was accepted as a refugee to Australia, and settled in Footscray, Victoria. While there she made contact with the Red Cross, who encouraged her to write a letter to her parents. Red Cross workers took the letter on a posting to Africa and tried to find Joyce's parents. Amazingly, they were still alive and received Joyce's letter, and replied to her:

Dear my beloved daughter Doru,
Most happiest greetings to find and hear from you after missing you a lot. For sure, after our separation we could not really locate your whereabouts otherwise we thought you're dead . . . Your sisters and brothers are all fine, they are also happy for the struggle to find our whereabouts.

Says Joyce: 'I was so happy, I couldn't believe it was true. When I opened the letter I knew it was really my mum, and that she was alive. I want to tell them we are very happy now. At last my heart is at peace.'

again after 2007, when the newly elected Labor Government started to dismantle the previous harsh rules. Arrivals dropped dramatically again when a Liberal–National Coalition Government was elected in 2013 and reintroduced strict measures.

The Australian people have been divided on the issue of refugee boat arrivals. One view is that refugees should be welcomed, as they are fleeing persecution. The other option, resettlement through official UN channels, can take many years, and leave asylum seekers vulnerable in overcrowded and sometimes dangerous camps, and it is Australia's international obligation to provide protection.

Others believe that it is more important to control Australia's border and that the flow of refugees by boat had to be stopped by strict policies. Refugees could then avoid the hazardous and sometimes fatal sea crossing in unsuitable boats and be processed in camps in other countries.

Multiculturalism

After the Second World War, immigrants were encouraged to assimilate and integrate into the broader Australian community. They were expected to do this by largely abandoning their original language and culture. This changed in 1973, when the Minister for Immigration, Al Grassby, shifted focus from assimilation to 'multiculturalism' – an emphasis on celebrating and supporting the cultural diversity that migrants brought with them. From the 1990s to the present, the emphasis has shifted again to one of social unity and cohesion through shared citizenship values. What exactly those values are, and how flexible any particular culture or viewpoint must be in order to reach a shared version, continues to be debated. In 2012 Labor Prime Minister Julia Gillard summed up her values on multiculturalism as *'The meeting place of rights and responsibilities, where the right to maintain one's customs, language and religion is balanced by an*

While many Australians celebrated Australia Day 1988 as the bicentenary of the settlement of Australia in 1788, others saw it as 'Invasion Day'.

equal responsibility to learn English, find work, respect our culture and heritage, and accept women as full equals.'

Australians have generally supported the idea of cultural diversity, which is evident in many public celebrations. Australia Day, 26 January, commemorates the landing of the First Fleet at Sydney Cove in 1788. This marked the beginning of British Australia, and also the destruction of much of Indigenous Australia. Many people see this 'Invasion Day' as being unworthy of Australia's national day, and would prefer to see an alternative national moment celebrated. For most people, however, Australia Day is neither British nor Indigenous, but has developed into a celebration of Australia as a successful multicultural community. Other events and festivals centring around different cultures, such as Chinese New Year and the National Multicultural Festival in Canberra, are also widely celebrated around the country.

INTERNATIONAL CONFLICTS AND PEACEKEEPING

Since 1947, Australia has provided more than 65,000 military, police and civilian personnel in more than 50 United Nations and other peace and security operations.

Peacekeeping operations

First Gulf War

In August 1990, Iraq invaded Kuwait. This action was condemned by the United Nations, and Australian warships joined a UN force to blockade Iraq by stopping and searching any ships bringing prohibited goods to or from Iraq.

Bougainville

Bougainville was part of Papua New Guinea, but a strong separatist movement wanted independence for the mineral-rich island. Thousands of people died as a direct or indirect result of the conflict between 1989 and 1998.

In 1997, the two sides met to discuss settlement of the conflict. Peacekeepers from New Zealand, Australia, Fiji and Vanuatu helped set up the truce and the subsequent peace, and to maintain it. Part of the peace agreement included the destruction of weapons, and a fair and free election of a new government. Bougainville is now an autonomous region of New Guinea.

East Timor

In 1975, Indonesia invaded East Timor, a Portuguese colony. Portugal was ending its rule, and Indonesia feared instability and the establishment of a left-wing government at its border. Indonesia claimed East Timor as an Indonesian province. Australia chose not to oppose this invasion, preferring to maintain its relationship with Indonesia.

Many East Timorese resisted Indonesian control, and waged a guerrilla war against the occupying troops and their local supporters. In 1999, Indonesia at last allowed East Timor to vote on the issue of independence from Indonesia – and the vote was overwhelmingly in favour. The vote unleashed mass burning, looting, beatings and even murder by

A cartoonist's critical depiction of atrocities committed by the Indonesian Government in East Timor titled 'Scorched Earth'. Signed by Nicholson, dated 1999.

pro-Indonesian locals ('militias') and by some Indonesian troops. Australia led a United Nations operation, called INTERFET (International Force East Timor), to provide protection for East Timor. Once order had been established the peacekeeping effort shifted to helping the East Timorese Government establish its authority. In 2002, East Timor became the new nation of Timor Leste.

Solomon Islands
In 2003 the Solomon Islands, in the Pacific Ocean and off the east coast of Papua New Guinea, was a dangerous and chaotic place. A corrupt police force meant that there was no security for the public, and the government had no control outside the capital, Honiara. Australia, New Zealand and 13 other nations from the Pacific Islands Forum organised a force to restore control and order.

Wars

Australia has also been involved in several wars as well as peacekeeping missions.

The Second Gulf War or Iraq War

On 20 March 2003, a combined force of American, British and Australian troops under United States leadership invaded Iraq in what was termed 'the Second Gulf War'. Their objective was to locate and destroy suspected 'weapons of mass destruction' (WMDs). Several other western nations, including France and Germany, opposed the mission, claiming that there was no proof that the WMDs existed, and that invasion was not justified. In Australia, opinion was generally favourable, but there was also some strong opposition.

Within three weeks coalition forces had seized Baghdad and the corrupt and brutal dictatorship of Saddam Hussein was overthrown. However, no weapons of mass destruction existed.

The coalition's victory was followed by a difficult 'nation building' and counter-insurgency campaign to prevent Iraq sliding into a vicious civil war between the former rulers, the minority Sunnis, and the majority Shia.

By May 2011, all non-US coalition forces had withdrawn from Iraq and the US military withdrew all forces on 18 December 2011, thus ending the Iraq War. Sectarian violence and civil conflict escalated within Iraq once the western forces withdrew.

Four Australian servicemen died in the conflict in Iraq between 16 July 2003 and 31 July 2009.

Afghanistan

The war in Afghanistan has been Australia's longest military engagement. It was an element in the 'War on Terror', which started following the multiple terrorist attacks in New York and Washington DC on 11 September 2001. Even though 15 of the 19 terrorists who attacked the World Trade Centre and the Pentagon on 11 September were Saudi Arabian nationals, the focus of the war became Afghanistan, where the group known as the Taliban had helped train and shelter the main international terrorist organisation, al-Qaeda, and its leader, Osama bin Laden. Australia invoked the Australia, New Zealand and United States Security Treaty (ANZUS) to support the US effort and Australian combat troops joined the forces of 'the coalition of the willing'.

In October 2001, coalition forces under US leadership invaded Afghanistan and ejected the ruling Taliban regime. The mission then evolved into civil aid, such as construction of hospitals and schools, and the reconstruction of wells, and training local forces so that they could take control of their own country.

Australia withdrew all but some training forces in 2013. The war cost 42 Australian deaths, and over 250 soldiers seriously wounded. Many servicemen and women continue to suffer physical and/or psychological problems as a result of their service. More than 100 veterans have committed suicide – far more than were killed during the conflict. Taliban insurgents have increased their attacks on Afghani Government forces since the withdrawal of western combat forces.

Humanitarian assistance

In addition to formal peacekeeping operations, Australia has been involved in many emergency humanitarian and natural disaster rescue operations in the Asia-Pacific region. These have included assistance in Vanuatu after Cyclone Pam in 2015, in the Philippines after Typhoon Haiyan in 2013; Christchurch, New Zealand, after the earthquake of February 2011; Japan after the earthquake and tsunami of March 2011, and Indonesia after the 'Boxing Day tsunami' of December 2004.

Foreign aid

Australia is one of the largest donors of foreign aid in the Pacific Islands region, contributing several billion dollars each year to projects that aim to assist economic growth, infrastructure development (such as building roads and bridges), education, health and the empowerment of women.

Weapons bans and controls

Australia has supported the international limitation, control and banning of nuclear, chemical, biological and anti-personnel weapons. The process involves the Australian Parliament 'ratifying' the United Nations measures on these issues – making the measure part of Australian law.

Australia ratified the United Nations Treaty on the Non-Proliferation of Nuclear Weapons in 1973. The objective of this landmark treaty is to prevent the spread of nuclear weapons and weapons technology, to promote cooperation in the peaceful uses of nuclear energy and to further the goal of achieving nuclear disarmament and general and complete disarmament. Australia ratified the treaty banning nuclear tests in 1998.

Australia has also ratified UN treaties banning chemical and biological weapons, landmines and cluster weapons – small explosive bombs that are dropped or spread over an area. Some of Australia's peacekeeping activities, such as those in Cambodia following the civil war that overthrew the brutal Khmer Rouge regime in 1979, have been in de-mining areas, and teaching local people the skills of de-mining.

Australia also applied this principle of restriction of weapons at home. In 1996, a gunman killed 35 people and wounded 23 others at the Tasmanian heritage tourist site, Port Arthur. Prime Minister John Howard immediately forced the states to put a ban on all semi-automatic weapons, and to accept a restrictive system of gun licence and ownership controls.

Antarctica

Seven nations claim sovereignty over Antarctica: Australia, Britain, New Zealand, Chile, France, Norway and Argentina. Australia claims 42 per cent of the Antarctic territory, more than any other nation. Britain claimed these areas in 1841, and in 1933 transferred their claim to Australia. In 1947, Britain also transferred Heard Island and McDonald Island to Australian control. The 1961 Antarctic Treaty, which Australia has ratified, does not accept any nation's claim to Antarctica.

Australia first sent expeditions to the area in 1913, and has established three year-round bases for its continuing exploration activities.

Originally, dog sleds were the primary means of transport for the researchers at these bases. The dogs were valued both for their work and for their companionship, but the fragile nature of the Antarctic environment meant that all non-native animals (other than humans) had to be removed. Australia's last dogs were removed in 1993.

Australia's claim to Antarctica includes territorial waters extending 200 nautical miles out to sea. Australia has declared an Antarctic whale sanctuary in these waters, but only four nations accept this claim. Japan is not one of them, and this has led to tension over the continuing presence of Japanese whaling expeditions. Japan claims that its whaling is scientific, and therefore allowable. This has been challenged by other countries that claim it is not.

Australia has been active in advocating that Antarctica remains demilitarised and free from mineral exploration. It has also opposed illegal fishing and whaling.

Australia's main activity in Antarctica is scientific research into the animals (such as penguins and whales), fish and plants of the area (including krill and plankton), glacier formation, climate changes (including establishing a 2000-year climate record from a study of ice cores), and the nature of the oceans.

Papua New Guinea

The southern half of eastern New Guinea, the Territory of Papua, came under Australian control in 1902. In 1920 Australia was given a League of Nations mandate to rule the northern part, the former German New Guinea. In 1942 Japan invaded and occupied much of it. Australia fought fierce battles to regain control by 1945. The area was combined in 1949 and Australia was given trusteeship of Papua New Guinea by the United Nations.

After the war the United Nations actively promoted decolonisation – the return of colonial areas to their Indigenous majorities, and the granting of independence to these countries. Australia granted independence to Papua New Guinea in 1975 as part of an international movement of decolonisation.

HUMAN RIGHTS AND LAND RIGHTS

Australia has ratified many United Nations declarations relating to human rights since the UN founded its Declaration on Human Rights in 1948, and made commitments both nationally and internationally towards offering humanitarian assistance and development aid, upholding the rights of Indigenous peoples, striving for gender equality and fair treatment of refugees and asylum seekers.

Women's rights

Women's rights have slowly moved towards equality with men's. The requirement for women to leave work once they married had been removed by 1966. Equal pay for equal work was fully legislated by 1972. This affected one and a half million women workers, and was implemented over the following years. The ratio of female to male earnings increased from 60 per cent to 80 per cent in six years after the decision.

Women's workforce participation rose. There were more jobs available, and many of the jobs were professionally based rather than manual labour. As women started to gain more equal pay, work became a more attractive option. Women started marrying later (average age 21 in 1961, 29 in 2010), having children later (average age of first childbirth was 23 in 1960, and 29 in 2010), and having fewer children (average of 3.4 in 1960 and 1.9 in 2010.) In 1973, the Australian Government introduced the maternity leave scheme, which meant that women employed in the public service could return to their jobs after they had given birth.

More women attended university, and by 1987 there were more women than men enrolled in tertiary education. Female

One of the great movements of the period was the demand for the social, political and economic equality of women. This badge celebrates the first major Sydney International Women's Day march held in 1972.

students were an overwhelming majority in fields such as education and health, but were small minorities in fields such as engineering and surveying.

In 1983 Australia ratified the United Nations Convention on the Elimination of All Forms of Discrimination Against Women, and in 1984 passed the *Commonwealth Sex Discrimination Act*, which made it illegal to discriminate on the basis of gender.

These measures helped promote the equality of women with men, especially in employment, but women continued to be paid less than men overall, and to be more likely to work part-time rather than full-time.

The growing awareness and acceptance of women's rights also led to the uncovering of dark areas that had been hidden by society. In 1966 an Australian Bureau of Statistics survey found that 23 per cent of married women had experienced at least one act of violence at some stage from their partners. This prompted campaigns about domestic violence against women and the establishment of more women's refuges.

The position of Indigenous Australians

The gap in education, health, employment and social conditions between many Indigenous Australians and other Australians continues to exist, but has reduced since 1972 through government action and Indigenous activism.

Racial Discrimination Act 1975

This Commonwealth Act made it illegal to discriminate against anyone on the grounds of race, colour, descent or national origin. The Act covers areas of public life such as employment, education, accommodation, getting or using services (in areas such as transport), shops and access to public places. It also covers harassment in the workplace.

Royal Commission into Aboriginal Deaths in Custody

A government inquiry was set up in 1987 to investigate the high number of deaths of Aboriginal people in prisons and police stations. There were accusations that unjustified violence by police and warders towards prisoners had caused at least some of these deaths.

The 1991 report found that Aboriginal prisoners did not suffer a greater death rate than other prisoners, and that there was no case in which illegal violence by authorities had caused any deaths. However, it raised serious questions about police and prison systems regulating the care of prisoners. It found that Aboriginal people did have a far higher rate of imprisonment than others. It also found that in 43 of the 99 cases, the people who died in custody were members of the Stolen Generations, that many had poor education, and that they had usually been in prison many times. The report made more than 300 recommendations of ways to reduce the Indigenous imprisonment rate, most of which have not been implemented.

Stolen Generations

In 1997, the Australian Government released its *Bringing Them Home* report on the Stolen Generations – Aboriginal and Torres Strait Islander children who had been forcibly removed from their homes as a result of government policies between the late 19th century and the 1970s.

These policies were aimed at removing Aboriginal and Torres Strait Islander children of mixed descent from their natural families, and placing them in government or religious institutions, or with foster families.

The stated aims of these policies were to remove children from disadvantaged and dangerous conditions, and to help them assimilate into mainstream society. But there was also an underlying intention to speed up what was thought to be the inevitable demise of Aboriginal and Torres Strait Islander people and culture. The result was that tens of thousands of children were simply taken from their parents, many of whom never saw their offspring again. Apart from the emotional trauma they inflicted, these policies also meant that parents could not pass on their culture and language to their children who were instead taught mainstream culture and values and were trained to become agricultural labourers and domestic help for European settlers. The *Bringing Them Home* report concluded that:

> 'When a child was forcibly removed that child's entire community lost, often permanently, its chance to perpetuate itself in that child. The Inquiry has concluded that this was a primary objective of forcible removals and is the reason they amount to genocide.'

We do not know exactly how many children were taken from their families in this way. Estimates vary from about one in ten to three in ten of Aboriginal and Torres Strait Islander children. Under government control, the children usually received very little education.

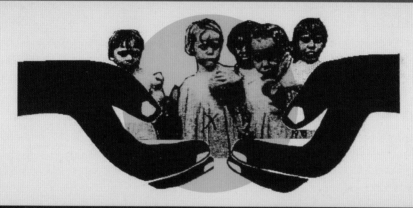

VICTORIAN STOLEN GENERATIONS RALLY
Friday May 26, 2000

**Meet at the Treasury Gardens at 10.30am
to proceed through the streets of Melbourne.
To be followed by a Family Day at the Treasury**

'Rebuilding Our Families — Rebuilding Our Future'

Come and support our struggle for justice!

Bring a white flower to place at the steps of parliament in remembrance
and respect for those who endured the loss and pain of separation.
Show the government that we are a community that feels strongly
about this issue and that you support the implementation
of the recommendations from 'The Bringing Them Home' Report.

BRING ALONG BANNERS AND FLAGS SHOWING YOUR SUPPORT FOR THE STOLEN GENERATIONS.

Survival — Unity — Dignity

Organised by:
**The Victorian Stolen Generations Committee and
The Bringing Them Home Victoria Committee.**

A poster for the Stolen Generations rally held in Victoria on Sorry Day, 28 May 2000. This rally was complemented by the Corroboree Bridge Walk across the Harbour Bridge in Sydney on the same day, in support of Indigenous Australians and Reconciliation.

The *Bringing Them Home* report heard evidence of terrible conditions in many government and religious institutions, including physical, sexual and psychological abuse. Children were isolated from their families and their culture. Because of the trauma from this experience, many of them developed psychological issues and grew up to be violent and abusive, prone to drug and alcohol addiction, and in poor health.

The Stolen Generations is an aspect of Australian history that continues to generate discussion and debate, and influences legislation and policies aiming to improve Indigenous health and welfare.

Northern Territory Emergency Response

In 2007, the Northern Territory Government released its *Little Children Are Sacred* report, which found that sexual abuse of children in many Aboriginal communities had reached critical levels. The Australian Government responded by authorising an intervention in the Northern Territory to ban alcohol and pornography, isolate 50 per cent of welfare money for food, as well as increase police and medical attention.

This was controversial because it overrode the *Racial Discrimination Act*, and because to some it seemed to be blaming all Aboriginal people for the terrible conditions and circumstances and the behaviour of some.

Land rights

While there was pressure for improving Aboriginal and Torres Strait Islander human rights from the 1960s onwards, there was also a growing belief that Indigenous people should have the legal right to control their traditional lands.

Homelands movement and land returns

In 1970, the first 'homeland' movement developed, with small numbers of Indigenous people choosing to leave dysfunctional larger settlements and return to their own Country. They wanted to maintain their traditional cultural practices, and their ties and obligations to the land.

By 2014, there were about 10,000 people living in about 500 homelands communities.

Supporters claimed that the homelands were a healthier and safer way of living, and helped maintain traditional culture. Critics claimed that these small communities were not economically and socially sustainable settlements, with a lack of basic water and electricity services, educational and health facilities, and employment opportunities.

The Australian Government passed the *Aboriginal Land Rights Act (NT) 1976*, which for the first time recognised Aboriginal claims to ownership of their land if it had not been previously sold. In 1975, the government handed back the land at Wattie Creek, now known as Dagaragu, as the result of the Wave Hill strike by the Gurindji. In 1985, the government handed back control of Uluru (Ayers Rock) and Kata Tjuta (the Olgas) to the local Anangu people. Uluru and Kata Tjuta are both listed as World Heritage sites for their environmental and cultural significance.

The Mabo case and the Wik decision are two significant moments in Indigenous land rights history. These cases have helped to establish the Native Title Tribunals, which have

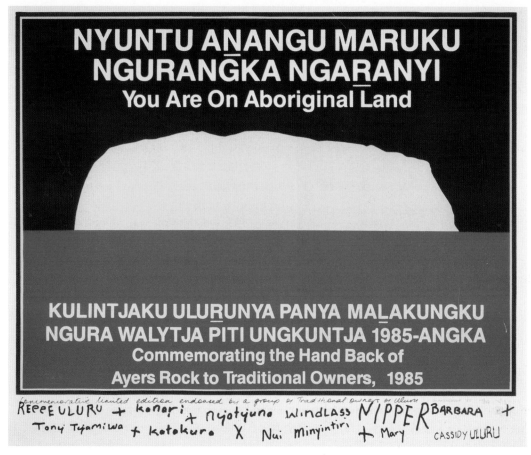

A poster celebrating the return of control of the Uluru Kata Tjuta National Park to the traditional owners, the Pitjantjatjara.

enabled many traditional owners to achieve a variety of rights over their land and, most importantly, the right to reclaim it.

The Mabo case

Eddie Koiki Mabo (born 1936; died 1992) was a Torres Strait Islander from the island of Mer, who challenged the right of the Queensland Government to claim ownership of traditional land.

Queensland had taken legal control of the Torres Strait Islands in 1879. It claimed that this meant that the land on the islands became Crown land – land owned by the government. Mabo and four other traditional landowners challenged this in the High Court in 1982. They lost the original case and another challenge in the Queensland Supreme Court.

Finally, in 1992, the High Court decided that the basis of British settlement of Australia in 1788 had been under the legal principle of 'terra nullius', which meant 'land belonging to no-one'. The judges decided that this was not appropriate, as the land in 1788 clearly did have owners. They rejected 'terra nullius' and the consequence was that 'native title' or Indigenous ownership of land could still exist in certain circumstances – where there was a

373

A portrait of Eddie Mabo, signed by C.B. Robinson, 1993.

continuing relationship with the land, and where the Crown (the Government) had not sold it. This decision did not change Britain's right to claim sovereignty over Australia, but it did restore land ownership to some Indigenous people. It also meant that Queensland's 1879 claim to land on Mer was not valid where a local person could establish that traditional and continuing ownership of the land.

The High Court's decision led to the Australian Government passing the *Native Title Act 1993*, which applied to all parts of Australia, not just Mer as the High Court decision had done. The Act stated that Aboriginal and Torres Strait Islander people had legal ownership of their traditional land, provided that it had not been previously legally sold, and that the people claiming the land could show a continuing connection to it.

More than 15 per cent of the Australian landmass is currently covered by native title claims. Many areas have been returned to their traditional owners, but there are criticisms of the process: that it takes far too long for the Native Title Tribunal to come to a decision, that it is difficult to prove unbroken connection to the land given the disruption that was forced on many Indigenous people, and that it sets different groups against each other when both lay claims to the same area. It also has not affected the land rights claims of urban Indigenous people and others whose continuity with their traditional country was broken by the process of colonial settlement.

The Wik decision

In 1996, the High Court considered another land rights claim. This was by the Wik people of Cape York Peninsula. The land they claimed had never been sold, but it had been leased out as pastoral land. The High Court decided that as the land had never been sold, the Wik people still retained their native title to it and that they could continue to practise their traditional ceremonies and ways of life, but only to the extent that they did not interfere with the pastoralists' use of the property. In other words, both parties had to share the land.

Towards Reconciliation

The increasing improvement in human rights and land rights was matched by a move towards 'reconciliation' – meaning towards justice, unity and respect between Aboriginal and Torres Strait Islander and non-Indigenous Australians.

National flags

In 1971 a new Aboriginal flag was flown for the first time. It was designed by Luritja artist Harold Thomas. The symbolic colours represent the people (black), the earth (red) and the sun (yellow).

The Torres Strait Islander flag was designed by a 15-year-old school boy, Bernard Namok, in 1992. The flag represents the land (green), the sea (blue), peace (white) and the people (black). The dhari (headdress) is a traditional Torres Strait Island design, and the five-pointed star represents navigation by a seafaring people, and the five major island groups.

Both flags were officially recognised in 1995, symbolising the importance of Aboriginal and Torres Strait Islander people in the nation.

Barunga Statement

In 1988 Prime Minister Hawke accepted the Barunga Statement, a document prepared by a number of Aboriginal groups in the Northern Territory. The statement called for a range of rights, compensation and self-determination measures, and a treaty. Hawke committed his government to working towards a treaty recognising the groups' 'prior ownership, continued occupation and sovereignty and affirming our human rights and freedom'. No treaty was ever presented, and there are still occasional calls for a treaty.

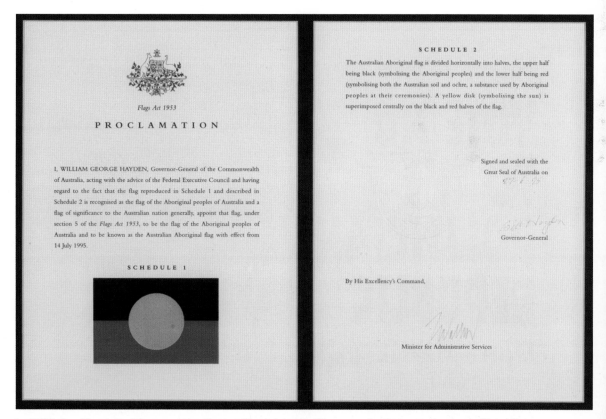

In 1995 the Aboriginal flag and the Torres Strait Islands flag were both recognised as official flags of Australia.

Council for Aboriginal Reconciliation

In 1991, a Council for Aboriginal Reconciliation was set up (replaced in 2000 by Reconciliation Australia) to work towards building better relationships between the wider Australian community and Aboriginal and Torres Strait Islander peoples for the benefit of all Australians. Its aim was to have a formal Reconciliation by 2001. In 1996 it introduced National Reconciliation Week, which is held each year between 27 May (the anniversary date of the 1967 Referendum) and 3 June (the Mabo decision date). This is in addition to NAIDOC Week, which is held each year between the first and second Sunday in July since 1975 and run by an entirely Indigenous committee.

Redfern speech

In 1993 Prime Minister Paul Keating made a famous speech in Redfern, an inner Sydney suburb with a traditionally strong Aboriginal and Torres Strait Islander presence, in which he accepted the role of the European possession in dispossessing Aboriginal people. He spoke of the smashing of their traditional way of life, of the bringing in of diseases and alcohol that have blighted so many lives, of Europeans committing murders, taking the children and practising discrimination and exclusion. This led to the establishment in 1998 of a national 'Sorry Day'.

Constitutional Preamble

In 1999 a proposed change to the Preamble of the Constitution, acknowledging prior Indigenous occupation of Australia, was defeated. This was largely because it was coupled

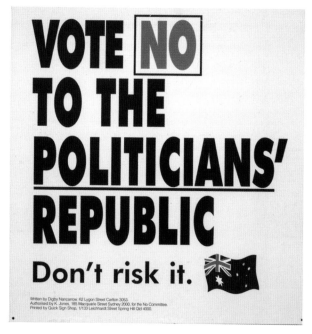

A placard and a T-shirt displaying different attitudes to the 1999 referendum's question on becoming a republic.

with the very controversial republic proposal that suggested Australia break ties with the British monarch, and the Preamble proposal received little attention and explanation. Both proposals were defeated, with the republic gaining a 45 per cent 'Yes' vote, and the Preamble a 39 per cent 'Yes' vote.

Stolen Generations apology

In 2008 Prime Minister Kevin Rudd apologised on behalf of the nation for the damage and hurt suffered by the Stolen Generations. This was a momentous occasion for Indigenous communities nationwide as the Australian Government had finally and officially recognised its responsibility in the dispossession, loss and trauma of many Indigenous families throughout the 20th century.

Constitutional recognition

During 2014 and 2015, pressure increased for a set of changes to the Constitution that would remove the few remaining

The Order of Australia presented to Neville Bonner in 1984.

Aboriginal and Torres Strait Islander political firsts

Name	Year	Achievement
Neville Bonner	1971	Appointed to the Senate, then elected in 1973
Hyacinth Tungatalum	1974	Elected to the Northern Territory Parliament
Eric Deral	1974	Elected to the Queensland Parliament
Ernie Bridge	1988	Appointed a Minister in the Western Australian Government
Marion Scrymgour	2003	Appointed a Minister in the Northern Territory Government
Ken Wyatt	2010	Elected to the House of Representatives
Adam Giles	2013	Appointed Chief Minister of the Northern Territory Government
Nova Peris	2013	Elected to the Senate

discriminatory elements, and acknowledge Aboriginal and Torres Strait Islanders within the Australian Constitution. Prime Minister Tony Abbott said that such changes were important because they would 'complete the Constitution'. The referendum was proposed to be held on the symbolic date of 27 May 2017 – the 50th anniversary of the 1967 referendum.

Closing the gap

The improvement in human rights and land rights, and the move towards Reconciliation are all positive steps. However, the 2011 census showed a range of areas where Aboriginals and Torres Strait Islanders were much worse off than other Australians. These included:

- 25 per cent of Aboriginal and Torres Strait Islander people completed Year 12, compared to 52 per cent for other Australians
- Aboriginal and Torres Strait Islanders had a higher rate of lower income levels than non-Indigenous Australians (below $799 per week), and a lower rate of higher income levels (above $800)
- The unemployment rate of Aboriginal and Torres Strait Islander people was 17 per cent, compared to 5 per cent for other Australians
- Aboriginal and Torres Strait Islander people continue to have a lower life expectancy, a higher infant mortality rate, a higher rate of many preventable diseases, and a higher rate of child welfare interventions
- Aboriginal and Torres Strait Islander people continue to be heavily over-represented in crime rates and incarceration in prisons.

These figures only partly present the real picture. They include the majority of Aboriginal and Torres Strait Islander people who live in cities and towns, most of whose work, health, education and social welfare situations are similar to non-Indigenous residents. That means that the level of disadvantage experienced by the relatively small number (about 30 per cent) who live in more remote areas, and often economically and socially dysfunctional communities, is severe.

CULTURAL CHANGES

In the final quarter of the 20th century and into the early 21st century, Australia's popular culture and entertainment has continued to be dominated by homegrown Australian culture, American and, to a lesser extent, British influences.

Film

Australian films and mini-series had a renaissance, with many popular films presenting an identifiable and distinct Australian character and themes. Some well known films were *The Chant of Jimmie Blacksmith, Picnic at Hanging Rock, My Brilliant Career, Mad Max, Crocodile Dundee, Strictly Ballroom, Muriel's Wedding* and *The Adventures of Priscilla: Queen of the Desert*. The films of the 1970s and 1980s often used historical events to present a strongly nationalistic message – especially *Gallipoli* and *Breaker Morant*.

TV

The development of video cassette recorders (VCRs) in the early 1980s allowed people to record programs and watch them later, while filtering out advertisements. Out of this progressed high-resolution DVD systems, which, along with hi-tech TVs that allowed the viewer to record shows, revolutionised the concept of home entertainment.

But the evolution of television and films also contributed to Australians' decreasing fitness and health, as they sat around more rather than being active. The 'Life. Be in it.' campaign was developed in 1975 to get people off the couch and doing more outdoor activities. Its 'hero' was Norm, an overweight and sedentary character who was encouraged to get up and out to experience and enjoy life, even if it was to fly a kite with the kids, walk the dog or do some gardening. The campaign was revived in 2000, due to concerns about Australia's rising rates of obesity.

Radio

Other technological developments included the introduction of FM (frequency modulation) radio stations, which could broadcast a much better quality sound. Alternative stations such as 2JJ, later 2JJJ, then Triple J developed, as did a range of community-based stations reflecting ethnic and cultural diversity.

Music styles proliferated and there was something for everybody: pop, rock, hip hop, electronic dance music, country and western, metal, ska, jazz, classical, soul, grunge and more. Several radio stations specialised in rock music.

Technology

The greatest technological development was the mass availability of computers in the 1970s, and the improvement of the internet for general use in the 1990s.

Apple released their Apple II home computers – one of the first commercially successful home computers in the world – in 1977, and the first IBM personal computers (PCs) followed in 1983.

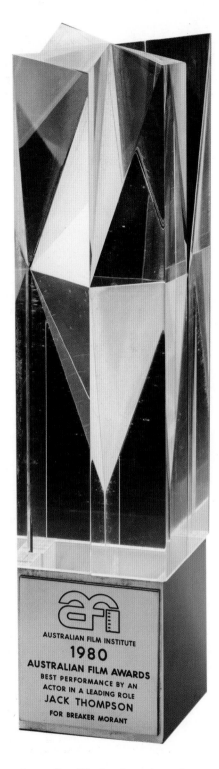

Australian Film Institute Award, 1980, to Jack Thompson, for his leading role in *Breaker Morant*.

379

Life.Be in it. Exercisements

The 'Life. Be In It.' campaign was established to encourage Australians to adopt a healthier lifestyle.

Computer and internet access revolutionised the spread and accessibility of information and entertainment, and has changed social interactions through the use of social media, such as Facebook, Twitter and Instagram. Computers and advanced technology have also changed the way people work (for example, eliminating the typing pools that used to exist in every major office) and affected greatly how we live our daily lives. Perhaps one notable change is the shift from paper currency to digital forms of payment – the use of credit cards and PayPass to pay for goods and services.

Mobile phones appeared in 1987. The first models were the size of a house brick and cost the equivalent of over $4000 today. The miniaturisation and improvement of the mobile phone has seen ownership go from six in every thousand Australians in 1989 to more than 130 mobiles for every 100 people in 2014.

Australia's first computer

CSIRAC, Australia's first computer and one of the earliest in the world, was built by the Council for Scientific and Industrial Research (CSIRO) in 1949. It needed enough electricity to power a suburban street, and had only a fraction of the brainpower of the cheapest modern electronic organiser. It took up a whole room and needed its own air-conditioning system. It was used to perform complex calculations, such as for weather forecasting and banking, which had previously been done on mechanical adding machines. It was turned off for the final time in 1964 and is now on display in the Museum of Victoria in Melbourne.

Indigenous pop culture

In the past 40 years Australian popular culture has been increasingly influenced by Indigenous culture. One major way was through the unique painting styles of artists such as Rover Thomas Clifford Possum Tjapaltjarri and Emily Kame Kngwarreye, whose works were inspired by stories from their Country. The Bangarra Dance Company formed in 1989, and created a fusion of traditional Indigenous and modern western dance.

One of the most popular songs in the early 1990s was 'Treaty' by rock band Yothu Yindi, which was comprised of Indigenous and non-Indigenous members. In 2001 'Treaty' was voted by the Australian Performing Rights Association (APRA) as one of the top 30 Australian songs between 1922 and 2001. This and other songs such as Midnight Oil's 'Beds Are Burning', Paul Kelly's 'From Little Things Big Things Grow' and the Warumpi Band's 'My Island Home' reflected the push towards reconciliation and greater land rights.

The Deadly Awards was established in 1995, and is held every year to recognise Aboriginal and Torres Strait Islander achievement in music, sport, entertainment and

Albert Namatjira

The life of Albert Namatjira (born 1902; died 1959) tells us much about the complexity of life of Aboriginal and Torres Strait Islanders in the 20th century.

Namatjira was born at Hermannsburg (now Ntaria) in the Northern Territory, was educated at the Lutheran Mission, became a Lutheran, and was an initiated Arrernte man.

He had a natural artistic ability, and worked as a blacksmith, carpenter, stockman and cameleer at the mission station for rations, and on neighbouring pastoral properties for wages.

In 1934 he met a visiting artist, Rex Battarbee, who taught Albert to paint. Namatjira painted the landscape of the Macdonnell Ranges, and had his paintings exhibited in prestigious art galleries in Adelaide and Melbourne. He produced about 2000 paintings during his lifetime. His paintings had gained so much popularity that he was presented to Queen Elizabeth II in Canberra during her visit in 1954.

Namatjira was given the status of a white citizen in 1957 – a first for an Indigenous person in the Northern Territory – which freed him from the normal restrictions on 'full-blooded' Aboriginal people.

One of these was the right to buy alcohol. In 1958 Namatjira was charged with supplying alcohol to a prohibited person, despite the cultural requirement for Namatjira to share his possessions with family. (At one stage he was personally providing for 600 people.) He was imprisoned for two months.

Other examples of discriminatory actions against him were that he was refused a grazing licence in 1949–50, and prevented from building a house on land he owned at Alice Springs, forcing him to move to a fringe camp nearby at Morris Soak.

Namatjira died aged 57, and is buried in the Lutheran section of Alice Springs cemetery. His talent and influence on Australian art is commemorated in many ways, including on a 1968 limited edition postage stamp released by Australia Post.

community. The international success of Indigenous artists such as Jessica Mauboy, Deborah Mailman, Jimmy Chi and David Gulpilil show just how much Indigenous culture has become representative of Australian talent in general.

Sport

The 1970s was a low point for Australian sport. The Montreal Olympics of 1976 were the first Olympics in which Australia failed to win a gold medal since the Berlin Olympics in 1936.

This shook sports administrators and they developed the Australian Institute of Sport. It opened in 1981 with the goal of bringing professionalism to the training and preparation of elite athletes. This includes much scientific research into physiology, diet, biomechanics and other areas; more than 2000 research papers have been produced by AIS staff.

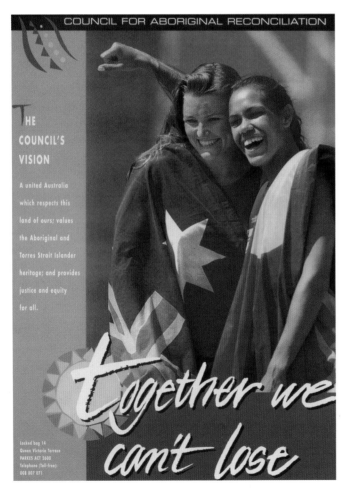

A poster promoting Reconciliation between Indigenous and non-Indigenous Australia, featuring athletes Cathy Freeman and Melinda Gainsford-Taylor.

International events

Australia won two gold medals at the 1980 Moscow Olympics and peaked at the 2000 Sydney Olympic Games, when the country finished fourth with 16 gold medals, and a total of 58 medals, behind the United States, Russia and China.

Australia has hosted Olympic Games and Commonwealth Games since the mid-1950s. Olympic Games were held in Melbourne (1956) and Sydney (2000). Commonwealth Games were held in Perth (1962), Brisbane (1982) and Melbourne (2006). The 2018 Commonwealth Games will be held in the Gold Coast.

The introduction of colour television in the 1970s increased the commercialisation and the popularity of spectator sport in Australia. Top sportsmen and women became full-time athletes earning six- and even seven-figure payments, as well as lucrative commercial sponsorships. In 1977 World Series Cricket became a breakaway television-based commercial rival to the traditional form, until the two came together again in 1979.

Impact on the economy

The significance of international events for the Australian economy can be seen in the statistics for another large international sporting event hosted in the country – the 2003 Rugby World Cup. The event sold 1.8 million tickets for $200 million, drew 65,000 international visitors, generated $494 million in other sales (such as food and accommodation), and created 4500 full- and part-time jobs across New South Wales, Queensland and Victoria.

Such events created Australian sporting heroes, stimulated the creation or improvement of sporting and entertainment facilities in the host city, generated tourism, increased spending in the local economy, and provided an international interest in and showcasing of Australia.

Indigenous sportspeople

Sport also provided an important way for some Aboriginal and Torres Strait Islanders to excel. Boxer Lionel Rose became the nation's darling when he won a world title in 1968 (and was named Australian of the Year, the first of six Indigenous Australians to receive this honour). Evonne Goolagong won 14 grand slam tennis titles between 1970 and 1980. Nova Peris became the first Aboriginal woman to win an Olympic gold medal, as part of the Hockeyroos side in 1996. The Ella brothers, Mark, Glen and Gary, all represented Australia in Rugby Union in the 1980s. Mark also captained the team, being the first Aboriginal player to captain an Australian team in any sport. Cathy Freeman brought all Australia together with her win in the 400 metres at the Sydney Olympics in 2000, and when she lit the Olympic flame in the opening ceremony.

Aboriginal and Torres Strait Islander players are well represented in Australia's two most popular national sports, Australian Rules football and Rugby League.

CONSERVATION AND ENVIRONMENTAL MOVEMENTS

Australians' awareness of and attitudes towards environmental conservation and sustainability has increased throughout the years due to growing scientific research and greater access to information.

Lionel Rose's International Bantamweight Championship Title Match boxing trophy, 1968.

Australian inventions and innovations of the 1970s–2000s

1978
Cochlear implant
Otherwise known as the 'bionic ear', this device is implanted into the ear to stimulate the auditory nerve so that the recipient can hear. It was invented by Graeme Clark, whose prototype of the implant had been created from money raised in a Channel Ten telethon.

1988
Polymer bank notes
The Reserve Bank of Australia and CSIRO collaborated to create plastic bank notes, making them stronger, cleaner and safer from counterfeiting than paper currency.

1992
Wi-Fi
CSIRO scientists developed the standard wi-fi model designed by Dutch researcher Victor Hayes, allowing the successful reception and transmission of digital information without wires and cords.

1999
Spray-on skin
Plastic surgeon Fiona Wood, alongside scientist Maria Stoner, developed a technique that allowed burns victims to recover faster from their injuries. This involved using a small patch of the victim's skin to grow new healthy cells, and then spraying the new cells on to the damaged areas.

Environmental disasters

Catastrophic international environmental disasters such the drying up of the Aral Sea between Kazakhstan and Uzbekistan over the last 50 years showed the frightening effects of environmental change. The Aral was approximately 68,000 square kilometres in 1960; by 2008, after its feeder rivers had been used for Soviet Union irrigation projects, it covered only 7000 square kilometres, split over two discrete areas.

Oil spills such as the Exxon Valdez disaster in 1989, which contaminated thousands of kilometres of water and coastal areas and killed birds, fish, seals and other creatures, also showed the fragility of nature and its vulnerability to human interference. Fortunately Australia has not suffered any comparable events, though there are fears that an oil spill affecting the Great Barrier Reef could one day cause great damage.

CFCs

In the 1960s, scientists discovered the increasing concentration of chlorofluorocarbons (CFCs) in the atmosphere, which was mainly due to increased use of chemicals in refrigeration and as aerosol propellants. These CFCs were creating 'holes' (really, reduced or thinner concentrations) in the ozone layer of the Earth's upper atmosphere over Antarctica, allowing harmful solar ultraviolet rays to filter through. These rays could cause skin cancers, and also destroy plankton, a basic food source in the sea. In 1987, international diplomats met and created the Montreal Protocol, which called on all nations to ban the use of CFCs. Less harmful alternatives were adopted and the ozone layer has slowly started to repair itself. It is anticipated that it will reach safe pre-1980 levels again between 2050 and 2065.

Climate change

The most persistent current environmental threat is climate change.

The scientific theory behind climate change is that the increasing release of greenhouse gases by industrial processes trap heat in the atmosphere. Greenhouse gases include carbon dioxide (CO_2) and methane (CH_4), which are freed into the atmosphere when fossil fuels (such as coal, wood, oil and gas) are burnt. Climate models predict that this will raise temperatures on earth and in the seas, and have a harmful effect on meteorological events, biological systems and the way humans live.

A United Nations specialist body, the Intergovernmental Panel on Climate Change (IPCC), meets periodically to try to get nations to reduce their greenhouse gas emissions. Most of this greenhouse gas production has come from the long process of the Industrial Revolution, which has helped create the wealth of the developed nations. Greenhouse gas can be reduced by the greater use of renewable energy, especially through the use of the wind and the sun, but these technologies are currently expensive and limited in their capacity to generate the amount of electricity needed.

Australian developments

Australian environmental disasters have been caused by drought, fire, flood, heat, cyclones, disease, introduced species and overclearing of the land, which has destroyed native habitats and caused erosion.

Increasing awareness of the environment

Early European Australians did not have the knowledge and understanding of the environment that Aboriginal and Torres Strait Islander people had developed over thousands

2011 census results

The census is conducted by the government every five years and gathers statistical information about Australian citizens such as their age, gender, religion and background. Here are some interesting facts from the 2011 Census:

- Of the 21,507,717 people in Australia, 49.4 per cent were male and 50.6 per cent were female. Aboriginal and Torres Strait Island people made up 2.5 per cent of the population.

- Just under 70 per cent of residents were born in Australia.

- 76.8 per cent of the population spoke only English at home; other languages included Mandarin, Italian, Arabic, Cantonese and Greek.

of years, so early farming and resource use was often destructive and wasteful. At least 17 of the 270 mammal species that lived in Australia in 1788 became extinct over the next 200 years.

Attitudes started to change as Europeans increased their knowledge of their natural environment. Field naturalist societies developed from the 1880s. These societies would study specific areas to learn how the Australian environment worked.

Walkers started to explore the bush and realised the value in conserving the natural habitat. In 1879, bushland in New South Wales was proclaimed the country's first national park. This area has since been renamed the Royal National Park and is the world's second oldest national park after Yellowstone National Park in the United States.

Periodic culls of native animals, especially koalas, led to the development of fauna advisory committees. These came too late to stop the extinction of the thylacine, or Tasmanian tiger, in 1936, but the koala was declared a protected species in all states by 1937, and the Tasmanian devil was protected in 1941.

From the 1920s international and local tourism developed into an important industry, especially as trains and cars made remote areas accessible to the ordinary person.

Lake Pedder

The earliest stimulus to the development of an environmental conservationist movement in Australia was the proposed development of Lake Pedder. Lake Pedder was a natural lake in the Tasmanian highlands. In 1972 it was flooded to develop a hydro-electricity scheme. Popular protests to the flooding led to the creation of the United Tasmania Group (UTG), one of the first Green political parties. Members of the UTG went on to create the Australian Greens Party. The Greens are today one of the four most important Australian political parties.

Natural disasters in Australia

Below are a few notable natural disasters that have struck different parts of the country since colonisation.

Year	Natural disaster	Area affected	Death toll
1852	Flood	Gundagai, New South Wales	89
1866	Storms	New South Wales coast	77
1899	Cyclone Mahina	Bathurst Bay, Queensland	410
1938	Heat wave	Victoria	438
1974	Cyclone Tracy	Darwin, Tiwi Islands	71
2009	Black Saturday bushfires	Victoria	173

Franklin Dam

In 1978, the Tasmanian Government planned to create a dam on the Gordon River that would flood the area below and destroy a wild river. The government claimed that the dam would create jobs and bring industry to Tasmania, as well as generate low-cost hydro-electric power.

Protesters and various conservation organisations united to fight the proposal, arguing that it would not have the claimed economic benefits, and that it would destroy one of the last remaining wilderness rivers and its environment. Protesters blockaded the works; many were dragged off and then came straight back to continue the blockade.

In 1983, Prime Minister Bob Hawke vowed to stop the dam being built. The federal government passed the *World Heritage Properties Conservation Act*, and placed the area under Commonwealth, not Tasmanian, control. Tasmania challenged the law but the High Court ruled 4:3 that it was a legitimate use of the Commonwealth's law-making power.

Australia now has 41 natural and human world heritage areas with sites in every state and territory.

Green bans

There were urban environmental movements as well. The green bans movement developed in Sydney in the 1970s. This was a period of rapid urban growth and development. However, new developments required the demolition of existing buildings, public spaces or disruption of the natural environment.

A key person in the green bans movement was the head of the New South Wales Builders' Labourers Federation, Jack Mundey. His workers, who needed to pull down the old and build the new, refused to work on sites where the building was historic and worthy of preserving, where natural areas would be destroyed or where public community space would become commercialised and privatised. Green bans were undertaken with the cooperation or at the request of resident groups who had been dismissed by their local

Mask worn by activist Benny Zable at the Franklin Dam protests.

A protest against the damming of part of the Franklin River.

members of parliament. The first area to be protected was a small patch of urban bushland called Kelly's Bush. Green bans also saved much of The Rocks area, the Royal Botanic Gardens and some inner-city houses.

Climate change

Australia produces a small overall percentage of greenhouse gas emissions (about 1 per cent of the world's total). But it is also a high per capita producer, as coal is so abundant for energy production in Australia and overseas, and Australians are mass consumers of goods.

Supporters of efforts to lower Australian greenhouse gas emissions argue that Australia has a moral obligation to help limit expected world temperature rises that might have severe global impacts. Opponents of strong cuts argue that Australia's contribution is minimal, and that renewable energy as an alternative to coal and gas can be unreliable and expensive.

Some also argue that the best solution is nuclear power, which does not produce greenhouse gas emissions. Australia is a world-leading producer of uranium, which is processed to become nuclear fuel, but does not produce nuclear power itself (although hospitals do use nuclear medicine and produce waste). Others oppose nuclear power, arguing that it is potentially deadly if there are accidents, and that the waste is very hard to dispose of and can lead to severe environmental damage and health risks.

Improvements in land use

Many colonial farmers did not understand the land and cleared it ruthlessly. Over time an increasing number of farmers developed a knowledge and greater understanding of their land and learned how to farm it sustainably.

Modern improvements in farming techniques from the 1980s included the careful application of herbicides to kill weeds rather than ploughing and disturbing the soil. New machinery sows and harvests crops more efficiently by using lasers and GPS technology to reduce the compacting or erosion of soil. Farmers introduced broadleaf rotation crops such as lupins, peas and canola that replaced nitrogen in the soil and avoided diseases that could develop from repeated mono-cropping. Farmers have also adopted technology that continuously monitors the soil and crops, so they know exactly when and where to use water and fertilisers in a way that maximises effectiveness and reduces usage and waste. Herbicides and nutrients can be delivered by GPS technology to places where they are needed, to within two-centimetre accuracy.

These and other improvements have increased crop yields as well as protecting the soil, thereby increasing agricultural sustainability.

Landcare movement

The Landcare movement developed in the 1980s in response to increasing land degradation. Groups of volunteers revegetated areas. The 1990s were declared the Decade of Landcare with the aim of planting a billion trees. 'Keep Australia Beautiful', 'Tidy Towns' and 'Clean Up Australia' campaigns from the 1960s onwards have also helped to improve the environment by increasing social awareness and encouraging community action to take care of the land. This has been applied to rivers, and people are more aware of the need to reduce salinity (concentration of salts in water) as a result of land use practices.

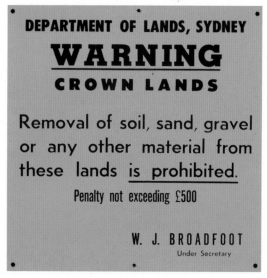

Part of a developing environmental awareness was the realisation of the need to protect soil.

CSIRO and CRCs

Research has helped promote sustainability. Much of the scientific work of the Commonwealth Scientific and Industrial Research Organisation (CSIRO) has been directed at rural improvements, such as pest-resistant and drought-tolerant crops. Australia has also established Cooperative Research Centres (CRCs), which conduct practical scientific research into major areas of sustainability – including mining and energy, agriculture, climate systems, water, salinity, the Great Barrier Reef, savannah lands and rainforests.

AUSTRALIA IN THE FUTURE

An expression of Australian identity

On 15 September 2000, an estimated 3.5 billion people watched Australia present itself to the world during the Olympic Games opening ceremony in Sydney.

The ceremony began when a lone horseman galloped into the arena, followed by 120 riders carrying a white flag with the five Olympic rings in aqua blue. The symbolism was clear – the horsemen and women were proud representatives of rural Australia, the flags representing the world-uniting sea.

Then a huge banner was unfurled, with the word 'G'day' set within a stylised arch of the Sydney Harbour Bridge – one of the country's most notable landmarks.

The scene changed to a Deep Sea Dreaming segment, celebrating the importance of the sea, the Great Barrier Reef and, with 13-year-old Nikki Webster in the middle of it on a towel, the Australian beach.

Next came The Awakening. This was led by Indigenous songman and Elder Djakapurra Munyarryun, who took Nikki Webster by the hand to lead her through the ancient past. The stadium was symbolically cleansed with the burning of eucalyptus leaves. A giant banner showing a Wandjina Spirit, the creative spirit from the Kimberley region, rose from the ground.

The Tin Symphony depicted Captain Cook as a white invader aboard his strange *Endeavour* ship full of weird contraptions, including a caged white rabbit, symbolising the foreboding change in the natural order of things. Iconic Australian objects also featured – corrugated iron, windmills, rainwater tanks, outback dunnies and shearing sheds. There were dancing Ned Kellys and a ballet of Victa lawnmowers.

Then came people from Africa, Oceania, the Americas Europe and Asia, symbolising the immigration that has helped shape multicultural Australia, while Nikki Webster sang 'Under Southern Skies'. The 2500 performers in the arena had formed the Australian landmass as they sang, while the Southern Cross stars rose in the sky.

The final segment had 1000 young and energetic tapdancers performing while a bridge was built to link the old Australia to the new. Djakapurra of the older generation and Nikki of the younger generation – the Indigenous culture and the European settler culture – met together on the bridge under the word 'Eternity'.

The presentation in 2000 showed how Australia had progressed from a settler country to a multicultural nation. It reflected how Australians of the start of the new millenium saw themselves and their history, and how they wanted the world to see them.

Australia is constantly changing and developing, reflecting each new generation's values and visions for the future. What will you make of Australia in the future?

'Land Rights' by Eunice Yunurupa Porter, 2011. In June 2005 the Australian Federal Court recognised the Ngaanyatjarra people's exclusive right to 180,000 square kilometres of land between the Great Victoria Desert and the Gibson Desert. This painting depicts the celebrations at Puntjilpi, an outstation near Mantamaru.

Select bibliography

Adam-Smith, P. *The Anzacs*, Penguin, 2014

Archer, M. et al, *The Evolution of Australia: 110 Million Years of Change*, Australian Museum, 2002

Arrow, M., *Friday on our Minds: Popular Culture in Australia since 1945*, UNSW Press, 2009

Australian Dictionary of Biography online: http://adb.anu.edu.au

Bashford, A., & Macintyre, S. (eds), *The Cambridge History of Australia Volume 1: Indigenous and Colonial Australia*, CUP, 2013

Bashford, A. & Macintyre, S. (eds), *The Cambridge History of Australia Volume 2: The Commonwealth of Australia,* CUP, 2013

Bate, W., Lucky City: *The First Generation at Ballarat*, MUP, 1978

Bean, C. E. W, *The Official History of Australia in the Great War*, 12 vols, Angus & Robertson, 1922–1947 Beaumont, J., *Australia's War 1939–1945*, Allen & Unwin, 1996

Beaumont, J., *Broken Nation: Australians in the Great War*, Allen & Unwin, 2013

Blainey, G., *Triumph of the Nomads*, Macmillan, 1975

Blainey, G., *A History of Victoria*, CUP, 2013

Blainey, G., *The Story of Australia's First People: The Rise and Fall of Ancient Australia*, Viking, 2015

Blewett, R., *Shaping a Nation: A Geology of Australia*, Geoscience Australia, 2012

Bolton, G., *Land of Vision and Mirage: Western Australia since 1826*, University of Western Australia Press, 2008

Boyce, J., *Van Diemen's Land*, Black Inc., 2008

Boyce, J., *1835: The Founding of Melbourne and the Conquest of Australia*, Black Inc., 2011

Broome, R., *Aboriginal Australians: A History since 1788*, Allen & Unwin, 2010

Cane, S., *First Footprints: The Epic Story of the First Australians*, Allen & Unwin, 2013

Clements, N., *The Black War: Fear, Sex and Resistance in Tasmania*, UQP, 2014

Clendinnen, I., *Dancing With Strangers*, Text Publishing, 2003

Clode, D., *Prehistoric Giants: The Megafauna of Australia*, Museum Victoria, 2010

Colebatch, H. G. P., *Australia's Secret War: How Unions Sabotaged our Troops in World War II*, Quadrant Books, 2013

Crotty, M. & Larsson, M. (eds), *Anzac Legacies: Australians and the Aftermath of War*, Australian Scholarly Publishing, 2010

Davison, G. et al (eds), *Australians 1888*, Fairfax Syme and Weldon, 1987

Dean, P. (ed), *Australia 1942: In the Shadow of War*, Cambridge University Press, 2013

Edwards, P., *Australia and the Vietnam War*, NewSouth Books, 2014

Evans, R., *A History of Queensland*, CUP, 2007

Evans, R. & West, A., *Constructing Australia*, The Miegunyah Press, 2007

Flood, J., *The Original Australians. Story of the Aboriginal People*, Allen & Unwin, 2006

Frankel, D., *Remains to be Seen: Archaeological Insights into Australian Prehistory,* Longman Cheshire, 1991

Frost, A., *Botany Bay: The Real Story*, Black Inc., 2011

Frost, A., *The First Fleet: The Real Story*, Black Inc., 2011

Gammage, B. & Spearitt, P. (eds), *Australians 1938*, Fairfax, Syme and Weldon, 1987

Gammage, B., *The Broken Years: Australian Soldiers in the Great War*, MUP, 2010

Gammage, B., *The Biggest Estate on Earth: How Aborigines Made Australia*, Allen & Unwin, 2011

Grey, J., *The Australian Army*, Oxford University Press, 2001

Grose, P., *An Awkward Truth: The Bombing of Darwin – February 1942*, Allen & Unwin, 2009

Ham, P., *Kokoda*, ABC, 2004

Ham, P., Vietnam: *The Australian War*, HarperCollins, 2007

Hasluck, P., *The Government and the People*, Vol. 1 and Vol. 2, Australian War Memorial, 1952 and 1970

Hinzell, T., *Australian Agriculture: Its History and Challenges*, CSIRO Publishing, 2007

Hirst, J., *The Sentimental Nation: The Making of the Australian Commonwealth*, OUP, 2000

Hirst, J., *Freedom on the Fatal Shore: Australia's First Colony*, Black Inc., 2008

Howard, J., *The Menzies Era: The Years that Shaped Modern Australia*, HarperCollins, 2014

Irving, H., *The Centenary Companion to Australian History*, CUP, 1999

Johnson, M., *Australia's Ancient Aboriginal Past: A Global Perspective*, Australian Scholarly Publishing, Melbourne, 2014

Karskens, G., *The Colony: A History of Early Sydney*, Allen & Unwin, 2009

Keneally, T., *Australians Volume 1: Origins to Eureka*, Allen & Unwin, 2009

King, J., *The Western Front Diaries*, Simon & Schuster, 2010

Kingston, B., *A History of New South Wales*, CUP, 2006

Knox, M., *Boom: The Underground History of Australia – From Goldfields to GFC,* Viking, 2013

Lake, M., *Getting Equal: The History of Australian Feminism*, Allen & Unwin, 1999

Larsson, M., *Shattered Anzacs: Living With the Scars of War*, UNSW Press, 2009

Long, G., *The Six Years' War*, Australian War Memorial, 1973

Lourandos, H., *Continent of Hunter-Gatherers: New Perspectives in Australian Prehistory*, CUP, 2009

Marchant, L., *France Australe*, Artlook Books, 1982

McKernan, M., *The War Never Ends: The Pain of Separation and Return*, University of Queensland Press, 2001

McKernan, M., *Australians at Home: World War 1*, The Five Mile Press, 2014

McKernan, M., *Australians at Home: World War II*, The Five Mile Press, 2014

McLean, I. W., *Why Australia Prospered: The Shifting Sources of Economic Growth*, Princeton University Press, 2013

Mulvaney, J. & Kamminga, J., *Prehistory of Australia*, Allen & Unwin, 1999

Nelson, H., *Prisoner of War: Australians Under Nippon*, ABC, 1990

Norris, R., *The Emergent Commonwealth: Australian Federation, Expectations and Fulfilment 1889–1910*, MUP, 1975

Nugent, M., *Captain Cook Was Here*, CUP, 2009

Parker, D., *Governor Macquarie: His Life, Times and Revolutionary Vision for Australia*, Woodslane, 2012

Parsonson, I., *The Australian Ark: A History of Domesticated Animals in Australia*, CSIRO Publishing, 1998

Pearson, M. & Lennon, J., *Pastoral Australia: Fortunes, Failures and Hard Yakka*, CSIRO Publishing, 2010

Pedersen, P., *The Anzacs: Gallipoli to the Western Front*, Viking, 2007

Pembroke, M., *Arthur Phillip: Sailor, Mercenary, Governor, Spy*, Hardie Grant Books, 2013

Potts, D., *The Myth of the Great Depression*, Scribe, 2009

Powell, A., *The Shadow's Edge: Australia's Northern War*, Charles Darwin University Press, 2007

Powell, A., *Far Country: A Short History of the Northern Territory*, Charles Darwin University Press, 2009

Prest, W., *Housing, Income and Savings in War Time: A Local Survey*, Melbourne University Department of Economics, 1952

Prior, R., *Gallipoli: The End of the Myth*, UNSW Press, 2009

Quick, J. & Garran, R., *The Annotated Constitution of the Australian Commonwealth*, Angus & Robertson, 1901

Rees, P., *The Other Anzacs: Nurses at War 1914–1918*, Allen & Unwin, 2008

Reynolds, H., *A History of Tasmania*, CUP, 2012

Reynolds, H., *Forgotten War*, New South Publishing, 2013

Sawer, G., *Australian Federal Politics and Law 1901–1929*, MUP, 1956

Schedvin, C. B., *Australia and the Great Depression*, Sydney University Press, 1970

Smith, B., *Australia's Birthstain: The Startling Legacy of the Convict Era*, Allen & Unwin, 2008

Souter, G., *Lion and Kangaroo: The Initiation of Australia 1901–1919*, Collins, 1976

Spenceley, G., *The Depression Decade*, Nelson, 1981

Stanley, P., 2010, *Bad Characters: Sex, Crime, Mutiny, Murder and the Australian Imperial Force*, Allen & Unwin

Stephens, A., *The Royal Australian Air Force*, Oxford University Press, 2001

Stevens, D. (ed), *The Royal Australian Navy*, Oxford University Press, 2001

Thompson, P., *Pacific Fury: How Australia and her Allies Defeated the Japanese Scourge*, William Heinemann Australia, 2008

White, P. & Mulvaney, D., *Australians to 1788*, Fairfax, Syme &Weldon, 1987

Williams, P., *The Kokoda Campaign 1942: Myth and Reality*, Cambridge University Press, 2012

Index

Image credits

NMA images of objects

p2 cast of Diprotodon foot SF 30:9, photo by Jason McCarthy; p10 pelt of a thylacine (Tasmanian tiger), which was shot in the Pieman River – Zeehan area of Tasmania in 1930, photo by George Serras; p11 fish scoop, photo by George Serras, p12 profile shot of an Aboriginal man displaying tribal scarring across his body, photo by Herbert Basedow; p13 head ornament made with macropod teeth, photo by Lannon Harley; p16 grass covered shelter, photo by Herbert Basedow; p16 the Aboriginal inhabitants; p17 hafted stone hatchet, photo by Lannon Harley; p18 cylindrical fibre basket, photo by Dean Golja; p19 Kimberley point – stone, photo by Jason McCarthy; p20 wooden model canoe, photo by Dean Golja; p21 wood carving – female human figure, photo by Dean Golja, p22 a Corrobirree or Dance of the Natives of Australia; p23 photograph of rock art, photo by Jason McCarthy; p24 coloured pastel drawing representing the markings on the underside of an old possum skin cloak, photo by Dragi Markovic; p27 Malo-Bomai

p28 Maris Pacifici quod vulgo Mar del Zur, photo by George Serras; p29 Discovery of Australia series VI – Torres, in the San Pedro, passes through Endeavour Straits, and sights Australia. 17 Sep., 1601, photo by Sam Birch; pp30–31 Malayan-type pigmented hollow cylindrical wood pipe with metal bowl, photo by Dean Golja; p32 bark painting 'Makassan praus' by Birrikidji Gumana, Yirrkala, 1966, photo by Jason McCarthy; p35 Staffordshire figurine of Captain Cook, photo by George Serras; p35 cannon from HMB *Endeavour*, which was jettisoned on the Great Barrier Reef in 1770 and recovered in 1969, photo by George Serras; p36 circular silk sampler map of the eastern hemisphere that indicate the routes of Captain James Cook's three voyages; p38 Wedgwood and Bentley blue jasper medallion portrait of navigator and explorer Captain James Cook. RN., photo by George Serras; p38 Wedgwood and Bentley blue jasper medallion portrait of naturalist and botanist Joseph Banks, photo by Dean McNicoll; p39 hand-coloured engraving titled 'A view of the Hulks, at Woolwich in Kent, with some of the Convicts heaving up a Ballast, and others on Show wheeling it to the places where the Embankments are made by them', photo by Jason McCarthy; p41 convict love tokens from David Freeman, photo by Jason McCarthy; p43 Australian silver commemorative medallion marking Australia's 150th Anniversary in 1938, featuring the landing at Sydney Cove of Captain Arthur Philip on January 26 1788, photo by Jason McCarthy; p44 Sydney Cove – central panel, photo by George Serras; p45 Sketch of Sydney Cove, Port Jackson from Book titled 'The Voyage for Governor Philip to Botany Bay: with an Account . . .', photo by Lannon Harley; p47 Journal of a Voyage to New South Wales, photos by George Serras; p49 needlework sampler on woollen evenweave fabric featuring boats and the text 'Botany Bay', photo by Dragi Markovic; p51 'Portrait of Bennilong [sic]' by Samuel Neele (artist and engraver) from G A Cooke, Modern and Authentic System of Universal Geography, 1802, photo by Jason McCarthy; p52 N'lle Hollande Baie des Chiens-Marins Presqu'ile Peron Entrevue avec les Sauvages, photo by Katie Shanahan; p57 19th Century folk art diorama which portrays Governor William Bligh's arrest during the Rum Rebellion in 1808, photo by Dragi Markovic

pp58–59 manacles from Campbell Street Gaol, photo by Katie Green; p60 Hyde Park, Sydney, NSW in 1942, photo by Sam Birch; p61 convict hand-stitched shift shirt of woven fabric of white and blue stripes, photo by Jason McCarthy; p62 convict's parti-coloured black yellow woollen work jacket, from Campbell Street Gaol, Hobart, late 1850s, photo by Dean McNicoll; p63 black leather lash with wooden handle, photo by Jason McCarthy; p64 document relating to the pardon of convict Thomas Jacques of Van Diemen's Land, photo by Rasha Ajaj; pp66–67 British Pattern 1842 .75 smooth bore percussion musket used by the 12th Foot (East Suffolk Regiment) with bayonet, photo by Lannon Harley; p68 Lantern slide entitled Relics of Convict Discipline with a black and white photograph, photo by George Serras; p70 Matthew Flinders; p70 stream anchor from Matthew Flinders *Investigator*, photo by Dragi Markovic; p71 bronze full size statue of Matthew Flinders' cat Trim, photo by Katie Green; p72 Proclamation regarding South Australia and the native population, photo by Jason McCarthy; p74 document known as the 'Batman Land Deed', between John Batman and Aboriginal 'chiefs' of the Kulin nation, Port Philip area, 1835, photo by George Serras; p75 postcard of John Batman, photo Jason McCarthy; p77 Charles Sturt Discovered Darling River 1828 Explored Murray R 1829 [Ex]pedition into Central Australia 1844, photo by Sam Birch; p79 Aboriginal breastplate for 'King John Cry, Chief of the Duedolgong Tribe, Argyle', photo by Jason McCarthy; p80 Staffordshire figure of seated male porcelain figure, photo by George Serras; p81 The Convict Ship, photo by Sam Birch; p82 Silver snuff box from the '. . . Emigrants of THE LADY ANN TO Capt. Wm. Maxton, Octr. 1854', photo by Jason McCarthy; p83 *Ditton* 25th March 1908, photo by Sam Birch; p84 PROP sea cucumber Makassan traders: dried trepang, photo by George Serras; p86 1813 Holey dollar, photo by Deon Rohmursanto; p87 Gunter's chain, photo by Jason McCarthy; p88 Circular Quay, Sydney, NSW in 1848; p89 (top) Hobart; p89 (bottom) South Perth, W. Australia; p90 (top) postcard of Adelaide: The Proclamation Tree; p90 (bottom) Brisbane Q; p93 Port Arthur paupers

p94 handmade wooden gold mining cradle on rockers, photo by Jason McCarthy; p95 Australian mining: prospecting for gold; p96 gold pan associated with Claude Dunshea, photo by Lannon Harley; p96 four alluvial gold nuggets from Emu Creek (Grenfell), 1867, photo by Lannon Harley; pp98–99 Race to the Gold Diggings board game, photo by Lannon Harley; p99 Ivanhoe Gold Mine; p100 Postcard featuring a black and white photograph of 'The Golden Eagle nugget', photo by Jason McCarthy; p102 Republic of Australia, photo by Jason McCarthy; p103 Western Australia's Phenomenal Gold Yield, photo by Jason McCarthy; pp 104–105 Harvest of Endurance: A History of the Chinese in Australia 1788–1988 'Before the Gold Rush', photo by Matt Kelso; p106 Chinese labour indenture certificate between Ng Hong and JB Simpson issued in Sydney in 1851; p109 (top) Australia – A Bush Post Office; p109 (right) The Timber Industry at the Huon, Tasmania, photo by Jason McCarthy; p110 Granted for Gallant and Faithful Services, photo by Lannon Harley; p111 Ned Kelly's death mask, photo by Dean McNicoll; p112 sword with scabbard presented to Sergeant Arthur Steele by grateful pastoralists following the capture of Ned Kelly, photo by Lannon Harley; p113 water bottle used by explorer Robert O'Hara Burke on his 1860–1861 expedition to the Gulf of Carpentaria, photo by Lannon Harley; p114 carved and mounted emu egg depicting the journey of Burke and Wills, photo by Jason McCarthy; p116 The Smith Premier typewriter, photo by Jason McCarthy; p117 Poster titled 'Telephone services link together the people of all nations', photo by Lannon Harley; p119 Siemens Brothers Morse Code printer, photo by Jason McCarthy; p120 photograph of a telegraph pole with three men on it, photo by Jason McCarthy; p122 preparation of the Ransomes, Sims and Jefferies 4 NHP portable steam engine for display in Large Objects Display Zone, the Main Hall, Acton, photo by Jason McCarthy; p123 Jubilee from 1850 to 1905, photo by Sam Birch; p124 Ferrier's Lever Wool Press, serial no. 1831, made by Humble & Sons, Geelong, c.1912, photo by Attila Kiraly; p127 illuminated address to Graham Berry, from William Barak and Coranderrk residents, 1886, photo by Rasha Ajaj; p129 In the Woollen Mill, photo by Sam Birch; p131 (top) Harvest Time in Australia, photo by Sam Birch; p131 (right) Pattison Shield presented to Victor Trumper 1898–1899, photo by Jason McCarthy; p133 mounted specimen – platypus – whole specimen mounted, photo by Jason McCarthy; p135 Artesian Bore, Australia, photo by Jason McCarthy; p136 photographic postcards, Christmas Greetings: Australian Sheep Shearing Shed, photo by Jason McCarthy; p137 two piece pink full length wool dress (bodice and skirt) with cream lace trimming, photo by George Serras; p138 Broken Hill Silver Mines NSW, photo by Jason McCarthy; p139 slate with a wooden frame with a hole at the top, photo by Jason McCarthy; p140 postcard – Father, teacher says I've gotter bring a penny wi' me to school termorrer, photo by Jason McCarthy; p141 Residence Roofed with Marseilles Tiles by Wunderlich Limited; p143 Camel Team in the Back Blocks, WA, photo by Jason McCarthy; p144 family portrait taken about 1895, photo by Rasha Ajaj; p150 shearers' dispute at Hughenden Strike Camp

p152 medallion presented to Bransby Beauchamp Cooper after England vs Victoria cricket tour match, 1873, photo by George Serras; p153 postcard 'Sunny Australia – A Bush Home', kangaroo, photo by George Serras; p154 Pre-Federation Australian flag from the Klondike goldfields; p155 ceramic umbrella stand in the form of a kangaroo, made by Doulton, England, 1885, photo by Jason McCarthy; p157 brass carriage clock in leather box used by Lord Forrest, photo by Lannon Harley; p158 Australasian Federated Butchers Union, Queensland Certificate of Recognition, photo by Jason McCarthy; p160 The Ten Best Citizens of Victoria – Hon. Alfred Deakin, photo by Sam Birch; p161 cartoon titled 'Combine, Australia!', photo by Dragi Markovic; p169 commemorative mug for the Federation of Australia in 1901, photo by Jason McCarthy; p171 (bottom) Queensland Federation medallion, photos by Jason McCarthy

p174 limited edition print of the painting 'Opening of First Commonwealth Parliament' by Tom Roberts, photo by Jason McCarthy; p178 (top left) Australian three half pence postage stamp featuring King George V and two pence kangaroo and map stamp, photos by Katie Shanahan; pp178–179 'Cycloramic View of Canberra Capital Site looking from Vernon', 1911, photo by Jason McCarthy; p180 (top) photograph – group of adults and children – Empire Day 1907; p180 Australia for the Australians, White Australia, photo by George Serras; p182 glass plate negative – Aboriginal prisoners, Northern Territory, photographed by Herbert Basedow; p183 sugar cane cutting knife, photo by Lannon Harley; p187 black and white photograph of Daisy Bates standing near tent; p189 Bird's Eye View of Port Pirie; p192 Sunshine stripper harvester, photo by Lannon Harley; p195 'Call Again Old Man – Thanks for a Million'; p196 map of Orient Line routes, photo by Jason McCarthy; p197 souvenir of United States Fleet's Visit to Australia 1908, photo by Jason McCarthy; p199 (top right) Debrie Parvo model 'L' camera and accessories, photo by George Serras; p199 The Dash for the South Pole, photo by Jason McCarthy; p200 Sir Douglas Mawson, photo by Sam Birch; p201 Adelaide Electric Trams, Opened March 9, 1909, First Car Driven by Mrs Price, photo by Jason McCarthy; p202 poster advertising 'To Western Australia by Trans-Australian Railway', photo by Lannon Harley; p203 (top) The Bridge Newtown, Sydney, NSW, photo by Jason McCarthy; p203 New South Wales Postal Service red painted metal pillar box with an arched top, photo by Jason McCarthy

p204 postcard with text 'Allies in Defence against Defiance' and featuring an image of King George V, photo by Jason McCarthy; p205 Don't Falter, Go and Meet the Hun menace, photo by Jason McCarthy; p207 German Kulture – Retribution, photo by Jason McCarthy; p208 group portrait of Australian soldiers in uniform with rifles in hand; p209 Matrosen Division of the Kaiserliche Marine [Imperial German Navy], 1914; p210 Advance Australia!, photo by Jason McCarthy; p211 white china cup commemorating the sinking of SMS *Emden* by HMAS *Sydney* at Keeling, Cocos Island on 9 November 1914, photo by George Serras; p212 portrait of a soldier, woman and child; p216 Fob medallion awarded to Corporal M O'Toole, photo by George Serras; p218 Box for Trencho, photo by Jason McCarthy; p219 postcard featuring a comic pen and ink sketch of a soldier shaving in a trench while shells explode close by 'A Close Shave', photo by Jason McCarthy; p220 toy brown velvet kangaroo covered with fundraising badges from World War One, photo by Jason McCarthy; p227 Anzac Day – Lest We Forget Gallipoli, 25 April, 1915, photo by Lannon Harley; p228 The Greatest Mother in the World – The Red Cross 1918, photo by Jason McCarthy; p230 Certificate of Honour awarded by the Commonwealth of Australia to Lesley Robertson for Services Rendered in Connection with the Sale of War Savings Certificates, 1919; p231 I will help until the war is won, photo by Lannon Harley; p232 Mourning Locket – inside view; Les Darcy, photo by Dean McNicoll; p233 Mothers and Widows badge issued to the mother of 9956 Driver Alison Hope Oliver, AIF, who was killed in France, photo by Jason McCarthy; p235 peace jubilations: the crowd wating official announcement in Martin Place and Moore Street, Sydney, NSW, photo by Katie Shanahan; p236 commemorative souvenir red, white and blue triangular paper 'Peace Hat, 1918', photo by Jason McCarthy; p238 When the boys come home, photo by Jason McCarthy; p239 First World war roll of honour board, Carrington Lodge, Protestant Alliance Friendly Society of Australasia (PAFS), photo by Jason McCarthy

p240 Anzac Day Commemoration at Bundaberg, photo by Jason McCarthy; p243 Epping school, Class 5 in 1921, photo by Jason McCarthy; pp244–245 Old Parliament House, Canberra, photo by Jason McCarthy; p247 postcard depicting William S. Hart of Paramount-Artcraft Pictures, photo by Jason McCarthy; p248 (top) QSL card for VK2ME, The Voice of Australia, A.W.A., photo by Jason McCarthy; p248 (left) Ginger Meggs, photo by George Serras; p250 Joan Richmond in album containing black and white photos with handwritten annotations; p251 gold and silver-plated brass handbuilt model of the Fokker tri-motor monoplane 'Southern Cross', flown by Sir Charles Kingsford-Smith, photo by George Serras; p252 black metal 'Winner' brand, hand-operated sewing machine, photo by Lannon Harley; p253 two women wearing swimsuits and sitting on the beach under a parasol; p254 kerosene tin and table model kerosene lamp, photos by Jason McCarthy; p255 See the better farming train, photo by George Serras; p256 colour poster with the caption 'Buy Australian Sultanas', issued by the Empire Marketing Board, photo by Lannon Harley; p257 white wooden 'make-do' stool made by soldier settler Harry Newman at Narrogin, Western Australia, in 1922, photo by Jason McCarthy; pp258–259 Boondara, showing horse teams pulling wagons loaded with wool bales, photo by Jason McCarthy; pp260 and 261, girl's fancy dress garment, hand-painted with cartoons and caricatures showing the work of the Heidelberg Unemployment Bureau, photos by George Serras; p264 (bottom) Phar Lap's heart, photo by George Serras; pp 266 and 267 political handbill titled 'Cash at Crank's bank', which was produced for the 1931 federal election, photos by Sam Birch; p269 matchbox holder depicting Two Champions, photo by Jason McCarthy; p270 coffee service produced to commemorate the opening of the Sydney Harbour Bridge in 1932, photo by George Serras; p271 black and white photograph of Francis De Groot cutting ribbon at opening of Sydney Harbour Bridge, 1932; p273 photograph – Sesquicentenary parade, Sydney, 1938, photo by Jason McCarthy; p274 women and girls, Hermannsburg, Northern Territory 1923 reproduced from glass plate negative

p276 Raising the Japanese Midget Submarine, photo by Jason McCarthy; p277 postcard for 'Fund for the relief of Polish victims of the war', photo by Jason McCarthy; p279 two members of Vienna Boys Choir, photo by Katie Shanahan; p280 instruction booklet titled 'Armstrong's How to Draw 'Em Short-Hand Way', photo by Sam Birch; p281 You love them – Fight for them!, photo by Lannon Harley; p283 travel document issued to Mr Capelluti to enable him to travel to his place of work, 18 September 1945, photo by Adria Hu; p289 Second World War Prisoner of War Banknote, photo by Sam Birch; p290 envelope titled 'United for Victory Interlocking Jigsaw', photo by Sam Birch; p297 telegram addressed to Lieutenant Commodore J Donovan regarding the birth of his son, 1942, photo by Sam Birch; p298 poster titled 'Help Australia – Help yourself . . . buy War Savings Stamps and Certificates', photo by Jason McCarthy; p299 Coal is Vital to Victory; p300 National Security (Man Power) Regulations 1943, photo by Lannon Harley; p301 (top) 1948 Queensland Clothing Ration Card, photo by Lannon Harley; p301 (right) War Relief fundraising certificate issued to Mary Knowles in 1944, photo by Adria Hu; p302 mosquito net wedding dress, photo by Katie Green; p303 tin of beef dripping sent to the Lawton family in Uxbridge, London, in a Red Cross parcel from Hobart in 1942, photo by Jason McCarthy; p205 USA Marines passing The Exchange, Sydney, photo by Walter Davies; p306 (top) disembarkation tag worn by Erin Craig when arriving in San Francisco on the SS *Lurline* in 1946, photo by Lannon Harley; p306 (bottom) stuffed toy pig prize won by Erin Craig for having the reddest hair of children aboard SS *Lurline*, 1946, photo by Lannon Harley; p310 Hiroshima Never Again, photo by Jason McCarthy; p312 Royal Australian Air Force Certificate of Service and Discharge, photo by Jason McCarthy; p315 Spanish refugees in Toulouse, circa 1940s

p316 Prototype No 1 Holden sedan, photo by Lannon Harley; p317 government information poster 'Australia Land of Tomorrow', 1948, photo by Dean McNicoll; p319 Certificate of Registration for A. Jedrzejowski, photo by Rasha Ajaj; p320 Latvian white, red and grey costume blouse, photo by George Serras; p321 a large light box showing the respective locations of the Snowy Mountains Scheme, photo by Lannon Harley; p322 World Tunnel Record Holder medallion awarded to A. S. Novikov, 1956, photo by Lannon Harley; p323 Song of Australia card issued to Mr Capelluti after his naturalisation from the Good Neighbour Council, 1962, photo by Adria Hu; p324 house with a fence and gate partially visible in the foreground, photo by Jason McCarthy; p325 'Doc' (Doctor) Evatt seated in front of a newspaper; p326 Discussion Poster No. 42 – Trusteeship, UN stands guard over the rights of the primitive people – August 22, 1949, photo by Jason McCarthy; p330 souvenir necktie for staff of the Maralinga atomic test facility, photo by Jason McCarthy; p335 Vietnam Moratorium Withdrawal All Troops Now, photo by Jason McCarthy; p336 Shirley Strickland's Australian Olympic Team athlete's white running singlet, 1956, photo by Jason McCarthy; p338 Warburton Mission: Leaving Time by Judith Yinyika Chambers, photo of artwork by Jason McCarthy; p340 Australian Aborigines League banner made by Bill Onus, photo by Lannon Harley; p341 Yirrkala bark petition, 1963, photo by Lannon Harley; p342 wooden and padded cinema seats, photo by Lannon Harley; p343 'Gurindji Land Rights Now', photo by Lannon Harley; p344 native station hands quartering and butchering a beast, Victoria River Downs station, NT; p347 (top) Welcome to our Royal visitors, 1954; p347 (bottom) smiling woman; p350 The Beatles: Away with the Words, photo by Jason McCarthy; p351 vinyl record featuring 'How Great Thou Art' and 'I'll Walk With God' by Harold Blair, photo by Jason McCarthy; p352 (top) Morris Model FE Pye outside broadcast van used by ABC-TV, photo by George Serras; p352 (bottom) sample of rock collected on the moon during the Apollo XV11 Mission, 1972; p353 souvenir silk scarf with rolled edges, from the 1956 Olympic games, Melbourne, photo by Jason McCarthy

p354 Save the Franklin – Damn the Government; Save the Franklin damn the government, created by Bob Clutterbuck, State Library of Victoria – H89.281/187, photo by Jason McCarthy; p356 Liberal Party leaflet produced for the 1975 Federal Election; p359 bamboo hybrid stringed musical instrument called a 'dan tre', an original creation by Vietnamese refugee Minh Tam Nguyen, photo by George Serras; p360 ship's wheel from the fishing vessel *Hong Hai*, photo by George Serras; p361 cartoon titled 'UnAustralian' by Katauskas, photo of work by George Serras; p363 poster with image of J. Samuels 'Produced as Part of the "We Have Survived" series . . . 1988', photo by Jason McCarthy; p365 Scorched Earth, photo of work by Jason McCarthy; p369 Women's Liberation March on March 11, photo by George Serras; p371 Victorian Stolen Generations Rally, photo by Jason McCarthy; p373 commemorative poster presented to Sir Ninian Stephens on the occasion of the handing back of Uluru to its traditional owners in 1985, artist: Chips Mackinolty; p374 Eddie Mabo, by CB Robinson, photo of work by Katie Shanahan; p375 *Flags Act 1953* – Proclamation, photo by Jason McCarthy, p376 Vote No to the Politician's Republic and Republic of Australia (t-shirt), photos by Jason McCarthy; p377 Order of Australia medal awarded to Neville Bonner, photo by Lannon Harley; p379 Australian Film Institute Award, 1980, to Jack Thompson for his role of leading actor in the film *Breaker Morant*, photo by Jason McCarthy; p380 Life. Be in it. Excercisements, photo by Sam Birch; p382 Council for Aboriginal Reconciliation poster; photo by Jason McCarthy, p383 Lionel Rose's International Bantamweight Championship Title Match, 2 July 1968 boxing trophy, photo by George Serras; p387 gas mask used as part of a protest costume, photo by Jason McCarthy; p388 protests during the campaign to save the Franklin River, photo by Sam Birch; p389 Department of Lands, Sydney Warning Crown Land, photo by Jason McCarthy; p391 'Land Rights' by Eunice Yunurupa Porter, Warakurna Artists, photo of work by Katie Shanahan

List of other images

pvi–1 continental drift © Designua, Dreamstime.com; p7 Megalania image from 2008 Megafauna stamp series reproduced with permission of Australia Post; © Australian Postal Corporations 2008; illustrator: Peter Trusler; p9 Aborigines using fire to hunt kangaroos © National Library of Australia, an2962715-s20; p34 The Dirk Hartog plate [Western Australia, 2] © National Library of Australia, an23181560; p156 Henry Lawson: Mitchell Library, State Library of NSW – P1/952; p156 Louisa Lawson © National Library of Australia, vn4464670; p163 Sir Samuel Walker Griffith, John Oxley Library, State Library of Queensland, Neg 68307; p164 Alfred Deakin, NAA: AA1984/624/A2; p165 Charles Kingston © National Library of Australia, an23379300; p166 Catherine Helen Spence © National Library of Australia, an14617296; p168 Andrew Inglis Clark © National Library of Australia, an13917935; p170 Invitation to the Commonwealth of Australia © National Library of Australia, an13143248-6; p171 The stockmen's procession passing along Spring Street, State Library of Victoria, H27418; p176 Australian flag, http://www.australianflag.org.au/the-flag-traditional-images/; p176 Edmund Barton, NAA: A5954/1299/2 PHOTO PL375/1; p177 1908 and 1912 Australian Coat of Arms, www.itsanhonour.gov.au/coat-arms/index. cfm#history; p185 Mary Lee, State Library of South Australia, B 70646; p185 Vida Goldstein © National Library of Australia, an23371660; p214 maquette for 'Simpson and his donkey 1915', sculpture, bronze, 41.5 x 25 x 36cm © Australian War Memorial (ART40983); p224 young soldiers mounted on horses, State Library of South Australia, PRG 280/1/8/64; p264 Don Bradman: Dixson Galleries, State Library of NSW – DG ON4/2356; p285 Reg Saunders © Australian War Memorial (AWM 003967); p291 Teddy Sheean © Australian War Memorial (AWM 044154); p314 Vivian Bullwinkel © Australian War Memorial (AWM P03960.001); p328 Jessie Street © National Library of Australia, an23371692